Biologically Inspired Networking and Sensing:

Algorithms and Architectures

Pietro Lio
University of Cambridge, UK

Dinesh Verma
IBM Thomas J. Watson Research Center, USA

Medical Information Science
REFERENCE

Senior Editorial Director:	Kristin Klinger
Director of Book Publications:	Julia Mosemann
Editorial Director:	Lindsay Johnston
Acquisitions Editor:	Erika Carter
Development Editor:	Joel Gamon
Production Editor:	Sean Woznicki
Typesetters:	Jennifer Romanchak
Print Coordinator:	Jamie Snavely
Cover Design:	Nick Newcomer

Published in the United States of America by
Medical Information Science Reference (an imprint of IGI Global)
701 E. Chocolate Avenue
Hershey PA 17033
Tel: 717-533-8845
Fax: 717-533-8661
E-mail: cust@igi-global.com
Web site: http://www.igi-global.com

Library of Congress Cataloging-in-Publication Data

Biologically inspired networking and sensing: algorithms and architectures / Pietro Lio and Dinesh Verma, editors.
    p. cm.
  Includes bibliographical references and index.
  Summary: "This book offers current perspectives and trends in biologically inspired networking, exploring various approaches aimed at improving network paradigms, addressing communication networks, performance modeling, and distributed computing in networking"--Provided by publisher.
  ISBN 978-1-61350-092-7 (hardcover) -- ISBN 978-1-61350-093-4 (ebook) -- ISBN 978-1-61350-094-1 (print & perpetual access) 1. Computer network architectures. 2. System theory. 3. Bionics. I. Lir, Pietro. II. Verma, Dinesh, 1965-
TK5105.52.B56 2012
004.6'5--dc23
                    2011025333

British Cataloguing in Publication Data
A Cataloguing in Publication record for this book is available from the British Library.

All work contributed to this book is new, previously-unpublished material. The views expressed in this book are those of the authors, but not necessarily of the publisher.

Table of Contents

Section 1
New Biologically Inspired Architectures

Section 2
Bio-Inspired Network Resource Optimization

Section 3
Biologically Inspired Routing Protocols

Preface

Computer communication networks have transformed human civilization, and enabled information to be shared across the globe at the speed of a mouse-click. They have transformed the way society functions, and their effects can be seen in all aspects of our life. This transformation can truly be called a miracle.

In spite of their far-reaching impact, the computer networks that provide the foundation of the World Wide Web and the Internet have many limitations. The networks were not designed to accommodate mobile users, they are extremely vulnerable to security threats, they break relatively easily, requiring extensive manual labor to resolve many of these disruptions, and have very limited ability to respond to changing conditions like huge swings in their workloads.

Researchers in the networking area are continuously striving to find ways to improve the attributes of computer communication networks and find ways to address the limitations. These new explorations are gradually helping to address the weaknesses of the network infrastructure. The investigations to improve the network include incremental improvements to the extant protocols and systems, as well as fundamentally different ways to looking at the networks.

Some of the researchers exploring a fundamentally different way to resolve the limitations of modern day networks have been looking towards biological systems for inspiration. This has results in an exciting new area of biologically inspired computer networks. Such networks are designed and developed using principles that are commonly found in natural and biological systems.

This book provides a current snapshot of some of those research activities. By bringing together the research activities from a variety of institutes around the globe, we hope to provide a good coverage of the various approaches that are being explored to improve the networking paradigms.

COMPARING BIOLOGICAL AND COMPUTER NETWORKS

The impetus to draw inspiration from biological networks comes from the fundamental observation that biological systems just do a better job at many functions than the best designed electronic computers and computer networks.

Perhaps the most obvious example of a domain where biological networks have an advantage is the human immune system. The immune system is able to react to attacks from a variety of viruses and bacteria, including those that it may have never encountered before. It is able to identify the intruders, and take action against them in a very effective manner. Even though the number and varieties of the viruses and bacteria keep on multiplying due to mutations and natural evolution, the immune system is able to manage these variations with relative ease. In stark contrast, computer networks have a very difficult time identifying malware, intrusions, and other attacks, and struggle to cope up with the new security threats that keep on surfacing all the time. In some instances, the security mechanisms become a nuisance rather than a useful feature.

Another unique area where biological systems have an advantage is in their ability to adjust themselves in the face of a changing external environment. When the external temperature is hot, the body sweats to cool itself down, and when the external temperature is low, the body shivers to restore and gain some heat. Not counting some extreme situations, the human body (and many other biological systems) is able to adapt to an amazing degree. On the other hand, the computer networks of today are rarely able to cope with a dynamically changing workload, and their ability to deal with extreme external changes is very limited.

There are some aspects of networking in which current computer networks outperform biological networks, e.g. the fidelity and speed at which information can be communicated in electronic networks is much more reliable and higher-speed than biological networks. The goal of biologically inspired networks is not to belittle those advantages, but to explore those aspects that can be made better by drawing inspiration from biology.

Some of the recent advances made in improving the design of networks using biologically inspired paradigms are compiled in this book. The next section explains the structure of the book and the content of the different chapters.

STRUCTURE OF THE BOOK

This book consists of thirteen chapters which provide a good overview of the current state of the art in biologically inspired computer networks. For organizational purposes, the work is divided into three different categories.

The first category consists of chapters that are proposing new architectures for computer networks that are based on biologically inspired techniques. These chapters include description of work that is trying to develop a new paradigm for computer communications.

The first chapter *A Networking Paradigm Inspired by Cell Communication Mechanisms* describes molecular communications - a new paradigm for networking in which information is encoded to and decoded from molecules, rather than electrons or electromagnetic waves. This paradigm is being used to explore new models for nano-networking and in synthetic biology. The chapter provides an overview of the current state of the art, and the models used in the current state of the art for molecular communications.

The second chapter, *Organic Network Control: Turning Standard Protocols into Evolving Systems* presents a new architecture that allows for automatic adaptation of protocol parameters in dynamically changing environment. It is based on an observer-controller paradigm and uses evolutionary algorithms for adaptation. The chapter provides some examples where such protocols can be used, and also surveys the current state of the art in the area.

The third chapter *Robust Network Services with Distributed Code Rewriting* looks at a way to design distributed software systems that are based on continuous replication of a code base. They use the concept of *quines* – a piece of software that prints its own code, and leverage *quines* to create a system that dynamically rewrites itself in a regulated manner simultaneously exploiting competition as well as cooperation.

The fourth chapter *Neural Networks in Cognitive Science – An Introduction* provides an overview of an architecture for cognitive modeling that leverages neural networks. It is an instance of biologically inspired neural networks being used in various domains and applications.

The fifth and final chapter in this section, *The Dendritic Cell Algorithm for Intrusion Detection* is a new architecture to perform the security functions in computer networks. It uses an algorithm modelled after the body's immunity functions, and provides a new approach to detect anomalies in network traffic.

The next section of the book consists of chapters that are focused on resource optimization in computer networks. Any computer network operates under an environment of constrained resources such as bandwidth, power, and computation capacity at nodes. In different types of networks, different resources are the bottlenecks which need to be optimized. In the context of military or satellite networks, bandwidth is usually the bottleneck. In the context of commercial wireless sensor networks, battery power becomes the most constrained resource, while for high speed optical networks, the computation and switching capacity at intervening electronics is the bottleneck resource. Therefore, new approaches that allow optimal use of scarce resources are valuable to explore in all types of computer networks.

The first chapter in this section, *TCP Symbiosis: Bio-Inspired Congestion Control Mechanism for TCP* looks at ways to improve the congestion control scheme used in the widely deployed TCP protocol using biologically inspired techniques. The authors use concepts borrowed from biophysics, such as the Lotka-Volterra competition model, to improve the congestion control behavior, and show that the new biologically inspired approach has better stability and scalability characteristics than the prevailing congestion control schemes.

The second chapter in this section, *From Local Growth to Global Optimization in Insect Built Networks* discusses how insect colonies optimize themselves in a completely distributed and decentralized manner. They provide an in-depth analysis of the local behaviors of insects that leads to an eventual overall optimization of the global network in the colony.

The next chapter, *Network Energy Driven Wireless Sensor Networks* examines the subject of managing energy in wireless sensor networks. The approach proposed is that of scavenging energy available from unwanted radio frequency waves, a model inspired by the behavior of emperor penguins. In networks where energy is at a premium, such harvesting approaches can provide significant value.

The final chapter in this section, *Congestion Control in Wireless Sensor Networks Based on the Lotka Volterra Competition Model* provides an alternative approach to congestion control in wireless sensor networks. The Lotka Volterra model is a mathematical model that characterizes the population of different species in an ecosystem. The model, when applied to the task of managing bandwidth resources and congestion during communication, provides an interesting paradigm to manage scarce resources.

The third section of this book looks at the task of routing in computer networks. Routing is the process by which packets emanating from a source in the computer network are eventually delivered to their destination for unicast communication, or to multiple destinations in the case of multicast communications. The routing protocols for traditional networks like the Internet have become standardized and well-established, specially for the paradigm of unicast or point-to-point communications. There is still a lot of room for routing innovation in other types of communication paradigms such as multicast or unicast. Furthermore, as new types of computer networks emerge, e.g. mobile ad-hoc networks, disruption tolerant networks, or nano-scale molecular networks, each with their own specific idiosyncrasies, new types of routing protocols need to be investigated for them.

The first chapter in this section, *Autonomously Evolving Communication Protocols: The Case of Multi-Hop Broadcast* looks at the routing needs of broadcast networks which are relevant in tactical military environments, wild-life monitoring, and other instances of mobile ad-hoc networking. They propose an alternative approach for routing using autonomous machine intelligence built upon on-line evolutionary approaches such as natural selection and genetic programming. Creating a genetic programming language and a selection mechanism for multi-hop broadcast protocols allows them to create a system that outperforms traditional networks under some conditions.

The next chapter, *Application of Genetic Algorithms for Optimization of Anycast Routing in Delay and Disruption Tolerant Networks* provides another algorithm based on genetic programming, with the difference being the type of networks that are targeted. This chapter looks at the routing problem in disruption tolerant networks.

The third chapter in this section, *Data Highways: An Activator–Inhibitor–Based Approach for Autonomic Data Dissemination in Ad Hoc Wireless Networks* uses the paradigm used in cell morphogenesis to create paths for information dissemination in ad-hoc networks. The concept provides a completely decentralized approach to establishing paths that lead to data sinks, a peculiar behavior that is commonly found in ad-hoc sensor networks.

The last chapter in this section, *Scented Node Protocol for MANET Routing* provides an approach based on modified ant colony algorithms to create effective routes in mobile ad-hoc networks.

Taken together, the thirteen chapters in this book provide a current snap-shot of network research drawing its inspiration from biological systems.

WHO IS THE BOOK FOR?

This book is intended for researchers in the academia, industry, and governments who want to understand the issues in networking, and obtain an overview of the recent advances in the field of networking that are inspired by biological systems. This book will introduce some new advances in networking. Researchers in the field of communication networks, performance modeling and distributed computing will find the chapters in this book to be of particular relevance.

WHO IS THE BOOK NOT FOR?

This book is not intended for a biologist or a researcher who is new to the principles of computer communications network. It does not provide a tutorial or introduction to the design of current computer networks, a topic that can take several books on its own. It also does not deal with incremental advances to existing deployed networks. Most of the ideas covered in this book will require a radical change in the networking infrastructure to implement.

This book is a compendium of research papers and surveys. As such, it is not a comprehensive introduction to the subject of biologically inspired communication networks. It is instead targeted for researchers who already have some understanding of the area and are looking for focused, detailed research papers on specific aspects of it.

Pietro Lio
University of Cambridge, UK

Dinesh Verma
IBM Thomas J. Watson Research Center, USA

Acknowledgment

This work was sponsored by the U.S. Army Research Laboratory and the UK Ministry of Defence and was accomplished under Agreement Number W911NF-06-3-0001. The views and conclusions contained in this document are those of the author(s) and should not be interpreted as representing the official policies, either expressed or implied, of the U.S. Army Research Laboratory, the U.S. Government, the UK Ministry of Defence, nor the UK Government.

Pietro Lio
University of Cambridge, UK

Dinesh Verma
IBM Thomas J. Watson Research Center, USA

Section 1
New Biologically Inspired Architectures

Chapter 1
A Networking Paradigm Inspired by Cell Communication Mechanisms

Tadashi Nakano
Osaka University, Japan

ABSTRACT

This chapter provides a brief review of molecular communication, a networking paradigm inspired by cell communication mechanisms. In molecular communication, information is encoded to and decoded from molecules, rather than electrons or electromagnetic waves. Molecular communication provides bio-compatible and energy-efficient solutions with massive parallelization at the nano-to-micro scale; it is expected to play a key role in a multitude of domains including health, the environment, and ICT (Information Communication Technology). Models and methods of molecular communication are also reviewed, and research challenges that need to be addressed for further advancement of the molecular communication paradigm are discussed.

INTRODUCTION

Molecular communication is an emerging technology that exploits biological materials or living matter to enable communication among biological nanomachines (or nanomachines in short) (Hiyama, 2005). Nanomachines are small-scale devices that exist in nature or are artificially synthesized from biological materials. Some examples of nanomachines found in nature are biological cells, molecular motors that produce mechanical work (e.g. myosin), and biochemical molecules, complexes, and circuits that are capable of processing chemical signals. Examples of artificially synthesized nanomachines include synthetic molecules, genetically engineered cells,

DOI: 10.4018/978-1-61350-092-7.ch001

artificial cells, and bio-silicon hybrid devices that are programmed to produce intended biochemical reactions.

In molecular communication, information is encoded to and decoded from molecules, rather than electrons or electromagnetic waves. Since nanomachines are made of biological materials and not amenable to traditional communication means (i.e., electrons or electromagnetic waves), molecular communication provides mechanisms for nanomachines to communicate by propagating molecules that represent information. Molecular communication allows networking of nanomachines and potentially enables new applications in various domains including health (e.g., nanomedicine and tissue engineering), the environment (e.g., monitoring and quality control), ICT (Information Communication Technology)(e.g., implantable biological sensors and actuator networks), and military situations (e.g., biochemical sensing).

Molecular communication exhibits unique features that are not commonly found in telecommunication technology as it currently stands. The distinctive features of molecular communication compared to current telecommunication technology are highlighted in Table 1.

- Communication components: Molecular communication allows networking of nanomachines while telecommunication is to communicate using silicon-based electric devices. Nanomachines in molecular communication are nano-to-micro scale devices that exist in biological systems or

are artificially synthesized from biological materials.

- Signal types: Molecular communication uses chemical signals to communicate information, unlike telecommunication technology which uses electrical or optical signals. Using signal molecules as carriers of information opens up new possibilities in ICT. For instance, signal molecules carry physical properties that encode a high density of information. Also, signal molecules may carry some functionality. For example, a DNA sequence that codes some biological functions can be transmitted to a receiver nanomachine which acquires new functionality (e.g., a functional protein) as a result of gene expression.

- Communication speed and range: The speed and range of molecular communication are extremely slow and strictly limited compared to existing telecommunication technology. The speed and range of molecular communication vary depending on the communication mechanisms used. The fastest and longest range communication is achieved through neural signaling which propagates electro-chemical signals (i.e., action potentials) at 100 m/sec over several meters, while the free diffusion of molecules based on Brownian motion is extremely slow and contained within a limited range.

- Communication media: In molecular communication, chemical signals propagate in

Table 1. Molecular communication and telecommunication

Communication	Telecommunication	Molecular Communication
Communication components	Electronic devices	Bio-nanomachines
Signal types	Optical/electrical signals	Chemical signals
Communication speed	Speed of light (3×10^8 m/s)	Extremely slow
Communication range	m ~ km	nm ~ μm
Communication media	Air or cables	Aqueous

an aqueous environment, while electrical signals in telecommunication (or electromagnetic waves) propagate through a metallic cable (or in air). In molecular communication, a communication medium normally contains thermal noise which influences significantly how signal molecules propagate in the communication medium. In addition, a communication medium contains other molecules which may react with signal molecules, affecting the communication performance.

- Other features: Biocompatibility is another unique feature of molecular communication. Since molecular communication uses communication mechanisms derived from biological systems, it can directly interact with our cells, tissues and organs. Molecular communication also operates with chemical energy, unlike telecommunication which requires electric energy and power sources. Chemical energy in molecular communication may be supplied by the environment where the molecular communication operates. For example, molecular communication systems deployed in a human body may harvest energy from the human body, requiring no external energy

sources. Furthermore, molecular communication may be energy efficient with low heat dissipation. For example, molecular motors, transport mechanisms found in biological cells, convert ATP energy to mechanical work at nearly 100 percent efficiency.

MOLECULAR COMMUNICATION

Figure 1 depicts a basic form of molecular communication. In this paradigm, the sender and receiver nanomachines communicate by propagating signal molecules via a communication channel. The sender and receiver often represent a group of molecular mechanisms performing n-to-n communication. The signal molecules are transmitted by a sender (or senders) of communication, propagated through the communication channel, and received by the recipient(s) of communication. The communication channel provides a mechanism for signal molecules to propagate while it typically contains noise sources such as thermal noise and other molecules that interfere with the propagation of signal molecules.

Figure 1. Molecular communication

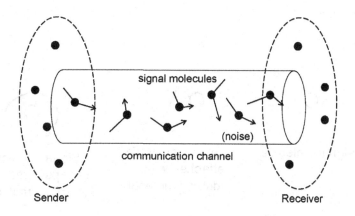

Signal Molecules

Examples of signal molecules that take part in cell communication include endocrine hormones, local mediators (e.g., cytokines), neurotransmitters (e.g., dopamine, histamine) and intracellular messengers (e.g., Ca^{2+}, and cyclic AMP). DNA and RNA molecules are also signal molecules that store and transfer genetic information in the cell.

Some options and techniques are available to facilitate communication between nanomachines (Figure 2). The first option is to use an addressing mechanism to specify the recipient of a signal molecule. Such a generic addressing scheme can be implemented using DNA sequences (Hiyama 2008). Single-stranded DNA, indicating the address of a receiver, is attached to a signal molecule. The receiver has a DNA sequence complementary to the single-stranded DNA on the signal molecule, allowing it to form double-stranded DNA upon reception of the signal molecule at the specified receiver. The DNA-based addressing scheme provides a large address space, as the current DNA technology can synthesize a DNA sequence with 10,000 base pairs.

The second option is to use an interface molecule to encapsulate a signal molecule. An interface molecule provides a generic abstraction for communication, allowing nanomachines to exchange a variety of molecules using the same communication mechanism, irrespective of the types of signal molecules inside. Such an interface molecule can be implemented using a spherical lipid bilayer or a vesicle similar to the membrane structure that encloses a biological cell (Moritani 2006). In addition, an interface molecule can prevent signal molecules from undergoing unintended reactions with other molecules present in the environment during propagation.

Nanomachines

Examples of nanomachines include cells, genetically engineered cells or artificial cells with an outer membrane that separates the interior of the nanomachine from the outside environment. To communicate, nanomachines need to receive (sense), process and send signal molecules. Figure 3 shows an example of nanomachine architecture as well as possible options and techniques for receiving, processing and sending signal molecules.

In receiving (sensing), a nanomachine captures signal molecules in the environment. If the signal molecules are membrane permeable, no specific mechanism is necessary for their uptake, and they are thus able to act directly on the interior of the nanomachine. In other cases, different options are available. One such option is to use surface receptor molecules (i.e., membrane receptors), which bind the signal molecules, resulting in signal

Figure 2. Signal molecules

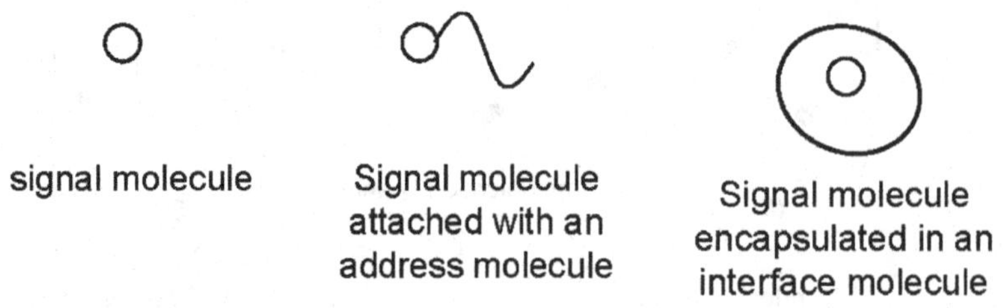

signal molecule

Signal molecule attached with an address molecule

Signal molecule encapsulated in an interface molecule

Figure 3. Nanomachine architecture based on the cell

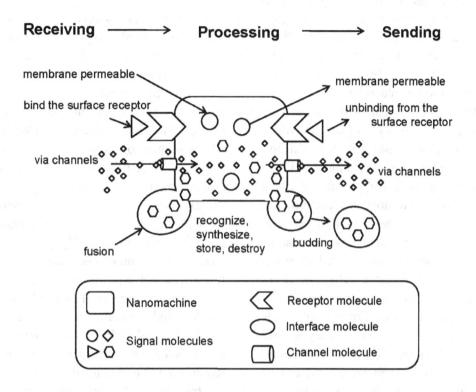

transduction in the nanomachine. Another option is to open surface channels (e.g., membrane-bound channels) that allow the signal molecules to flow into the nanomachine. Further, for capturing signal molecules contained in an interface molecule (e.g., a vesicle), a nanomachine's outer membrane may fuse with the vesicle, allowing the signal molecules within to be transported into the nanomachine's interior.

In processing, a nanomachine biochemically reacts with the received signal molecules, thereby changing its chemical state. Some molecules must therefore be recognized, synthesized, stored or destroyed by a nanomachine in the processing mechanism. As a result of processing molecules, a nanomachine may subsequently release molecules as well as produce mechanical activity that gives rise to division, migration or aggregation.

In sending, a nanomachine releases signal molecules into the communication channel (or the environment). Similar to the receiving process, sending membrane-permeable signal molecules does not require any mechanism as the signal molecules diffuse through the outer membrane. In other cases, a number of mechanisms are available for sending signal molecules from the interior of a nanomachine to the outside environment. For example, a nanomachine may unbind signal molecules that are attached to the surface receptor molecule, which then diffuse to the environment. Also, a nanomachine may release signal molecules by opening surface channels (or by using pumps), which allows the signal molecules to diffuse away. Furthermore, a nanomachine may release signal molecules to the outside environment by budding an interface molecule (e.g., a vesicle) containing the signal molecules.

In order to engineer nanomachines capable of receiving, processing and sending molecules, two principal approaches are available. One is to genetically modify biological cells that are already capable of these three functions, and the other is to produce cell-like structures using biological materials capable of performing these functions.

The first approach to engineering nanomachines has been used and demonstrated in Synthetic Biology (Andrianantoandro, 2006), wherein a sending function is implemented by modifying a metabolic pathway of a biological cell which then synthesizes and releases specific signal molecules. A receiving and processing function is also implemented by genetic engineering, allowing a cell to capture signal molecules and produce intended reactions. Synthetic biology has also demonstrated that many other functions can be introduced into biological cells, such as logic gates, toggle switches, and oscillators. These functions can be used to increase the complexity of sending and receiving processes. For example, logic gates can be embedded to produce programmed responses based on received signal molecules. Toggle switches (i.e., 1 bit memories) can be used to retain a communication-related memory such as whether a nanomachine is in a state of sending or waiting. Oscillators (i.e., clocks) can be used to control the timing of release. However, introducing multiple functions requires that issues related to interferences with existing functions are resolved, and this could be technically difficult.

The other approach to engineering nanomachines is to create simplified cell-like structures from biological materials. One example of this approach is to use a lipid bilayer (Mukai, 2009). The lipid bilayer can be made to form into a spherical lipid bilayer (i.e., a vesicle) and functional proteins can be embedded into the vesicle membrane or are captured inside the vesicle. By restricting the number of functions that are embedded in a vesicle, it is not necessary to consider the millions of complex processes occurring in a natural biological cell; to this extent it is virtually impossible to achieve in a nanomachine anything like the functional complexity present in a natural biological cell.

Communication Channels

A communication channel provides a mechanism for signal molecules to propagate between cells. Figure 4 shows two major modes of propagation; passive and active. In the passive mode, signal molecules diffuse randomly based on Brownian motion. No external mechanism is necessary, yet to propagate signal molecules over long distances, a large number of molecules are necessary, or a sufficiently long period of time is required. In addition, the propagation of large signal molecules in high-viscosity environments is extremely slow. On the other hand, in the active mode, signal molecules are directionally propagated in an energy consuming manner (e.g., via ATP hydrolysis). The active propagation may decrease the time necessary for signal molecules to reach the receiver and concomitantly increase the probability of signal molecules successfully reaching the receiver, although such processes typically require communication infrastructure (e.g., guide and transport molecules) and chemical energy.

Several mechanisms have been designed and engineered for propagating signal molecules. For instance, a passive propagation mechanism has been engineered using a line of biological cells whose interiors are directly connected by cell-to-cell communication channels (Nakano, 2008). The line of cells, called the cell wire, propagates signal molecules along the line. Since the diffusion of signal molecules is restricted to the connected interiors of cells and there is no diffusion to the outside environment, the mechanism can effectively propagate signal molecules between cells. A passive propagation mechanism has also been enhanced by incorporating an amplification process during propagation. In this case, signal molecules propagate in a wave-like fashion through repetitive processes of diffusion and amplification (Nakano, 2009).

Active propagation mechanisms have also been engineered. One example of such a mechanism uses molecular rails as guide molecules

Figure 4. Communication channels

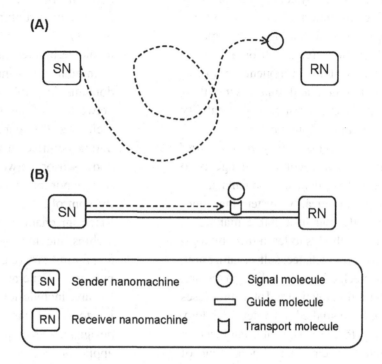

that self-organize into a network, and molecular motors that act as transport molecules that actively transport signal molecules along the guide molecules (Enomoto, 2006). This mechanism is similar to active transport processes in biological cells. By controlling self-organization processes to create a topology of molecular rails, molecular motors may be selectively propagated along the designed topology to desired locations on a network. In another engineered active propagation mechanism, the arrangement of microtubules and motors is inverted; a glass surface is coated with the molecular motors that act as guide molecules (Hiyama, 2008). The motors push filaments of molecular rails that move along the surface. In this arrangement, the filaments load signal molecules at one nanomachine and unload them at another. The filaments thus act as transport molecules. Various patterns of molecular motors may be created that gather transport molecules towards a specific nanomachine.

FUTURE RESEARCH DIRECTIONS

Research on molecular communication is in its infancy and there are a number of challenges that need to be addressed.

1. *Component design and engineering*: The first challenge is to identify, design, and engineer (or fabricate) building blocks necessary to provide full communication functionality. For this, traditional electrical communication systems may be examined as a reference system, and corresponding system components are designed by exploiting biological materials and mechanisms. In addition to signal molecules, nanomachines and propagation mechanisms discussed in this article, potentially useful components include amplifiers, switches, memory, power sources, and mechanisms for recycling molecules. General research challenges in this category

include identifying biological materials and mechanisms to be used in constructing such systems, designing system components using biological materials and mechanisms, applying bio-nanotechnology or biologically inspired methods (e.g., self-organization) to fabricate system components in a cost-effective manner, and quantifying their capacity and characteristics (e.g., durability in a biological environment).

2. *Component integration, protocols and architecture*: The second challenge is to integrate independent components into a working communication system that functions robustly and in a stable manner. A promising method is to learn from biological systems; for instance, self-organization, feedback mechanisms, modular architecture, evolution and adaptation and other processes that have been studied in Systems Biology may apply to the design and engineering of a robust system. In addition, some of the knowledge and mechanisms available from communication engineering may also be helpful in designing communication protocols or mechanisms. General research challenges in this area therefore include investigating a robust design architecture that allows communication components to self-organize and function even under the influence of noise, and developing protocols and mechanisms for interfacing components.

3. *Application development*: Another challenge is to develop innovative applications of molecular communication systems. Molecular communications provide a means of biocompatible communication by which nanomachines interact directly with biological systems. Thus, molecular communication systems are highly anticipated in medical domains. For instance, nanomachines capable of molecular communication may be implanted in a human body to interact with cells, tissues and organs for the purpose of monitoring the health of an individual. Also, nanomachines made of living matter may self-organize to form three-dimensional functional structures (e.g., tissues and organs) for the purpose of regenerative medicine, biomedical studies, and in vivo information processing. There are many other domains that molecular communication or networking of nanomachines may impact, including ICT (e.g., unconventional computing, biomolecular computing, biological body sensor networks), the environment (e.g., environmental monitoring and quality control), NEMS/MEMS (Nano/Micro Electromechanical Systems) (e.g., lab-on-a-chips and micro-total-analysis-systems) and for military (e.g., biochemical sensing) purposes. General research challenges in this area include developing standard libraries, tools and frameworks for enabling the design and development of a wide range of applications.

4. *Information theory:* Lastly, it is important to build theoretical foundations of molecular communication. Shannon information theory may apply as it has contributed significantly to the advancement of the current telecommunications technology. General research challenges in this area include understanding and designing molecular codes, quantifying and analyzing channel capacity, and identifying efficient design schemes for molecular communication under the influence of thermal noise.

CONCLUSION

The idea of using biological molecules in communication technology, namely molecular communication, first appeared in 2005 and a line of research from that time has begun addressing various issues in this field. Current experimental efforts are focused on addressing typical physical layer issues of computer communications in addition to addressing issues related to the design and engineering of system components (Hiyama, 2008; Moritani, 2006; Mukai, 2009; Nakano, 2008; Nakano, 2009; Enomoto, 2006). Theoretical efforts are also underway to investigate information representation using molecules, and to analyze the information transfer capacity in nano-to-microscale environments (Eckford, 2007; Atakan and Akan, 2008; Moore, 2009). Although research on molecular communication is in its infancy and a number of research issues exist, continuing efforts will lead to integrated systems in which various components of molecular communication coordinate to provide full communication functionality. Molecular communication has significant potential since it can interact directly with biological systems. Its areas of application are broad, including the ICT, health, environment and military domains.

REFERENCES

Andrianantoandro, E., Basu, S., Karig, D. K., & Weiss, R. (2006). Synthetic biology: New engineering rules for an emerging discipline. *Molecular Systems Biology*, *2*, E1–E14. doi:10.1038/msb4100073

Atakan, B., & Akan, O. B. (2008). *On molecular multiple-access, broadcast, and relay channels in nanonetworks*. In International Conference on Bio-Inspired Models of Network, Information, and Computing Systems, 16.

Eckford, A. (2007). *Nanoscale communication with Brownian motion*. In 41st Annual Conference on Information Sciences and Systems, (pp. 160-165).

Enomoto, A., Moore, M., Nakano, T., Egashira, R., Suda, T., & Kojima, H. … Oiwa, K. (2006). *A molecular communication system using a network of cytoskeletal filaments*. In 2006 NSTI Nanotechnology Conference, vol. 1, (pp. 725-728).

Hiyama, S., Inoue, T., Shima, T., Moritani, Y., Suda, T., & Sutoh, K. (2008). Autonomous loading, transport and unloading of specified cargoes by using DNA hybridization and biological motor-based motility. *Small*, *4*(4), 410–415. doi:10.1002/smll.200700528

Hiyama, S., Moritani, Y., Suda, T., Egashira, R., Enomoto, A., Moore, M., & Nakano, T. (2005). *Molecular communication*. In 2005 NSTI Nanotechnology Conference, vol. 3 (pp. 392-395).

Moore, M., Suda, T., & Oiwa, K. (2009). Molecular communication: Modeling noise effects on information rate. *IEEE Transactions on Nanobioscience*, *8*(2), 169–180. doi:10.1109/TNB.2009.2025039

Moritani, Y., Hiyama, S., & Suda, T. (2006). *Molecular communication among nanomachines using vesicles*. In 2006 NSTI Nanotechnology Conference.

Mukai, M., Maruo, K., Kikuchi, J., Sasaki, Y., Hiyama, S., Moritani, Y., & Suda, T. (2009). Propagation and amplification of molecular information using a photo-responsive molecular switch. *Supramolecular Chemistry*, *21*(3-4), 284–291. doi:10.1080/10610270802468439

Nakano, T., Hsu, Y. H., Tang, W. C., Suda, T., Lin, D., & Koujin, T. … Hiraoka, Y. (2008). *Microplatform for intercellular communication*. In Third Annual IEEE International Conference on Nano/Micro Engineered and Molecular Systems (pp. 476-479).

Nakano, T., Koujin, T., Suda, T., Hiraoka, Y., & Haraguchi, T. (2009). A locally induced increase in intracellular Ca^{2+} propagates cell-to-cell in the presence of plasma membrane ATPase inhibitors in non-excitable cells. *FEBS Letters*, *583*(22), 3593–3599. doi:10.1016/j.febslet.2009.10.032

ADDITIONAL READING

Akyildiz, I. F., Brunetti, F., & Blazquez, C. (2008). Nanonetworks: a new communication paradigm. *Computer Networks*, *52*(12), 2260–2279. doi:10.1016/j.comnet.2008.04.001

Hiyama, S., & Moritani, Y. (2010). Molecular communication: Harnessing biochemical materials to engineer biomimetic communication systems. *Nano Communication Networks*, *1*(1), 20–30. doi:10.1016/j.nancom.2010.04.003

Moore, M., Enomoto, A., Suda, T., Nakano, T., & Okaie, Y. (2007). Molecular communication: new paradigm for communication among nanoscale biological machines. In Bidgoli, H. (Ed.), *The Handbook of Computer Networks* (*Vol. 3*, pp. 1034–1054). John Wiley & Sons Inc.

KEY TERMS AND DEFINITIONS

Molecular Communication: A new communication paradigm based on mechanisms and materials from biological systems.

Nanomachines: Small-scale devices that exist in nature or are artificially synthesized from biological materials. **Chemical Signals:** Biochemical molecules used in molecular communication. **Brownian Motion:** Random movement of a molecule.

Passive Propagation: A mode of propagating molecules based on Brownian motion, requiring no chemical energy.

Active Propagation: Another mode of propagation that consumes chemical energy to directionally move molecules.

Molecular Motors: A protein family to achieve active propagation. Molecular motors move directionally along the molecular rails.

Chapter 2
Organic Network Control:
Turning Standard Protocols into Evolving Systems

Sven Tomforde
Leibniz Universität Hannover, Germany

Jörg Hähner
Leibniz Universität Hannover, Germany

ABSTRACT

In recent years, the number of network applications and appliances has increased tremendously. This has lead to a large number of new network protocols on all layers, introducing a varying set of possible protocol stack configurations for different usage scenarios. Also, the functionality of each one of these protocols has become more complex. The fear of losing the fight against complexity here has lead to a number of initiatives discussing the future of the Internet.

The Organic Computing initiative focuses on new design approaches for complex systems, in which the complexity is not only an issue during the design time of the system. Instead, the complexity is handled partly at runtime using novel architectures and algorithms that allow for evolving systems.

In this chapter, we present the Organic Network Control (ONC) architecture, which is based on a three-layered Observer/Controller-Architecture and the usage of Evolutionary Algorithms. Without touching the internal behavior of the protocol itself, this approach allows for the automatic adaptation of protocol parameters towards a changing environment at runtime. Based on the background of related work, we will first describe the generic ONC architecture, followed by a step by step description of how to apply this concept to an existing system. Two examples are explained of how ONC can be applied to existing protocols and what effect this application has on the system's performance. Finally, the chapter concludes with an outline of current and future work and a summary of the concept.

DOI: 10.4018/978-1-61350-092-7.ch002

INTRODUCTION

The development of networking during the past decades shows that the number of protocols being proposed for different applications on all layers has increased largely. This is partly due to the ubiquitous availability of networked devices for a wide spectrum of applications and ranges from classical desktops and servers in wired networks to small handheld and embedded devices in wireless networks, such as mobile phones and sensor nodes. This development is accompanied by the users' requirements of a better convergence of all these networks and applications.

Most protocols offer a large number of parameters that allow for adapting them to different usage scenarios, e.g. they allow for changing settings for timeouts, number of nodes to connect with, and retransmission counters. However, these parameters are seldom changed at runtime. Instead, they are mostly investigated and set at design time or – at best – changed manually at runtime. This leads to a rather static configuration even though the situation in the network is constantly changing. These dynamics are not only characterized by changes in, for example, available bandwidth, network topology, and channel quality over time. Additionally, new applications – and protocols respectively – are introduced. The class of Peer-to-Peer applications is probably one of the most dynamic classes of applications contributing to the changes in the protocol landscape during the past years. In essence, well established protocols, e.g., for Web traffic, have to co-exist with protocols that no one would have thought of some years back in the first place.

During the past years, the Organic Computing (OC) Initiative (Schmeck, 2005) has proposed a number of techniques, architectures, and algorithms that support the development of complex systems. One of the key ideas is that the complexity of (current and) future systems, such as the Internet, does not allow for a design-time-only approach when it comes to, for example, testing and optimization. Instead, the OC approach provides means for building systems that adapt and improve at runtime, using for example machine learning techniques. This also includes the seamless integration of new components (like protocols) into an existing system and is frequently referred to as Self-Organization.

In this chapter we present the Organic Network Control (ONC) system (Tomforde et al., 2009b), a three-layered Observer/Controller architecture that allows for "wrapping" existing protocols into a framework which enables a large degree of Self-Organization in existing networks. The architecture has a generic character: it has also been applied to other scenarios like, e.g., vehicular traffic control (Prothmann et al., 2009). The process to apply this to other domains is similar to adapting the ONC framework to network protocols.

The "wrapping" is achieved by adapting the numerous parameters of existing protocols at runtime and in dependence of the current status of the network node, e.g. a router or a user's PC, running the ONC system. As a basis, the so-called *Observer* collects information locally available at the network node, like available bandwidth and CPU resources. In turn, the so-called *Controller* uses this information and a performance measure for the protocol "under observation and control" to evaluate its current performance. If knowledge about similar situations is available from the past or if the performance falls below a threshold, the ONC system applies changes to the configuration of the protocol. In the case of observing a drop of performance below a given threshold, the ONC system makes use of Learning Classifier Systems (LCS) (Wilson, 1995) and Evolutionary Algorithms (EA) (Eiben & Smith, 2003) to find and evaluate better parameter sets. This process does not require any knowledge about the internal behavior of the protocol and takes place at runtime (although it may be supplemented with knowledge acquired during design time).

In the next section, we will give a brief overview of related work. Afterwards, we will introduce the ONC architecture in detail. For each of the architecture's layers, a step-by-step description of how to integrate a protocol into the architecture is given. This is followed by an illustration of the overall integration process for ONC using two particular examples: one from the domain of Peer-to-Peer (P2P) systems and one from the domain of broadcast protocols for mobile ad-hoc networks (MANets). This is also accompanied by examplary results showing automatically evolved parameter sets and their performance in a range of situations. These performance results are then compared to performance results of the example protocol provided in the literature. The chapter closes with an outlook to future work and research directions and gives a conclusion for the present work.

BACKGROUND

The Organic Network Control system provides a generic solution to control network protocols and adapt them to dynamically changing environments. The approach is based on locally available knowledge only and is able to learn the best control strategies and to self-optimize its own behavior. Within this section, we introduce the background of the Organic Network Control system and give a short overview of related work. Therefore, we start with a description of how network protocols are configured and which techniques are used. Afterwards, related work is introduced and compared to the approach presented in this chapter.

Determine Protocol Parameter Configurations

The performance of a network protocol depends highly on the configuration of its parameter set. Therefore, the optimization of protocol parameter sets is a main task for the development of a new network protocol or the adaptation of an existing

one. To determine the best-fitting set of parameters, a network engineer can try to manually choose parameters and continue using a directed trial-and-error approach. Alternatively, he can rely on an automated system as the effort for a manual optimization increases exponentially with the number of parameters and the size of the configuration space per parameter.

Since testing in real environments is not feasible due to monetary and safety-based reasons, in most cases simulation tools are used to model the reality and analyze the protocol's behavior based on different settings of protocol parameters. The most popular and widely-used tools to simulate networks in research are *NS-2* (Fall, 1999) and *Omnet* (Varga, 2001). An overview and comparison of network simulation tools can be found in (Weingärtner et al., 2009). Besides manual analysis of protocol configurations using simulation tools, a couple of automated approaches have been presented, where authors of a new or adapted protocol developed a system to automatically fine-tune their solutions. Considering the techniques used for the ONC system, the approach of Montana & Redi (2005) is connected as they also use an Evolutionary Algorithm (EA) to optimize a full custom communication protocol for military MANets. A similar optimization of a protocol for underwater communications using an EA is described by Sözer et al. (2000). Turgut et al. (2002) discuss the usage of a Genetic Algorithm to optimize their MANet-based clustering protocol. They all compare their achieved results to a manual optimization. The authors' intention in these cases has been to optimize a specific protocol and not to create a generic system. In contrast to the ONC system, the approaches are specific to the particular protocols, but do not aim at providing a generic framework which is adaptable to different protocol types.

Automatic Protocol Adaptation

In recent years, automatically performed *on-line* adaptation of network protocols has become a highly dynamic field of research. A broader community has been generated in the course of IBM's Autonomic Computing (AC) initiative (Kephart & Chess, 2003). Compared to the off-line configuration as described within the previous section, on-line adaptation is a significantly more complex task – due to time and computational restrictions. Besides ONC, different directions of research are known to cope with the problem: adaptive protocols, composition of protocol stacks, or centralized solutions to adapt protocol configurations.

Adaptive Protocols

The most obvious way of adapting network protocols to changes in the environmental conditions is to develop environment-sensitive, adaptive protocols - thus, several examples can be found in literature. In 1996, e.g., Goyan et al. (1996) presented an adaptive network layer protocol that aims at minimizing buffer requirements within the networks without losing packets. Simultaneously, end-to-end delay and jitter of frames are minimzed. They achieve their goals by introducing a receiver-oriented, adaptive, and credit-based flow control algorithm on protocol-level.

Bandyopadhyay et al. (2001) focused on medium access control (MAC) layer protocols when presenting their work for wireless ad-hoc networks. Their approach relies on keeping track of nodes in the direct neighborhood and considering this information for the protocol logic in order to avoid interference due to other communicating nodes. Another protocol for the MAC-layer of wireless ad-hoc networks has been presented by van Dam & Langendoen (2003). They focus on contention-based media access. To handle load variations in time and location, an adaptive duty cycle is used by dynamically ending the active part of it.

Another example has been introduced in (Huang et al., 2009). The authors presented an adaptive MAC-layer protocol framework. Since radio node density and service requirements can vary widely over time, they defined the need of an adaptation to changing environments. Their protocol prototype can switch between CSMA and TDMA within a radio platform scenario. Whiteson and Stone (2004) introduced an on-line learning mechanism to increase the performance of a routing protocol. Based on the Q-routing techniques presented in (Boyan & Littman, 1994), they learn the best routes by receiving immediate answers from the next hop. Both approaches rely on the existence of a protocol extension covering the learning/adaptation information.

Farago et al. presented a mechanism to automatically adapt the parameter settings of a MAC protocol to dynamically changing conditions (Farago et al., 2000). They use a meta-protocol which performs an on-line optimization of the most important MAC protocol parameters. Therefore, no knowledge about the future network conditions and their fluctuations over time is needed in advance. The optimization itself is performed on-line during runtime without the need to exchange messages with a centralized element or other nodes. The approach relies on the existence of different MAC protocol versions, which can be exchanged dynamically at runtime depending on the observed status of the environment. In contrast to the ONC system, the approach is based on the pre-defined protocol versions and is only working for MAC protocols.

All these protocols provide specific solutions - they are designed to enable adaptive behavior just for one task, mainly situated at the MAC layer. They are reactive approaches and rely on pre-estimated configurations and actions. Thus, these approaches cannot be adapted to other layers or tasks.

Protocol Composition

Besides considering adaptivity aspects at protocol-level, e.g. Heinzelman (2000) investigated alternative architectural approaches. She developed LEACH (Low-Energy Adaptive Clustering Hierarchy), which is an application-specific protocol architecture for micro-sensor networks and wireless video delivery. Here, the adaptation is done at a meta-level by adapting the conditions under which the protocol operates.

Based on the observation that a development of new protocols for all possible adaptation and learning processes is not feasible, a research field called *protocol stack composition* emerged covering the upcoming tasks by exchanging protocols and stacks dynamically (Rosa et al., 2007). In contrast to the ONC system, which keeps the existing and currently used techniques and optimizes their behavior, a re-combination of protocols is performed. Although the target deviates from the ONC approach (e.g., the protocol stack exchange has impact on all involved systems and can hardly be done locally), the approach enables adaptivity aspects at protocol-level. The most important representatives are *Appia* (Miranda et al., 2001), *Cactus* (Hiltunen et al., 2000), *Ensemble* (van Renesse et al., 1998), and *Horus* (van Renesse et al., 1996). Besides the locality aspect, some characteristics of the approaches separate them from the requirements of the ONC framework: the protocols and their configurations have to be known from the beginning and further extensions with a new behavioral repertoire are not possible.

The approach presented in (Schöler & Müller-Schloer, 2005) is founded upon the basic ideas of protocol stack composition, but it already focuses on the techniques used within the ONC system. The authors describe their adaptive monitoring architecture for protocol stack configuration and demonstrate the integration into the Observer/Controller pattern of Organic Computing. The learning part is covered by a Fuzzy Learning Classifier System (Casillas et al., 2004). Due to the usage of the same architectural pattern (Observer/Controller), the approach has some similarities with the ONC system. But, unlike the ONC framework, the approach is built again without offering the opportunity of handling different protocols and extending the set of possible solutions autonomously and on demand.

Centralized Systems for Protocol Adaptation

In fact, there are only few approaches to be named that aim at adapting network protocol configurations dynamically. Sudame & Badrinath (2001) present a first TCP- and UDP-based study and define the need of dynamic adaptation, but detailed examination and a demonstration of the re-usability for other protocols are currently not addressed. Currently, there exist only two approaches covering a similar target as ONC: the systems introduced by Ye & Kalyanaraman (2001) and by Georganopoulos & Lewis (2007). The former one introduces an adaptive random search algorithm, which tries to combine the stochastic advantages of pure random search algorithms with threshold-based knowledge. The approach is based on the initial system as presented in (Ye et al., 2001). In contrast to our approach, Ye et al. (2001) propose a centralized system that tackles the optimization task for each node. To allow for such a division of work between a central server and the particular network nodes, problems like, e.g., bandwidth usage, single point of failure, or local knowledge accessible from server-side have to be covered.

The second system has been presented in (Georganopoulos & Lewis 2007) and introduces a dynamic optimization framework for the reconfiguration of network protocols at all layers of the protocol stack. In order to optimize the performance of the system according to given goals, different entities can be adjusted (applications, protocols, etc.) or replaced. Again, the system relies mainly on a centralized element being responsible for the optimization tasks. The focus of the initial paper has been set on cross-layer optimization for the protocol stack, but less on considering environmental conditions. Hence, the authors demonstrated the performance of the solution by applying it to two different layers of the protocol stack: the link and the network layer. A detailed proof of the approach and insights on the currently vague black box *dynamic optimization engine* are still missing, consequently a suitability of the approach cannot be estimated - although some criteria (centralized element, low re-usability of existing protocols, etc.) are again contradicted for the ONC requirements.

THE ORGANIC NETWORK CONTROL SYSTEM

The Organic Network Control (ONC) system is designed to control the configuration of network protocols dynamically at runtime. Based on the principles of Organic Computing (Schmeck, 2005) and Autonomic Computing (Kephart & Chess, 2003), it relies on self-organization and is able to analyze its own behavior. Within this section, we explain the objectives of the system in detail and define its scope. Afterwards, the architecture is introduced and all contained layers are discussed, followed by an exemplary evaluation of ONC's performance using two different scenarios.

Target Definition and Scope

The target of the ONC system is to increase the subjacent network protocol's performance significantly by adaptation. As described before, protocols are configured using *static* parameters in order to receive an acceptable performance for all foreseen situations. This solution represents a configuration that works well *on average* – ONC's focus is to find the best configuration for each situation. Hence, the goal is to determine that protocol parameter configuration, which leads to

the maximum performance of the system in this situation, or approaches the system's performance towards this maximum. Besides the optimality-aspect, the ONC system is able to deal with changing environments – in contrast to existing static solutions, unforeseen changes over time are covered by a learning component, which is able to direct the system into a self-optimizing direction. Learning always requires the possibility to try different solutions and receive a feedback of how well the chosen action has performed. Since a trial-and-error approach is not feasible in technical systems due to safety reasons, ONC is equipped with a sandbox-learning mechanism, which learns mainly from simulation and does not interfere with the real system. The investigation of different optimization, learning, and simulation techniques is part of the research.

In order to achieve the desired behavior, the system reacts on changes in the observed situation at runtime. We assume that large networks and dynamic environments lead to such complex continuously changing situations that a centralized system is not capable of configuring all distributed nodes – which leads to the need of a decentralized solution where each node acts for itself. Therefore, so-called *self-x properties* (Schmeck, 2005) are needed. Consequently, the ONC system is able to control, evaluate, and improve its own behavior by using concepts like machine learning and optimization. The resulting behavior is meant to be traceable – an engineer has to be able to understand why the system performs a particular action and from which set of actions it chooses in a particular scenario. In order to achieve the comprehensibility of the system's decisions, a rule-based approach is used for the adaptation component.

The system is co-operable with existing solutions, especially with non-adaptable systems (not running the additional ONC component). The application of ONC itself and consequently the expandability of the system in combination with the effort to apply the adaptation mechanism to existing solutions are manageable – the few tasks for adapting ONC to new protocols will be discussed in detail in the remainder of this section.

The ONC system can be applied to various types of protocols. Based on the locality aspect above, some restrictions regarding the applicability of ONC for different protocols can be derived. The performance of the particular protocol instance has to be measured locally without additional global knowledge. Additionally, the protocol has to come with configuration parameters, which have to be available for the adaptation process of the ONC system. Furthermore, the fitness function (also called *evaluation function, reward,* or *learning feedback*), which is used to derive information about the quality of applied actions and the current system status, has to possess characteristics like: being continuously differntiable, simple computability, and low structural change over time. The differentiability is necessary, since we assume that situations, which are close to others within the configuration space, can be covered by using the actions known for the nearby situations, i.e. if a node performing a mobile ad-hoc network protocol has no neighbors in sending distance, but it knows (e.g. due to disturbances on the channel) about a neighbor nearby, it might be useful to delay the message and to consequently close the gap before sending. Simple computability is needed, since the fitness function has to be calculated very often and an immediate reaction is necessary. Finally, the rule-based learning approach relies on re-using already known rules, which implies that the action is always the correct one for the given situation. An ageing of the basic fitness landscape modeled by the fitness function can be covered if this ageing does not completely change the landscape (only slightly changing landscapes are manageable since the learning takes time).

Based on the terms defined for Organic Computing in (Schmeck & Müller-Schloer, 2007), a formal description is defined. Let S be the network protocol instance controlled by the *control mechanism* (*CM* – here realized as the ONC system). S performs the protocol logic, which is configured using a set of parameters P (e.g. delay times, hello-interval, buffer-sizes, etc.). The behavior of S is affected by the *environment,* which aggregates all entities outside of S and its *control mechanism* (ONC). At any time t, the values of all the relevant attributes of the system constitute its *state z(t)*, i.e. if there are n attributes used to describe the state of S, $z(t)$ is a vector in some n-dimensional state space Z (also called *parameter space* or *configuration space* of S).

These parameters include internal values (measured figures for, e.g., buffer sizes, queue lengths, utilization of resources like CPU, etc.) and can include environmental figures that can be measured locally or received from neighbors (e.g. the distribution of neighbors in MANets, the neighbors' energy status in wireless sensor networks, etc.). Some of these parameters are used as *evaluation criteria* (also called objectives) $\acute{\eta}1, ..., \acute{\eta}k,$ which are provided by a higher external entity (the user). The evaluation criteria are assumed to map the system state into the set of real numbers. The evaluation of the system might rely on additional computational functions based on these criteria, but this does not have impact on the model. Additionally, an *evaluation (or fitness) function f(z(t))* is needed, which calculates the current system performance based on these evaluation criteria. For simplicity, we assume that the functional space of f is known in advance, including its maximum and minimum boundaries (e.g. in a P2P-based scenario an evaluation function can refer to maximizing the download rate, where the minimum of the download rate is equal to zero and the maximum is given by physical characteristics of the channel).

Finally, the evaluation criteria are used to define a hierarchy of subspaces of Z characterizing the performance of the system:

1. **Target Space (TS):** The goal of the ONC system is to optimize the system's performance, which is quantified by the fitness function f. Based on the user's definition of which

system performance he favors, the relative performance $f(z(t))$ can be determined. This function characterizes the current state $z(t)$ in relation to the user's goal. If the goal is fulfilled, e.g. the download speed in the aforementioned P2P-scenario is above a given threshold θt, the corresponding state $z(t)$ is part of *TS*. Hence, no control actions of the control mechanism are needed.

2. **Acceptance Space (AS):** The system state $z(t)$ is called acceptable if an acceptance criterion or threshold θa is satisfied: $\theta a < \theta t$ if the fitness function is to be maximized, $\theta a > \theta t$ otherwise. The set of all acceptable states satisfying the threshold θa is called *acceptance space* (AS). Obviously, *TS* is a subset of *AS*. In many cases, the protocol client's performance using the standard parameter configuration will lead to acceptable states.

3. **Survival Space (SS):** If the system is in an inacceptable state and it is still possible to modify the system state $z(t)$ such that at some later time t' the resulting state $z(t')$ is acceptable, the system state belongs to the survival space. For example, the *CM* could have changed its queue sizes to zero and no packages are stored anymore (and consequently none are processed) – the system performance will be low, but it can return to *AS* by re-increasing this value.

4. **Dead Space (DS):** If *S* cannot return into an at least acceptable state, it is not part of one of the previous sets and therefore belongs to the *Dead Space*.

The target of ONC is then to adjust *P* depending on the observed state $z(t)$ in such a way that at the next evaluation time t' the corresponding system state $z(t')$ will be part of *TS*. How this is achieved in detail is described in the remainder of this section by explaining the architecture and its components.

System Architecture

The ONC system uses the three-layered architecture depicted in Figure 1. The bottom layer (Layer 0) encapsulates the particular network protocol, for example, a broadcast algorithm or a P2P protocol. The particular internals of the protocol do not need to be available. However, it is required that the parameters of the protocol can be altered by the ONC system. Also, local information describing the current situation of the node needs to be accessible. In order to evaluate the current performance of the protocol, the developer or administrator needs to provide a performance measure (also called fitness or evaluation function), quantifying good and bad performance.

Layer 1 of the ONC architecture includes two main components: an Observer and a Controller which is realized as a Learning Classifier System (LCS). The Observer collects local information and current settings of the protocol and aggregates them into a vector describing the current situation at the node. This situation vector then serves as input to the LCS. Based on this input, the LCS evaluates the current performance of the protocol using the fitness function and selects a parameter set for the protocol that fits the current situation vector best (and therefore promises the best-possible performance). In case of no parameter sets are available in the LCS suiting the current needs, new classifiers need to be created. In contrast to the original LCS algorithm, however, the ONC architecture does not allow new classifiers (pairs of situation/conditions and parameters/actions) to be created randomly by Genetic Algorithms. Instead, control is transferred to Layer 2 of the ONC architecture.

Layer 2 of the ONC architecture consists of a network simulation tool and an Evolutionary Algorithm and constitutes the "creative" component of the system. The transfer of control from Layer 1 to Layer 2 contains a situation vector describing a yet unknown situation. In that sense, the question "What would you do in this situation?" is

Figure 1. The architecture of the ONC system

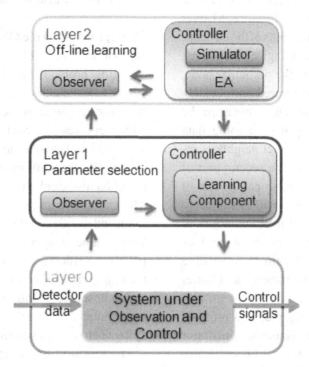

given to Layer 2. Layer 2 creates an appropriate simulation scenario from the situation vector and triggers the Evolutionary Algorithm to repeatedly evolve a number of parameter sets for the network protocol. These parameter sets are evaluated in the simulator. This bears the advantage that newly created parameter sets are not directly used in the live system, as this could cause the system to perform badly or even malfunction. Only those parameter sets that qualify in the simulator of Layer 2 are passed back to Layer 1 and may then be applied in the real world. Therefore, the Layer 2 allows for a kind of "sandbox"-learning without the risk of applying arbitrary parameter sets to the live system.

The remainder of this section gives more details on the three layers of the architecture. The description of each layer is divided into three parts. The *Scope* summarizes the main purpose of each layer, the *Task* highlights its functionality, and the *Engineer* paragraph describes what needs to be adapted in order to integrate a new protocol into the architecture.

Layer 0: System under Observation and Control (SuOC)

Scope: The ONC framework provides a generic solution to control network protocols and adapt them to dynamically changing environments. The controlled protocol is called the *System under Observation and Control (SuOC)*. Due to the generic concept of the proposed system, it is not restricted to a particular set of protocols, which means protocols on all layers (from media access up to applications) can be controlled in the same way as, e.g., wire-based protocols or MANets.

Task: By encapsulating the SuOC, Layer 0 has to fulfill two basic tasks. It has to provide a possibility to observe it and to apply control actions to the SuOC. The observation part is responsible for measuring the current performance of the system in terms of a defined fitness function. For P2P protocols, this may be the received download rate, for routers running the TCP/IP protocol it may be the net throughput. Additionally, a description of the SuOC's current status is needed, taking all necessary information into account, which might influence the performance. For instance, MANet protocols rely strongly on the status of the environment in terms of available (topological) neighbors, their positions in relation to the particular node, and their settings of the performed protocol. By contrast, the TCP/IP router has to measure the properties of all incoming and outgoing data streams and settings of the direct neighbors responsible for those streams. The second part of the task is to define the variable parameters of the controlled protocol, as they will be subject to adaptations performed by the Layer 1 component. Almost each existing network protocol provides variable parameters like delay times, re-sending intervals, intervals for 'hello'-messages, or buffer sizes to fine-tune its behavior.

Engineer: In order to integrate a new protocol into the framework, an engineer/administrator has to describe its observation and control process. First, he has to define the fitness function in order to allow for a suitable evaluation of the system's performance at runtime. In some cases, a trade-off between conflicting goals needs to be reflected in the fitness function (e.g. for sensor network protocols the two conflicting goals are: maximizing the number of observed events while minimizing the energy consumption). To achieve the best configuration, we propose a simulation-based setup. Especially after adding Layer 1, the system's learning component tends to favor only one goal, if the contrary aspects are not balanced well enough in the fitness function.

Secondly, the engineer has to provide two interfaces: one for accessing the protocol parameters and one for collecting information about the local system status. The former interface enables the framework to adapt the behavior of the protocol. In the latter interface, the engineer has to define what is (or could be) relevant and influences the protocol's performance. The ONC framework provides interfaces and predefined implementations for protocol groups (e.g. MANets, P2P networks) to allow for an easy integration.

Layer 1: On-line Adaptation

Scope: Layer 1 of the ONC framework provides the functionality to adapt the protocol by actively changing protocol parameters. It contains two components to achieve the best possible adaptation strategy: an Observer and a Controller. The Observer is responsible for monitoring the SuOC using the interfaces provided for Layer 0. Additionally, it aggregates information and augments them based on historical observations and predictions. The Controller takes the pre-processed data as input and decides on the best adaptation strategy. This is done using a Learning Classifier System (LCS) – a rule-based on-line machine learning technique. In this context, a rule defines under which observed situation which action (in terms of parameter settings) will lead to a predicted system behavior quantified by the fitness function.

Task: The Observer receives a description of the situation for the particular node, combined with a measurement of the system's performance. Since the measured figures might be noisy or subject to disturbances, it has to process the incoming data. To enable a sophisticated view on the measured figures, historical data is taken into account as well as predicted trends for a subset of the figures (depends on the possibility to predict a trend, e.g. the movement of a mobile node can often be predicted based on observations of the past movements).

Based on the inputs determined by the Observer, the Controller selects the best strategy (parameter setting). Within the ONC framework, this task is covered by a LCS. In our framework, it is an adapted accuracy-based XCS as introduced in (Wilson, 1995). The rule-based character is important, since we have to guarantee a system behavior strictly avoiding undesired effects. For instance, a system with full freedom in choosing its actions might try to adapt buffer sizes to zero and transmission delays to infinity leading to a non operable system. For other learning techniques like *Artificial Neural Networks*, a validation of what the system will do in all possible situations is not possible due to the black box character of the learning mechanism. Additionally, the system's behavior has to be comprehensible and traceable for administrators and engineers: a rule-based approach is easy to understand. Current research focuses on comparing the existing LCS variant to other learning techniques that are applicable in our framework.

Due to the restrictions named before, the LCS itself has been adapted by removing the rule generation mechanism (which is the randomized part) and replacing it with the simulation-based rule evolving mechanism included in Layer 2. Details on the technical realization can be found in (Tomforde et al., 2009a). The task of this layer is to draw conclusions from the system's performance and the previous adaptation of the protocol – it learns and self-optimizes its behavior.

Engineer: In order to enable the learning component of Layer 1, the engineer has to specify a distance measurement function. This function is used to compare the similarity of two situation descriptions, representing the SuOC's status (performance, settings, etc.) and the environmental conditions (e.g. location of neighbors). Based on this function, the LCS can decide if the condition part of a rule is fulfilled or not, since it is only allowed to choose rules with similar condition parts. Additionally, an optional prediction model can be provided to increase the adaptation speed. This is important, since the rule-based adaptation is performed in cycles defined by a certain threshold in order to allow for a feasible measurement of the system's performance. In most cases, the applied action does not have enough time to change the behavior of the system, if the cycles are too short. Based on the concept of providing a generic solution to control network protocols, the Layer 1 mechanism itself is designed as a black box, which means that the distance measurement function (which already exists for a set of pre-defined protocol groups) and the prediction model (likewise existing) are the only parts, a network engineer or administrator has to deal with.

Layer 2: Off-Line Learning

Scope: As, for safety reasons, Layer 1 does not have the possibility to create new rules, it only works on the existing set of rules. This leads to a conflict with the initial target definition, since the ONC framework has to provide a solution for dynamically changing environments where situations will occur that have not been foreseen at design time. This means, we need a safe mechanism to generate new rule sets for observed situations that are not covered by the existing rule set or for situations where the matching rules have shown a bad performance. Our approach relies on a self-organized and autonomous sandbox-learning mechanism: Layer 2 combines an optimization technique (we use an Evolutionary Algorithm, see (Eiben & Smith, 2003)) with a standard network simulation tool (the state-of-the-art solution NS-2, see (Fall, 1999)) to generate new situation-specific and tested parameter sets.

Task: The task of the second layer is to learn new parameter sets off-line. In contrast to Layer 1, Layer 2 has no hard time restrictions (Layer 1 reacts immediately). Therefore, an optimization technique can be used to generate new parameter sets and test them for the given situation by using simulations. The approach has to find the best-fitting parameter set under certain constraints, like the best solution found within a given time-interval, a given number of iterations, or after achieving a particular performance threshold. The simulator generates a scenario reflecting a more abstract view of the currently observed situation and runs the protocol with the parameter set to be tested. Afterwards, the performance is measured in terms of the fitness function as defined for Layer 0 and compared to the performance of the protocols standard configuration. This is the last check to guarantee that only well-fitting parameter sets are added to the rule-base of Layer 1.

Additionally, Layer 2 contains an own Observer, which is responsible for monitoring the whole device processing the network protocol. Since the rule learning task is time and performance consuming, this can only be done, if the system can provide free resources. For instance, the Layer 2 can only execute a task on MANet nodes, if the user does not need the system's resources. Alternatively, the second layer can be outsourced to other participants. For instance, controlling sensor node protocols using ONC will not allow for a distributed rule-generation solution, since sensor nodes have very hard energy- and computation restrictions. Here, the supply with new rules can be covered using periodic update messages provided by the destination of the observation messages (which is a central and more powerful element in most cases).

Engineer: In order to enable the usage of Layer 2, the engineer has to provide a simulation model. Within the ONC system, the standard tool NS-2 is used; other simulators can be easily integrated. The network simulator NS-2 has a large set of integrated or available standard protocols, but for recently developed or proprietary protocols, a simulation model probably does not exist. The engineer has to provide a realistic model (as it is also used during the protocol development process), which can be adapted to the observed situation by generating an appropriate scenario.

Exemplary Evaluation of the ONC System's Performance

The ONC system has been applied to different protocols: MANet protocols (Tomforde et al., 2010), a P2P protocol (Tomforde et al., 2009a), a Smart Camera protocol (Tomforde et al., 2009c) and a sensor network protocol (Tomforde et al., 2010b). In all cases, we have demonstrated the potential of the approach by measuring the increase in the system's performance due to the dynamic adaptation performed by the ONC system. For this chapter, we chose two protocols from different domains and different layers of the protocol stack to demonstrate the benefit of ONC and its generic character.

The first part of the exemplary evaluation deals with the P2P protocol BitTorrent (Cohen, 2003). We define a simple scenario in order to show the benefit of using ONC already for just a small set of observed figures. More details on the application of ONC to BitTorrent can be found in (Tomforde et al., 2009a). The second part of the evaluation applies ONC to broadcast algorithms in MANets, particularly the R-BCAST protocol (Kunz, 2003). More details about this scenario can be found in (Tomforde et al., 2010).

Scenario 1: Peer-to-Peer Network Protocols

The first scenario is used to apply the ONC system to a protocol from the application layer of the protocol stack. Here, BitTorrent (Cohen, 2003) has been chosen as an example for the whole domain. BitTorrent is a well-known and widely-used protocol, which is responsible for up to 53% of all P2P traffic on the Internet (Pouwelse et al., 2005), based on measurements in June 2004.

Protocol: BitTorrent is a very popular P2P protocol for distributing large files to many users. Since previous P2P protocols had problems regarding, e.g., fairness or efficiency, BitTorrent's approach relies on a fairness-based distribution of data. Files are split into small parts, so called *chunks*. The search mechanism to find data files within the P2P overlay-network is based on specific web servers, the so-called *trackers*. A client needs the address of a tracker to get into the system, since the tracker manages a list of available parts for the particular files. A peer receives a list of other peers providing chunks of the sought-after file and can ask for more, if the received set did not contain enough peers, which are still alive. Individual chunks are exchanged based on a tit-for-tat approach to achieve fairness and to avoid free-riding: A peer is only uploading data to those peers from which it is receiving the highest download rate. All other peers are said to be *choked*. The process itself is organized by defining several parameters, which can be controlled by the peer (some only when setting up a new file for the overlay network). A last fundamental part of the protocol is necessary to understand the mechanism and to receive a basic understanding of the parameter list provided in the following: the *optimistic unchoking* technique. Here, the client reserves a minor part of its available bandwidth for sending pieces to randomly selected peers with the intention of discovering even better partners and to ensure that newcomers get a chance to join the group.

Parameter: The BitTorrent protocol contains several parameters, but not all have influence on the performance or can be controlled locally by each peer. Table 1 lists all parameters, which are subject to control actions by the ONC framework in our current implementation. The adaptation of further protocol parameters and the direct intervention of protocol logic within the simulator are subject to ongoing investigations.

Adaptation of ONC: To enable the control of BitTorrent using the ONC framework, we had to adapt it as described within the previous section. To encapsulate the protocol instance (our SuOC) using Layer 0, a fitness function is needed, as well as a description of the current situation the protocol instance is in. In order to keep the example simple, we decided to use only the received download rate of a file as fitness measurement. The status of the node and the environment are modeled using different attributes, e.g. num-

ber of available peers, their connections, the files currently downloading, to reflect the system view, or the CPU-, RAM-, or bandwidth-usage for the local view of the node itself. Again, we decided to keep the scenario as simple as possible and took only the bandwidth usage including up- and download utilization of the channel into account. All system figures are observed by Layer 0, but only the two figures for the bandwidth utilization are used as basis for the situation description and consequently the optimization process.

For Layer 1, a metric to quantify the similarity between two situation descriptions is needed. To receive one value for this distance of a situation (status of available up- and download for BitTorrent), an aggregated number has to be taken into consideration. Therefore, we decided to use the Euclidian Distance between both situations within the space, defined by the two axes given by the values for up- and down speed. For instance, the comparison of Situation(A) (upstream: 25KByte, downstream 100 KByte) and Situation(B) (upstream: 20 KByte, downstream: 80 KByte) leads to a value of 20.6.

Finally, Layer 2 needs a simulation model to configure the simulator. We used an implementation of the BitTorrent protocol for the NS-2 simulator (Eger, 2009). The scenario processed by NS-2 is configured using the observed figures provided by the Observer of Layer 1: the number of peers, their connections, which chunks they already downloaded, etc. Within this scenario,

Table 1. Parameter of BitTorrent controlled by ONC

Variable parameter	Description	Standard configuration
NumberOfUnChokes	Number of unchoked connections	4 connections
ChokingInterval	Interval for unchoking process	10 seconds
RequestPipe	Number of simultaneous requests	5 requests
NumberPeersPerTracker	Number of requested peers	50 peers
MinPeers	Min. number of peers for not re-requesting	20 peers
MaxInitiate	Maximum number of peers for initialization	40 peers
MaxConnections	Maximum number of open connections	1000 connections

we used a simplified and abstracted presentation in order to demonstrate the general behavior. By contrast, an application of the ONC system in a realistic environment will take other figures for the rule selection mechanism into consideration: the state of the environment (in terms of available peers and their configurations) or other local figures (e.g. CPU- or RAM-usage).

Setup: The evaluation scenario considers the usage of a standard PC during one day. The user fulfills tasks, which leads to a certain utilization of resources. Sporadic lookup of information and downloading of files has influence on the utilization of up- and downstream connections to the Internet, which are also used by the BitTorrent client running in the background to download a high amount of data (e. g. video recordings of lectures). The target of the ONC system is to adapt the BitTorrent client to the changes in the observed utilization of system resources. In this example, we aim at demonstrating the working concept and therefore restricted the observed figures to just measuring the current usage of up- and download speed (several other figures might have influence, like CPU-, and RAM-usage). This means,

the BitTorrent client can only use the remaining bandwidth - the assumed usage during the day by other processes is depicted in Figure 2.

The scenario contains 100 peers and one tracker. Three peers are *seeds*, meaning that they have the complete file available at start - all other peers do not have parts of the file. Each peer tries to download the same 500 MByte file during the simulation and starts over after finishing the download. All peers are connected with similar links: 400 KByte/sec bandwidth for the downstream and 40 KByte/sec for the upstream link (e.g. an ADSL line).

Results: To evaluate the ONC system's behavior in such a usage-scenario, we analyzed the received download rate for three consecutive days. The results are depicted in Figure 3. All three days were simulated using the same usage profile (see Figure 2); the only difference is that the ONC system improved over time by evolving new rules and using them for particular situations. At day 1, the system starts with a completely empty rule base. Since no rules are available, it reacts on all changes in the observation of the SuOC by applying the standard parameter set, which is

Figure 2. Assumed usage-profile of bandwidth during one day, the difference to the total values defined by the channel (Maximum Down-/Upload) can be used by BitTorrent

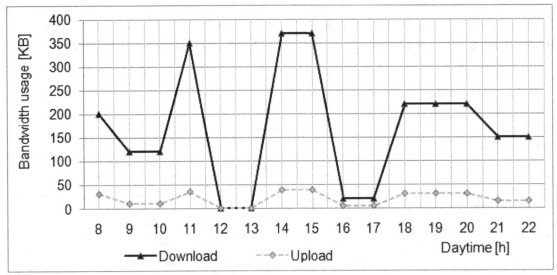

the fall-back solution in our approach. Since the generation and optimization of a new rule (find the best possible parameter set for the given situation) using Layer 2 takes time (depends on the complexity of the scenario and the expected quality of the rule), no rules are available during day 1. This means that the system's performance at day 1 (average download rate of 165.5 KByte/sec) is equal to using the standard protocol parameter configuration as listed in Table 1.

At the next simulated day, an improved situation-depending selection of parameter sets and the corresponding adaptation of the protocol can be observed. The system performance is increased by 7.2% (in comparison to day 1) to an averaged download rate of 177.4 KByte/sec. This demonstrates the desired effect that the ONC system recognizes already observed situations and uses the rules evolved by Layer 2. In some cases, the system does not have an appropriate rule for the observed situation, but can use a similar rule (nearby in terms of the distance measurement) – which can, e.g., be seen for the situation from 8 to 9 o'clock. Since the Layer 1 Controller is able to learn, it has to be allowed to choose not always the best-matching rule. With a lower prob-

ability, it might try a rule situated nearby (again in terms of the provided distance measurement). This leads to the effect that, e.g., in one case (during day 2) the Layer 2-generated rule has not been selected, although (see interval from 9 to 10 o'clock) it was already available.

Finally, at day 3 the system shows the desired behavior. It always chooses the best available rules (here, for each of the 14 different intervals an optimized rule has been evolved). The resulting averaged download rate is 199.3 KByte/sec, which is an increase of 20.4% compared to always using the standard configuration of the protocol (day 1). This demonstrates the need for and the potential of controlling networks by using ONC, since the static standard configuration does not lead to the best possible performance.

The diagram depicted in Figure 4 describes the resulting utilization of the (download) channel for all three days. Each line shows the sum over the standard utilization of the channel as depicted in Figure 2 and the performance of the BitTorrent client controlled by the ONC system as depicted in Figure 3. Again, the utilization of the channel and consequently the efficiency of the channel usage have been increased significantly.

Figure 3. Resulting download performance due to ONC control (BitTorrent protocol)

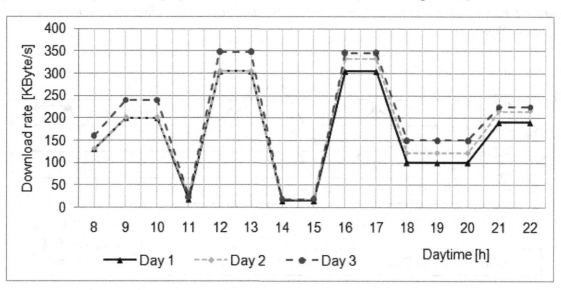

Scenario 2: Broadcast Algorithms for Mobile Ad-hoc Networks

In order to demonstrate the generic character of the ONC system, it has been applied to different protocols. Besides BitTorrent, especially MANet protocols are of interest for ONC's scope, since they are processed in highly dynamic environments and have to deal with uncertainties in their neighborhood due to movements or failures. Within the MANet domain, we decided to apply ONC to broadcast algorithms for MANets, since they provide a basic technology, which is used for other protocol types (e.g. for routing). Out of the set of MANet-based broadcast protocols, the *Reliable Broadcast* (R-BCast) Protocol as introduced by Kunz has been chosen (Kunz, 2003), since it is a representative for this research field. The target for the ONC system in this setup is to reduce the number of forwarded messages and simultaneously increase the number of successfully delivered broadcast messages.

Protocol: R-BCast is a representative for the research field of reliable broadcast protocols in MANets. In order to achieve reliability and increase the packet delivery ratio compared to other protocols, additional effort is made by equipping the nodes with extra buffers. These round-robin based buffers are used to store the last p unique packets received by the particular node. Therefore, the R-BCast protocol has significantly more variable parameters than standard broadcasting algorithms. In contrast to the previous scenario, the task to control this protocol is even more complex, but it also offers a higher potential benefit due to a dynamic adaptation.

Parameter: R-BCast is configured using several parameters defining its behavior. For this scenario, we selected the parameters listed in Table 2 as subject to control interactions of the ONC system. The protocol itself has more parameters, but not all have impact on the simulated performance or can be controlled locally by each node.

Adaptation of ONC: The first scenario demonstrated the benefit of ONC using a simple setup and only a few input parameters. Here, a more complicated setup is used in order to show that ONC is able to deal with more demanding tasks.

At Layer 0, again, two interfaces are needed: one for accessing the protocol parameters and one for collecting information about the local system status. The former interface enables the framework to adapt the behavior of the protocol,

Figure 4. Channel utilization for the three consecutive days (ONC controlled BitTorrent and standard usage from Figure 2)

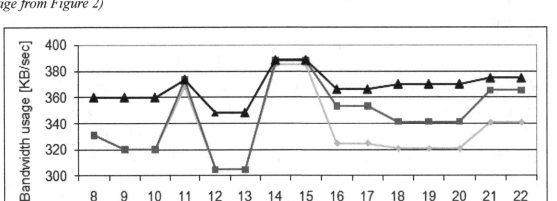

Table 2. Parameter of the B-Cast protocol controlled by ONC

Variable parameter	Description	Standard configuration
Delay	Maximum deceleration time between receiving and forwarding of a message, interval [0, delay]	0.1 sec
Allowed Hello-loss	Maximum number of Hello-messages, which may be lost until a node is assumed to be out of transmission range	3 messages
HelloInterval	Interval between two Hello-messages	2 sec
Δ Hello-Interval	Randomizes Hello-Interval	0.5 sec
Packet count	Number of the last x stored NACK messages	30 messages
Minimum difference	Minimum difference between NACK messages	0.7 sec
NACK timeout	Wait timeout until retransmission of NACK	0.2 sec
NACK retries	Number of retries of sending a NACK message	3 retries

which means the parameter settings can be adapted at runtime. In the latter interface, the engineer has to define what is relevant and influences the protocol's performance - we call this the situation of the system. The latter interface has to be more powerful than in the BitTorrent setup – in MANets the dynamics of the system are mainly represented by the changing neighborhood of nodes (the distribution of other nodes within sending range). Therefore, the sector-based description of the situation as depicted in Figure 5 has been developed. The radius of the outer circle is twice as large as the sending distance – we assume that a node is able to determine the current positions of its neighbors within sensing range relative to its own position (e.g. based on GPS, see (Pahlavan and Krishnamurthy, 2001)).

The situation as depicted in Figure 5 needs an additional measurement for the similarity of two entities (A, B). To be able to determine the distance, the possible influence of rotation and reflection are deducted initially. Afterwards, the formula for the distance of two situations (∂) can be defined with $r \in$ RADII and $s \in$ SECTORS as follows:

$$\partial(A, B) = \sum_r \sum_s (A_{r,s} - B_{r,s})^2 / r \text{ distance}$$

The function *r.distance* defines the radius size. $A_{r,s}$ represents the number of neighbors within the sector s of radius r for the situation description A. This means that the importance of a node's neighbor decreases if it is situated within an outer radius. The same fitness function can be used to measure the global effect of the ONC system on the overall performance, since the target is reflected by the formula above. ONC has to decrease the number of forwarded messages and simultaneously increase the number of successfully delivered broadcast messages.

Furthermore, the fitness function has to be defined to enable the learning process of Layer 1. In literature, several different functions to evaluate the performance of MANets have been proposed and applied. In this context, the standard functions are *Packet Delivery Ratio* and *Packet Latency* – both cannot be measured locally at each node. Therefore, we need another criterion, which can be determined based on locally available information only. The target of the function is to reduce the number of forwarded broadcasts and assure the delivery of the broadcast to each node at the same time. Therefore, we introduce the following formula:

$$\text{Fitness}(x) = \frac{\# recMess}{\# forMess}$$

Figure 5. Environment representation for ONC when controlling protocols for mobile ad-hoc networks

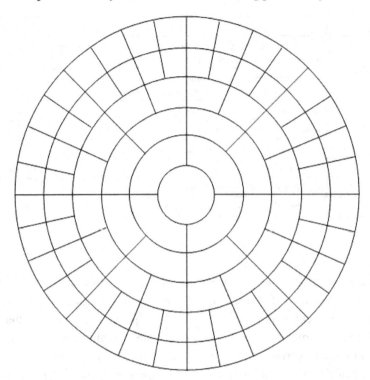

The fitness of a performed action is determined for the last evaluation cycle, defined by the variable x. Since a new parameter set has to be used for a certain duration until we can determine the effect of this configuration, we use evaluation cycles defining discrete time slots. This cycle duration depends on how dynamic an environment is: the faster it changes, the shorter is the cycle to be chosen. Considering the formula above, the node evaluates the sum of all messages being forwarded by all of the neighbors and the node to be evaluated within the last evaluation cycle (*#forMess*), and the sum of all messages being received by them (*#recMess*).

The last part of the adaptation process for ONC deals with the rule-generation component. Layer 2 has to configure adequate simulation scenarios for observed situations in order to evolve new rules. In the current version of ONC, the standard network simulation tool NS-2 (Fall, 1999) is used, but it can easily be exchanged by other solutions. Although NS-2 has a large set of integrated or available standard protocol models, a new one might have to be provided for recently developed or proprietary protocols. Since the development and the analysis of protocols rely on the existence of simulation models, we assume that the availability is given. The adaptation of the scenario is done using the configuration interface by considering the observed situation of the particular MANet node. In order to control broadcast algorithms in MANets, a randomized instance of the aforementioned sector-model is created. This model defines the distribution of the neighboring nodes and considers the movement direction of the node – this information is then transferred to the NS-2 instance to simulate the sub-network using the same coordinate system as for the observed system. Thus, the simulated sub-network is a randomized view on that part of the network the particular node has local information about.

Setup: The ONC framework is implemented in JAVA. The moving agents communicating via the MANet protocol are simulated using the Multi-Agent Simulation Toolkit *MASON* (Luke et al., 2004) with each agent's protocol instance representing a SuOC of the architecture as depicted in Figure 1. The respective Layer 1 Controller is an adapted Learning Classifier System as described in (Tomforde et al., 2009a). At Layer 2, the standard network simulation tool NS-2 (Fall, 1999) is used to evolve new parameter sets in combination with a standard Genetic Algorithm (population size: 15, new children per iteration: 7, mutation rate: 0.2 per child, all children via crossover with fitness-based selection of parents). We use two different simulation tools in order to avoid having exactly the same conditions while optimizing rules, since a complete copy of the current situation observed in the real environment within the simulator is not realistic. 100 agents have been created and applied to the simulated area which has dimensions of 1,000x1,000 cells (corresponds to 1,000x1,000 meters). The agents move according to a random-waypoint-model. The Physical/Mac layer is an IEEE 802.11 in ad-hoc mode at 2 Mbps.

Results: To evaluate the ONC system with the scenario presented before, we analyzed the system's performance for two cases under the same restrictions: a) all nodes are uncontrolled and use the manually optimized standard configuration of the protocol (without ONC system), and b) all nodes have an own instance of the ONC system to control their protocol configuration. During one run of the scenario (10,000 simulated seconds), 17,400 B-Cast-messages have been simulated. The performance measurement in Figure 6 and Figure 7 is calculated using the fitness function used for the local learning part. The diagrams consist of the simulation time in simulated seconds (X-axis) and the determined fitness values (Y-axis).

The diagram in Figure 6 plots the system's performance considering only one node. In principle, all simulated nodes show a comparable behavior; this specific node has been explicitly chosen to demonstrate the typical differences between an ONC-controlled and an uncontrolled node. During the simulation, the node gets separated from the rest of the network (no other nodes within sending distance) between simulation seconds 7,350 and 7,700. Within this interval, the fitness is 0 for both cases. But especially these situations demonstrate the benefit of ONC control.

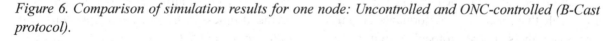

Figure 6. Comparison of simulation results for one node: Uncontrolled and ONC-controlled (B-Cast protocol).

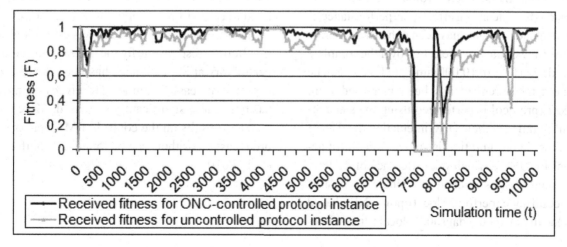

Figure 7. Network-wide comparison of simulation results: Uncontrolled and ONC-controlled (B-Cast protocol)

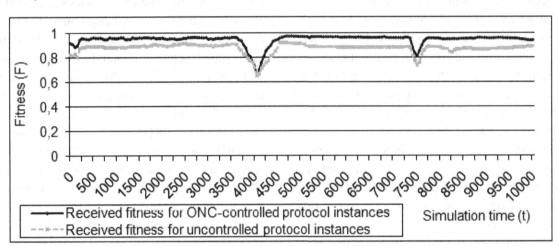

The delays have been lengthened so that the node receives more old messages when it arrives back in sending distance of another node resulting in a quicker recovery of the ONC-controlled system.

Considering again Figure 6, another observation can be made regarding the impact of the learning module. Learning is only possible, if the system gets a feedback on its actions and behavior – thus, it must be able to try different solutions. From this set of possible actions, not all will lead to the intended system performance – some might lead to an affected behavior. Here, e.g. at simulation second 1,800, the learning component tries a rule that results in a performance slightly worse than the standard protocol configuration. Besides these learning effects, the performance of the protocol instance has been enhanced in terms of the fitness function measured over the complete simulation time of 10,000 simulated seconds. The fitness measurement has been increased from 0.827 (protocol is performed using the standard configuration without ONC interactions) to 0.8991 (protocol configuration is subject to control actions by ONC), which is a difference of 8.71%.

These results refer to one single node only. Since all nodes perform a local optimization based on locally available data and a local fitness func-

tion, an increase in the local performance of one node has been expected. To be able to analyze the overall performance, an aggregated view on network-level is needed. Figure 7 plots the averaged performance of the network protocol instances on network-level. The averaging leads to the effect that the system's performance is only slightly influenced by a separation of nodes (e.g. between simulation seconds 3,850 and 4,200). Despite these separation effects, an increase in the system's performance can be observed. When all nodes perform just the standard protocol configuration without any adaptation, the resulting averaged fitness is 0.8760. The same simulation with additional ONC control for all nodes leads to an averaged fitness value of 0.9456, which is an increase of 7.94%. Both aspects of the fitness function are responsible for the increase: the number of forwarded messages has been decreased slightly, whereas the number of received messages has been more significantly increased. More details and results on the control of MANet-based broadcast algorithms can be found in (Tomforde et al., 2010).

FUTURE RESEARCH DIRECTIONS

Future research in the ONC System will be guided along two major dimensions: the scope of optimization and the means for structural reorganization. While currently only single protocols are considered for optimization, future work in the scope of optimization will include multiple protocols in a single protocol stack of a single node. A special focus will be set on the interdependencies of protocol layers. In addition to purely local cross layer approaches, the coordinated optimization of protocol stacks on multiple nodes in a subnetwork will be investigated. This cross-node approach involves, for example, the cooperation and orchestration of large populations of nodes. The structural reorganization currently only employs the parameter adaptation described in this chapter. Future research will also include the evolution of protocol logic, e.g., the adaptation of protocol state machines. Going even further, we will investigate means for the autonomous modification of message syntax and even the semantics of messages.

CONCLUSION

Within this chapter, we described the Organic Network Control (ONC) System which is used to adapt network protocols to dynamically changing environments. We discussed the proposed system architecture in detail and explained the necessary tasks, which an engineer has to process to enable the usage of ONC. Since the dynamic adaptation is a highly complex task, especially if large parts of the possibly occurring situations are unknown at design time, the system is equipped with capabilities to learn new strategies and self-optimize its behavior.

Reagrading the handling of complex tasks in nature, a distributed solution involving a large set of mostly simple entities leads to good solutions in most cases. Typically, these systems are characterized by a combination of evolution and self-optimization. Inspired by these elementary concepts, the ONC approach distributes the responsibility to find and apply the best-fitting control strategies to all participants: they decide autonomously based on local knowledge only. Additionally, the usage of Evolutionary Algorithms in combination with a simulation tool for the rule-generation process enables an evolving system over time.

To demonstrate the potential of the ONC approach, we applied it to the well-known Bit-Torrent protocol and a MANET broadcast protocol. In the former example, usage profiles for three consecutive days were used to present the self-optimizing character of the ONC system by achieving an increase in terms of the measured system performance on all three days. In the latter example, we have compared the performance of the ONC system to manual optimizations, which are typically carried out by protocol designers and network engineers. The results of the simulation studies show that the automated ONC system can reach at least the results of manual optimization and outperforms it for most of the cases.

REFERENCES

Bandyopadhyay, S., Hasuike, K., Horisawa, S., & Tawara, S. (2001). An adaptive MAC and bi-directional routing protocol for ad hoc wireless network using ESPAR antenna. In N. H. Vaidya, M. S. Corson, & S. R. Das (Eds.), *MobiHoc '01: Proceedings of the 2nd ACM International Symposium on Mobile ad hoc Networking & Computing*, (pp. 243–246). New York, NY: ACM.

Boyan, J. A., & Littman, M. L. (1994). Packet routing in dynamically changing networks: A reinforcement learning approach. [Morgan Kaufmann Publishers, Massachusetts, US.]. *Advances in Neural Information Processing Systems, 6*, 671–678.

Casillas, J., Carse, B., & Bull, L. (2004). *Fuzzy XCS: An accuracy-based fuzzy classifier system.* Paper presented at XII Congreso Espanol sobre Tecnologia y Logica Fuzzy (ESTYLF 2004), September 2004, Universidad de Jaen, ES.

Cohen, B. (2003). *Incentives build robustness in BitTorrent.* Paper presented at the 1st Workshop on Economics of Peer-to-Peer Systems, May 2003, Berkeley, US.

Eger, K. (2009). *Simulation of BitTorrent peer-to-peer networks in ns-2.* Retrieved from http://www.tuharburg.de/et6/research/bittorrentsim/index.html

Eiben, A. E., & Smith, J. E. (2003). *Introduction to evolutionary computing. Natural Computing Series (Vol. 2).* Berlin, Germany: Springer Verlag.

Fall, K. (1999). *Network emulation in the Vint/ NS simulator.* Paper presented at the Fourth IEEE Symposium on Computers and Communications, Washington, DC, US.

Farago, A., Myers, A. D., Syrotiuk, V. R., & Zaruba, G. V. (2000). Meta-MAC protocols: Automatic combination of MAC protocols to optimize performance for unknown conditions. *IEEE Journal on Selected Areas in Communications, 18*(9), 1670–1681. doi:10.1109/49.872955

Georganopoulos, N., & Lewis, T. (2007). *A framework for dynamic link and network layer protocol optimisation.* Paper presented at the 16th IST Mobile and Wireless Communications Summit, July 2007, Budapest, HU.

Goyal, P., Vin, H. M., Sheny, C., & Shenoy, P. J. (1995). *A reliable, adaptive network protocol for video transport.* In IEEE INFOCOM'96 - The Conference on Computer Communications Fifteenth Annual Joint Conference of the IEEE Computer and Communications Societies - Networking the Next Generation, (pp. 1080–1090). IEEE, Los Alamitos, US.

Heinzelman, W. B. (2000). *Application-specific protocol architectures for wireless networks.* PhD thesis, Massachusetts Institute of Technology, US.

Hiltunen, M. A., Schlichting, R. D., Ugarte, C. A., & Wong, G. T. (2000). *Survivability through customization and adaptability: The Cactus approach.* Paper presented at DISCEX'00: DARPA Information Survivability Conference and Exposition, 2000, vol. 1, (pp. 294–307). January 2000, Hilton Head, US.

Huang, K. C., Jing, X., & Raychaudhuri, D. (2009). *MAC protocol adaptation in cognitive radio networks: An experimental study.* Paper presented at the International Conference on Computer Communications and Networks, August 2009, San Francisco, US.

Kephart, J. O., & Chess, D. M. (2003). The vision of autonomic computing. [IEEE.]. *IEEE Computer, 1*(36), 41–50.

Kunz, T. (2003). *Reliable multicasting in MANETs.* PhD thesis, Carleton University, CA.

Luke, S., Cioffi-Revilla, C., Panait, L., & Sullivan, K. (2004). *MASON: A new multi-agent simulation toolkit.* Paper presented at The 2004 Swarmfest Workshop, May 2004, University of Michigan, US.

Miranda, H., Pinto, A., & Rodrigues, L. (2001). Appia: A flexible protocol kernel supporting multiple coordinated channels. In *Proceedings of the 21st International Conference on Distributed Computing Systems* (ICDCS 2001), April 16-19, 2001, Phoenix, Arizona, USA, (pp. 707–710). IEEE Computer Society, Los Alamitos, US.

Montana, D., & Redi, J. (2005). Optimizing parameters of a mobile ad hoc network protocol with a genetic algorithm. In H.-G. Beyer, & U.-M. O'Reilly (Eds.), *Genetic and Evolutionary Computation Conference, GECCO 2005, Proceedings,* Washington DC, USA, June 25-29, 2005, ACM, New York, US.

Pahlavan, K., & Krishnamurthy, P. (2001). *Principles of wireless networks: A unified approach*. Upper Saddle River, NJ: Prentice Hall PTR.

Pouwelse, J. A., Garbacki, P., Epema, D. H. J., & Sips, H. J. (2005). The BitTorrent P2P file-sharing system: Measurements and analysis. In M. Castro & R. van Renesse (Eds.), *Peer-to-Peer Systems IV, 4th International Workshop, LNCS 3640*, (pp. 205-216). Springer Verlag.

Prothmann, H., Branke, J., Schmeck, H., Tomforde, S., Rochner, F., Hähner, J., & Müller-Schloer, C. (2009). Organic traffic light control for urban road networks. In [Inderscience Publishers.]. *International Journal of Autonomous and Adaptive Communications Systems, 2*, 203–225. doi:10.1504/IJAACS.2009.026783

Rosa, L., Rodrigues, L., & Lopes, A. (2007). *Appia to R-Appia: Refactoring a protocol composition framework for dynamic reconfiguration* (Tech. Rep. No. 1). University of Lisbon, Department of Informatics.

Schmeck, H. (2005). *Organic computing - A new vision for distributed embedded systems*. Paper presented at the Eighth IEEE International Symposium on Object-Oriented Real-Time Distributed Computing (ISORC 2005), 18-20 May 2005, Seattle, WA, USA.

Schmeck, H., & Müller-Schloer, C. (2007). A characterization of key properties of environment-mediated multiagent systems. In D. Weyns, S. Brueckner, & Y. Demazeau (Eds.), *Engineering Environment-Mediated Multi-Agent Systems, International Workshop, EEMMAS 2007*, (pp. 17–38). Berlin/Heidelberg, Germany: Springer Verlag.

Schöler, T., & Müller-Schloer, C. (2005). An observer/controller architecture for adaptive reconfigurable stacks. In M. Beigl & P. Lukowisz (Eds.), *Systems Aspects in Organic and Pervasive Computing - Proceedings of the 18th International Conference on Architecture of Computing Systems (ARCS'05)*. Berlin, Germany: Springer Verlag.

Sözer, E. M., Stojanovic, M., & Proakis, J. G. (2000). *Initialization and routing optimization for ad-hoc underwater acoustic networks*. Paper presented at OPNETWORK 2000, August 2000, Washington, US.

Sudame, P., & Badrinath, B. R. (2001). On providing support for protocol adaptation in mobile wireless networks. [Hingham, MA: Kluwer Academic Publishers.]. *Mobile Networks and Applications, 6*(1), 43–55. doi:10.1023/A:1009861720398

Tomforde, S., Cakar, E., & Hähner, J. (2009b). Dynamic control of network protocols - A new vision for future self-organised networks. In J. Filipe, J. A. Cetto, & J. J. Ferrier (Eds.), *Proceedings of the 6th International Conference on Informatics in Control, Automation, and Robotics* (pp. 285-290). INSTICC.

Tomforde, S., Hoffmann, M., Bernard, Y., Klejnowski, L., & Hähner, J. (2009c). POWEA: A system for automated network protocol parameter optimisation using evolutionary algorithms. In S. Fischer, E. Maehle, & R. Reischuk (Eds.), *Beiträge der 39. Jahrestagung der Gesellschaft für Informatik e.V.* (GI) (pp. 3177-3192). Gesellschaft für Informatik e.V. (GI).

Tomforde, S., Hurling, B., & Hähner, J. (2010). *Dynamic control of mobile ad-hoc networks - Network protocol parameter adaptation using Organic Network Control*. Paper presented at the 7th International Conference on Informatics in Control, Automation, and Robotics, June 2010, Madeira, PT.

Tomforde, S., Steffen, M., Hähner, J., & Müller-Schloer, C. (2009a). Towards an organic network control system. In J. G. Nieto, W. Reif, G. Wang, & J. Indulska (Eds.), *Proceedings of the 6th International Conference on Autonomic and Trusted Computing (ATC09)* (pp. 2-16). Berlin/Heidelberg, Germany: Springer Verlag.

Tomforde, S., Zgeras, I., Hähner, J., & Müller-Schloer, C. (2010b). Adaptive Control of Sensor Networks. In: Proceedings of the 7th International Conference in Autonomic and Trusted Computing (pp. 77 - 91). Berlin / Heidelberg, Germany: Springer Verlag.

Turgut, D., Daz, S., Elmasri, R., & Turgut, B. (2002). Optimizing clustering algorithm in mobile ad hoc networks using genetic algorithmic approach. In C.-K. Mao, L.-S. Lee, & K. C. Chen (Eds.): *Global Telecommunications Conference (GLOBECOM '02)*, (pp. 62–66). IEEE, Los Alamitos, US.

van Dam, T., & Langendoen, K. (2003). An adaptive energy-efficient MAC protocol for wireless sensor networks. In I. Akyildiz, D. Estrin, D. Culler, & M. Srivastava (Eds.), *SenSys '03: Proceedings of the 1st International Conference on Embedded Networked Sensor Systems*, (pp. 171–180). New York, NY: ACM.

van Renesse, R., Birman, K. P., Hayden, M., Vaysburd, A., & Karr, D. (1998). Building adaptive systems using ensemble. [New York, NY: John Wiley & Sons, Inc.]. *Software, Practice & Experience*, 28(9), 963–979. doi:10.1002/(SICI)1097-024X(19980725)28:9<963::AID-SPE179>3.0.CO;2-9

van Renesse, R., Birman, K. P., & Maffeis, S. (1996). Horus: A flexible group communication system. [New York, NY: ACM.]. *Communications of the ACM*, 39(4), 76–83. doi:10.1145/227210.227229

Varga, A. (2001). *The OMNeT++ discrete event simulation system*. Paper presented at the European Simulation Multiconference (ESM'2001), June 2001, Prague, CZ.

Weingärtner, E., vom Lehn, H., & Wehrle, K. (2009). *A performance comparison of recent network simulators*. Paper presented at ICC 2009: IEEE International Conference on Communications, June 2009, Dresden, DE.

Whiteson, S., & Stone, P. (2004). *Towards autonomic computing: Adaptive network routing and scheduling*. Paper presented at the International Conference on Autonomic Computing (ICAC'04), May 2004, New York, US.

Wilson, S. W. (1995). Classifier fitness based on accuracy. *Evolutionary Computation*, 3, 149–175. doi:10.1162/evco.1995.3.2.149

Ye, T., Harrison, D., Mo, B., Sikdar, B., Kaur, H. T., & Kalyanaraman, S. … Vastola, K. (2001). *Network management and control using collaborative on-line simulation*. Paper presented at IEEE International Conference on Communications (ICC'01), May 2001, Helsinki, FI.

Ye, T., & Kalyanaraman, S. (2001). *An adaptive random search algorithm for optimizing network protocol parameters* (Tech. Rep. No. 1). Rensselaer Polytechnic Institute, US.

ADDITIONAL READING

Branke, J. (2002). Evolutionary Optimization in Dynamic Environments (Genetic Algorithms and Evolutionary Computation). Dordrecht, NL: Kluwer Academic Publishers Group.

Dracopoulos, D. C. (1997). *Evolutionary Learning Algorithms for Neural Adaptive Control*. Berlin/Heidelberg, DE: Springer Verlag.

Eiben, A. E., & Smith, J. E. (2003). *Introduction to Evolutionary Computation*. Berlin, DE: Springer Verlag.

Kurose, J. F., & Ross, W. K. (2008). *Computer Networking: A Top-Down Approach*. Boston, US: Pearson Education, Inc.

Lynch, N. (1996). *Distributed Algorithms (Morgan Kaufmann Series in Data Management Systems)*. San Francisco, CA, US: Morgan Kaufmann Publishers Inc.

Mitchell, T. M. (1997). *Machine Learning*. Columbus, OH, US: Mcgraw Hill Book Co.

Parashar, M., & Hariri, S. (Eds.). (2007). *Autonomic Computing: Concepts, Infrastructure, and Applications*. Boca Raton, FL, US: CRC Press Taylor & Francis Group.

Schuster, H. G. (2001). *Complex Adaptive Systems: An Introduction*. Saarbrücken, DE: Scator Verlag.

Tanenbaum, A. S. (2002). *Computer Networks*. Upper Saddle River, New Jersey, US: Prentice Hall International Publishers.

Tanenbaum, A. S., & van Steen, M. (2006). *Distributed Systems: Principles and Paradigms*. Upper Saddle River, New Jersey, US: Prentice Hall International Publishers.

Vasilakos, A., Parashar, M., Karnouskos, S., & Pedrycz, W. (Eds.). (2009). Autonomic Communication. New York, US: Springer Science+Business Media, LLC.

Würtz, R. P. (Ed.). (2008). *Organic Computing (Understanding Complex Systems)*. Berlin, DE: Springer Verlag.

Chapter 3
Robust Network Services with Distributed Code Rewriting

Thomas Meyer
University of Basel, Switzerland

Christian Tschudin
University of Basel, Switzerland

ABSTRACT

Nature does not know the concept of a dedicated controlling instance; instead, "control" is an emergent phenomenon. This is in stark contrast with computer networking where protocol control loops are (seemingly) in charge: while the functional aspect of a networking service can be well mastered, the dynamic behavior is still difficult to understand and even control. In this chapter, we present a methodology how to design distributed software systems that are dynamically stable and robust in execution. It is based on continuously replicating a system's own code base in order to thwart unreliable execution and even accidental code changes. The crucial part is to design the system such that it regulates its own replication. This can be achieved by an execution environment inspired by chemistry to which we add the concept of self-rewriting programs (Quines). With a link load balancing example we show how to exploit competition and cooperation in a self-rewriting service implementation.

INTRODUCTION

Natural systems are able to dynamically construct redundancy by assembling and reproducing their components. Often, components exist in several copies (flocks, but also blood or nerve cells), exploiting parallelism and minimizing the impact of the loss of a single item. For singular components (e.g. bones) and in order to fight the problem of aging, redundancy is achieved over time through procreation, yielding a new and possibly modified copy. In computer science however, software is considered to be static (and without wear). This view is recent: Back in the 1940s, von Neumann (1966) developed a theory of self-reproducing automata. He described a universal constructor,

DOI: 10.4018/978-1-61350-092-7.ch003

a machine able to produce a copy of any other machine whose soft- and hardware blueprint is provided as input. Being universal, the constructor is also able to generate a copy of itself.

Considerable research on self-replication was carried out on the framework of Cellular Automata (CA), in which remarkable results were achieved, also in terms of robustness and self-repair (Tempesti, Mange, & Stauffer, 1998). However, these results are hard to transfer from CA to the world of today's computer software. In the 1960s, with the desire to understand the fundamental information-processing principles and algorithms involved in self-replication, researchers started to focus on self-replicating code: how textual computer programs are able to replicate independent from their physical realization. The existence of self-replicating programs is a consequence of Kleene's second recursion theorem (Kleene, 1938), which states that for any program P there exists a program P', which generates its own encoding and passes it to P along with the original input. The simplest form of a self-replicating program is a Quine, named after the philosopher and logician Willard van Orman Quine, and made popular by Hofstadter (1979): A Quine is a program that prints its own code. Quines exist for any programming language that is Turing complete and it is a common challenge for students to come up with a Quine in their language of choice. The *Quine Page* provides a comprehensive list of such programs in various languages (Thompson, 2010).

Contribution

In this work, we put Quines in a parallel execution environment, permitting an ensemble of Quine copies to achieve surprising robustness with respect to code and packet loss and even execution errors. Our contribution consists in the demonstration of an operational system based on Quines that runs highly reliable network services with provable dynamic properties. More precisely, we will introduce an artificial chemistry embodied as

interconnected "molecule vessels" in which we place carefully crafted self-replicating programs. Packets, or "molecules", react with each other and produce new packets, thus executing the program. Useful computations are piggybacked to the Quine structures in order to implement the network services. Due to the special scheduling of the reactions in the artificial chemistry according to the "law of mass action" in real chemistry, our system inherits the dynamic properties from chemistry such that we can apply the related analysis tools that were developed in the past two centuries. The law of mass action links the microscopic (scheduling) events with the observable behavior at macro scale. Using perturbation analysis, we can then proceed in identifying equilibria and their stability.

Structure of this Chapter

We present our work along the following argumentation path: After having highlighted the context of our approach and related work, we proceed with introducing a new "style" of implementing network services that we call *chemical networking protocols*. Next, we present "chemical Quines" and we extensively study their long-term stability, both in a single node as well as in a distributed setting. We also look at competing Quines and show that the aggressive growth of Quines leads to a winner-takes-all dynamics. We then investigate cooperative couplings of Quines and put these insights to work with a link-load-balancing service for which we show its resilience to packet *and* code loss.

CONTEXT AND RELATED WORK

In this section, we reference the relevant corner stones for our work where we could draw important insights, namely self-reproduction, fault tolerance, artificial chemistries and their dynamics, the dynamics of competing populations and finally cooperation patterns. The programming language

"Fraglets", which we have used to implement our system, was described by Tschudin (2003) and is summarized in the next section.

Since the work of von Neumann (1966), many variants of universal constructors for self-reproduction have been proposed and elaborated. For an overview, see Freitas and Merkle (2004) or Sipper (1998). Langton (1984) argued that natural systems are lacking a universal constructor and relaxed the requirement that self-replicating structures must be equipped with a universal constructor. Instead, self-replication may arise from dynamic loops instead of static tapes; the information necessary to replicate the structure may be distributed in this loop and may not be present in explicit and distinct entities of a passive, un-interpreted blueprint and its active version of interpreted instructions. This observation led to a new surge of research on such self-replicating structures (Perrier, Sipper, & Zahnd, 1996; Sipper, 1998).

In computer science and engineering, the method of choice to achieve robustness, resilience and fault tolerance of services is to build up redundancy in order to mask errors (Johnson, 1996; Pradhan, 1996; Wilfredo, 2000): Multiple identical or similar redundant systems are performing the same task. The result is compared, often by a centralized observer. This architecture inevitably leads to the problem that the central decision maker may also be error prone, requiring an observer of the observer, and so on, leading to infinite regression. Hence, we need a solution where the central observer that steers the redundancy is redundant too and is blended into the system

Artificial chemical computing models (Banâtre, Fradet, & Radenac, 2006; Calude & Paun, 2001; Dittrich, 2005; Holland, 1992; Paun, 2000) express computations as chemical reactions that consume and produce objects (data or code) that are organized in a multiset. Dittrich, Ziegler and Banzhaf (2001) classified chemical computing as applications of Artificial Chemistry, a branch of Artificial Life (ALife) dedicated to the study of the chemical processes related to life and organizations in general. In the same way as ALife seeks to understand life by building artificial systems with simplified life-like properties, Artificial Chemistry builds simplified abstract chemical models that nevertheless exhibit properties that may lead to emergent phenomena, such as the spontaneous organization of molecules into self-maintaining structures (Dittrich & Speroni di Fenizio, 2007; Fontana & Buss, 1994). The applications of artificial chemistries go beyond ALife, reaching biology, information processing (in the form of natural and artificial chemical computing models) and evolutionary algorithms for optimization, among other domains. Chemical models have also been used to express replication, reproduction and variation mechanisms (Dittrich & Banzhaf, 1998; Dittrich et al., 2001; Hutton, 2002; Teuscher, 2007; Yamamoto, Schreckling, & Meyer, 2007).

The dynamics of natural chemical reactions is governed by the law of mass action (Waage & Guldberg, 1864; English translation by Abrash, 1986), which states that the reaction rate is proportional to the reactant concentration. Several algorithms have been proposed to simulate chemical reactions on the microscopic level: Gillespie (1977) describes an exact stochastic simulation algorithm that accurately mimics the randomness of reactions, which stems from the Brownian motion of the colliding reactant molecules. Several variants and improvements of this algorithm have been proposed since then (Gibson & Bruck, 2000; Gillespie, 2007). Originally, the aim of these algorithms was to simulate real chemical reactions. In this work, we use them as scheduling algorithms for our chemical programs. Consequently, program execution is an inherently stochastic process; there is no guarantee, which reaction will be executed next and when. However, since on the macroscopic time scale these algorithms simulate the law of mass action, the average dynamic behavior can be described by the same Ordinary Differential Equations (ODEs) that are used to deterministically approximate real chemical reactions.

A novel element of our work is the use of hard limits to an artificial chemical vessel's capacity. Environments with limited resources that host replicating entities lead to natural selection, as was shown by research on population dynamics by Fernando and Rowe (2007); Stadler, Fontana, and Miller (1993); Szathmáry (1991). In our case, the population consists of software components: Healthy software survives whereas errors are displaced. This naturally leads to software homeostasis – the intrinsic self-regulation of code in order to maintain a stable, healthy state.

Natural selection inevitably induces a competitive environment where software instances fight for resources and where this struggle may lead to the extinction of healthy but inefficient or rarely used code. There are, however, well-known methods that show the emergence of cooperation (Wagner, 2000) in a competitive environment, such as the theory of hypercycles (Eigen & Schuster, 1979). Furthermore, in computer network research, mechanisms to control redundancy on the level of data-packets are well known. Transmission control protocols such as TCP (Postel, 1981) are not only able to recover from packet losses, but also to adapt the transmission rate to the limited bandwidth of the network (Jacobson, 1988), providing fairness for the competitive environment of the underlying IP network. Within our setting, we are able to transpose these methods, currently only used for data stream control, down to the code execution level, granting fairness among the software parts that fight for limited (memory) resources.

CHEMICAL NETWORKING PROTOCOLS

Traditionally, protocol execution is handled by a state machine that upon the reception of a packet synchronously changes its internal state and performs some communication activity. Here we introduce a "molecule metaphor" where each packet is treated as a virtual molecule. Virtual molecules react with other molecules in a reaction vessel (node). A reaction may produce other molecules being delivered to the application or being sent over the network. In such a chemical perspective, we obtain a web of reactions that together perform a distributed computation (called network service).

Modeling Chemical Communication

Instead of encoding a deterministic state machine, or having a sequential program that processes an incoming packet, each network node contains a finite multiset of molecules $S=\{s_1,\ldots,s_n\}$ (=packets). In addition, each node defines a set of reaction rules $R=\{r_1,\ldots,r_m\}$ expressing which reactant molecules can collide and which molecules are generated during this process. Such a reaction is typically represented as a chemical reaction equation such as

$$C_i + X_i \rightarrow C_i + X_j$$

The above reaction in node i consumes, if present, two molecules C and X from the local multiset, regenerates C and sends molecule X to neighbor node j. In a simple two-node network topology, the above example spans the following reaction network that works as follows:

$$C_1 + X_1 \rightarrow C_1 + X_2$$

$$C_2 + X_2 \rightarrow C_2 + X_1$$

A received molecule is in a first step passively placed into the multiset of the node. For example, the second rule is not executed immediately after node 2 receives a new X-molecule. It is rather scheduled for a later time determined by an exact stochastic reaction algorithm, for instance those proposed by Gillespie (1977) or Gibson and Bruck

(2000). The reaction scheduler draws the delay between two occurrences of the same reaction from an exponential probability distribution. The role of this delayed execution is to enforce the law of mass action at the macroscopic level: Molecules C_1 and X_1 react with an average rate equal to the product of their abundance $r_1 = c_1 x_1$. The rate of packets sent from node 1 to node 2 is equal to r_1 while the packet stream in the opposite direction exhibits a rate of $r_2 = c_2 x_2$. It can be shown that the overall reaction system spanned by the two local reaction rules strives towards equilibrium where the number of X-molecules in either node is inversely proportional to the number of the corresponding C-molecules.

Fraglets: A Chemical Programming Language

So far, we demonstrated a static reaction network where abstract reaction rules were "installed" permanently in each node. Here, we extend this model aiming at dynamically changing the set of reaction rules. We present the Fraglets language (Tschudin, 2003, 2007), an artificial chemistry according to the definition of Dittrich et al. (2001), whose corresponding chemical machine is executable and which serves as a simple platform to run chemical protocols.

Each molecule $s \in S$, or packet, is a string of symbols over a finite alphabet Σ. The first symbol of the string defines the string rewriting operation applied to this molecule by the virtual chemical machine; it can be thought of an assembler instruction. For example, the molecule [fork a b c d] transforms itself and splits into the two molecules [a c d] and [b c d]. The list below shows some essential instructions and their actions.

$$[\text{match } \alpha \ \Phi] + [\alpha \ \Theta] \rightarrow [\Phi \ \Theta]$$

$$[\text{fork } \alpha \ \beta \ \Theta] \rightarrow [\alpha \ \Theta] + [\beta \ \Theta]$$

$$[\text{nop } \Theta] \rightarrow [\Theta]$$

$$[\text{send k } \Theta]_i \rightarrow [\Theta]_k \text{ if } (i,k) \in E$$

$\alpha, \beta \in \Sigma$ are arbitrary symbols, $\Phi, \Theta \in \Sigma^*$ are symbol strings, $i, k \in V$ denote network nodes, and $(i,k) \in E$ communication links of the network graph $G = (V, E)$. Molecules starting with "match" or any non-instruction identifier are in their *normal form*. The "match" instruction can be used to join two molecules by concatenating the second to the first after removing the processed headers. Subsequent instructions immediately reduce the product further until they again reach their normal form. For example, the two molecules [match pkt send 2 pkt] and [pkt data] in node 1 imply the reaction

$$[\text{match pkt send 2 pkt}]_1 + [\text{pkt data}]_1$$

$$\rightarrow [\text{send 2 pkt data}]_1$$

(transmit to neighbor 2) $\rightarrow [\text{pkt data}]_2$

Such a chemical language allows us to "program" the reaction graph. Molecules now have a structure; they *contain* information such as piggybacked user data. However, the dynamics of the reaction network is still governed by the law of mass action and thus, the protocol's behavior is chemically controlled.

CHEMICAL QUINES AND THEIR STABILITY

In this section, we first demonstrate how to write Quine programs in the Fraglets artificial chemistry. Then, by limiting the memory resources of the reaction vessel, we turn these Quines into software elements that steer their own redundancy and by this way become intrinsically self-healing. We also quantify the Quines' robustness by calculating their average survival time using phase-type distributions.

In ordinary sequential programming languages, a Quine is a single piece of code outputting its own source code. In the parallel world of an artificial chemistry, a Quine becomes a *set of molecules* that is able to replicate itself. An example that illustrates this concept is the combination of a "blueprint molecule" B = [x fork nop match x] and its active variant A = [match x fork nop match x] (Yamamoto et al., 2007). The two molecules react with each other and, according to the Fraglets rewriting rules, regenerate themselves.

By repeating the fork instruction three times, the above Quine can be converted into a duplicating Quine as shown in Figure 1. The duplicating Quine generates two copies of itself in each round while consuming the original copy. The schematic illustration on the right side of Figure 1 shows the corresponding chemical reaction network that is dynamically equivalent to the Fraglets rewriting loop on the left side. Note that only bimolecular reactions are scheduled according to the law of mass actions; unimolecular rewriting rules such as "fork" are immediately executed, hence these intermediate steps (molecules) are omitted in the schematic notation.

Because the reactions are scheduled according to the law of mass action, the duplication rate increases with the growing number of Quine instances. Consequently, the population of Quines

grows hyperbolically (Szathmáry, 1991), meaning that it theoretically reaches infinite abundance in finite time.

As a limit to this unbounded growth, we introduce a *non-selective dilution flux* to the reaction vessel, which destroys arbitrary molecules as long as the total number of molecules exceeds a pre-defined vessel capacity. This leads to a selective pressure: Only molecules that are part of a self-replicating set have a chance to remain present – all other molecules will eventually be displaced.

The dynamic behavior of the duplicating Quine in a vessel of limited capacity N is described by the catalytic network equation (Stadler et al., 1993), a deterministic approximation expressed by Ordinary Differential Equations (ODEs) where x_A is the number of A-molecules and where x_B denotes the number of blueprints B

$$\dot{x}_A = \overbrace{x_A x_B}^{\text{growth}} - \overbrace{\frac{x_A}{N} \Phi}^{\text{death}}$$

$$\dot{x}_B = \underbrace{x_A x_B}_{\text{growth}} - \underbrace{\frac{x_B}{N} \Phi}_{\text{death}}$$

subject to the conservation relation $x_A + x_B = N$. The total dilution flux $\Phi = 2 x_A x_B$ is equal to the net production rate in the vessel. The system exhibits three dynamic fixed points, one at $x_A = x_B = N /$

Figure 1. The duplicating Quine grows hyperbolically by generating two replicas in each cycle while the original copy is consumed

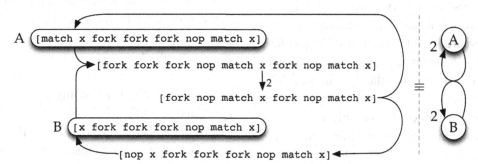

2 and two pathological cases at $x_A^* = N$, $x_B^* = 0$, and $x_A^* = 0$, $x_B^* = N$.

The first fixed point is locally stable according to a standard perturbation analysis (Strogatz, 1994) and is characterized by both molecules – the blueprint and its active variant – being present with the same abundance. The stability property essentially means that the system returns to equilibrium condition: Even if we perturb the system by removing some instances of either species, the opponent forces of hyperbolic growth and non-selective dilution flux let the system autonomically find back to this equilibrium. In other words, the system intrinsically maintains its own redundancy without an external controller!

The Odds of Unlucky Scheduling

The two pathological fixed points from the analysis above deserve some more attention. The deterministic ODE model predicts that they are not locally stable, which may lead to the conclusion that these states cannot be reached. However, in our stochastic execution environment, these fixed points will eventually be reached and represent states where one of the molecule species is completely absent such that the system becomes deadlocked and finds itself in a so called "absorption state". Consequently, the lifetime of a chemical Quine is finite, even when no faults occur.

In order to quantify the baseline robustness of the duplicating Quine, we now calculate the mean first-passage time to one of those absorption states. A chemical reaction network obeying the law of mass action can be modeled stochastically by a continuous time discrete space Markov jump process on the non-negative $|S|$-dimensional integer lattice where $|S|$ is the number of molecular species. The Chemical Master Equation (CME) (Gillespie, 1992) describes the dynamics of this stochastic model.

Our simple chemical Quine only consist of two species and the total number of molecules is fixed to N. This allows the system to be modeled by a finite birth-death Markov chain where $X_A(t)$

$\in [0,N]$ is a random variable denoting the number of A-molecules, whereas the number of blueprints (B) is given by $X_B(t) = N - X_A(t)$. In this context, the birth rate λ_i represents the average rate of losing a B-molecule and gaining an A-molecule in state i whereas the death rate μ_i describes a movement in the opposite direction. These transition rates for the states $[1,N-1]$ are given as

$$\lambda_i = i(N - i)\frac{N - i - 1}{N + 2}\frac{N - i}{N + 1}$$

$$\mu_i = i(N - i)\frac{i + 1}{N + 2}\frac{i}{N + 1}$$

The distribution of the first passage time from an initial state (here: $k = N / 2$) to one of the absorption states is given by the phase-type distribution according to Neuts (1981): We first build the transition rate matrix $\mathbf{Q}$, the off-diagonal elements of which are the transition rates ($q_{i,i+1} = \lambda_i$, $q_{i,i-1} = \mu_i$) and the diagonal elements are given by the sum over the off-diagonal elements such that its row sum is zero. Next, we separate the transient states from the absorbing states; thereby we summarize all absorbing states to one single state. Finally, we rewrite the transition matrix to the form

$$\mathbf{Q} = \begin{pmatrix} \mathbf{S} & \mathbf{S}_0 \\ \mathbf{0} & \mathbf{0} \end{pmatrix}$$

where $\mathbf{S}$ is the transition matrix among the transient states and $\mathbf{S}_0 = -\mathbf{S} \cdot \mathbf{1}$ is the vector of transition rates to the absorbing state. The mean time to absorption is now given by the expression

$$E[T_{abs}] = -\mathbf{p}\mathbf{S}^{-1}\mathbf{1}$$

where $\mathbf{p}$ is the initial probability distribution with $p_k = 1$ and $p_{i \neq k} = 0$.

We developed a tool that given the reaction network and the vessel capacity N automatically builds the corresponding Markov chain and its transition matrix S. We then use Scilab (Campbell, Chancelier, & Nikoukhah, 2006) to calculate the mean time to absorption based on the generated transition matrix.

Figure 2 shows the mean time to absorption for the duplicating Quine in vessels with different capacities. The figure illustrates that the mean time to absorption exponentially increases with the vessel capacity N. In fact, already for $N = 37$ the mean survival time exceeds the current lifetime of the universe. For small values of N, we complemented these analytical calculations with 1000 simulation runs in Fraglets; the empirically measured average survival time accurately matches the predicted survival time.

We expect the robustness of a Quine to decrease with the presence of execution errors. We study two types of errors: (1) With probability p, each Fraglets instruction fails to produce the right result; instead, a neutral fraglet is generated, that is unable to replicate or to react with other molecules. (2) The symbols of a vessel's fraglets become subject to alteration with rate δ, turning the affected fraglet again into a neutral molecule.

Figure 3 shows the rewriting steps of the duplicating Quine that is subject to execution errors. The dashed arrows indicate that instead of the intended rewriting result, an error product E is generated. The corresponding reaction network is

$$A + B \xrightarrow{p(2-p)} E$$
$$A + B \xrightarrow{(1-p)^2 p} 2E$$
$$A + B \xrightarrow{(1-p)^3 p^2} 2E + 2B$$
$$A + B \xrightarrow{(1-p)^3 p(2-p)} A + E + 2B$$
$$A + B \xrightarrow{(1-p)^5} 2A + 2B$$

We cannot model the system by a one-dimensional birth-death Markov chain anymore because now three species are involved: A, B, and the error product E. However, the survival time, i.e., the first-passage time to an absorption state, can be calculated from the transition matrix of the corresponding two-dimensional Markov state

Figure 2. Mean survival time of a Quine with respect to the vessel capacity

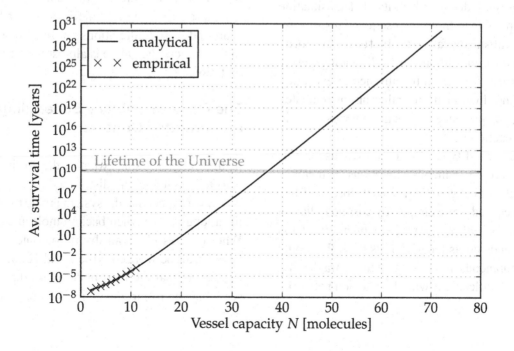

Figure 3. Duplicating Quine where each rewriting step may be subject to an execution error (dashed lines) with probability p. We assume that the error product E is not able to react with the other molecules.

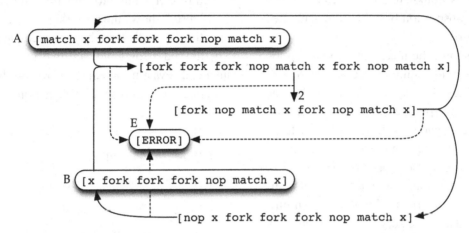

array. An absorption state is still defined as a state where either A- or B-molecules are absent.

Figure 4 shows the mean survival time of a duplicating Quine in vessels of different capacities plotted with respect to different execution error probabilities. The robustness of the Quine barely decreases for realistic execution error probabilities and only sharply drops for error probabilities above 1%. The diagonal line in Figure 4 illustrates the survival rate of a single Quine instance that just replicates but does not heal itself. This situation is comparable to traditional sequential software, which realistically fails at the first occurrence of an execution error. Although the self-healing Quines eventually die even in the absence of execution errors, they live much longer than un-instrumented code in the presence of execution errors, even in small reaction vessels.

The second type of error we discuss in this section are spontaneous alterations of memory bits with rate δ. Such Single Event Upsets (SEUs) can be caused, for example, by cosmic radiation (Normand, 1996). The rate at which a fraglet is hit depends on its length l, thus is $l\delta$. We model the spontaneous mutations that turn a fraglet into a neutral molecule E with the reaction network

$$A + B \xrightarrow{\ 1\ } 2A + 2B$$
$$A \xrightarrow{\ 8\delta\ } E$$
$$B \xrightarrow{\ 7\delta\ } E$$

Figure 5 shows the mean survival time of our duplicating Quine, now plotted with respect to different symbol mutation rates (we assumed that each fraglets symbol is encoded by eight bits). To appraise these curves, we recall that, according to Normand (1996), the Singe Event Upset (SEU) rate caused in microelectronic devices by radiation is around $5 \cdot 10^{-16}$ alterations per bit and second. In this region, the Quine is almost unaffected by mutations.

The Odds of Unlucky Scheduling in a Distributed Context

In this section, we study whether the survival time of a Quine is higher in a distributed context. Intuitively, we expect that the system is able to survive for a longer time when backup molecules exist: When one vessel hits an absorption state, another vessel in the network could be still alive and would be able to heal the inert node by sending it the seed that can restart the Quine's loop. However,

Figure 4. Mean survival time of a duplicating Quine, in a vessel of capacity N and subject to execution errors with probability p. The fluctuations for N = 30 are due to floating point precision limits in Scilab.

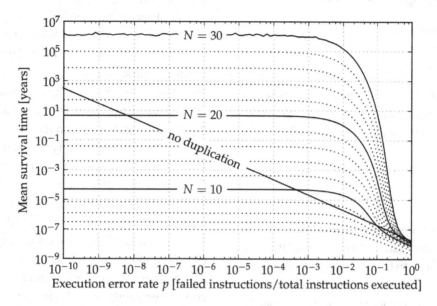

Figure 5. Mean survival time of a duplicating Quine, in a vessel of capacity N and subject to spontaneous symbol alterations at rate δ

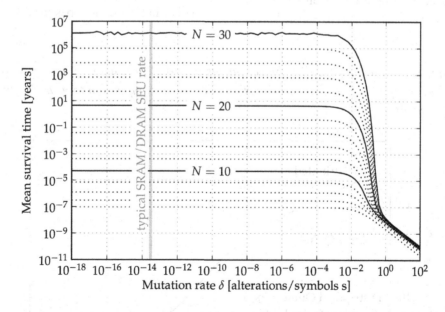

we found out that the strategy of spreading seeds is important for this scheme to work.

We analyzed the robustness of two different types of distributed Quines. Common to both types is that each node i contains a reaction between the Quine's active molecule A_i and the corresponding blueprint B_i. The difference is that in the first case we produce the seed replicas locally and broadcast them to neighbor nodes. Once arrived, the seeds unfold and generate two instances of either molecule type:

$$A_i + B_i \rightarrow \sum_{\{j|(i,j)\in E\}} (2A_j + 2B_j)$$

The second distributed Quine type only sends one seed to its neighbor nodes whereas the other seed is used to replicate the Quine locally:

$$A_i + B_i \rightarrow A_i + B_i + \sum_{\{j|(i,j)\in E\}} (A_j + B_j)$$

Figure 6 shows the mean survival time against different mutation rates of the two distributed Quine types in a two-node network topology, as well as the curve of a one-node duplicating Quine for comparison purpose. The total capacity of the reaction vessel(s) is the same for all three cases, namely $N = 10$ molecules: This is, for the one-node Quine, the single vessel provides the whole capacity, whereas for the two distributed

cases, the capacity is evenly distributed between the two participating nodes.

We observe that the single Quine always outperforms the distributed Quine of type 1, which sends both seed copies to the neighbor. The distributed Quine of type 2, however, is the most robust variant for moderate symbol alteration rates. This stems from the fact that the second type has to digest only two received molecules at once, whereas the first type receives four instances at a time. The more excessive molecules the dilution flux has to remove, the higher is the fluctuation around the steady state and, consequently, the more likely one of the absorption states is reached. Thus, the good recipe for robust distributed Quines is to replicate locally in order to maintain the population and to send only one copy to the neighbor nodes for the case the neighbors deviate from the fixed point or even reached a local absorption state.

Figure 7 shows the robustness surface of the two distributed Quine types for different symbol

Figure 6. Mean survival time of the distributed Quines in two vessels with a total capacity of N = 10 molecules, subject to spontaneous symbol alteration at rate δ in comparison to a single Quine with the same total capacity of N = 10

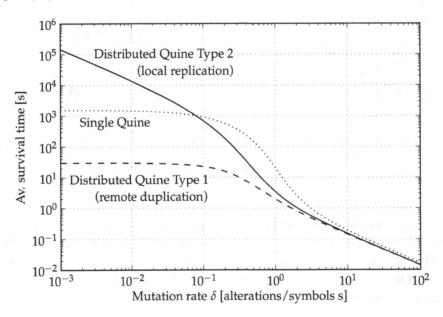

alteration rates and packet loss probabilities. Packet loss only has a marginal effect on the robustness, especially for the second type, which replicates locally. The second type only needs the received Quine seeds to bootstrap the local Quine when accidentally hitting a local absorption state.

Competing Quines: The Winner Takes All

As we showed above, the aggressive growth of the duplicating Quine is instrumental for letting it self-heal. However, when placing two different instances of duplicating Quines into a common reaction vessel, only one will survive while the other will be literally squeezed out. This is due to the finding that independently and hyperbolically growing populations with finite resources lead to the survival of the common (Szathmáry, 1991): The first Quine that reaches a sufficiently high concentration will dominate the others and lead to their extinction even if their replication rate is higher.

Figure 8 illustrates the fight between two Quines in the same vessel for different start concentrations but constant total vessel capacity $N = 20$. We observe that the robustness of the Quines heavily depend on their initial concentration – the (initial) allocation of memory slots for Quine 2 grows linearly from left to right – and that the non-selective dilution flux does not guarantee fairness among the Quines *per se*.

This winner-takes-all behavior is problematic because we would like to compose multiple self-healing Quines, each working on some part of a problem to solve. As we show in the following section, this is in fact possible if the Quines co-operate.

DESIGN PATTERNS FOR A COOPERATIVE COUPLING OF QUINES

In this section, we introduce three design patterns to couple Quines and, in an application case,

Figure 7. Mean survival time of the distributed Quines in two vessels with a total capacity of N = 10 molecules, subject to packet loss with probability p and spontaneous symbol alteration at rate δ

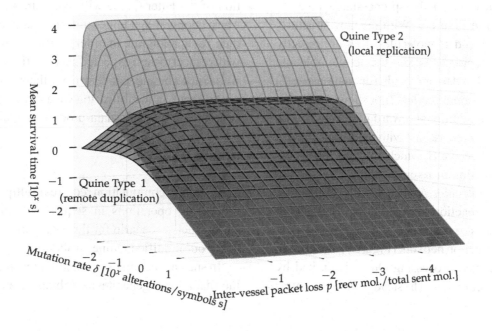

Figure 8. Mean survival time of two competing Quines in a vessel with capacity N = 20 with respect to different initial partitions

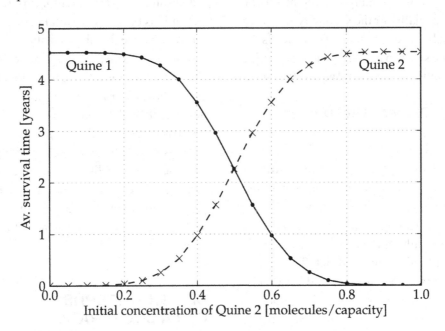

show that even competitive Quines can be used to build useful, self-healing networking protocols. But first, we demonstrate how our self-healing Quines can be enriched to perform an actual and useful computation.

A small modification to the duplicating Quine's structure leads to a data-processing Quine, as is depicted in Figure 9. With the new structure, the set of A and B molecules does not directly replicate anymore. Instead, the active molecule A reacts with a data molecule (or "data packet") D, computes some product (not shown) and also generates an additional reward molecule R. The reward molecule reacts with and consumes a blueprint molecule B, which contains the necessary information to re-create the active and the blueprint molecule. As usual with duplicating Quines, the reaction between R and B results in two instances of A and B.

In this reaction network (Figure 9), the growth rate of the data-processing Quine is limited by the data injection rate. The steady-state concentra-

tion of the Quine becomes proportional to its steady-state growth rate (not considering the dilution flux). If the growth rates of two Quines differ by magnitudes (for example, if data molecules for one Quine are injected more frequently than data molecules for another Quine), the concentration of the latter Quine will likely drop to zero. Thus, cooperating Quines must mutually control their replication rate in order to achieve fairness with respect to their expected survival time, which we want to be independent from their data processing rate. In the following we analyze various coupling methods for data-processing Quines.

String of Quines

Frequently, a computation requires multiple data-processing operations in sequence; Figure 10 shows such a scenario for three operations, each using our modified Quine structure.

In such a reaction network topology, the common data stream generates a symbiotic relationship

Figure 9. Data processing Quine: The active molecule A processes a data molecule D resulting in a reward R. The blueprint B contains all information necessary to generate two copies of A and B when reacting with R.

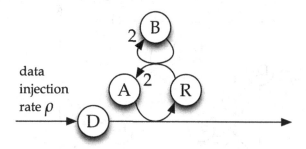

Figure 10. String of Quines: Three data-processing Quines are indirectly linked by sequentially processing the same data stream.

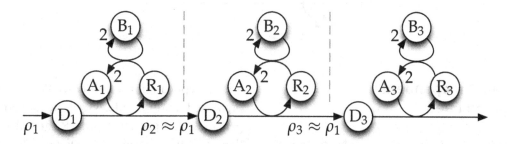

among the Quines: The second Quine is only able to duplicate if the first Quine generated a product molecule and duplicated in turn. The third Quine only duplicates after the second duplicated before. Thus, the growth rate of all Quines is approximately equal to the data injection rate.

Hypercycle

If Quines do not process the same data stream sequentially, we need another method of symbiotically coupling the Quines. Eigen and Schuster (1979) proposed a cyclic linkage of reactions as an explanation of self-organization of prebiotic systems in which RNA strands and enzymes cooperate. We translate this idea to the world of Quines in Fraglets: As shown in Figure 11, a hypercycle of Quines consists of several data-

processing Quines, which do not generate their own duplication reward R_i. Instead, each Quine cyclically generates the reward for another Quine.

The advantage of such a cyclic dependence is that none of the Quines is able to replicate much faster than the others, which leads to their sustained coexistence in the reaction vessel. The disadvantage comes from the fact that an active molecule A_i is consumed when a data packet is processed and is not immediately available for the next data packet. Thus, on the long run, Quine i cannot process a data stream faster than twice the data processing rate of the predecessor Quine. That is, the hypercycle Quines impose strong restrictions on the range of data streams they are able to process as the most active element is doomed to starve.

Figure 11. Hypercyclic Quines: Four data-processing Quines are symbiotically linked by mutually letting them generate their reward to duplicate in a cyclic fashion.

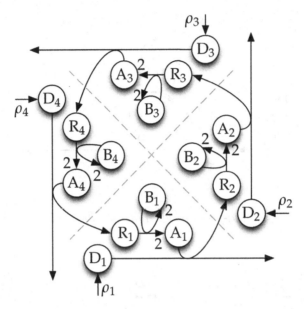

Data-Rate-Independent Duplication Feed

The main disadvantage of the hypercyle, starvation of the most active molecules, arises from the fact that these molecules are produced by one specific other Quine in the hypercycle. This dependency can be broken by separating replication from duplication: When processing a data packet, the Quine shall immediately replicate and regenerate the consumed active molecule. This maintains a constant number of active molecules if there is no dilution flux and no (mutation or execution) error. To cope with the relatively rare error events we have to provide a separate stream of duplication rewards for the fraglet; these duplication rewards increase the number of active molecules and blueprints. Because we want all coupled Quines to survive, we have to guarantee that they all receive their duplication rewards with the same rate, i.e., they are fairly fed.

Figure 12 shows such a "duplication feed pattern". Two Quines process independent data streams and replicate individually by generating a local replication reward molecule R_i^r for each processed data molecule. A separate support Quine generates duplication rewards R_i^d and distributes them equally to the involved Quines. The support Quine is self-duplicating, paced by an externally provided stream of trigger molecules. Ideally, its "feeding rate" would be adjusted to the expected error rate. If the error rate cannot be estimated, the data processing Quines could be reprogrammed in order to automatically produce this trigger, although the latter method will probably result in a feeding rate that is higher than needed.

An Example of Robust Link Load Balancing with a Chemical Protocol

We now make use of the cooperation patterns for Quines in order to implement a *self-healing protocol* that balances a packet stream over two different network paths such that packet loss is minimized.

As depicted in Figure 13, we inject packets at rate *r* into node 1 where two Quines, one for each path, compete for them and send them over the

Figure 12. Separation of replication and duplication: the two data-processing Quines only replicate; a duplication feed is provided by a separate supporting Quine on the right.

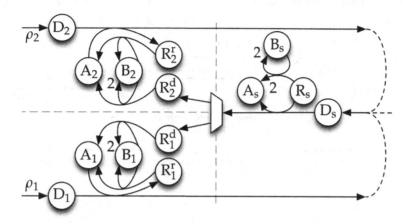

corresponding path. Instead of replicating as fast as possible by generating their own reward, the Quines wait for and react with acknowledgment packets that serve as duplication rewards. The third Quine in node 2 sends these acknowledgments back over the reverse path and delivers the packet to the application.

This scheme leads to a perfect packet balance between the two paths. When the reaction vessel in node 1 is saturated, its molecules belong either to Quine Q_{1a} or to Q_{1b}, as other molecules have been squeezed out. Let us denote the relative concentrations by x_1 and x_2, respectively, satisfying $x_1 + x_2 = 1$. Since replication is triggered by the received acknowledgments, these concentrations are

$$x_i = \frac{r_i{}'}{\sum_j r_j{}'}$$

where $r_j{}'$ is the rate of acknowledgments received over path p_j.

Let us assume that the bandwidth of path p_1 is infinite whereas p_2 drops packets exceeding a rate of b packets/s. We examine the overload situation where the total rate $r > 2b$. Consequently, the rate of acknowledgments is $r_1{}' = r_1$ and $r_2{}'$

$= \min(r_2, b)$. Due to the law of mass action, the fraction of packets sent over p_1 is proportional to the concentration of Quine Q_{1a}:

$$r_1 = x_1 r = \frac{r_1}{r_1 + \min(r_2, b)} r$$

Hence, $r_1 = r - b$ and $r_2 = r - r_1 = b$. Quine Q_{1b} reduced its concentration so as to only forward packets up to the bandwidth limitation of path p_2.

The load balancing protocols reaches (chemical) equilibrium, where it provides the optimal traffic partition. Deviations from the equilibrium, for example by lost molecules on one network path, are compensated by increasing the population of Quines that forward packets over the opposite path. Moreover, the code itself is organized in circuits of self-replicating molecules: In the face of execution and mutation errors, the system will eventually regenerate the lost code and, after some transition time, autonomously finds back to equilibrium. In fact, packet loss as well as code loss is treated by the same mechanism and in the same way.

Figure 14 depicts the protocol's response to an extraordinary error where the system loses the majority of its molecules. In an OMNeT++ (Varga, 2001; Varga & Hornig, 2008) simulation we fixed

Figure 13. Data packets to node 2 are injected at rate r into node 1. Quines 1 and 2 (concentration x_1 and x_2, respectively) compete for and forward packets at rate r_1 and r_2 over paths p_1 and p_2, resp. The Quine's replication is controlled by acknowledgments received at rate r_1' and r_2', respectively.

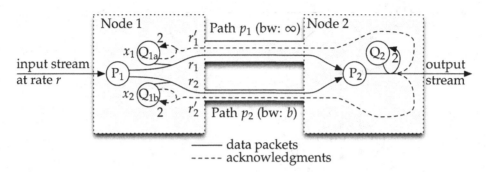

the input rate r to 200 pkts/s and the bottleneck capacity to $b = 40$ pkts/s. At time $t = 50$s, 80% of all molecules (code and data) are neutralized in node 1. The forwarding rates, as can be seen in the figure, remain unaffected while the code fully regenerates itself within 10 seconds!

The load balancing protocol discussed in this chapter may also be used for other tasks. Meyer, Yamamoto, and Tschudin (2008) use it as a self-adapting forwarding engine of a self-healing routing protocol implementation. We point out that the protocol, although self-healing, is not as elaborate as existing load-aware protocols in many respects. However, a noteworthy observation is that it implements *intrinsic bandwidth estimation* by relying on the rate of actual data packets, akin to ACK pacing in TCP (Aggarwal, Savage, & Anderson, 2000), whereas other existing bandwidth estimation techniques numerically calculate the bandwidth based on the rate of separate probe packets or on their inter-arrival time (Easwaran & Labrador, 2004).

FUTURE RESEARCH DIRECTIONS

In this section, we point out two areas where further research efforts are needed: Hardware anchor and instruction set design linked to a more probabilistic mindset to networking services.

Hardware Level Artificial Chemistries

Our move to study fault tolerance at the pure software level implicitly makes assumptions on the underlying execution environment: Ideally, each molecule would be carried by a "physical" thread. However, in our implementation we place a single virtual machine (VM) per node that serves full vessels. An error in the vessel will hurt many molecules instead of single items. Therefore, one should investigate hardware chip designs where "molecule threads" and "memory access" is highly parallel and as decoupled as possible. Note that due to the self-healing properties of our software, the hardware implementation can exhibit spurious errors. This relates to efforts of Chakrapani, Korkmaz, Akgul, and Palem (2007), who proposed probabilistic chips, i.e., CMOS devices whose behavior is rendered probabilistic by noise. The advantage of such chips is their feasible manufacturing process in the nanometer scale and their lower energy consumption achieved by a lower operating voltage. The problem of such hardware is that it may expose physical noise up to the instruction level, an environment where traditional programming paradigms and languages obviously fail.

Figure 14. OMNeT++ simulation: Relative concentrations of the forwarding Quines in node 1 during the loss of molecules and the corresponding packet forwarding rate (unaffected).

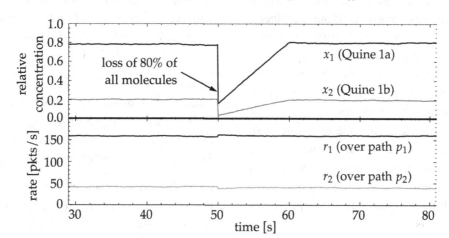

Instruction Set Design and Probabilistic Network Services

Recently we observed that some instructions are more fragile to bit errors than others (e.g., the "fork" tag). A redundant binary encoding scheme (forward error correction or just bit error flagging) for Fraglet symbols would lower the fraction of harmful mutations. For example, a fraglet starting with a corrupted symbol would be non-reactive but still exposed to the non-selective dilution flux and will eventually be displaced.

An even more radical approach would be to let an instruction encode a probability distribution of actions on (Fraglets) strings. Currently, we are far from devising such an execution scheme for practical use, but it would resonate well with the mindset that exposing some randomness of networking services to the end user, e.g., accepting packet loss in a video-stream, instead of providing delivery guarantees, is just fine.

CONCLUSION

In this work, we showed that Quines, i.e., self-replicating programs, are much more than a mere intellectual challenge for computer science students. When interpreted in a chemical context and equipped with self-induced dynamic behavior, they provide the basis for self-healing programs and protocols.

We presented different Quine variants in the Fraglets system, an artificial chemistry especially targeted for networking applications. With the help of a law of mass action scheduler, the population of a specially designed duplicating Quine grows hyperbolically. Put in a virtual reaction vessel with limited capacity, this Quine has intrinsic self-healing properties without relying on an external controller.

Because of the behavioral equivalence of the Fraglets reaction regime to real chemical reactions, we are able to use the same mathematical tools used to analyze chemical reactions. For example, phase-type distributions can be used to quantify the survival probability of Quines. In a networking context, certain self-replicating programs are able to survive longer than on a single machine: "Going distributed" is a strategy that brings about more robustness. We also demonstrated the use of Quines for real networking protocols, for example a link load balancing protocol that recovers from execution errors and spurious alteration of bits in the memory.

Unlike other bio-inspired approaches that extract the essence of a natural mechanism and then try to import it into existing networking machinery, we make a step forward by putting chemical laws in the core of packet processing engines: It seems that such an approach simplifies the transfer of desirable robustness properties from nature to manmade systems. Network service robustness must be understood as a code-rewriting task with homeostatic properties where the software continuously and actively has to maintain its healthy state. We believe that this is a necessary requirement for the future's truly adaptive and evolving protocols.

REFERENCES

Abrash, H. I. (1986). Studies concerning affinity. *Journal of Chemical Education, 63*, 1044–1047. English translation of the original paper by Waage and Guldberg (1864).

Aggarwal, A., Savage, S., & Anderson, T. (2000). Understanding the performance of TCP pacing. In *Proceedings of the 9th Annual Joint Conference of the IEEE Computation and Communication Societies (INFOCOM 2000)* (pp. 1157–1165).

Banâtre, J. P., Fradet, P., & Radenac, Y. (2006). A generalized higher-order chemical computation model. *Electronic Notes in Theoretical Computer Science, 135*(3), 3–13. doi:10.1016/j.entcs.2005.09.016

Calude, C. S., & Paun, G. (2001). *Computing with cells and atoms: An introduction to quantum, DNA and membrane computing.* Bristol, PA: Taylor & Francis/Hemisphere.

Campbell, S., Chancelier, J.-P., & Nikoukhah, R. (2006). *Modeling and simulation in Scilab/Scicos.* New York, NY: Springer.

Chakrapani, L. N., Korkmaz, P., Akgul, B. E. S., & Palem, K. V. (2007). Probabilistic system-on-a-chip architectures. *ACM Transactions on Design Automation of Electronic Systems, 12*(3), 1–28. doi:10.1145/1255456.1255466

Dittrich, P. (2005). Chemical computing. In J.-P. Banâtre, P. Fradet, J.-L. Giavitto, & O. Michel (Eds.), *Unconventional programming paradigms, Vol. 3566. Lecture notes in computer science* (pp. 19–32). Berlin / Heidelberg, Germany: Springer.

Dittrich, P., & Banzhaf, W. (1998). Self-evolution in a constructive binary string system. *Artificial Life, 4*, 203–220. doi:10.1162/106454698568521

Dittrich, P., & Speroni di Fenizio, P. (2007). Chemical organization theory. *Bulletin of Mathematical Biology, 69*, 1199–1231. doi:10.1007/s11538-006-9130-8

Dittrich, P., Ziegler, J., & Banzhaf, W. (2001). Artificial chemistries – A review. *Artificial Life, 7*, 225–275. doi:10.1162/106454601753238636

Easwaran, Y., & Labrador, M. (2004). Evaluation and application of available bandwidth estimation techniques to improve TCP performance. In *Proceedings of the 29th annual IEEE international conference on local computing networks*, (pp. 268–275).

Eigen, M., & Schuster, P. (1979). *The hypercycle: A principle of natural self-organization.* Berlin, Germany: Springer.

Fernando, C., & Rowe, J. (2007). Natural selection in chemical evolution. *Journal of Theoretical Biology, 247*, 152–167. doi:10.1016/j.jtbi.2007.01.028

Fontana, W., & Buss, L. W. (1994). The arrival of the fittest: Toward a theory of biological organization. *Bulletin of Mathematical Biology, 56*, 1–64.

Freitas, R. A., Jr., & Merkle, R. C. (2004). *Kinematic self-replicating machines.* Georgetown, TX: Landes Bioscience. Retrieved June 22, 2010, from http://www.molecularassembler.com/KSRM.htm

Gibson, M. A., & Bruck, J. (2000). Efficient exact stochastic simulation of chemical systems with many species and many channels. *The Journal of Physical Chemistry A, 104,* 1876–1889. doi:10.1021/jp993732q

Gillespie, D. T. (1977). Exact stochastic simulation of coupled chemical reactions. *Journal of Physical Chemistry, 81,* 2340–2361. doi:10.1021/j100540a008

Gillespie, D. T. (1992). A rigorous derivation of the chemical master equation. *Physica A: Statistical Mechanics and its Applications, 188,* 404–425.

Gillespie, D. T. (2007). Stochastic simulation of chemical kinetics. *Annual Review of Physical Chemistry, 58,* 35–55. doi:10.1146/annurev.physchem.58.032806.104637

Hofstadter, D. (1979). *Gödel, Escher, Bach: An eternal golden braid.* New York, NY: Basic Books.

Holland, J. H. (1992). *Adaptation in natural and artificial systems.* Cambridge, MA: MIT Press.

Hutton, T. J. (2002). Evolvable self-replicating molecules in an artificial chemistry. *Artificial Life, 8,* 341–356. doi:10.1162/106454602321202417

Jacobson, V. (1988). Congestion avoidance and control. In *Applications, technologies, architectures, and protocols for computer communication: Symposium proceedings on communications architectures and protocols,* (pp. 314–329), New York, NY: ACM.

Johnson, B. W. (1996). An introduction to the design and analysis of fault-tolerant systems. In *Fault-tolerant computer system design* (pp. 1–87). Upper Saddle River, NJ: Prentice-Hall, Inc.

Kleene, S. C. (1938). On notation for ordinal numbers. *Journal of Symbolic Logic, 3,* 150–155. doi:10.2307/2267778

Langton, C. G. (1984). Self-reproduction in cellular automata. *Physica D. Nonlinear Phenomena, 10,* 135–144. doi:10.1016/0167-2789(84)90256-2

Meyer, T., Yamamoto, L., & Tschudin, C. (2008). A self-healing multipath routing protocol. In *Proceedings of the 3rd International Conference on Bio-Inspired Models Of Network, Information and Computing Systems (BIONETICS '08)* (pp. 1–8). Brussels, Belgium: ICST.

Neuts, M. F. (1981). *Matrix-geometric solutions in stochastic models.* New York, NY: Dover Publications Inc.

Normand, E. (1996). Single event upset at ground level. *IEEE Transactions on Nuclear Science, 43,* 2742–2750. doi:10.1109/23.556861

Paun, G. (2000). Computing with membranes. *Journal of Computer and System Sciences, 61,* 108–143. doi:10.1006/jcss.1999.1693

Perrier, J.-Y., Sipper, M., & Zahnd, J. (1996). Toward a viable, self-reproducing universal computer. *Physica D. Nonlinear Phenomena, 97,* 335–352. doi:10.1016/0167-2789(96)00091-7

Postel, J. (1981). *Transmission control protocol. RFC 793.* IETF Standard.

Pradhan, D. K. (1996). *Fault-tolerant computer system design.* Upper Saddle River, NJ: Prentice-Hall, Inc.

Sipper, M. (1998). Fifty years of research on self-replication: An overview. *Artificial Life, 4,* 237–257. doi:10.1162/106454698568576

Stadler, P. F., Fontana, W., & Miller, J. H. (1993). Random catalytic reaction networks. *Physica D. Nonlinear Phenomena, 63,* 378–392. doi:10.1016/0167-2789(93)90118-K

Strogatz, S. H. (1994). *Nonlinear dynamics and chaos. Studies in nonlinearity.* Westview Press.

Szathmáry, E. (1991). Simple growth laws and selection consequences. *Trends in Ecology & Evolution, 6,* 366–370. doi:10.1016/0169-5347(91)90228-P

Tempesti, G., Mange, D., & Stauffer, A. (1998). Self-replicating and self-repairing multicellular automata. *Artificial Life, 4,* 259–282. doi:10.1162/106454698568585

Teuscher, C. (2007). From membranes to systems: Self-configuration and self-replication in membrane systems. *Bio Systems, 87,* 101–110. doi:10.1016/j.biosystems.2006.09.002

Thompson, G. P. (2010). *The Quine page.* Retrieved June 22, 2010, from http://www.nyx.net/~gthompso/quine.htm

Tschudin, C. (2003). Fraglets - A metabolistic execution model for communication protocols. In *Proceedings of the 2nd Annual Symposium on Autonomous Intelligent Networks and Systems (AINS).*

Tschudin, C. (2007). *Fraglets home page.* Retrieved June 22, 2010, from http: // www. fraglets. net

Varga, A. (2001). The OMNET++ discrete event simulation system. In *Proceedings of the European Simulation Multiconference* (ESM 2001).

Varga, A., & Hornig, R. (2008). An overview of the OMNET++ simulation environment. In *Proceedings of the 1st International Conference on Simulation Tools and Techniques for Communications (SIMUTOOLS '08),* (pp. 1–10).

von Neumann, J. (1966). *Theory of self-reproducing automata.* Champaign, IL: University of Illinois Press.

Waage, P., & Guldberg, C. M. (1864). Studies concerning affinity. *Forhandlinger: Videnskabs – Selskabet i Christiania, 35.*

Wagner, K. (2000). Cooperative strategies and the evolution of communication. *Artificial Life, 6,* 149–179. doi:10.1162/106454600568384

Wilfredo, T.-P. (2000). *Software fault tolerance: A tutorial. Technical report.* NASA.

Yamamoto, L., Schreckling, D., & Meyer, T. (2007). Self-replicating and self-modifying programs in fraglets. In *Proceedings of the 2nd International Conference on Bio-inspired Models of Network, Information, and Computing Systems (BIONETICS '07).*

KEY TERMS AND DEFINITIONS

Quine: A computer program that generates its own source code as output; named after the philosopher and logician Willard van Orman Quine (1908-2000).

Replication: The process of generating an identical copy of itself. Self-replicating programs are well known in the form of viruses. Artificial chemical Quines make use of self-replication to establish redundancy.

Reproduction: The process of generating a modified copy of itself. Variation may stem from external sources, such as mutation due to radiation, or may be intrinsically caused, such as crossover during sexual reproduction. Reproduction in an environment with limited resources leads to evolution.

Code Robustness: Ability of software to tolerate execution errors or changes of its own code base.

Artificial Chemistry: Computer model to simulate real chemistry or to mimic chemical reactions in order to process information. An artificial chemistry is defined by a set of molecular species, a set of reactions among them and an algorithm that describes how and when the reactions are applied to the molecules.

Fraglets: An artificial chemistry designed for efficient packet processing in computer networks. Packets are represented as virtual molecules. Molecules are shaped as strings of instruction symbols. They determine the rewriting operation applied to the molecules when colliding with other molecules. Virtual reactions are scheduled according to the law of mass action.

Law of Mass Action: Mathematical model, discovered by Waage and Guldberg (1864), that relates the reaction rate to the concentration of molecules. According to this law, the reaction rate is proportional to the product of the reactant concentrations. In a simulator, potentially "executable reactions" must be delayed in order to match the rate imposed by the law of mass action.

Equilibrium: A system state in which opposing forces are balanced. This condition is satisfied in a stable dynamic fixed point of the system. Chemical networking protocols are designed such that the solution of a distributed problem is presented as equilibrium of the chemical reaction network.

Chapter 4
Neural Networks in Cognitive Science:
An Introduction

Nooraini Yusoff
University of Surrey, UK

Ioana Sporea
University of Surrey, UK

André Grüning
University of Surrey, UK

ABSTRACT

In this chapter we give a brief overview of the biological and technical background of artificial neural networks as are used in cognitive modelling and in technical applications. This will be complemented by three instructive case studies which demonstrate the use of different neural networks in cognitive modelling.

INTRODUCTION

Neurobiology

Classic neuroanatomic research tells us that the nervous system of animals essentially consists of the nerve cells, the so-called neurons, and that these are connected to each other along axons and dendrites (longer and shorter tree-like branching excrescences of the neuron body) via so-called synapses (Shepherd, 1994). This is certainly a simplified picture, but – while research about the degree of neural minutiae of importance for supporting cognitive process is still on-going – it is a useful working hypothesis that neural computation takes place mainly through neurons and synapses. Most artificial network models that aim to explain nervous processing or utilise in artificial intelligence concentrate on these two ingredients (Müller et al., 1990; Rojas, 1996).

It appears that – compared to a computer in a technical sense – a single neuron is only capable of a very restricted set of computations, but that the complexity of the nervous system lies in the

DOI: 10.4018/978-1-61350-092-7.ch004

precise way how these neurons are connected to each other through their synapses. Hence where a classical computer has one or a few complex processor kernels connected in a comparatively simple way, nervous systems have a high number of simple elementary processors connected in a complex way.

How do these components, neurons and synapses interact? First of all the neurons fire a spike, i.e. send an electrical potential pulse down their axons and via the synapses to the dendrites of connected other neurons. More precisely, the cell bodies of neurons have an electrical potential difference against the surrounding medium. This electrical potential is a function of the input such a neuron receives from other neurons (usually through the synapses on its dendrites). If the electrical potential exceeds a certain threshold, the neuron generates an electro-chemical pulse, the spike, which propagates along its axon. This pulse is then transmitted as input to the next neuron through a synapse, and the strength (or weight) of such a synapse determines how much the potential of the post-synaptic cell changes subsequently. The receiving cell usually needs a number of such pulses within a certain time in order to reach its own firing threshold and pass on a spike to its successor neurons i.e., neurons often function approximately as leaky integrators of incoming spikes within a certain characteristic time (Gerstner & Kistler, 2002).

It is important to note that a synapse is a site of close contact of the pre-synaptic axon and post-synaptic dendrite which are however separated by the so-called synaptic cleft. Signal transmission at the synapse happens as follows: The change of electrical potential due to the spike in the pre- synaptic neuron causes it to release a chemical neurotransmitter at the site of the synapse which then diffuses across the synaptic cleft. If it arrives at the site of the synapse in the post-synaptic neuron, it there causes a change of electrical potential in the cell body. Synapses can be excitatory, i.e. the transmitted spike increases

the post-synaptic potential, or inhibitory, where the potential is decreased.

To summarise for use in artificial neural networks, neurons communicate among each other by sending spikes, short electrical pulses of stereotypical form. Receiving neurons sum this spikes within a time window, weighted by the strength of the synapses over which they were received, and if they have received enough input – and dependent on the parameters of the neuron (i.e. firing threshold, internal state history etc) – then fire a spike themselves.

How is information encoded in the nervous system? What is a significant neural firing pattern? This is still an open question, and its answer might depend on where one looks in the nervous system. It is known that there are parts of the nervous system that use the firing rate, i.e. the average number of spikes a neuron emits in a time interval to encode for example the intensity of a sensory stimulus. However also precise spike times or time-locked spiking of various neurons are important for information encoding, for example in the owl auditory system, where precise runtime differences are encoded in precisely timed spikes needed for echo-location (Carr, 1993).

In artificial neural networks, for their technical simplicity often rate-neuron based models are preferred over spiking ones, since here the output variable of neuron is only a real number for every time step whereas for spiking models the precise timing of spikes and hence the cell internal states needs to be modelled (Gerstner & Kistler, 2002).

Learning

Long-term learning in nervous systems seems to be mainly following a Hebbian paradigm (Hebb, 1949; Kempter et al., 1999; Gerstner et al., 1996; Markram et al., 1997): If one neuron fires a spike and a connected neuron fires subsequently, the first neuron has provided useful information to the second and therefore the strength of the synapse between the two increases etc. Variations of this scheme have been observed in natural nervous systems that make use of statistical correlations, such as the above, in the firing patterns of two connected neurons and thereby changing the strength of synaptic connection between them. Such plasticity of synapses and neurons can also be affected by local concentrations of neurotransmitters, signals from third neurons and so on (Gu, 2002).

Currently it is an open problem how precisely (unsupervised) learning on the neuronal and synaptic level "conspires" to yield the flexible goal-driven (supervised) learning behaviour which we observe in higher cognitive processing (Harris, 2008). As far as artificial neural network models are concerned, usually weights of synapses and neural firing thresholds are adapted, following a local Hebbian-type rule. Alternatively synaptic and neural parameters are adapted as to minimise a global error functional. This however requires localised feedback of the global error-signal, and it is currently not clear how this is achieved in natural neural networks.

General Properties

While natural neural networks as a whole are reliable information processors – otherwise humans and animals could not survive in the complex environments they are in, this is not the case for single neurons and synapses. In fact it is assumed that the firing or not of a single neuron or even its death does not alter information processing. Neurons and synapses often also work only in a stochastic sense: be it through external noise in the system or through intrinsic stochasticity e.g. in the release of transmitter vesicles at the synapses (Allen & Stevens, 1994; Schneidman et al., 1998). Hence neuronal networks as such must be noise- and fault-tolerant.

A consequence of the noise and fault tolerance is that the networks can deal with problem domains that cannot be described in a rule-based manner or only so with lots of exceptions to rules to deal

with special cases (e.g. English pronunciation, irregular past tense forms of English verbs etc). They often find solutions to a problem where analytic treatment is not possible or no ansatz for a structured solution exists due to lacking experience with the problem domain (e.g. handwriting recognition). They find solutions in a self-organised way. A down side is of course that it is also hard to understand how a neural network solves a given problem unless a lot of analytical effort is made towards understanding its trained dynamics. In this sense, there is no proof of 100% reliability or correctness of trained neural networks – so you do not want a neural network to inform a jet's auto-pilot.

If dynamics of biological or artificial neural networks are analysed, this will often be with tools from mathematical non-linear dynamical systems theory, iterated mappings and differential equations (Jost, 2005), and theoretical results about for example oscillatory behaviour, fixed point behaviour, learning convergence, types of solutions found have successfully been analysed to a certain degree for various types of artificial neural networks. Also theory of symbolic computation has been applied to several types of networks, and for many Turing-equivalence has been established (Kilian & Siegelmann, 1996; Maass, et al., 2002). While neural networks can be analysed in terms of discrete symbolic computation (Hopcroft & Ullmann, 1979), this does not mean that due to their continuous nature this is the approach that does justice to their nature: neural networks are understood better in terms of sub-symbolic, associative and gradual computation rather than symbolic, rule-based and discrete computation.

Artificial Neural Networks

Biologically Plausibility

The brain consists of a vast number of neurons and synapses (and other structures not mentioned that also contribute to nervous computation). Neuron and synapse can be classified into different types, but each neuron of each type will come with a different set of parameters like firing thresholds, plasticity, synaptic weight, synaptic delays. Large scale neuronal models exist that model individuals neurons very exact, however such models are computationally costly (Markram, 2006), so that large nets of these cannot feasibly simulated in a standard technical application. Hence neuron and network models vary according to the biological detail they take on board.

Biologically realism is always then an issue when understanding nervous or cognitive function is in the focus. For technical applications often only the concept of a large number of simple processing units interconnected in a complicated way is important.

Supervised vs Unsupervised Learning

Networks can and have been hand-coded, e.g. for cognitive modelling or robot control or formal proof of Turing-equivalence, however the great appeal of neural networks is that they can learn. Learning can be done in a supervised way or in an unsupervised way.

In supervised learning, some prior knowledge of the problem and sample solutions are available in the form of pairs of input data and target output data. In the learning process the input data is presented to the network which is left to calculate its output. The output is then compared to calculate the error E between the actual and the target output data, for example using the Euclidean distance if the data is in vector format. In gradient descent approaches to learning (Williams & Peng, 1990), network parameters such as synaptic weights w, firing thresholds are changed proportionally to their contribution to the error, i.e. $\Delta w = -\eta \partial E / \partial w$. This training process is then repeated until E converges to zero or – more usual – drops under a certain value. Mathematically speaking, a network trained in a supervised regime learns a mapping from input to output minimising a given

error functional in an approximative way – it is essentially doing function approximation.

The trained network can then be run on additional validation data to check its accuracy and generalisation beyond the training data. Ultimately the network will be run with input data for which the output data is not yet known. A typical example would be handwriting recognition where the network is given handwritten characters and their label, i.e. the corresponding printed character or ASCII code. Characters could come from a data base with samples from different writers. After training the network could then for example operate in a hand-held device and recognise a different writer's characters.

An example of such a network is given further down as a case study to understand the cognitive McGurk Effect, using a prototypical multi-layered feed-forward network with the back-propagation learning algorithm.

A different type of supervised processing of a neural network is pattern completion. In this case the input data is a cue to the expected output data. The output data fall into a number of classes which are given to the network. Its task is to complete a partial or noisy input pattern to the corresponding complete pattern as output. This is useful for pattern completion, pattern recognition or denoising a pattern. A typical representative of such an auto-associative network is a Hopfield network which will be presented in a case study using such a network to model another cognitive effect, the Stroop effect, see the auto-associative network modelling the Stroop effect.

In unsupervised learning, no input-output pairs are given or known. The network's tasks is to find structure in a given data set and for example cluster the data into a number of classes or find principle or independent components in a data set, or do some other dimensional reduction of the data. Mathematically speaking, the unsupervised network does some form of non-linear higher-order statistical analysis of the data (Deco & Obradovic, 1996). A typical example would be a Kohonen network. Another example would be a purely Hebbian approach to learning where connections strengthen between (part) patterns that co-occur frequently. A case study using such an approach is presented in the recurrent associative network modelling the McGurk effect.

However distinction between supervised and unsupervised is not always so clear-cut and many approaches exist that are in-between. While fully supervised networks need the fully specified and correct target answer in order to learn, in reinforcement learning schemes the network only gets feedback about how well or badly it is doing, and this is the only clue to finding a correct solution (Sutton & Barto, 2002). Thus reinforcement learning could be classified as semi-supervised. Furthermore unsupervised learning schemes can be subject to increased or decreased plasticity of synaptic weight depending on how well the network does, so that originally unsupervised learning schemes can be given a (semi-)supervised touch (Legenstein et al., 2005) – this is a matter of interpretation. And thus there is a finally a second case-study utilising an originally unsupervised learning scheme, this time however using spiking neurons instead of rate neurons as well as some form of interaction in associative spiking network described below.

Recurrence

Another important feature to distinguish different neural networks is how the deal with data in time. Artificial neural networks may act on data one at a time, with no explicit or implicit memory of its state or data from previous times (other than in its parameters fixed during learning). This is for example the case the network in the feedforward model for the McGurk effect which utilises a feedforward structure, so that outputs or intermediate states are not fed back to the network in a subsequent time step.

Networks may have a recurrent structure and operate in time, i.e. some output will be part of the network state in a subsequent time step. The feedforward network in the McGurk model can for example easily be transformed into a recurrent network with an implicit memory of past states and data by connecting some neurons in the output or hidden layer back to the hidden layer (Elman, 1990). Such network could then be used in time series prediction.

Applications of Artificial Neural Networks

Artificial neural networks have always had a dual purpose: to help us understand the brain and as artificial intelligence computing devices in their own right. Applications of artificial neural networks in cognitive science or in technical areas have concentrated mainly on models that make use of rate code neurons only due to the perceived mathematical simplicity and the availability of powerful general purpose learning algorithms. While artificial networks of spiking neurons are important to understand computation in the brain, they have so far not played a prominent role in technical applications. It is understood however that potential applications might lie in applications which rely on precise timing of events, such as in fault-tolerant communication networks that have to deliver precise information using unreliable communication channels.

In the following we present three instructive case studies of how different artificial neural networks can be used in cognitive modelling following the connectionist stream of cognitive science. The connectionist stream holds that in order to understand cognitive processing we must aim to understand and be inspiring the neural machinery (Ellis & Hunt, 1993). This is opposed to the so-called symbolicist stream of cognitive science which tries to understand cognitive processing in terms of (rule-based) symbolic computation.

Feedforward Network modelling: the McGurk Effect

The McGurk effect is a speech perception illusion that occurs when an auditory stimulus, such as /ba/, is combined with a different visual stimulus of lips and mouth movements, such as /ga/. When presented with such incongruent auditory-visual input, people often perceive a different sound, in this case /da/ (McGurk & MacDonald, 1976).

In order to investigate the McGurk effect the main theories about its occurrence, the speech perception illusion was modelled with artificial neural networks (Sporea & Gruning, 2010). The analysis of the effect consists of determining the moment of audio-visual stimuli integration and also the influence of language and the frequency of phonemes.

Several studies have been conducted in order to establish the moment of the auditory-visual integration during the processing of speech. While some researchers believe that the signals are processed parallel and independently and the integration occurs at a later stage (Massaro & Stork, 1998), others suggest that the integration is produced at an early point in the speech processing (Bernstein, 1989; Green & Miller, 1985). Other studies suggest that the phonological repertoire influences the appearance of the McGurk effect. One such evidence is shown in Sekiyama and Tohkura (1991), where Japanese subjects have been tested for the McGurk effect. The results indicate that in noise-free environments the "Japanese McGurk effect" is weaker than the English one. The perception of the incongruent auditory-visual signals, produced by a Japanese speaker, was dominated by the auditory stimuli, in contrast with English subjects who perceived the fused sounds (MacDonald & McGurk, 1976, 1978).

Model

In order to test the main theories regarding the point at which the integration of the stimuli occurs, two feedforward networks structures have been used and compared (Figure 1).

The neurons in the feedforward network are simple processing units structured in successive layers, where each neuron in one layer is connected to all neurons in the subsequent layer. The synapses between the connected neurons are represented by the weight of a connection. The set of input units is called the input layer and the set of output units are called the output layer. The input units are just injecting the information into the network, without performing any computation. The output is read off from the output units. All other layers that do not have direct connections from or to the outside are called hidden layers. Except the input layer, the neurons in all other layers compute their input as the weighted sum of output of the previous layer:

$$g = f(\textstyle\sum_i w_i x_i), \tag{1}$$

where f is the activation function, w_i are the weights and x_i are the activations of the previous layer. One of the most popular activation functions is the sigmoid, due to its continuity and differentiability:

$$s(x) = 1 / (1 + \exp(-x)). \tag{2}$$

The networks are trained with the backpropagation algorithm (Willams, 1990) which is using the method of gradient descent to minimize the error function in the weight space. The learning problem consists of finding the optimal combination of weighs in order for the neural network to approximate a given function as close as possible. When the input pattern is presented to the network, the output o_i is usually different from the expected output pattern t_i. The purpose of the back propaga-

Figure 1. (A) Late integration model. (B) Early integration model.

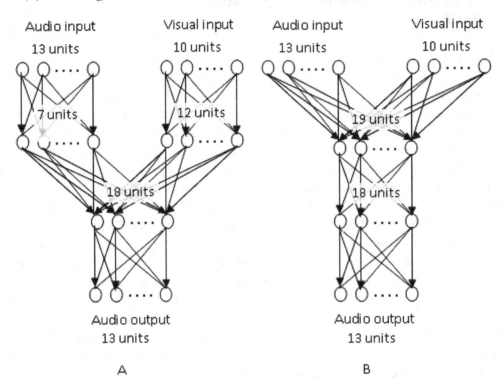

tion algorithm is to make t_i and o_i identical; this is done by minimizing the error function of the network, which is defined as follows:

$$E = \tfrac{1}{2} \sum_i (o_i - t_i)^2 \qquad (3)$$

One defines auxilary quantities, the back-propagated errors δ_j for each neuron j as $\delta_j = o_j (1 - o_j)(o_j - t_j)$ for the output neurons and then layerwise in a recursive way as $\delta_j = o_j (1 - o_j)\sum_i w_i \delta_i$, where δ_i is the backpropagated error from the previous layer of neurons. With these δ_j the individual weight changes can be expressed as:

$$\Delta w_{ij} = -\eta \; \partial E / \partial w_{ij} = -\eta \; \delta_i \, o_j, \qquad (4)$$

where η is the learning rate, which defines the step length of each iteration in the gradient descent.

Method

The two models have two groups of inputs represented by binary vectors, consisting of the auditory and visual stimuli, and one set of output, the auditory pattern which represents the recognized sound. The network in Figure 1A has two individual and parallel hidden layers, and one integration layer and it corresponds to the late integration hypothesis. The network in Figure 1B has an integration layer instead of the parallel hidden layers, without any individual pre-processing of the two stimuli; this corresponds to the early integration hypothesis. The two neural networks have the same number of neurons and have been trained and tested in the same conditions as described below.

The network's input consists of patterns representing the auditory stimulus (the phoneme, which is the smallest unit of sound) and the visual stimulus (the viseme (Fisher, 1968), the basic unit of speech in the visual domain).

The phonemes are represented by a 13-element vectors which encode speech features utilized by the International Phonetic Alphabet (International Phonetic Association, 1999). The auditory patterns incorporate vectors that indicate the voice, the manner and the place of articulation. The visemes correspond to groups of phonemes, as the visual input contains less information than the auditory input. Therefore, several phonemes are mapped to one viseme, for example the phonemes /f/ and /v/ are in the same visual group. The visual patterns are represented by randomly generated vectors with 10 elements.

The neural network models have been trained with a randomly generated sequence of a hundred patterns consisting of congruent audiovisual stimuli, replicating the way human subjects hear and see people producing sounds. The training sequence contains all the consonants from one language (e.g. English with 24 phonemes or Japanese with 16 phonemes).

The neural networks have been tested using the following steps:

1. Initialise the network with random synaptic weights, within the range of -0.1 and 0.1 uniformly distributed.

2. Generate a new random training sequence of a hundred congruent patterns.

3. Train the network with the back-propagation algorithm with a learning rate of 0.1. The learning stops when the total mean squared error of the training set is sufficiently small (0.1). This step corresponds to a subject being exposed to speech with consistent audiovisual input.

4. After each session of training the network is tested with the sets of incongruent patterns considered to produce the McGurk effect, the winning phoneme being determined as having the smallest Euclidean distance from

the original vector to the output vector. This step corresponds to a subject being tested with incongruent stimuli as in the experiments conducted by McGurk & MacDonald (1976, 1978).

Results

The results are averaged across 100 trials, the networks being trained with a new generated sequence of patterns and new random weights. The tables below show the percentage of recognized phonemes corresponding to the McGurk effect, when trained with all the consonants from the English or Japanese phonetic alphabet and tested with three sets of incongruent auditory-visual signals.

Table 1 shows the summarized results corresponding to the late and early integration models. For all three set of incongruent auditory-visual patterns, there can be seen a significant difference between the results of two neural network models.

In the following tables the auditory response means that the network response is closest (in Euclidean distance) to the congruent pattern corresponding to the auditory part of the incongruent pattern - for example for the incongruent audio-visual pair /b/-/g/, the auditory response is /b/, the visual response means that the network response is closest to the congruent pattern corresponding to the visual part of the incongruent pattern - /g/ in this case, the fused response is the intermediate sound different from the auditory and visual patterns considered as the McGurk perceptual illusion - /d/ for this incongruent pattern.

Using the late integration neural network, the influence of language on the McGurk illusion is investigated by training the model with English phonemes using the frequency of phonemes as found in conversational English (Mines et al., 1978) and with Japanese phonemes with the frequencies found in the Japanese newspaper Asahi (Tamaoka &Makioka, 2004). The network is tested with the same incongruent stimuli. Table 2 shows the summarized results of the simulations when the network is trained and tested in the same conditions as described above.

When comparing the results of the same network trained with English phonemes with uniform frequencies, a stronger McGurk effect can be noticed for all three sets of incongruent auditory-visual phonemes for the network trained with the English consonants with frequencies found in conversational English.

The difference between the two phonetic alphabets is that unlike English, the Japanese language does not contain certain phonemes, such as /r/ or /l/, and contains others that do not exist in English, such as /N/ (International Phonetic Association, 1999). As a consequence, the incongruent sets of plosive consonants (auditory-visual /b/-/g/ and /p/-/k/) resulted in considerably lower fusion responses than the results of the equivalent model when trained with English phonemes. In the case of nasal incongruent pair (auditory-visual /m/-/n/), the result are similar to the corresponding English trained network.

Discussion

The simulations of the late and early integration theories resulted in different responses when tested with incongruent auditory-visual patterns. Although both neural networks learn very well to recognize the congruent patterns, the McGurk effect in the early integration model is almost absent. These results support the theory of the independent parallel processing and late integration of the audiovisual signals (Massaro & Stork, 1998). When the late integration model is trained

Table 1. The output when trained with a random sequence of patterns having equal probability of appearance. The training is stopped when the network has reached the performance criterion on the congruent data.

	Audiovisual input	Auditory response	Visual response	Fused response	Other
Late integration	/b/-/g/	42%	3%	39%	5%
	/p/-/k/	32%	11%	46%	11%
	/m/-/n/	27%	65%		8%
Early integration	/b/-/g/	99%			1%
	/p/-/k/	90%			10%
	/m/-/n/	99%			1%

Table 2. The output when trained with a random sequence of patterns having English and Japanese phonemes' frequencies.

	Audiovisual input	Auditory response	Visual response	Fused response	Other
English phonemes	/b/-/g/	10%	2%	68%	20%
	/p/-/k/	8%	5%	83%	4%
	/m/-/n/	12%	83%		5%
Japanese phonemes	/b/-/g/	18%	37%	27%	18%
	/p/-/k/		81%	11%	8%
	/m/-/n/	32%	65%		3%

with auditory-visual patterns having the frequency of phonemes found in conversational English the network response to the incongruent stimuli is much closer to the experimental data (Macdonald & McGurk, 1978).

The results of the simulations using the Japanese phonetic alphabet are partly consistent with empirical data showing that in noise free environments the McGurk effect is weaker for Japanese listeners (see Sekiyama & Tohkura, 1991). The late integration model responded with a weaker McGurk effect for two sets of incongruent patterns, which is consistent with the experiments conducted with Japanese listeners illustrating that speech perception is almost entirely limited to the auditory stimuli when presented with incongruent signals.

RECURRENT ASSOCIATIVE NETWORK MODELLING MCGURK EFFECT

In this section we present a different model of the same cognitive effect as before, however using a different network model (Sporea & Gruning, 2010b): Instead of a feedforward network model with back-propagation we are now using a network with a more pronounce associative component (McClelland & Rumelhart, 1985). The different perceived sounds when presented with incongruent auditory visual stimuli suggest a strong association between auditory and visual inputs since the perceived sounds is influence by the visual information.

Model

The distributed model of memory and information processing model (McClelland & Rumelhart, 1985) is assumed to associate the auditory and visual stimuli. The representation of the patterns is similar to the one used in our previous model. The new patterns are vectors with elements of

-1 and 1, instead of the previous representation with elements of 0 and 1, which is for technical convenience.

In this type of neural network each unit is connected to all other units in the network. The units receive an external input, within the range of -1 to +1 and an internal input representing the weighted sum of the activations of the other units in the module. The net input of the neuron n_i, represents the sum of all the internal inputs and the external input:

$$n_i = e_i + \sum_j w_{ij} a_j, \tag{5}$$

where e_i is the external input, a_j is the activation of the neuron j and w_{ij} is the weight between the neurons i and j, representing the synapse.

If the net input is positive the activation of this unit is then incremented by an amount proportional to the distance left to the ceiling activation of +1. If the net input is negative the activation is then decremented by an amount proportional to the distance left to the floor activation of -1. The equations used for updating the activations are:

$$\Delta a_i = E n_i (1 - a_i) - D a_i, \text{ if } n_i > 0, \Delta a_i = E n_i [a_i - (-1)] - D a_i, \text{ if } n_i \leq 0, \tag{6}$$

where E and D are global parameters that represent the rates of excitation and decay, respectively.

The processing ends when the pattern of activation the network produced settles down and stops changing. In the present simulations, the network runs for a maximum of 50 processing cycles. The units have activations values within the range of -1 to +1, with the value 0 representing a neutral resting value (McClelland & Rumelhart, 1985).

After computing the net input, n_i, of the unit i, the activations of the units are updated. In this case the target output of the network is the same as the input pattern. As this network does not require an external target output the learning is unsupervised. If one considers that external target output is the input pattern, the learning can be regarded as supervised. The weights between the neurons are adjusted using the delta rule, a type of correlation based learning, in order to determine the amount and direction of the change of the connection weights. The weights are modified according to the following formula:

$$\Delta w_{ij} = S\,(e_i - \sum_j a_j\,w_{ij})\,a_j, \qquad (7)$$

where S is a constant that controls the amount of the modifications in the weights.

The algorithm based on the delta rule is minimizing the difference between the external and the internal input. As a consequence, when partial or distorted patterns are presented, part of the units will be active and will tend to reproduce the rest by the connections between units.

Method

The distributed memory system has been trained in a similar manner as the previous models, with congruent audiovisual patterns arranged in a randomly generated sequence of a hundred patterns. The training set contains the consonants from English as found in the International Phonetic Alphabet (International Phonetic Association, 1999).

The distributed memory system has been tested using the following steps:

1. Initialize the internal weights with null values;
2. Generate a new random training set of congruent patterns;
3. Train the network for 10 learning cycles with the delta rule; this step corresponds to a subject being exposed to speech with consistent audiovisual input.
4. After each session of training the network is tested with the congruent patterns, with auditory patterns (the visual part has null values), distorted patterns, and with three incongruent auditory visual pairs of stimuli considered to produce the McGurk illusion.

A stable pattern of activations is considered to be achieved when there is no difference in the updated activations or when it reaches a maximum of 50 processing cycles. The produced pattern is determined as having the smallest Euclidean distance from the original pattern;

5. The results are averaged across a hundred trials.

Results

In order to confirm the theory that the phonemes' frequencies influence the appearance of the Mc-Gurk effect the network has been trained with two random sequences of patterns, one with equal probability of appearance and the other one having English phonemes' frequencies as found in conversational English (Mines et al., 1978).

Studies performed on audiovisual speech perception show that in noise-added audio-visual condition Japanese speakers experience a much stronger McGurk effect than in noise-free condition, suggesting that people rely on the visual input in the presence of auditory uncertainty (Sekiyama, Tohkura, 1991). Therefore, noise has been added to the incongruent patterns, both on the auditory and visual part. Table 3 shows the obtained results averaged across a hundred trials.

Furthermore, the model has been tested with incongruent patterns in relation with prime congruent patterns. Because the activations are calculated based on the values of the previous activations, the neural network is sensitive to priming effects (McClelland & Rumelhart, 1985). The distributed model of memory is represented as a composition of patterns of activations determined by the processing of each input presented to the neural network. Each time an input is presented to the network, the activations are changed corresponding to the present stimuli and also to the current state of the memory. The new state of the memory is thus determined according to the processing of the given patterns. As McClelland and

Table 3. The output of the network after training with congruent patterns and tested with noisy incongruent patterns. Reproduced from Sporea & Gruning (2010b)

	Audiovisual input	Auditory response	Visual response	Fused response
Trained with patterns with uniform frequencies	/b/-/g/	25%	25%	50%
	/p/-/k/	94%	1%	5%
	/m/-/n/	14%	86%	
Trained with patterns with English phonemes' frequencies	/b/-/g/	14%	41%	45%
	/p/-/k/	14%	41%	45%
	/m/-/n/		100%	

Table 4. The output of the network after training with congruent patterns and tested with noisy incongruent patterns after presenting a prime. Reproduced from Sporea & Gruning (2010b).

	Audiovisual input	Auditory response	Visual response	Fused response
Trained with patterns with uniform frequencies	/b/-/g/	2%		98%
	/p/-/k/	14%		86%
	/m/-/n/	21%	79%	
Trained with patterns with English phonemes' frequencies	/b/-/g/			100%
	/p/-/k/			100%
	/m/-/n/		100%	

Rumelhart (1985) explained, the experience of perceiving an item affects the subject's later performance. If, for example, a word is perceived twice within a reasonable interval of time, the prior presentation makes it possible for the subject to recognize the word faster, or from a briefer presentation. McClelland and Rumelhart (1985) showed that this model provides an account for the existence of priming effect as a function of congruity between the prime event and the test event.

The priming effect on the appearance of the McGurk effect has been investigated by presenting the network with the fused congruent pattern before testing with the incongruent audio-visual pair of phonemes. Table 4 shows the results obtained across a hundred trials.

The processing of the prime pattern before presenting the incongruent stimulus resulted in a much stronger McGurk effect for the network trained with the sequence of patterns with equal probability of appearance. The network trained with the sequence of patterns having English phonemes' frequencies responded only with the fused patterns.

Discussion

In comparison to the feed forward networks, the distributed memory system is able to learn the same set of patterns considerably faster. The autoassociator has significantly less weights to adjust and the delta rule requires fewer computations to be performed than the back propagation algorithm.

The results of the simulations are consistent with empirical studies on audiovisual speech perception in noise conditions (Sekiyama & Tohkura, 1991) as the fused responses to noisy incongruent patterns can be observed as dominant for most of the incongruent pairs of phonemes.

One explanation for this behaviour can be found in the network's ability to recognize incomplete and distorted patterns. The patterns presented to the neural network were both incongruent and distorted. As the network tried to complete both parts of the input, the audio and visual patterns, the response was the fused pattern corresponding to the McGurk effect. Since the encoding of the auditory patterns reflects the way phonemes are produced by the human vocal tract, it can be concluded that the network behaves in a similar manner as human subjects.

When the network is also presented with a prime congruent pattern, the model responds with a considerably stronger McGurk effect. However, there is not sufficient evidence from psycholinguistic experiments to suggest that the McGurk illusion is sensitive to priming effects. On the other hand, priming events were likely to occur in speech perception experiments as the order of stimuli was chosen randomly (Macdonald & McGurk, 1978). The priming event acted as a facilitator for the neural network to recognize the fused pattern.

As in the previous simulation, there have been two types of training sets. When the network is presented with the pairs of incongruent patterns known to produce the McGurk effect, the network responded with the fused pattern more consistently and stronger for two out of three incongruent sets of patterns. The distributed model of memory is thus susceptible to the frequency of the presented patterns as one might expect a human subject to be. The results of two kinds of neural network are consistent, suggesting that phonemes' frequencies influence the strength of the McGurk effect.

AUTO-ASSOCIATIVE NETWORK MODELLING STROOP EFFECT

The Stroop effect was first described in 1935, highlighting the brain's limited ability to suppress automatic responses (Stroop, 1935). In a Stroop test, subjects are required to respond (verbally or via button presses) to a sequence of stimuli. The stimuli are coloured colour-words in three conditions; control (e.g. a non coloured colour-word – e.g. RED written in black or a non colour-word – e.g. BOOK written in red), conflicting (e.g. a colour-word RED written in green) and congruent (e.g. a colour-word RED written in red). Subjects are asked either to read the colour words or to name their colours while the reaction times and error rates of performing the task are observed. The findings from Stroop studies show that there is an increased reaction time in naming the colour of the printed colour-word denoting a different colour, while the subjects could easily read the word and ignore the colour. Also the congruence of the word and its colour reduces the time of response processing to the colour name.

We present here a model of this effect using an auto-associative Hopfield network (Yusoff, Grüning & Browne, 2009a; 2009b).

Hopfield Neural Network (HNN)

Hopfield neural network (Hopfield, 1982) is one of the auto-associative neural network models. A neuron in the network is either in an active state (+1) or inactive (0, -1). The network consists of binary neurons and each neuron is connected to every other neuron by a symmetric connection (as depicted in Figure 2). The connections are weighted with positive (excitatory) and negative (inhibitory) sign values. The total weighted input determines the current state of a neuron based on the net threshold value.

In a Hopfield network, a memory consisting of M patterns is formed through pattern association. All memory patterns x are correlated to each other using equation below. The correlation derives a set of weights (W) as a product of pattern vector associations (Hopfield, 1982; Popoviciu & Boncut, 2005).

$$w_{ij} = \sum_{k=1}^{M} x_i(k)x_j(k), \; i \neq j, \; w_{ii} = 0, \; i,j = 1,n \qquad (8)$$

Figure 2. A general Hopfield neural network with symmetric structure where $w_{ij} = w_{ji}$ for $i \neq j$, and $w_{ij} = 0$ for $i = j$.

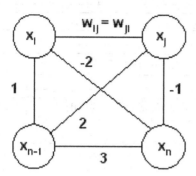

The memory can then be recalled through a asynchronous update mechanism. A pattern *xr* is presented to the system, at any given time, each bit (representing a neuron in biological system) in *xr* is randomly selected and updated based on the total activation it has received from other triggering neurons. The total activation *net*, is computed using the equation below

$$net_i(t) = \sum_{i \neq j} w_{ji} (xr_j(t)) \tag{9}$$

where $net_i(t)$ is the *net* input to neuron *i* at time *t*, w_{ji} is the connection strength between neuron *j* to neuron *i*, xr_j is the state of neuron *j* (+1 or -1). In an update cycle, the state of neuron *i* is readjusted according to:

$$xr_i(t+1) = \Theta (net_i(t)) = \{+1, net_i(t) > 0; -1, net_i(t) < 0; xr_i(t), net_i(t) = 0\}. \tag{10}$$

The pattern *xr* is updated until its convergence, that is there is no further changes in the state of all neurons in *xr* i.e. $xr(t) = xr(t+1)$.

Model

To model the Stroop effect, we developed a colour-word memory set of four random 56-bit patterns. Each pattern represents a colour concept compris-

ing three parts, the colour word (<WORD> - 16 bits) and its visual colour (<colour> - 16 bits) and a pattern (<Background> - 24 bits) that models process noise from ongoing background activity in the brain. It can be seen as a simple model of the attentional resource that one needs to perform colour naming and word-naming tasks. An example of a memory is as depicted in Figure 3.

The underlying idea is that the underlying cognitive representation of the colour has to be activated in order to trigger an action (speak out the colour / press a button) and the full pattern of colour activation can be triggered by completing part-patterns that correspond to a visually perceived colour <colour> or the meaning of the read word <WORD>. If these are conflicting, they will compete to drag the pattern completing processes into different directions. The Stroop HNN based model is illustrated in Figure 4.

The network consists of 56 neurons (bit), *x*, ($n_x = 56$, with $n_{Background} = 24$, $n_{WORD} = 16$ and $n_{colour} = 16$) interconnected to each other (with no self-connection). w_{ij} represents the strength of connection between neuron *i* and *j*. Depending on the task, word reading (WR) or colour naming (CN), at time *t*, the network is presented with a different test pattern stimulus, *xr*. During Hopfield asynchronous update, each randomly selected bit, xr_i, is updated until *xr* has converged to a closest memory pattern measured by Euclidean Distance within a maximum of 300 update iterations (with probability of $1/n \approx 0.02$ for each bit to be selected in each iteration).

Method

For Stroop stimuli representations, from each memory set, 20 test patterns are generated to observe the recall performance. The performance is observed under three conditions of stimuli: control – absence of irrelevant stimulus to the attended task (e.g. for a word reading; <Background><RED><minimal noise>, 4 test patterns), conflicting – incongruent colour concept

Figure 3. An example of a memory for coloured colour words with their associated background.

<RED>	<red>	<Background: RED-red>
— — + — + + + — + — + — + — — —	— — + — — + — — — + — + — — + —	— — — — + — — + — + — — — — + — — — + — — —

<GREEN>	<green>	<Background: GREEN-green>
— — — — + — — — + — — — + — —	— — — — + + — — + — + — — — — + —	— —

<BLUE>	<blue>	<Background: BLUE-blue>
— — + — — + — + — + — + — + —	+ — — + + — + — + — — + — — + —	— + — + — + — — — + + — — + — + — — + — — + — —

<YELLOW>	<yellow>	<Background: YELLOW-yellow>
— — + + — + — — + — + + — — — +	— — + — + — — — + — — + — + — +	— — — + + + — — + — — + — — + — — — — + — — —

Figure 4. Hopfield neural network based Stroop model.

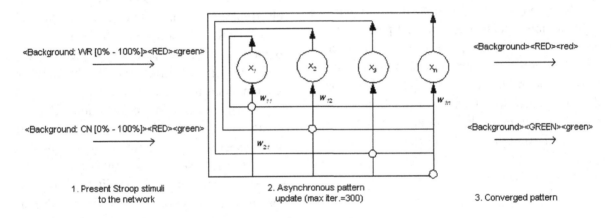

1. Present Stroop stimuli to the network
2. Asynchronous pattern update (max iter.=300)
3. Converged pattern

(e.g. <Background><RED><green>, 12 test patterns) and congruent – compatible colour concept (e.g. <Background><RED><red>, 4 test patterns). Performance is measured based on the number of bit-flips required in HNN updated asynchronously to converge to the closest (measured by Euclidean Distance) target memory pattern (Collier, 1997). This simulates the reaction time (RT) taken by a subject to perform any of the tasks.

In our model, a part-pattern <Background>, <WORD> or <colour> is defined by its distribution of on-bits. The actual test patterns are derived from this by randomly flipping some of the on-bits to zero with a probability p. To model test-patterns that correspond to a word-reading task, the part-patterns are subjected to this noise as follows: In the

<WORD> component the flip probability is 0.25 for each bit, and 0.86 in average for the <colour> component to model the subject's focusing on the input channel for <WORD> which is assumed to reduce noise in this channel. Test-patterns that model colour naming are derived from the imprinted memory by flipping on-bits to zero with probability of 0.75 for <colour> and 0.63 in average for <WORD> to model that despite focusing on the <colour> input channel the more automated cannot be suppressed to a high degree.

For test patterns for the congruent condition are generated simply by choosing <WORD> and <colour> part-patterns as above that stand for the same colour (4 combinations). Test patterns for the conflicting condition are derived by choosing those part patterns that stand for different colours (4*3 combinations) and finally control patterns are generated by choosing either the <WORD> or the <colour> component as above and setting the other component with noise by having maximum probability of 0.25 random switching on some bits (4 combinations).

Finally, the <Background> component is a simple model of global processing noise due to background activity, limited attention and so on, and hence a test pattern's <Background> component deviates the more from the (unique) imprinted one the less focused an individual is. Different levels of distraction are then modelled by different bit-flip probabilities p for the <Background> component. In our simulation, the p is varied from 1 (all on-bits flipped to zero) to 0 (no on-bit flipped to zero, i.e. maximal possible focus on the task).

Results

To study the influence of <Background> in response processing, with the Stroop task-related settings of colour concept, we ran a series of simulations with 10 different set of memories and their Stroop stimuli. The average number of bit-flips required by the HNN asynchronous update recalling the closest correct memory was recorded as the reaction time. The maximum number of update iterations for each test pattern is 300 iterations for each trial (with a total of 100 trials for each test pattern) with equal probability for a bit to be updated provided the 56-bit length vector.

Effects of Background Noise on Stroop Stimuli Processing

Generally, for both tasks word reading (WR) and colour naming (CN), less deviation from the imprinted <Background> pattern leads to a decrease in response (i.e. convergence) times (see Figure 5). However the effect of stimuli conditions varies between WR (Figure 5 left) and CN (Figure

5 right). The response to WR is processed faster compared to CN for all levels of distraction in <Background>. WR requires less processing time due to greater initial activation of <WORD>, meanwhile the higher processing time in CN is a result of the great bit-flip noise of the <colour> and less suppression of <WORD> (irrelevant stimulus) raising interference making it more difficult to reach a local attractor corresponding to a colour representation.

For WR, there is no significant influence (ANOVA, $p > 0.05$) of the Stroop conditions (control, conflict and congruent) on the reaction time. It is shown that, at each distraction level, the responses to any Stroop stimulus are recalled with similar reaction times. Meanwhile there is a significant difference ($p < 0.01$) found in CN for the conflicting condition (control and congruent conditions no effect, $p_{(control, congruent)} > 0.05$). For CN, interferences constantly occur at all distraction levels in conflicting stimulus conditions, Otherwise, greater similarity to the imprinted colour memories facilitates the response processing in the congruent stimulus condition.

Stroop Performance

Figure 6 shows human (left) reaction times (in msec) and model (right) reaction times (in number of bit-flips until convergence). For our model, in rational to the human average performances with variety of cognitive abilities, we consider the average of the reaction time in processing the response for both WR and CN at all levels of background noise. The results show that the words are always read faster than colours are named, (for the model data: WR: $RT_{control}$=7.05, $RT_{conflict}$=7.26, $RT_{congruent}$=6.53; CN: $RT_{control}$=13.05, $RT_{conflict}$=18.32, $RT_{congruent}$=10.39). The increase in reaction time can be found in the conflicting stimuli conditions both for humans and the model.

In our Stroop simulation, we also measured the frequency (*freq*) of correct recalls to target responses. The results indicates that longer pro-

Figure 5. Performance results of the Stroop task with <Background> noise modulation from p = 0 (fully focused) to p = 1 (maximum distraction) for (Left) word reading (WR) and (Right) colour naming (CN), in three stimuli conditions; control, conflict and congruent.

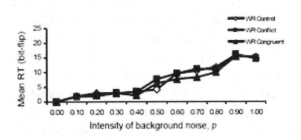 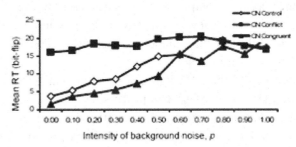

Figure 6. Performance results for Stroop task. (Left: Results from empirical study by Dunbar & MacLeod (1984), Right: Results of the model's simulation)

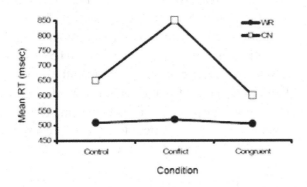 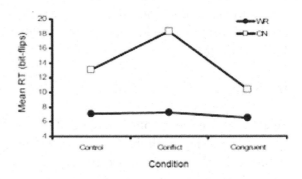

cessing time leads to higher recall error rate. The correct recalls recorded in WR are as follows; $WR_{freq(control,correct)}$ = 87.82, $WR_{freq(conflict,correct)}$ = 87.43, $WR_{freq(congruent,correct)}$ = 91.87, whilst for CN we obtained; $CN_{freq(control,correct)}$ = 70.64, $CN_{freq(conflict,correct)}$ = 23.25, $CN_{freq(congruent,correct)}$ = 81.02. Hence, we could conclude that the variability in initial activation of Stroop stimuli and their correspond background levels explains the differences in reaction times and frequency of correct recalls in both WR and CN. Asynchronous updates of bits in <Background>, <WORD> and <colour> vectors simultaneously, simulate the dynamics of cognitive process in Stroop phenomenon for active inhibition, facilitation and interference.

Discussion

HNN has been used to simulate the interferences and facilitations in processing responses to Stroop stimuli. For this purposes, a cognitive colour concept broken down into three components standing for activation coming in through the word reading and the colour naming channels and a third component accounting for attentional resource.

The results showed that our simple model is able to model the interference and the facilitation and reflects human reaction time data on the Stroop effect. We therefore suggest that the Stroop effect could simply be viewed as an associational or pattern completion effect (Ellis & Humphreys, 1999). A Hopfield network has a set of imprinted memories which serve as attractors for it bit-flip update dynamics. These attractors correspond to fixed cognitive colour concept that among other things (which can also be thought to be subsumed in the background noise) has components that correspond to the word corresponding to that colour as well as components that correspond to the visual percept of that colour.

In the congruent cases, inputs from both the word reading and colour naming coincide and would drag cognitive activity easily towards the corresponding full colour concept. In the control case, which corresponds to reading colour words in a neutral colour (i.e. black) or to seeing words with no colour association printed in colour, no problem arises either since again the activity is easily attracted to the colour concept corresponding to the non-neutral channel. Finally in the conflicting configuration a conflict arises because the combined activity has components that would drag it to different (mutually exclusive) attractors of the HNN corresponding to different cognitive colour concepts.

Depending on the intensity of the two different competing channels which might stem from attention to the task or from different degrees of automaticity of the two conflicting channels, the one or the other subpattern wins and the resulting pattern is dragged to the attractor that corresponds to the "stronger" subpattern. Hence the suggested model describes the Stroop effect without any particular assumption about processing pathways or cognitive architecture by using a general purpose associative neural network metaphor.

MODELLING STIMULI ASSOCIATION USING SPIKING NEURAL NETWORK (SNN)

Recordings of cells in the associative cortex from neuropsychological experiments (e.g. Erickson & Desimone; 1999; Sakai & Miyashita; 1991, and Naya, Yoshida & Miyashita (2001; 2003), have found two types of task-related activity namely retrospective and prospective. Retrospective activity is related to previously shown stimulus meanwhile prospective activity is related to a stimulus that is expected to appear. Prospective activity is not triggered directly by external stimuli but could be invoked by activations of other associated events.

In our approach (Yusoff & Grüning, 2010), we model both retrospective and prospective activities using Spiking Neuron Network (SNN). We use a supervised associative learning paradigm as a combination of spike emission rate dependent and Spike Timing Dependent Plasticity (STDP) approaches, a form of temporal Hebbian learning (Bi & Poo, 1998; Caporale & Dan, 2008). For learning simulation in network with simple Izhikevich's spiking neuron (Izhikevich, 2003), we integrated the rate dependent based associative learning by Mongillo, Amit and Brunel (2003) with STDP rules suggested in Paugam-Moisy, Martinez and Bengio (2008).

Supervision in learning is implemented through intensified current into paired target neuron subpopulations. For this, we pre-allocate the excitatory neurons in the network into their subpopulation, and learning is performed by associating two different stimuli, where synchronizations of network activity among inter and intra-subpopulation of neurons is the key measure to learning convergence.

Model

Izhikevich Spiking Neuron Model (IM)

Izhikevich's spiking neuron model (IM) (Izhikevich, 2003) was proposed based on two principles; computationally simple, and yet capable of producing rich firing behaviours of real biological neurons. Dynamics of cell potential are given by variable v in:

$$v_i' = 0.04v_i^2 + 5v_i + 140 - u_i + I_i \qquad (11)$$

where,

v_i = membrane potential of neuron i

u_i = membrane recovery variable of neuron i;
$u_i'=a_i(b_iv_i-u_i)$; a and b are parameters

I_i = synaptic currents or (and) injected external currents to neuron i.

When the cell potential reaches +30 mV, the neuron generates a spike and the voltage is reset to a value c, the resting potential (between -70 and -60), and the recovery variable is reset to d, the after-spike reset of the recovery variableif v_i $\geq +30$ mV, then $v_i \leftarrow c_i$ and $u_i \leftarrow u_i + d_i$ (12)

Spikes are transmitted to other neurons via synapses with a weight w. The input current I_i at time t is then simply the sum of the weights all neurons that fired and external currents.

Network Architecture

We created a network of 1000 Izhikevich spiking neurons with similar synaptic structure of excitatory-inhibitory neural network as proposed in works by Brunel and Lavigne (2009), Izhikevich (2003) and Mogillo, Amit and Brunel (2003) as follows. The network consists of 800 excitatory neurons and 200 inhibitory neurons with random and sparse connectivity. Each neuron is randomly connected to 20% of excitatory neurons and 20% of inhibitory neurons. For a case study, the excitatory neurons population is divided into four subpopulations (160 units each) that each represents an object (e.g. #1 and #2 in Figure 7). The underlying cognitive assumption is that a group of neurons are selective to a particular object or concept. Meanwhile the inhibitory subpopulation acts as the global network inhibition. For simplicity, we allocate neurons into subpopulations (i.e. P_n) as follows: P1: neurons 1-160, P2: neurons 161-320, P3: neurons 321-480 and P4: neurons 481-640, while neurons from 801-1000 are inhibitory and

the remaining neurons are non-selective to any object stimulus. A schematic view of the neural network is shown in Figure 8.

The network comprises of excitatory neurons pool and inhibitory neurons pool. #1 and #2 are subpopulations of excitatory neurons that are selective to a certain object stimulus. The connection strengths of excitatory synapses on excitatory neurons, excitatory synapses on inhibitory neurons, inhibitory synapses on excitatory neurons, and inhibitory synapses on inhibitory neurons, are labelled by $W_{1/a}$, W_{EI}, W_{IE}, and W_{II}, respectively. W_1 is the synaptic connection within the same subpopulation and W_a is the synaptic connection between two associated subpopulations.

Method

In a learning session with each trial of 500 milliseconds (ms) simulated time in 1 ms step, the network is trained to learn a pair of stimuli. The network receives noisy external currents, $\gamma\zeta_i(t)$, where γ is the strength of currents, and $\zeta_i(t)$ is the Gaussian noise with $\mu=0$, $\sigma=1$. The learning trial is run in the following four intervals:

1. Pre-stimulus: Both excitatory and inhibitory neurons receive external currents with $\gamma_{Ne}=3$) and $\gamma_{Ni}=1$,. The noisy current models the noisy thalamocortical input (Izhikevich, 2003) and serves as some background activity with no preferred stimulus.

2. Presentation of the first member of a stimulus pair: For $t > 150$ to $t \leq 350$ ms, the strength of external currents to target stimulus subpopulation 1 is intensified to $\gamma\zeta_i(t)$ with γ =30 and $\zeta_i(t)$ is the distribution with random values in the range of 0 and 1, uniformly distributed of the current. The intensified current simulates the attentional bias by having more enhanced cortical activity in the subpopulation of neurons that is selective to a certain stimulus.

Figure 7. Schematic view of the proposed excitatory-inhibitory neural network model with random sparse connectivity

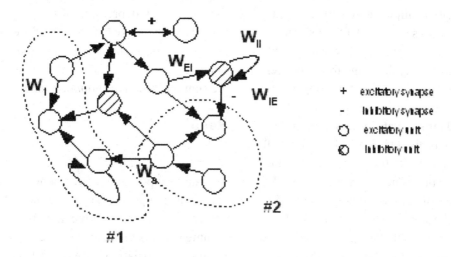

Figure 8. Learning time bins with overlapping windows, $T_{N.S}$ is the beginning of a time bin which ends at $T_{N.E}$ with $T_{N.E} - T_{N.S} = 100$ ms, and $T_{N.S}$ increasing in steps of 50 ms (Mogillo, Amit & Brunel, 2003).

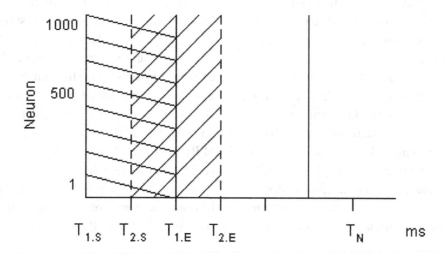

3. Delay interval: To model the interstimuli interval between representation of stimuli. The network is stimulated with only background activity

4. Presentation of the second member of a stimulus pair: For $t>250$ to $t \le 450$ ms, the target stimulus subpopulation 2 is stimulated with the same range of current as its associated subpopulation.

For a testing phase, the network is also stimulated with similar amount of intensified currents but for every ms of the simulation time ($t=500$ ms).

Synaptic Plasticity

Synaptic plasticity is implemented on excitatory to excitatory synapses (i.e. $W_{I/a}$). Other synapses (W_{EI}, W_{IE}, and W_{II}) are set to random values with moduli drawn uniformly the range from between 0 and 1 and with signs of connections depending on the type of the neuron (excitatory or inhibitory). In the 500 ms simulated time learning trial, the time window is divided into 100 ms ($T=100$) with overlapping bins at 50 ms intervals (Figure 8). For each learning time bin, we estimate the average spike rate of every excitatory neuron (S_{pre} and S_{post}) from the spikes in the bin divided by T (Mogillo, Amit & Brunel, 2003).

We derive the synaptic changes, ΔWs from a function of time difference, $\Delta t = t_j^{(f)} - t_i^{(f)}$, where $t_j^{(f)}$ and $t_i^{(f)}$ are the last firing times of post-synaptic neuron j and pre-synaptic neuron i, respectively, within the learning time bin (Figure 9) (Paugam-Moisy, Martinez & Bengio, 2008). In our approach, to control the infinite growth of synaptic values, we set the min and max weights to $w_{min}=0$ and $w_{max}=3$, respectively.

If both pre- and postsynaptic neurons emit spikes above the high rate threshold T_+ and only if the time difference of the last firing between the pre- and postsynaptic neurons is above 0 ($\Delta t > 0$), we highly potentiated a synapse W (if $W(t)) = 0$) to the maximal synaptic strength ($w_{max} = 3$). Meanwhile, if the pre synaptic (postsynaptic) neuron emits spikes with rate above T_+ whilst the postsynaptic (pre synaptic) neuron spike emission

rate is below T_+ but above the low threshold, T_a, ΔW is derived from 13.2 (weak potentiation). On the other hand, depression of W is applied when $\Delta t < 0$ and the spike rate of any of pre- and postsynaptic neurons reaches above T_+ and the other below T_a (see 13.3). The synaptic plasticity rules are summarised in the equations shown in Box 1.

Results

For learning initialisation, 20% of neurons within the same subpopulation are connected with synaptic values W_I in the range of 0 and 1. The initial values of W_I represent some random connectivity assumed to result from any previous learning. Results of association learning with novel stimuli P1 and P3 are depicted in Figure 10.

Currents to excitatory subpopulation neurons of P1 is intensified for 200 ms ($t>150$ to $t<= 350$ ms), then P3 is stimulated for the same duration ($t>250$ to $t<= 450$ ms). A) In the early phase of learning, after one trial, neurons in subpopulations P1 and P3 fire asynchronously as both stimuli are novel and activity are only dependent on the external currents. B) After ten trials, neuronal activity within each subpopulation is more synchronised as the result of learning. Activation of P3 (within $t>150$ to $t<= 250$ ms) and activation of P1 (within $t>400$ to $t<= 500$ ms) indicate association of P1 ↔ P3.

From Figure 10, during the early phase of learning, neurons fired asynchronously after the stimulations to both P1 (within $t>150$ to $t\leq 350$

Box 1.

$$W_{ij}(t+1) = \begin{cases} w_{max}, & \Delta t > 0 \\ max(w_{min}, min(w_{max}, W_{ij}(t)+ \Delta W), & \begin{aligned}&[(S_{pre} \geq T_+, T_a < S_{post} < T_+) ; \\ &(T_a < S_{pre} < T_+, S_{post} \geq T_+)], \Delta t > 0\end{aligned} \\ max(w_{min}, min(w_{max}, W_{ij}(t) - |\Delta W|), & \begin{aligned}&[(S_{pre} \geq T_+, S_{post} \leq T_a) ; \\ &(S_{post} \geq T_+, S_{pre} \leq T_a)], \Delta t < 0\end{aligned} \end{cases}$$

$$W_{ij}(t) = 0, (S_{pre} \geq T_+, S_{post} \geq T_+), \tag{13.1}$$

$$\tag{13.2}$$

$$\tag{13.3}$$

Figure 9. A function of time difference between last firing of pre-, $t_i^{(f)}$, and post synaptic neuron, $t_j^{(f)}$, $\Delta t = t_{post} - t_{pre} = t_j^{(f)} - t_i^{(f)}$, on excitatory neurons (Paugam-Moisy, Martinez & Bengio, 2008), Figure 2.

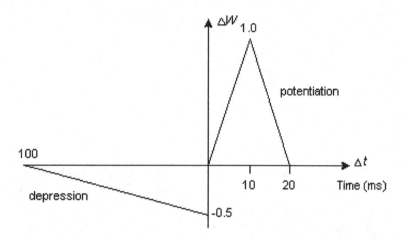

Figure 10. Neuronal network activity after one and ten learning trials for stimuli pair P1 ↔ P3

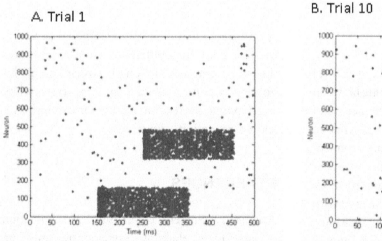

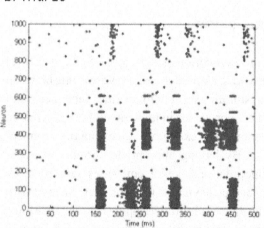

ms) and P3 (*t>250 to t ≤450 ms*). The retrospective and prospective activities can only be significantly observed after ten trials. The retrospective activity can be found through synchronised firings within the same subpopulation. Meanwhile the prospective activity is shown by a spill-over of activity from P1 to P3 (and otherwise) indicating learned association of stimuli pair of P1 ↔ P3. Results of pattern recalls are exhibited in Figure 11.

In comparison with the recall to unlearned and non-associated stimuli as depicted in Figure 11B, it is shown by synchronous activity among neurons in the same subpopulations that the network has learned each stimulus. Also the association of stimuli pair e.g. P1 ↔ P3 through synchronous activity between associated subpopulations.

Figure 11. Pattern recalls after associative learning with intensified current to target subpopulation. A) Recalls to learned and associated stimuli pair, B) Recalls to novel and non-associated stimuli.

A.

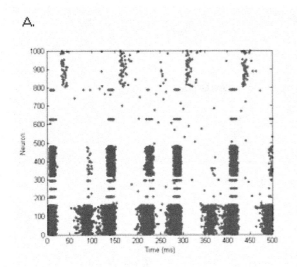

B.

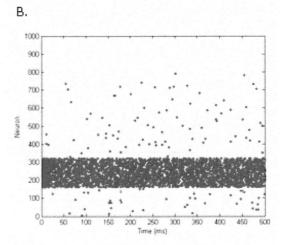

Discussion

In the simulation paradigm of Spiking Neural Networks, we model associative learning between two stimuli. We combine rate dependent and STDP approaches in implementation of synaptic plasticity on excitatory to excitatory connections. By having appropriate currents to target subpopulations, spike emissions rate by both pre- and postsynaptic neurons are measured with some thresholds in overlapping learning time bins. The results show retrospective network activity in neurons observed within the same subpopulation through synchronous activity. From Figure 11A, we can see that, when currents are flowed into a subpopulation e.g. P1, there is a synchronous activity among neurons in P1 as the result of learned association within the same subpopulation. In contrast in Figure 11B, neurons within the same subpopulation only fire asynchronously for unlearned pattern P2. Meanwhile, prospective activity is shown by spill-over of activity in two associated subpopulations. P3 gets active as the P1 is triggered (Figure 11A). Stimulation of neurons in subpopulation P1 has resulted a pro-

spective activity in P3 due to learned association between both subpopulations. This demonstrates that long-term associations between stimuli involving synaptic plasticity could be triggered by overlapping short-term activity involving only short-term activity dynamics.

REFERENCES

Allen, C., & Stevens, C. F. (1994). An evaluation of causes for unreliability of synaptic transmission. *Proceedings of the National Academy of Sciences (PNAS) USA, vol. 91*, (pp. 10380–10383).

Bernstein, L. E. (1989). Independent or dependent feature evaluation: A question of stimulus characterization. *The Behavioral and Brain Sciences, 12*, 756–757. doi:10.1017/S0140525X00025632

Bi, G. Q., & Poo, M. M. (1998). Synaptic modifications in cultured hippocampal neurons: Dependence on spike timing, synaptic strength and postsynaptic cell type. *The Journal of Neuroscience, 18*, 10464–10472.

Brunel, N., & Lavigne, F. (2009). Semantic priming in a cortical network model. *Journal of Cognitive Neuroscience, 21*(12), 2300–2319. .doi:10.1162/jocn.2008.21156

Caporale, N., & Dan, Y. (2008). Spike timing–dependent plasticity: A Hebbian learning rule. *Annual Review of Neuroscience, 31*(1), 25–46. doi:10.1146/annurev.neuro.31.060407.125639

Carr, C. E. (1993). Processing of temporal information in the brain. *Annual Review of Neuroscience, 16,* 223–243. doi:10.1146/annurev.ne.16.030193.001255

Collier, N. (1997). Convergence time characteristics of an associative memory for natural language processing. *Proceedings of Fifteenth International Joint Conference on Artificial Intelligence,* (pp. 1106-1113).

Crick, F. (1989). The recent excitement about neural networks. *Nature, 337,* 129–132. doi:10.1038/337129a0

Deco, G., & Obradovic, D. (1996). *An information-theoretic approach to neural computing.* Heidelberg, Germany: Springer.

Dunbar, K., & MacLeod, C. M. (1984). A horse race of a different color: Stroop Interference patterns with transformed words. *Journal of Experimental Psychology. Human Perception and Performance, 10,* 622–639. doi:10.1037/0096-1523.10.5.622

Ellis, H. C., & Hunt, R. R. (1993). *Fundamentals of cognitive psychology.* Boston, MA: McGraw-Hill.

Ellis, R., & Humphreys, G. (1999). *Connectionist psychology* (pp. 23–30). UK: Psychology Press.

Elman, J. L. (1990). Finding structure in time. *Cognitive Science, 14,* 179–211. doi:10.1207/s15516709cog1402_1

Erickson, C. A., & Desimone, R. (1999). Responses of Macaque Perirhinal neurons during and after visual stimulus association learning. *The Journal of Neuroscience, 19*(23), 10404–10416.

Fisher, C. G. (1968). Confusions among visually perceived consonants. *Journal of Speech and Hearing Research, 11,* 796–804.

Folk, C. L., Remington, R. W., & Johnston, J. C. (1992). Involuntary covert orienting is contingent on attentional control settings. *Journal of Experimental Psychology. Human Perception and Performance, 18,* 1030–1044. doi:10.1037/0096-1523.18.4.1030

Gerstner, W., Kempter, R., Leo van Hemmen, J., & Wagner, H. (1996). A neuronal learning rule for sub-millisecond temporal coding. *Nature, 383,* 76–78. doi:10.1038/383076a0

Gerstner, W., & Kistler, W. (2002). *Spiking neuron models: Single neurons, populations, plasiticity.* Cambridge, UK: Cambridge University Press.

Gray, F. (1953). *Pulse code communication.* (U.S. Patent 2,632,058, March, 1953).

Green, K. P., & Miller, J. L. (1985). On the role of visual rate information in phonetic perception. *Perception & Psychophysics, 38,* 269–276. doi:10.3758/BF03207154

Gu, Q. (2002). Neuromodulatory transmitter systems in the cortex and their role in cortical plasticity. *Neuroscience, 111*(4), 815–835. doi:10.1016/S0306-4522(02)00026-X

Harris, K. D. (2008). Stability of the fittest: Organizing learning through retroaxonal signals. *Trends in Neurosciences, 31*(3), 130–136. doi:10.1016/j.tins.2007.12.002

Hebb, D. O. (1949). *The organization of behavior.* New York, NY: Wiley.

Hopcroft, J. E., & Ullmann, J. D. (1979). *Introduction to automata theory, languages, and computation.* Mass.: Addison-Wesley.

Hopfield, J. J. (1982). Neural networks and physical systems with emergent collective computational abilities. *Proceedings of the National Academy of Sciences of the United States of America, 79,* 2554–2558. doi:10.1073/pnas.79.8.2554

International Phonetic Association. (1999). *Handbook of the International Phonetic Association: A guide to the use of the international phonetic alphabet.* Cambridge, UK: Cambridge University Press.

Izhikevich, E. M. (2003). Simple model of spiking neurons. *IEEE Transactions on Neural Networks, 14*(6), 1569–1572. doi:10.1109/TNN.2003.820440

Jost, J. (2005). *Dynamical systems – Examples of complex behavior.* Springer.

Kempter, R., Gerstner, W., & van Hemman, J. L. (1999). Hebbian learning and spiking neurals. *Physical Review E: Statistical Physics, Plasmas, Fluids, and Related Interdisciplinary Topics, 59*(4), 4498–4514. doi:10.1103/PhysRevE.59.4498

Kilian, J., & Siegelmann, H. T. (1996). The dynamic universality of sigmoidal neural networks. *Information and Computation, 128,* 48–56. doi:10.1006/inco.1996.0062

Legenstein, R., Naeger, C., & Maass, W. (2005). What can a neuron learn with spike-timing-dependent plasticity? *Neural Computation, 17*(11), 2337–2382. doi:10.1162/0899766054796888

Maass, W., Natschlger, T., & Markram, H. (2002). Real-time computing without stable states: A new framework for neural computation based on perturbations. *Neural Computation, 14*(11), 2531–2560. doi:10.1162/089976602760407955

Macdonald, J., & McGurk, H. (1978). Visual Influences on speech perception process. *Perception & Psychophysics, 24,* 253–257. doi:10.3758/BF03206096

Markram, H. (2006). The blue brain project. *Nature Reviews. Neuroscience, 7*(2), 153–160. doi:10.1038/nrn1848

Markram, H., Lübke, J., Frotscher, M., & Sakmann, B. (1997). Regulation of synaptic efficacy by coincidence of postsynaptic APS and EPSPS. *Science, 275*(5297), 213–215. doi:10.1126/science.275.5297.213

Massaro, D. W., & Stork, D. G. (1998). Speech recognition and sensory integration. *American Scientist, 86,* 236–244.

McClelland, J. L., & Rumelhart, D. E. (1985). Distributed memory and the representation of general and specific information. *Journal of Experimental Psychology. General, 114,* 159–197. doi:10.1037/0096-3445.114.2.159

McGurk, H., & Macdonald, J. (1976). Hearing lips and seeing voices. *Nature, 264,* 746–748. doi:10.1038/264746a0

Mines, M. A., Hanson, B. F., & Shoup, J. E. (1978). Frequency of occurrence of phonemes in conversational English. *Language and Speech, 21*(3), 221–241.

Mongillo, G., Amit, D. J., & Brunel, N. (2003). Retrospective and prospective persistent activity induced by Hebbian learning in a recurrent cortical network. *The European Journal of Neuroscience, 18,* 2011–2024. doi:10.1046/j.1460-9568.2003.02908.x

Müller, B., Reinhardt, J., & Strickland, M. T. (1990). *Neural networks.* Springer.

Naya, Y., Yoshida, M., & Miyashita, Y. (2001). Backward spreading of memory-retrieval signal in the primate temporal cortex. *Science, 291,* 661–664. doi:10.1126/science.291.5504.661

Naya, Y., Yoshida, M., & Miyashita, Y. (2003). Forward processing of long term associative memory in monkey inferotemporal cortex. *The Journal of Neuroscience, 23*, 2861–2871.

Paugam-Moisy, H., Martinez, R., & Bengio, S. (2008). Delay learning and polychnization for reservoir computing. *Neurocomputing, 71*(7-9), 1143–1158. doi:10.1016/j.neucom.2007.12.027

Popoviciu, N., & Boncut, M. (2005). On the Hopfield algorithm: Foundations and examples. *General Mathematics, 13*(2), 35–50.

Rojas, R. (1996). *Theorie der neuronalen Netze: Eine systematischen Einfhrung*. Berlin, Germany: Springer.

Sakai, K., & Miyashita, Y. (1991). Neural organization for the long term memory of paired associates. *Nature, 354*, 152–155. doi:10.1038/354152a0

Schneidman, E., Freedman, B., & Segev, I. (1998). Ion channel stochasticity may be critical in determining the reliability and precision of spike timing. *Neural Computation, 10*, 1679–1703. doi:10.1162/089976698300017089

Sekiyama, K., & Tohkura, Y. (1991). McGurk effect in non-English listeners: Few visual effects for Japanese subjects hearing Japanese syllables of high auditory intelligibility. *The Journal of the Acoustical Society of America, 90*, 1797–1805. doi:10.1121/1.401660

Shepherd, G. M. (1994). *Neurobiology*. Oxford University Press.

Sporea, I., & Grüning, A. (2010a). Modelling the McGurk effect. In M. Verleysen (Ed.), *Proceedings of the 18th European Symposium on Artificial Neural Networks* (pp. 363-369). Bruges, Belgium: Dside pub.

Sporea, I., & Grüning, A. (2010b). A distributed model of memory for the McGurk effect. *Proceedings of IEEE International Joint Conference on Neural Networks*, (pp. 120-123). Barcelona, Spain.

Stroop, J. R. (1935). Studies of interference in serial verbal reactions. *Journal of Experimental Psychology, 18*, 643–662. doi:10.1037/h0054651

Sutton, R. S., & Barto, A. G. (2002). *Reinforcement learning: An introduction*. Cambridge, MA: Bradford Books, MIT Press.

Tamaoka, K., & Makioka, S. (2004). Frequency of occurrence for units of phonemes, morae, and syllables appearing in a lexical corpus of a Japanese newspaper. *Behavior Research Methods, 36*(3), 531–547.

Williams, R. J., & Peng, J. (1990). An efficient gradient-based algorithm for on-line training of recurrent network trajectories. *Neural Computation, 2*, 490–501. doi:10.1162/neco.1990.2.4.490

Yusoff, N., & Grüning, A. (2010). Supervised associative learning in spiking neural network. In K. Diamantaras, W. Duch, & L. Iliadis (Eds.), *ICANN2010*, Springer.

Yusoff, N., Grüning, A., & Browne, A. (2009a). Modelling the Stroop effect: Dynamics in inhibition of automatic stimuli processing. *Proceedings of the 2nd International Conference in Cognitive Neurodynamics (ICCN)*, LNCS, Springer.

Yusoff, N., Grüning, A., & Browne, A. (2009b). *Competition and cooperation in colour-word Stroop effect: An association approach*. Frontiers in Behavioral Neuroscience. Conference Abstract: 41st European Brain and Behaviour Society Meeting. doi: 10.3389/conf.neuro.08.2009.09.353

Chapter 5
The Dendritic Cell Algorithm for Intrusion Detection

Feng Gu
University of Nottingham, UK

Julie Greensmith
University of Nottingham, UK

Uwe Aicklein
University of Nottingham, UK

ABSTRACT

As one of the solutions to intrusion detection problems, Artificial Immune Systems (AIS) have shown their advantages. Unlike genetic algorithms, there is no one archetypal AIS, instead there are four major paradigms. Among them, the Dendritic Cell Algorithm (DCA) has produced promising results in various applications. The aim of this chapter is to demonstrate the potential for the DCA as a suitable candidate for intrusion detection problems. We review some of the commonly used AIS paradigms for intrusion detection problems and demonstrate the advantages of one particular algorithm, the DCA. In order to clearly describe the algorithm, the background to its development and a formal definition are given. In addition, improvements to the original DCA are presented and their implications are discussed, including previous work done on an online analysis component with segmentation and ongoing work on automated data pre-processing. Based on preliminary results, both improvements appear to be promising for online anomaly-based intrusion detection.

INTRODUCTION

Artificial Immune Systems (AIS) (de Castro and Timmis, 2003) are computer systems inspired by both theoretical immunology and observed immune functions, principles and models, which

DOI: 10.4018/978-1-61350-092-7.ch005

are applied to real world problems. The human immune system, from which AIS draw inspiration, is evolved to protect the host from a wealth of invading microorganisms. AIS are developed to provide the similar defensive properties within a computing context. Initially AIS were based on simple models of the human immune system. As noted by Stibor *et al.* (2005), "first generation algorithms", including negative selection and clonal selection do not produce the same high quality performance as the human immune system. These algorithms, negative selection in particular, are prone to problems with scaling and the generation of excessive false alarms when used to solve problems such as network based intrusion detection. Recent AIS use more rigorous and up-to-date immunology and are developed in collaboration with modellers and immunologists. The resulting algorithms are believed to encapsulate the desirable properties of immune systems including robustness, error tolerance, and self-organisation (de Castro and Timmis, 2003).

One such "second generation" AIS is the Dendritic Cell Algorithm (DCA) (Greensmith, 2007), inspired by the function of the dendritic cells (DCs) of the innate immune system. It incorporates the principles of a key novel theory in immunology, termed the "danger theory" (Matzinger, 2002). This theory suggests that DCs are responsible for the initial detection of invading microorganisms, in addition to the induction of various immune responses against such invaders. An abstract model of natural DC behaviour is used as the foundation of the developed algorithm. The DCA has been successfully applied to numerous computer security related, more specific, intrusion detection problems, including port scan detection (Greensmith, 2007), botnet detection (Al-Hammadi et al., 2008) and a classifier for robot security (Oates et al., 2007). According to the results, the DCA has shown not only good performance in terms of detection rate, but also the ability to reduce the rate of false alarms in comparison to other systems, including Self Organising Maps (SOM) (Greensmith et al., 2008).

The main aim of this chapter is to demonstrate the reason for why the DCA is a suitable candidate for intrusion detection problems. In order to clearly describe the algorithm, the background and a formal definition are given. In addition, improvements to the original DCA are presented and their implications are discussed. The chapter is organised as follows: firstly, background information about a series of well known AIS algorithms and intrusion detection are described in section 2; secondly, several population AIS approaches for intrusion detection are introduced in section 3; thirdly, the algorithm details and formal definition of the DCA are demonstrated in section 4; fourthly, issues with the current DCA and potential solutions are discussed in section 5; finally, a summary of the work and some future directions are given in section 6.

BACKGROUND

Intrusion Detection

Intrusion detection involves the detection of any disallowed activities in networked computer systems. Based on deployment, intrusion detection systems can be grouped into either host-based or network-based. Host-based intrusion detection refers to the systems that monitor and collect data from the host machine. Data can be log files that include system information, such as CPU usage, memory usage, incoming/outgoing network traffics, and information of processes that are running on the host. Conversely, network-based intrusion detection refers to the systems that monitor and collect network traffic data among multiple hosts that are required for protection. Each host is a source of monitoring and collecting data, termed 'sensor'. Generally, network traffic is represented by network packets, which contain information of communications between the sources and destinations, such as IP address, port, service etc. Nowadays, most intrusion detection systems are hybrids of host-based and network-based deployments (Bejtlich, 2005).

Another way of categorising intrusion detection systems is based on detection methods, namely signature-based detection and anomaly-based detection (NIST, 2001). Signature-based detection, also known as misuse detection, distinguishes an intruder by comparing patterns or signatures of the intruder with previously known intrusions. As soon as any matches occur, an alarm is triggered. Whereas, anomaly-based detection involves discriminating between normal and anomalous data, based on the knowledge of the normal data. Thus, firstly the system needs to generate profiles of normality by either training or statistical analysis. During detection, anything that deviates from the normal profile is classified as anomalous, and an alarm is launched. Both signature based and anomaly based detection have different strengths and weaknesses. Signature-based detection produces high detection rate and low rate of false alarms, but it can only recognise the intruders or attacks are previously seen. Anomaly-based detection is capable of novel intruders and attacks that have not been seen before, but it encounter the problem of generating relatively high rate of false alarms. This problem stems from the way in which normal profiles are generated, as in most cases the collected data are just a small sample and thus not representative of the whole problem. Current techniques are often unable to cope with the dynamic changes of normal profile in real world problems and complex systems, such as large computer networks in which massive amount of nodes and uncertainties are presented.

AIS Algorithms

AIS researchers believe that AIS are intended to perform similar functions to the natural immune, such as defence and maintenance of the host, in a computational context. Unlike genetic algorithms, there is no one archetypal AIS, instead there are four major AIS paradigms, including the Negative Selection Algorithm (NSA) (Hofmeyr & Forrest, 1999), the Clonal Selection Algorithm (CSA) (de Castro & Von Zuben, 2000), the algorithms based on idiotypic networks models (Hart & Timmis, 2008), and the Dendritic Cell Algorithm (DCA) (Greensmith, 2007). These algorithms map the defence function of the immune system, in which certain immune entities and their functions or behaviour are included. Commonly seen immune entities are antigens which are protein particles recognised by the immune system, immune cells that perform certain immune functions individually or collaboratively, and antibodies that are detectors capable of recognising and binding to antigens. These algorithms generally involve generating effective detectors that can recognise the invading intruders and induce reactions against potential threats.

The NSA are inspired by the behaviour of a population of immune cells, named "T-cells", which belong to the adaptive immune system. In order to become functional, natural T-cells undergo "negative selection" for maturation in the thymus. First of all, the immune system generates a population of naive T cells with random specificity. Any naive T-cells that are reactive to self components are then removed from the population during this process. Remaining T-cells should only react to non-self substances, which according self/non-self theory (Coico et al., 2003), are threats to the host. From an algorithmic point view, the NSA has the following steps:

1. The system initialises certain amount of random detectors, named "naive detectors";
2. The system generates a self set from the training data that only contains normal data instances;
3. The naive detectors are compared with the self set, to produce a population of detectors that only react to intruders, termed "mature detectors";
4. The data instances in the testing data are compared with each mature detector, and if any detector reacts to the incoming data instance, an alarm is triggered.

Comparisons in training and testing (detection) are accomplished by certain matching function, to assess the affinity of two compared candidates, where an activation threshold is applied.

The CSA are based on Burnett's theory of clonal selection and immune memory (Coico et al., 2003). This includes several adaptive and learning processes. It involves another population of immune cells, named "B-cells", which produce antibodies capable of detecting diverse and numerous patterns of invading threats. Immune memory is composed of "memory cells" that are able to remember the previously seen threats. The procedures of the CSA are as follows:

1. The system initialises certain amount of random solutions to a given problem;
2. These solutions are then being exposed to training;
3. In each generation, the best solutions are selected based on a affinity measure, to reproduce with multiple clones;
4. Current solutions then undergo a mutation process with high frequency, which is proportional to the affinity measure;
5. Optimal solutions are selected in the current population, to form memory cells;
6. The steps above keep repeating until a termination point is reached.

In brief, the system also uses pattern recognition mechanism for information processing, to make decisions of selecting the optimal solutions. The probability of a solution being replaced is proportional to its goodness. The better a solution is, the more clones are reproduced. As a result, majority of the population are optimal solutions.

Idiotypic network based algorithms are derived from the immune network theory proposed by Jerne (Jerne, 1974). It suggests that the immune system can be seen as a network in which immune entities interact with each other even when antigens are absent. The interactions can be initialised not only between antigens and antibodies, but also between antibodies and antibodies. This induces either stimulating or suppressive immune responses. They result a series of immunological behaviours, including tolerance and memory emer-

gence. There are three major factors that affect the stimulation level of B-cells (Timmis et al., 2008), which are the contribution of the antigen binding, the contribution of neighbouring B-cells, and the suppression of neighbouring B-cells. As the stimulation level of a B-cells increases, the amount of clones it produces increases accordingly. At the population level, this results a diverse set of B-cells. In addition, three mutation mechanisms are introduced, including crossover, inverse and point mutation. In principle, the idiotypic network based algorithms are similar to the CSA, apart from the interactions between solutions in the repertoire, which may result a higher convergence rate.

APPLICATIONS OF AIS TO INTRUSION DETECTION

Since AIS are designed though mimicking certain properties of the natural immune system, especially the detection mechanism for intruders, obvious applications of AIS can be intrusion detection problems (Kim et al., 2007). However, not all AIS paradigms are applicable, majority of the applications involve the NSA, the idiotypic network based algorithms and the DCA. In this section, a number of noticeable applications are described.

The NSA-Based Approaches

Initial development of an NSA based intrusion detection system was by Hofmeyr et al. (1999). The system aimed to solve problems that involve detecting malicious connections between one computer in the Local Area Network (LAN) and one external computer. Connections are represented as 49-bit binary strings that include the source IP, destination IP, source port, destination port and service type etc. Detection is performed through string matching between connection string s and detector string d, using r-contiguous bits rule (if s and d have the same symbols in at least r contiguous bits positions). The value r is a threshold that determines the specificity of a detector. The system has a training phase where negative selection mechanism is used. Later on, a real-valued NSA was proposed by González & Dasgupta (2003), in which data representation is changed from binary strings to real-valued numbers. The use of such data representation was intended to speed up detector generation process.

As pointed out in (Stibor et al., 2005), the NSA (no matter binary string version or real-valued version) have numerous problems: firstly they cannot avoid the curse of dimensionality, and not applicable to data with high dimensionality; secondly, the detector generation can result holes within the shape-space, so it is difficult to cover just non-self, and it either generates the population of detectors covering both non-self and unseen self (over-fit) or only covering partial non-self (under-fit); thirdly, the NSA still take extensive time period to generate the adequately complete set of detectors. Therefore, negative selection is insufficient and not suitable for anomaly detection.

The Idiotypic Network Approach

Ostaszewski et al (2008) proposed an adaptive and dynamic intrusion detection system based on idiotypic network. This system was designed mainly for the detection of a special type of attacks, namely "denial of service" (DOS). The DAPRA 1999 dataset (MIT Lincoln Lab, 1998) was used to test the system. As the aim was to provide comprehensive information of network behaviour, rather than raise alarms whenever inappropriate activities are identified, the evaluation of system performance also considered the amount of information generated during usual events.

The proposed system provides a means of gathering information about incoming, or proceeding attack from the very beginning, to take efficient countermeasures against threats. According to the experiments, monitoring activities of the idiotypic network helped to identify DOS attacks in the tested data, and different kinds of attacks showed their own particular impacts on the system. In addition, extra information can be extracted from the idiotypic network to facilitate the identification of anomalies.

The Danger Theory Approach

The DCA was developed to overcome the problems shown with the NSA. It was initially proposed and developed by Greensmith et al. (2005) where it was applied to a basic and standard machine learning dataset, the UCI Wisconsin Breast Cancer dataset (UCI). For this simple dataset, a classification accuracy of 99% was produced. The DCA was then applied to the ping scan detection (Greensmith et al., 2006) in computer security. The results showed that the algorithm could achieve 100% classification accuracy when appropriate thresholds are used. The DCA was later on applied to SYN scan detection (Greensmith & Aickelin, 2007) where the collected dataset consists of over five million data instances. The detection scenario was that the SYN scan was launched from a victim machine, where the DCA is used to monitor the behaviours of the victim. This scenario represents a scan performed by an insider, who can be a legitimate user of the system doing unauthorised activities. The algorithm produced high true positive rate and low false positive rate, and each experiment could be finished within acceptable time despite the large quantity of data it needs to process.

The DCA was also applied to Botnet detection (Al-Hammadi et al., 2008). Botnets are decentralised and distributed networks of subverted machines, controlled by a central commander, namely "botmaster". A single bot is a malicious piece of program that can transfer victim machines into zombie machines once installed. This work demonstrated the application of the DCA to the detection of a single bot, to assess its performance on this novel problem area. The results indicated that the DCA was able to distinguish the bot from the normal processes on a host machine. The

DCA was then applied to a benchmark intrusion detection dataset (Gu et al., 2008), KDD Cup 1999 (Hettich & Bay, 1999). KDD 99 has been widely used and understood, and it is one of the only few labelled datasets that are publicly available in the field of intrusion detection. A preliminary comparison is performed, among the DCA, the real-valued NSA with constant detectors and the C4.5 decision tree algorithm. The results show that the DCA produces reasonably good performance compared to others.

The applications of the DCA indicate the strengths of the algorithm as follows: firstly, the DCA does not require a training phase and the knowledge of normality and anomaly is acquired through basic statistical analysis, so the applications may be less time consuming than other supervised learning algorithms; secondly, the DCA performs linear calculations for its computation, making the system low weight and ideally for intrusion detection tasks. Both strengths make the DCA a suitable candidate for intrusion detection tasks, which mainly require high detection speed.

In summary, the DCA has shown reasonable detection accuracy in the past applications, and it has the advantage of not having a training phase shortening the application process and low weight in computation improving detection speed. As a result, if one needs a system such that a high requirement of detection speed is more crucial, the DCA can be a suitable solution.

THE DENDRITIC CELL ALGORITHM

The DCA is a population-based algorithm, designed for tackling anomaly-based detection tasks. It is inspired by functions of natural DCs of the innate immune system, which form part of the body's first line of defence against invaders. DCs have the ability to combine a multitude of molecular information and to interpret this information for the T-cells of the adaptive immune system, to induce appropriate immune responses towards perceived threats. Therefore, DCs can be seen as detectors for different policing sites of the body as well as mediators for inducing a variety of immune responses.

Algorithm Overview

Signal and antigen are two types of molecular information processed by natural DCs. Signals are collected by DCs from their local environment and consist of indicators of the health of the monitored tissue. DCs exist in one of three states of maturation to throughout their lifespans. In the initial immature state, DCs are exposed to a combination of signals. Based on the concentration of various signals, DCs can differentiate into either a "fully mature" form to activate the adaptive immune system, or a "semi-mature" form to suppress it. During their immature phase DCs also collect debris in the tissue which are subsequently combined with the environmental signals. Some of the "suspicious" debris collected are termed antigens, and they are proteins originating from potential invading entities. DCs combine the "suspect" antigens with evidence in the form of processed signals to correctly instruct the adaptive immune system to respond, or become tolerant to the antigens in question. For more information regarding the underlying biological mechanisms, please refer to (Greensmith, 2007 and Lutz and Schuler, 2002).

The DCA incorporates the functionality of DCs including data fusion, state differentiation and information temporal correlation. For the remainder of the chapter the term "DC" will refer to the artificial agent based cell, not the natural DCs. For the DCs in the DCA, as per the natural system, there are two types of input data, signal and antigen. Signals are represented as vectors of real-valued numbers, which are measures of the monitored system's status within certain time periods. We term this information as "system context" data. Antigens are categorical values that can be various states of a problem domain or the entities of interest associated with a monitored system. In real world applications, antigens represent what to be classified within a problem domain. For example, they can be process IDs in computer security problems (Al-Hammadi et al., 2008, Greensmith and Aickelin, 2007), a small range of positions and orientations of robots (Oates et al., 2007), the proximity sensors of online robotic systems (mokhtar2009), or the time stamps of records collected in biometric datasets (Gu et al., 2009). Signals represent system context of a host or a measure of network traffic (Al-Hammadi et al., 2008, Greensmith and Aickelin, 2007), measurements derived from various sensors in robotic systems (Oates et al., 2007, Mokhtar et al., 2009), or the biometric data captured from a monitored automobile driver (Gu et al., 2009). Signals are normally pre-categorised as "PAMP", "Danger" or "Safe" in the DCA. The semantics of these signal categories is listed as follows.

- PAMP: a measure that increases in value as the observation of anomalous behaviour. It is a confident indicator of anomaly, which usually presented as signatures of the events that can definitely cause damage to the system.
- Danger: a measure indicates a potential abnormality. The value increases as the confidence of the monitored system being in abnormal status increases accordingly.
- Safe: a measure that increases value in conjunction with observed normal behaviour. This is a confident indicator of normal, predictable or steady-state system behaviour.

Increases in the safe signal value suppress the effects of the PAMP and danger signals within the algorithm, as per what is observed in the natural system. This immunological property has been incorporated within the DCA in the form of predefined weights for each signal category, for the transformation from input signals to output

signals. The output signals are used to evaluate the status of the monitored system, to determine the presence of anomalies or misbehaviours.

A relationship of cause-and-effect is believed to exist between signals and antigens, where signals are the explicit effects that potentially result from the implicit cause of antigens. This is achieved if the input data is correctly mapped to the underlying problem domain. The goal of the DCA is to incorporate such a relationship to identify antigens that are responsible for the anomalies reflected by signals. Therefore, the algorithm operates in two steps, firstly it identifies whether anomalies occurred in the past based on the input data; secondly it correlates the identified anomalies with the potential causes, generating an anomaly scene per suspect.

This is achieved by deploying a population of artificial cells, DC objects, which operate in parallel as detectors. Diversity is generated within the DC population through the application of lifespans, which limit the amount of information an individual DC object can process. Different DCs are given different limits for their lifespan, which creates a variable time window effect, with different DC objects processing the signal and antigen data sources during different time periods across the analysed time series (Oates et al., 2008). It is postulated that the combination of signal/antigen temporal correlation and diversity of the DC population are responsible for the detection capability of the DCA.

Development Pathway

In this section a brief history is given of the development of the DCA and the numerous versions that have appeared over the past few years. An overview of this process is given in Figure 1.

Following the development of the initial abstract model the applicability of the DCA was first demonstrated in a prototype system (pDCA) (Greensmith, 2007). Here the pDCA was applied to a binary classification problem which demon-

Figure 1. Development pathway of the DCA

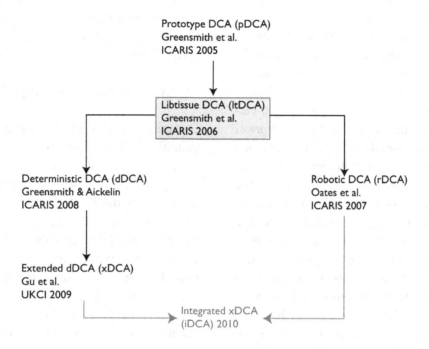

strated this population based algorithm was capable of performing two-class discrimination on an ordered dataset, using a timestamp as antigen and a combination of features forming three signal categories.

After the encouraging results achieved, the pDCA was further developed into a larger system, combined with the immune-inspired agent based framework libtissue. This version (ltDCA) was stochastic in nature and contained numerous somewhat unpredictable elements including random sampling of incoming antigen, signal decay and randomly assigned migration thresholds. While ltDCA yielded positive results in a number of applications, it contained too many arbitrary and random components, rendering detailed study of its behaviour as an algorithm almost infeasible. Initially the ltDCA was applied to problems in computer and network security including port scan detection and sensor network security.

In parallel to the development of ltDCA, this algorithm steadily increased in popularity especially within the AIS community, being applied

to a range of problems. This includes its use as a robotic classifier for physical security. To adapt the ltDCA for purpose, to obtain a reasonable mapping of signal and antigen data, a number of modifications were made, including the segmentation of the output information to provide localisation information for a detected anomaly and the integration of a re-implemented ltDCA with a Brookes style 'subsumption architecture'. This experiment in effect validated the use of the DCA as an anomaly detection technique and transformed its analysis stage into an online process.

Despite its successful application in a number of problem domains, several issues arose in particular with understanding the nature of the "signal and antigen" model of input, and how to interface the categories with given input data. Definitions for the data streams, initially heavily reliant on biological metaphors, were never sufficiently clear and the stochastic nature of ltDCA exacerbated this problem. Theoretical analysis implied that the ltDCA was simply an ensemble linear classifier, which contradicted some of the claims made previously about the manner by which the ltDCA functions.

In response to this, a large amount of randomness was removed from the algorithm and a simplified version developed, named the deterministic DCA (dDCA). This DCA variant is predictable in its use; one can follow a single antigen element throughout the system, and given a priori knowledge of the signals used and the antigen's relative position to all other antigen it is possible to predict its classification. It is shown that the dDCA does not have impaired performance in comparison to ltDCA, and it is possible to calculate crucial algorithmic information such as its real-time capability and run-time complexity values.

Still, the dDCA does not avoid the problems that accompany its interface to underlying datasets, nor does it solve the problem of having a non-adaptive analysis module. We propose that ultimately it is necessary to develop an integrated DCA (iDCA) which can automatically extract and select relevant components of underlying data and can adapt to appropriately produce anomaly discrimination in real time and adapt to changes in the underlying dataset. The difference in the dDCA in comparison to a hypothetical iDCA are numerous, therefore we propose to initially develop an intermediate version extended from the dDCA, termed xDCA which is described and used in this paper.

IMPROVEMENTS TO THE ORIGINAL DCA

Recently a series of improvements to the original DCA have been made, to respond to some of the criticisms. Firstly, a formal definition of the DCA is given to avoid the potential ambiguities of the algorithm. Secondly, an online analysis component based segmentation approaches is introduced to enable periodic and continuous analysis. Thirdly, automated data pre-processing methods based on dimensionality reduction and statistical inference techniques for automated signal selection and categorisation.

Formalisation of the Algorithm

One criticism of the DCA is the lack of a formal definition, which results in ambiguity for understanding the algorithm and thus leads to incorrect applications and implementations. A formal definition of the DCA should be provided for clearly presenting the algorithm. In this section, we define data structures of the DCA and formalise the algorithm. We concentrate on specifying the entire DC population using quantitative measures at the functional level, and basic set theory and computational functions such as addition, multiplication and recursion are used for clarity.

Data Structures

Define *Signal* $\subseteq R^3$ and *Antigen* $\subseteq N$ to be the two types of input data. Within a time period (*Time* $\subseteq R$), the input data can be defined as *S: Time* $\rightarrow$ *Signal* $\cup$ *Antigen*, and *S(t)* is an instance of input data where $t \in$ **Time**. Elements of **Signal** are corresponding to three signal categories of the DCA as mentioned, which are represented as three-dimensional (3D) vectors and usually normalised into a predefined nonnegative range. Elements of **Antigen** are categorical values, represented as natural numbers where ordering is ignored.

Define the weight matrix of signal transformation as W, a matrix with two rows and three columns, where $w_{ij} \in$ **R**. The weight matrix is used to transform three categories of input signal to two categories output signals. It is usually predefined by users, and kept constant during runtime. The entries are based on empirical results from the underlying immunology.

We use the notation **List***(A)* for a list of type *A*. Let **Population** be a set of DC objects and *N*=**Population** be the population size, a DC object consists of:

- a unique index $i \in \{1,2,...N\}$;
- a lifespan *I*: **Population** →**R**;
- an initial value of its signal profile *K*: **Population** →**R**, which is equal to zero;
- a list **List(Antigen)** for storing its antigen profile.

The signal profile is a measure of processed signal instances, whereas the antigen profile is a measure of sampled antigen instances. Each DC object is able to update its internal data structures by calling relevant operations.

The output of each DC is stored in a list of **N×R**. We use *lst(j)* to denote the *j*th element of *lst*, and π_1 and π_2 for projection functions to get the first and second dimension of a 2-D vector respectively.

Procedural Operations

To access the data structures of the DCA, a series of procedural operations are called. These procedural operations describe behaviours of the algorithm at the functional level. They are the most fundamental elements of the algorithm, each of which is executed in one step. The aim of formalising these operations is to present them as simple and clear as possible without losing details.

Let *Append (x,X)* be a generic function of appending an element *x* (2-D vector) to a list *X* (a list of 2-D vectors). The type of *x* determines the type of *X*, they can be **N×R** or **R×R**. It is different from "unite" of sets, as duplicates are not eliminated. The function operates by appending the new element to the current list, so it is executed in one step.

At the beginning ($t=0$), the algorithm initialises all DC objects in **Population** by assigning the initial values of *I(i)* and *K(i)*, namely "DC initialisation". The value of *I(i)* depends on the density function used to generate the initial lifespan of each DC object. Both uniform distribution and Gaussian distribution can be applied.

Definition 1 (signal transformation). *The signal transformation function is defined as*

O: Time →**R×R**.

$$O(t) = \begin{cases} S(t) \bullet W^T, & S(t) \in \textbf{Signal}; \\ \textbf{Null}, & \text{otherwise,} \end{cases}$$

where $\bullet$ is a multiplication operator for two matrixes. This operation is executed whenever $S(t) \in$ **Signal** holds, and it performs a multiplication between a 3-D vector and a transposed **2×3** matrix to produce another 2-D vector, which consists of two output signals, namely "*CSM*" and "*K*". In the case that $S(t) \in$ **Antigen** holds, the function returns **Null**.

Definition 2 (lifespan update). *The lifespan update function is defined as*

*F:***Time** × **Population**→**R**.

$$F(t,i) = \begin{cases} I(i), & t = 0; \\ I(i) - \pi_1(O(t)), & F(t-1,i) \leq 0; \\ F(t-1,i) - \pi_1(O(t)), & \text{otherwise.} \end{cases}$$

When $t=0$, the initial value of *F* is *I(i)* which is the initial lifespan of a DC object. It is repeatedly subtracted by *CSM* signal until the termination condition, *F (t-1, i)*≤0, is reached, and then it is reset to its initial value *I(i)*.

Definition 3 (signal profile update). *The signal profile update function is defines as*

G:**Time** × **Population**→**R**.

$$G(t,i) = \begin{cases} K(i), & t = 0; \\ K(i) + \pi_2(O(t)), & F(t-1,i) \leq 0; \\ G(t-1,i) + \pi_2(O(t)), & \text{otherwise.} \end{cases}$$

When $t = 0$, the value of G is $K(i) = 0$ which is the initial signal profile of a DC object. It is repeated added by k signal the termination condition is reached, and the it is reset to its initial value $K(i) = 0$.

Definition 4 (antigen profile update). *The antigen profile update function is defined as*

H:**Time** × **Population**→**List(Antigen)**.

$$H(t,i) = \begin{cases} Append(S(t), H(t-1,i)), & S(t) \in \textbf{Antigen}; \\ \textbf{Null}, & \text{otherwise.} \end{cases}$$

Initially H is empty, and when a new antigen instance arrives, it is sampled by a DC object and stored into its list until the termination condition is reached. The index of the DC object selected is defined as $i \equiv \theta$ (**mod**N), where θ is the number of antigen instances up to time t. This is termed the "sequential sampling" rule.

Definition 5 (output record). *Let $R(t,i) = \{(r,a)|r = G(t,i) \wedge a \in H(t,i)\}$ be the output of a DC object, and the output record function is defined as*

$(F(t,i) \leq 0) \wedge (t>0) \Rightarrow Append(R(t,i)<lst)$.

Where r is the signal profile and a is the antigen profile recorded by a DC object. This function is responsible for appending the output of a DC object (a 2-D vector) into the output list lst when the termination condition is reached. The processed information in lst is used to produce the final detection results in the analysis phase.

Definition 6 (antigen counter). *The antigen counter function for each antigen type*

$\alpha\epsilon$**Antigen**is *defined as* C: N× N→$\{0,1\}$.

$$C(j,\alpha) = \begin{cases} 1, & \pi_1(lst(j)) = \alpha; \\ 0, & \text{otherwise.} \end{cases}$$

Definition 7 (signal profile abstraction). *The signal profile abstraction function is defined as*

R: N× N→ R.

$$R(j,\alpha) = \begin{cases} \pi_2(lst(j)), & \pi_1(lst(j)) = \alpha; \\ 0, & \text{otherwise.} \end{cases}$$

Function C counts the number of instances of antigen type α, and function R calculates the sum of all k values associated with antigen type α. These two operations are performed for every single antigen type, and involve scanning ls$t$ in its entirety.

Definition 8 (anomaly metric calculation). *The anomaly metric calculation function of $K(\alpha)$ is defined as.*

$$\beta = \sum_{j=0}^{n-1} C(j,\alpha) \wedge \gamma = \sum_{j=0}^{n-1} R(j,\alpha)$$

$$\Rightarrow K(\alpha) = \frac{\gamma}{\beta}$$

As α is a known antigen type, we have $\beta \geq 1$. A threshold can be applied for further classification. The value of the threshold depends on the underlying characteristics of the dataset used. If $K(\alpha)$ is greater than the predefined threshold, it is classified as anomalous, other normal.

The procedural operations of the DCA are formally defined in previous section, so by combining them with for or while loops and if statements the algorithm can be presented as the following Pseudocode.

```
while input data do
      if antigen then
            antigen profile update;
      end
      if signal then
            signal transformation;
            foreach DC object do
                  lifespan update;
                  signal profile update;
                  if termination condition then
                        output record;
                  end
            end
      end
end
while output list do
      foreach antigen type do
            antigen counter;
            signal profile abstraction;
            anomaly metric calculation;
      end
end
```

Online Analysis Component

An online analysis component is essential for developing an effective intrusion detection system using the DCA. Such a component performs periodic analysis of the processed information presented by DCs, to continuously identify intrusions during detection. An effective and fully functioning intrusion detection system should be able to identify the intrusions as quickly as possible, as accurately as possible, and hence detection speed and detection accuracy are two major indicators of performance. By detection speed here we meant the time an intrusion detection system takes to identify intrusions or anomalies during detection. Most techniques can produce reasonable detection accuracy, if sufficient time is given. But in most case detection speed is more significant for assessing the performance of an intrusion detection system. If the system fails to identify the intrusions in time, no further responses against the intrusions can be made. This leads to the eventual success of attacks, which is a fatal failure of an intrusion detection system. In other words, if the intrusions are identified too late, even with 100% detection accuracy, it all becomes meaningless in terms of system defence. As a result, we propose integrating online analysis with the DCA, to improve detection speed without compromising detection accuracy.

If online analysis is to be performed during detection, one issue needs resolved, namely, when to perform analysis. This could be solved by introducing segmentation to the DCA. It is different from the moving time windows method described in (Gu et al., 2008), which is used in the pre-processing stage to smooth noisy input signals, as segmentation is performed in the post-processing stage for the purpose of periodic and continuous analysis. As the processed information is presented by matured DCs over time, a sequence of processed information is being generated during detection. Segmentation involves partitioning this sequence into relative smaller segments, in terms of the number of data items or time. All the generated segments have the same size, and the analysis is performed within each individual segment. Therefore, in each segment, one set of detection result ($K(\alpha)$ per antigen type) is generated, in which intrusions appeared within the duration of this segment can be identified.

First of all, segmentation can produce multiple sets of results, rather than one set of results produced by non-segmentation system. This enables the system to perform analysis online not offline, as all segments are processed during detection. In addition, segmentation distributes the analysis process into multiple steps, instead of performing at once. This can reduce the computation power and time required for the analysis process, so segmentation can effectively enhance detection speed. Moreover, as the processed information is presented by matured DCs at different time points over the duration, analysing the sequence of processed information at once ignores the temporal difference of each piece of processed information. As a result, the same antigen type that causes malicious activities at one point but does nothing at another point may be classified as normal rather than an intrusion. This can be avoided by applying segmentation, as it features periodic analysis that can cope with the inherited time differences. Therefore, the system can effectively discriminate malicious activities from normal ones, and hence the detection accuracy can also be improved.

The most important and in fact the only factor of segmentation is the segment size. It determines how soon the intrusions can be identified. The smaller the segment size, the sooner the intrusions can be identified, and vice versa. Moreover, the segment size may also influence the sensitivity of the final results. If the segment size is too large, the results can lose the sensitivity and thus the system loses the ability to identify true positives. However, if the segment size is too small, the results may be too sensitive, and the system can generate false positives.

In (Gu et al., 2009), the authors have shown that applying segmentation to the DCA makes significant differences to the results. In some cases, the system with segmentation may even produce better performance in terms of detection accuracy. In addition, segmentation enables the system to perform periodic analysis on the processed information presented by the DCs. As a result it can effectively improve detection speed without compromising detection accuracy. Therefore, segmentation is applicable to the DCA. Even though segmentation is not immune inspired, it can still make contribution to the field of AIS, as it can improve the system performance of the DCA. As a result, more effective intrusion detection systems can be developed, by integrating segmentation with the DCA. This method is also applicable to other second generation AIS algorithms.

Automated Data Pre-processing

The DCA encounters issues that accompany its interface to underlying datasets, as well as have a non-adaptive analysis module. Formal definition and theoretical analysis have shown that the algorithm itself is rather simple, and segmentation enables the DCA to efficiently and effectively process large datasets in terms of data size. However, data size is not the only concern when handling complex datasets, high dimensionality is often a bigger problem. Complexity occurs at the data pre-processing stage of the DCA when dimensionality reduction is required. Previously, the data pre-processing of the DCA is performed manually based on users' expert knowledge of a given problem domain, which is time consuming and sometime difficult to achieve. As a result, it is necessary to automate the data pre-processing stage, which extracts and selects relevant features, and adapts the algorithm to characteristics of the underlying data.

Originally the DCA does not rely on training data to define which of the input signals are potentially "dangerous". But expert knowledge of the problem domain is required to generate proper input data to the DCA during manual data pre-processing. It involves two steps, namely "antigen representation" and "signal selection and categorisation" for generating two types of input to the DCA. Since antigen representation involves identifying the objects to classify as normal or anomalous in the problem, it is usually easy to accomplish and thus does not require automation. The rest of this section is focused on the automation of signal selection and categorisation in the DCA.

Signal selection and categorisation involve firstly selecting or extracting the most interesting features from the original feature set of a given dataset, and then categorising these features into one of three signal categories of the DCA. Manual methods are problematic, as whenever the problem is changed, the whole process needs to be redone. Even for the same dataset, if cross-validation is used, the process needs to be performed for every single subset generated. In addition, it is not always possible to acquire adequate expert knowledge for a dataset to effectively perform signal selection and categorisation for the DCA. In order to automate signal selection and categorisation, techniques of dimensionality reduction and statistical inference are used, and an unsupervised "training phase" is introduced to obtain the underlying knowledge regarding normality and anomaly of a problem.

Let $X = I\{x_1, x_2, ..., x_m\}$ the original feature set of a problem. Dimensionality reduction involves generating a new feature space $Y = \{y_1, y_2, ..., y_d\}$ ($d<m$), which is supposed to be representative of the problem with minimum redundancy. Feature selection involves selecting a best subset of input features. Feature extraction creates new features based on transformations or combinations of the original features. The choice between feature selection and extraction depends on the problem domain and classifier. The possible techniques are listed as follows.

- Correlation Coefficient (with class labels) - feature selection
- Information Gain (with class labels) - feature selection
- Principal Component Analysis (PCA, without class labels) - feature extraction

Preliminary work has been carried out in Gu et al. (2009), in which the authors showed that it was possible to integrate PCA with the DCA for the purpose of automated data pre-processing. The PCA facilitated the reduction of data dimension of the raw data, to select proper features as the candidates of the input of the DCA. It was also used for the ranking of attributes based on the variability, which is mapped to the ranking of signal categories of the DCA for signal categorisation. In this way, the data pre-processing of the DCA is performed by simply using PCA and basic Min-Max normalisation, without the requirement of any expert knowledge of the problem domain. The results suggested that the integrated system of PCA and the DCA was successful in terms of anomaly detection, as the system can produce relatively high true positive rates and low false positive rates. As a result, the application of PCA to the DCA makes it possible to automatically categorise input data into user-defined signal categories, while still generating useful and accurate classification results.

More recently, automated data pre-processing methods based on feature selection/extraction and statistical inference techniques are developed. The idea is to use dimensionality reduction techniques to select the *most interesting* features from the original feature set as the candidates of input signals to the DCA, then perform greed search to find the best combination of these candidates corresponding to the signals categories where mean square errors (MSE) (Garthwaite et al., 2006) is employed as a performance measure. The new system is tested by a number of datasets, as well as compared with other existing machine learning techniques. The testing datasets include: the UCI Wisconsin Breast Cancer dataset (Blake et al., 1998) consists of 700 data instances and each data item has 10 features; the KDD 99 dataset derived from the DAPRA 98 Lincoln Lab data set for applying data mining techniques to the area of intrusion detection, it consists of about 5 million data instances, each of which has 42 features. Two versions of the KDD 99 dataset are used: a 10% subset whose data items are randomly and proportionally selected from the whole dataset; and the whole dataset. As these two datasets are much more complicated, 10-fold cross validation is performed to generate 10 subsets. For the purpose of baseline comparison, other existing techniques, including K-Nearest-Neighbour (KNN), decision trees, and Support Vector Machine (SVM) algorithms are used.

Table 1 shows the true positive rate and false positive rate of all methods applied to the breast cancer dataset. As expected, manual method produces high true positive rate and low false positive rate; PCA based method produces better result since its true positive rate is higher and false positive rate is zero; information gain based method has significantly lower true positive rate but comparable false positive rate; correlation based method has comparable true positive rate but significantly higher false positive rate.

As shown in Figure 2 and Figure 3, the manual method and other existing techniques produce

Table 1. Results of all methods on the breast cancer dataset

	True Positive Rate	False Positive Rate
Manual	0.963	0.033
PCA	0.985	0.000
Information Gain	0.789	0.008
Correlation	0.930	0.213

good performance in terms of both true positive rate and false positive rate. Whereas, automated methods produce the results that vary from one subset to another. The PCA based method produces high true positive rate and low false positive rate for most subsets, except one where the true positive rate is significantly lower. The information gain based method produces true positive rates within a relatively large range but still all above the boundary of random classifier (50%),

and it keeps the false positive rates at a low level. The correlation based method produces high true positive rates across, but simultaneously high false positive rates across all the subsets. The results show that it is possible to automate the data pre-processing of the DCA to produce useful. However, as this is work in progress, more investigation should be performed.

CONCLUSION AND FUTURE DIRECTIONS

In this book chapter, we reviewed some of the most popular AIS algorithms for intrusion detection problems, as well as demonstrating that the DCA is a suitable solution due to its unsupervised learning paradigm and low weight in computation. In order to present the DCA as simply and clearly as possible without losing detail, we used

Figure 2. Boxplot of true positive rates of all methods for KDD 10% dataset

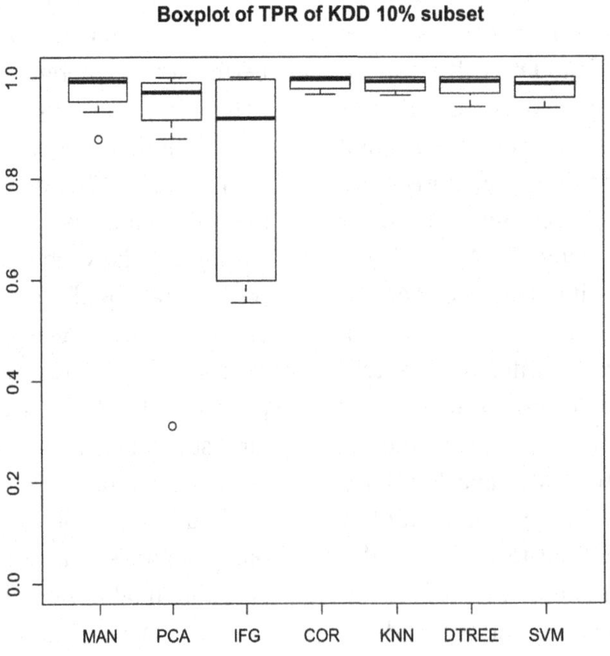

Figure 3. Boxplot of false positive rates of all methods for KDD 10% dataset

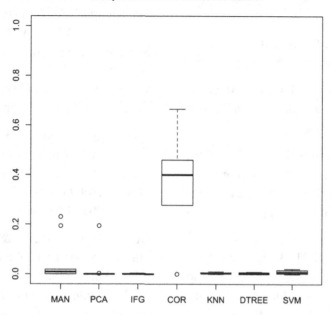

set theory and basic functions to formalise the algorithm. In addition, we demonstrated recent work for introducing an online analysis component to the DCA through segmentation, and the results indicate that the approach is promising especially for intrusion detection problems. Finally, ongoing work of automated data pre-processing of the DCA was described. With the automated data pre-processing, applications of the DCA are not dependent on the expert knowledge of the problem, and they become much less time consuming since manual procedures are replaced.

Much of the work regarding the further development of the DCA is still 'work in progress'. For example, only static segment sizes applied and tested for the online analysis component of the DCA, more adaptive mechanisms where segment size varies according the situations encountered during detection should be investigated. Additionally, only preliminary work has been performed for the automated data pre-processing of the DCA,

more techniques of feature selection and feature extraction and more appropriate mechanisms for signal categorisation should be evaluated.

REFERENCES

Al-Hammadi, Y., Aickelin, U., & Greensmith, J. (2008). DCA for bot detection. In *Proceedings of the IEEE World Congress on Computational Intelligence* (WCCI 2008. Bejtlich, R. (2005). *The Tao of network security monitoring: Beyond intrusion detection*. Pearson Education.

Blake, C. L., Hettich, S., & Merz, C. J. (1998). *UCI repository of machine learning databases*.

Cohen, R. I. (2004). *Tending Adam's garden: Evolving the cognitive immune self*. Paperback edition. Elsevier Academic Press.

Cohen, R. I. (2007). Real and artificial immune systems: Computing the state of the body. *Nature Reviews. Immunology, 7,* 569–574. doi:10.1038/nri2102

Coico, R., Sunshine, G., & Benjamini, E. (2003). *Immunology: A short course.* John Wiley & Sons.

de Castro, L. N., & Timmis, J. (2003). *Artificial immune systems: A new computational intelligence approach.* Springer-Verlag.

de Castro, L. N., & Von Zuben, F. J. (2000). *The clonal selection algorithm with engineering applications.* In Genetic and Evolutionary Computation Conference (GECCO) (pp. 36-37). Las Vegas, USA.

Farmer, J. D., Packard, N. H., & Perelson, A. S. (1986). The immune learning, adaptation, and machine learning. [Elsevier.]. *Physica D. Nonlinear Phenomena, 4,* 187–204. doi:10.1016/0167-2789(86)90240-X

Garthwaite, P. H., Jolliffe, I. T., & Jones, B. (2006). *Statistical inference* (2nd ed.). Oxford Science Publications.

González, F. A., & Dasgupta, D. (2003). Anomaly detection using real-valued negative selection. [Springer.]. *Genetic Programming and Evolvable Machines, 4,* 383–403. doi:10.1023/A:1026195112518

Greensmith, J. (2007). *The dendritic cell algorithm,* PhD Thesis, University of Nottingham, UK.

Greensmith, J., Aickelin, U., & Cayzer, S. (2005). Introducing dendritic cells as a novel immune-inspired algorithm for anomaly detection. In *Proceedings of the 4th International Conference on Artificial Immune Systems (ICARIS), LNCS 3627,* (pp. 153-167). Springer.

Greensmith, J., Aickelin, U., & Twycross, J. (2006). Articulation and clarification of the dendritic cell algorithm. In *Proceedings of the 5th International Conference on Artificial Immune Systems (ICARIS), LNCS 4163,* (pp. 404-417). Springer, Greensmith, J., & Aickelin, U. (2007). Dendritic cells for SYN scan detection. In *Proceedings of the Genetic and Evolutionary Computation Conference* (GECCO) (pp. 49-56). London, UK.

Greensmith, J., Feyereisl, J., & Aickelin, U. (2008). The DCA-SOMe comparison: A comparative study between two biologically-inspired algorithms. *Evolutionary Intelligence, 1*(2), 85–112. doi:10.1007/s12065-008-0008-6

Gu, F., Greensmith, J., & Aickelin, U. (2008). Further exploration of the dendritic cell algorithm: Antigen multiplier and moving windows. In *Proceedings of 7th International Conference on Artificial Immune Systems* (ICARIS 2008), (pp. 54-66).

Gu, F., Greensmith, J., & Aickelin, U. (2009). Integrating real-time analysis with the dendritic cell algorithm through segmentation. In *Proceedings of the Genetic and Evolutionary Computation Conference* (GECCO), (pp. 1203–1210).

Gu, F., Greensmith, J., Oates, R., & Aickelin, U. (2009). PCA 4 DCA: The application of principal component analysis to the dendritic cell algorithm. In *Proceedings of the 9th Annual Workshop on Computational Intelligence* (UKCI).

Hand, D. J., Manila, H., & Smyth, P. (2001). *Principles of data mining.* Cambridge, MA: The MIT Press.

Harel, D. (2003). *Computers Ltd.: What they really can't do. Revised paperback edition.* Oxford University Press.

Harel, D., & Feldman, Y. (2004). *Algorithmics: The spirit of computing* (3rd ed.). Addison Wesley.

Hart, E., & Timmis, J. (2008). Application areas of AIS: The past, the present and the future. *Applied Soft Computing, 8,* 191–201. doi:10.1016/j.asoc.2006.12.004

Hettich, S., & Bay, S. D. (1999). *The UCI KDD archive. Technical report.* Irvine, CA: University of California, Department of Information and Computer Science.

Hofmeyr, S. A., & Forrest, S. (1999). Immunity by design: An artificial immune system. In *Proceedings of Genetic and Evolutionary Computation Conference* (GECCO1999) (pp. 1289-1296). Orlando, USA.

Jerne, N. K. (1974). Towards a network theory of the immune system. *Ann. Immunol. (Inst. Pasteur), 125C,* 373-389.

Ji, Z., & Dasgupta, D. (2006). Applicability issues of the real-valued negative selection algorithms. In *Proceedings of Genetic and Evolutionary Computation Conference* (GECCO2006) (pp. 111-118). Washington, USA.

Kim, J. W. (2002). *Integrating artificial immune algorithms for intrusion detection.* PhD Thesis. University College London.

Kim, J. W., Bentley, P., Aickelin, U., Greensmith, J., Tedesco, G., & Twycross, J. (2007). Immune system approaches to intrusion detection - A review. *Natural Computing, 6,* 413–466. doi:10.1007/s11047-006-9026-4

Kornek, B., Storch, M. K., Weissert, R., Wallstroem, E., Stefferl, A., & Olsson, T. (2000). Multiple sclerosis and chronic autoimmune encephalomyelitis: A comparative quantitative study of axonal injury in active, inactive, and remyelinated lesions. *American Journal of Pathology, 157,* 267–276. doi:10.1016/S0002-9440(10)64537-3

Lutz, M. B., & Schuler, G. (2002). Immature, semi-mature and fully mature dendritic cells: Which signals induce tolerance or immunity? *Trends in Immunology, 23,* 445–449. doi:10.1016/S1471-4906(02)02281-0

Matzinger, P. (2002). Danger model: A renewed sense of self. *Science, 296,* 301–305. doi:10.1126/science.1071059

MIT Lincoln Lab Information System Technology Group. (1998). *The 1998 intrusion detection offline evaluation plan.* Retrieved from http://www.ll.mit.edu/IST/ideval/data/1998/

Mitchell, T. M. (1997). *Machine learning.* McGraw-Hill.

Mokhtar, M., Bi, R., Timmis, T., & Tyrrell, A. M. (2009). A modified dendritic cell algorithm for on-line error detection in robotic systems. In *Proceedings of the 11th IEEE Congress on Evolutionary Computation* (CEC), (pp. 2055–2062).

NIST. (2001). *Intrusion detection systems.* NIST Computer Science Special Reports SP 800–31, November 2001.

Oates, R., Greensmith, J., Aickelin, U., Garibaldi, J., & Kendall, G. (2007). The application of a dendritic cell algorithm to a robotic classifier. In *Proceedings of the 6th International Conference on Artificial Immune* (ICARIS), (pp. 204–215).

Oates, R., Kendall, G., & Garibaldi, J. (2008). Frequency analysis for dendritic cell population tuning: Decimating the dendritic cell. *Evolutionary Intelligence, 1*(2).

Rajewsky, K. (1996). Clonal selection and learning in the antibody system. *Nature, 381,* 751–758. doi:10.1038/381751a0

Somayaji, A., Hofmeyr, S., & Forrest, S. (1997). Principles of a computer immune system. In *Proceedings of New Security Paradigm Workshop* (pp. 75-82), Langdale, Cumbria.

Stibor, T., Timmis, J., & Eckert, C. (2005). A comparative study of real-valued negative selection to statistical anomaly detection techniques. In *Proceedings of 4th International Conference on Artificial Immune Systems (ICARIS2005). LNCS 3627*, (pp. 262-275). Springer.

Twycross, J., & Aickelin, U. (2006). Libtissue - Implementing innate immunity. In *Proceedings of the IEEE Congress on Evolutionary Computation* (CEC2006) (pp. 499-506). Vancouver, Canada.

Section 2
Bio–Inspired Network Resource Optimization

Chapter 6
TCP Symbiosis:
Bio–Inspired Congestion Control Mechanism for TCP

Go Hasegawa
Osaka University, Japan

Masayuki Murata
Osaka University, Japan

ABSTRACT

In this chapter, we introduce a robust, self-adaptive and scalable congestion control mechanism for TCP. We change the window size of a TCP connection according to the information of the physical and available bandwidths of the end-to-end network path. The bandwidth information is obtained by an inline network measurement technique. We also borrowed algorithms from biophysics to update the window size: the logistic growth model and the Lotka-Volterra competition model. The greatest advantage of using these models is that we can refer previous discussions and results for various characteristics of the mathematical models, including scalability, convergence, fairness and stability in these models. Through mathematical analysis and simulation experiments, we compare the proposed mechanism with traditional TCP Reno, HighSpeed TCP, Scalable TCP and FAST TCP, and exhibit its effectiveness in terms of scalability to the network bandwidth and delay, convergence time, fairness among competing connections, and stability.

INTRODUCTION AND RESEARCH BACKGROUND

Transmission Control Protocol (TCP) (Stevens, 1994) is the de facto standard transport layer protocol of the current Internet first designed in the 1970s: the first Request for Comments (RFC) on TCP was released in 1981 (Postel). TCP has also been frequently modified and enhanced to accommodate the development of the Internet (Jacobsen et al, 1992; Allman et al, 2001; Blanton et al, 2003).

TCP has various functions to realize reliable and efficient data transmission on the network. The congestion control mechanism (Stevens, 1994) is one of the most important. Its main purpose is to avoid and resolve network congestion and to distribute network bandwidth fairly

DOI: 10.4018/978-1-61350-092-7.ch006

among competing connections. To do that, TCP employs a window-based congestion control mechanism that adjusts data transmission speed by changing congestion window size. A congestion window indicates the maximum amount of data that can be sent out on a connection without being acknowledged.

TCP Reno is the most popular version of TCP in current operating systems. Its window size control algorithm allows a TCP sender to continue to additively increase its congestion window size until it detects a packet loss (or losses), decreasing it multiplicatively when a packet loss occurs. This is called an Additive Increase Multiplicative Decrease (AIMD) policy. In (Chiu & Jain, 1989), the authors argue that an AIMD policy is suitable for efficient and fair bandwidth usage in a distributed environment, if congestion indication signals are simultaneously distributed to all connections.

With increases in the heterogeneity and the complexity of the Internet, many problems have emerged in TCP Reno's congestion control mechanism (Shenker et al, 1990; Hoe, 1996; Guo & Matta, 2001; Fu et al, 2003; Floyd, 2003 for example). The primary reasons for these problems are that the congestion signals are only indicated by packet loss and that TCP Reno uses fixed AIMD parameter values to increase and decrease window size, whereas the window size should be changed according to the network environment. For example, it is well-known problem that the throughput of TCP connections decreases when it traverses wireless links, since TCP cannot distinguish congestionoriented packet loss caused by network congestion, and wireless-oriented packet loss caused by link loss and/or handoff. Another problem is the low throughput of TCP connections in large bandwidth and long delay networks. In (Floyd, 2003), the authors argued that a TCP Reno connection cannot fully utilize the link bandwidth of such networks, since the increasing parameter, which is one packet per a Round Trip Time (RTT), is too small and the decreasing parameter, which halves the window

size when a packet loss occurs, is too large for networks with a large bandwidth-delay product. Although many solutions have been proposed for their problems (Floyd, 2003; Kelly, 2003; Jin et al, 2004), most of them inherit the fundamental congestion control mechanism of TCP Reno: the AIMD mechanism triggered by the detection of packet losses in the network. The congestion control mechanism improves the throughput by adjusting the increasing and decreasing parameters statically and/or dynamically. However, most previous studies have focused on changing the AIMD parameters to accommodate particular network environments. Since these methods employ ad hoc modifications for a certain network situation, their performance when applied to other network environments is unclear.

Because window size indicates the maximum amount of packets that TCP can transmit for one Round Trip Time (RTT), an adequate window size for a TCP connection is equal to the product of the available bandwidth and the round-trip propagation delay between the sender and receiver hosts. TCP Reno measures the RTTs of the network path between sender and receiver hosts by checking the departure times of the data packets and the arrival times of the corresponding ACK packets. However,

TCP Reno does not have an effective mechanism to recognize the available bandwidth. This is an explanation of the fundamental problem: TCP Reno cannot adjust window size to an adequate value under various network environments. In a sense, traditional TCP Reno can be considered to be a tool that measures available bandwidth because of its ability to adjust the congestion window size to achieve a transmission rate appropriate to the available bandwidth. However, it is ineffective because it only increases the window size until packet loss occurs. In other words, TCP Reno induces packet loss in order to obtain information about the available bandwidth (-delay product) of the network. That is, even when the congestion control mechanism of TCP works perfectly, the TCP sender experiences packet losses in the network at some intervals. Since all modified versions of TCP using AIMD policy contain this essential problem, they cannot avoid periodic packet losses.

There are some TCP variants, including TCP Vegas (Brakmo et al, 1994) and FAST TCP (Jin et al, 2004), that utilize the RTT values for the congestion indication, based on the fact that, the RTTs for a TCP connection usually increase before packet losses occur when the network is congested. However, such RTT-based approaches cannot be applied to high-speed networks due to an inherent problem, i.e., changes in RTT values of the end-to-end network path becomes invisible as the network bandwidth becomes large. We believe, therefore, that if a TCP sender recognizes the bandwidth information of the network path quickly and adequately, we can create a better mechanism for congestion control in TCP.

Although numerous measurement tools that measure the physical and available bandwidths of network paths have been proposed in the literature (Melander et al, 2000; Jain & Dovrolis, 2002; Ribeiro et al, 2003; Carter & Crovella, 1996; Dovrolis et al, 2001; Jacobsen, 1997; King et al, 2005; Bhandarkar et al, 2005), we cannot directly employ these existing methods in TCP mechanisms, primarily because these methods utilize a lot of test probe packets. Moreover, these methods also require too much time to obtain one measurement result. Accordingly, we have proposed a method called Inline measurement TCP (ImTCP) that avoids these problems in (Cao et al, 2004; Cao et al, 2005). It does not inject extra traffic into the network, and instead it estimates the physical/available bandwidths of the network path from data/ACK packets transmitted by an active TCP connection in an inline fashion. Furthermore, since the ImTCP sender obtains bandwidth information every 1–4 RTTs, it can follow the traffic fluctuation of the underlying IP network well. We believe that, by directly measuring bandwidth information, the congestion control in TCP

becomes truly scalable to the bandwidth delay product of the network. AIMD- and MIMD-based mechanisms such as HighSpeed TCP (HSTCP) (Floyd, 2003) and Scalable TCP (STCP) (Kelly, 2003) are more scalable than TCP Reno, but they have serious problems in parameter tuning. Since no knowledge of the bandwidth information is obtained, the control parameters are configured based on implicit/explicit assumptions of the network environment. For example, in (Floyd, 2003), the recommended control parameters are to fill the network link with 10 Gbps bandwidth, 100 msec RTT, and a packet loss rate of 10^{-7}. One of the advantages of the proposed mechanism is that it is not necessary to configure the control parameters according to the network environment. In addition, because ImTCP is implemented at the bottom of the TCP layer, this measurement mechanism can be included in various types of TCP congestion control mechanisms.

In this chapter, we propose a new congestion control mechanism of TCP that utilizes the information of physical and available bandwidths obtained from an inline measurement technique. The proposed mechanism does not use ad hoc algorithms such as TCP Vegas and instead employs algorithms that have a mathematical background, which enable us to mathematically discuss and guarantee their behavior even though posing a simplification of the target system. More importantly, it becomes possible to give a reasonable explanation to our control parameter selections within TCP, instead of conducting intensive computer simulations and/or choosing parameters in an ad hoc fashion. We designed a window size control algorithm for the purpose of quickly adjusting the window size to an adequate value based on bandwidth information in order to fairly distribute bandwidth among competing connections.

For this, we borrowed algorithms from the logistic growth model and the Lotka-Volterra competition model (Murray, 2002), both of which are used in biophysics to describe changes in the population of species. The biophysics models were chosen based on their essential nature of stability and robustness, which is achieved even when they behave independently in an autonomous and distributed fashion. This is the case for the congestion control of TCP: each TCP connection behaves independently, but still we want to maximize the bandwidth utilization and the throughput of the connection. When applying the logistic growth and Lotka-Volterra competition models to the congestion control algorithm of our TCP, the population of a species can be viewed as the window size of a TCP connection, the carrying capacity of the environment as physical bandwidth, and interspecific competition among species as bandwidth sharing among competing TCP connections. Analytic investigation of the proposed algorithm can be performed based on previously reported discussions and results regarding various characteristics in biophysics of the mathematical models, including scalability, convergence, fairness and stability. Endowing TCP with these characteristics is the primary objective of the present study. In addition, we also present simulation results in order to evaluate the proposed mechanism and show that, compared with traditional TCP Reno and other TCP variants, the proposed mechanism utilizes network bandwidth effectively, quickly, and fairly.

The reminder of this chapter is organized as follows. In the next section, we introduce the mathematical models used in biophysics and the design of the proposed TCP congestion control mechanism. In the third section, we analyze and discuss the characteristics of the proposed mechanism. In the fourth section, we present its effectiveness and performance through various simulation experiments. The fifth section discusses areas for future study. In the final section, we present our conclusions of this chapter.

TCP SYMBIOSIS: BIO-INSPIRED CONGESTION CONTROL MECHANISM

In this paper, we intend to build a robust self-adaptive congestion control mechanism for TCP. In this sense, the proposed method is quite different from existing approaches. The concept of the window updating algorithm of the proposed method is borrowed from a biological system, which is often pointed out to be robust (Montresor et al, 2003), because in many biological systems, the actions of the entity (e.g., living organism) are not determined based on the results of direct interactions among entities, but rather on information obtained through the environment, which is a fundamental necessary condition for the system to be robust. The concept is often called "stigmergy" in the literature (see, e.g., (Bonabeau et al, 1999)). With respect to the current case, the window increase/decrease strategy is determined based on the physical and available bandwidth, rather than on the packet loss or RTTs, which are direct consequences of the activities of the TCP connections.

Of course the up-to-date and reliable available bandwidth is necessary in order to realize such a mechanism for TCP congestion control. Fortunately, the inline measurement method of TCP (ImTCP (Cao et al, 2004; Cao et al, 2005)) can quickly obtain such information within several RTTs. Then the resultant control method has good scalability with respect to both RTT and capacity, which has not been achieved in the previous proposals. This is the main motivation for developing a new TCP congestion control method. In this section, we briefly introduce the mathematical models borrowed from biophysics and present the proposed mechanism.

Brief Introduction to the Lotka-Volterra Model

Logistic Model

The logistic equation is a formula that represents the evolution of the population of a single species over time. Generally, the per capita birth rate of a species increases as the population of the species becomes larger. However, since there are various restrictions on living environments, the environment has a carrying capacity, which is usually determined by the available sustaining resources. The logistic equation describes such changes in the population of a species as follows (Murray, 2002):

$$\frac{d}{dt} N = \varepsilon \left(1 - \frac{N}{K} \right) N \tag{1}$$

where t is time, N is the population of the species, K is the carrying capacity of the environment, and ε is the intrinsic growth rate of the species ($0 < \varepsilon$).

Lotka-Volterra Competition Model

The Lotka-Volterra competition model is a well known model for examining the population growth of two or more species that are engaged in interspecific competition. In the model, Equation (1) is modified to include the effects of both interspecific competition and intraspecific competition. The basic two-species Lotka-Volterra competition model with both species N_1 and N_2 having logistic growth in the absence of the other is comprised of the following equations (Murray, 2002):

$$\frac{d}{dt} N_1 = \varepsilon_1 \left(1 - \frac{N_1 + \gamma_{12} N_2}{K_1} \right) N_1 \tag{2}$$

$$\frac{d}{dt} N_2 = \varepsilon_2 \left(1 - \frac{N_2 + \gamma_{21} N_1}{K_2} \right) N_2 \tag{3}$$

where N_i, K_i, and ε_i are the population of the species, the carrying capacity of the environment, and the intrinsic growth rate of the species i, respectively. In addition, y_{ij} is the ratio of the competition coefficient of species i with respect of species j.

In this model, the population of species 1 and 2 does not always converge to a value larger than 0, and in some cases one species becomes extinct, depending on the values of y_{12} and y_{21}. Commonly, when the following conditions are satisfied, two species can survive in the environment (Murray, 2002):

$$\gamma_{12} < \frac{K_1}{K_2}, \gamma_{21} < \frac{K_2}{K_1} \tag{4}$$

Assuming that the two species have the same characteristics, they have the same values: $K=K_1=K_2, \varepsilon=\varepsilon_1=\varepsilon_2$, and $y=y_{12}=y_{21}$. Then, Equations (2) and (3) can be written as follows:

$$\frac{d}{dt} N_1 = \varepsilon \left(1 - \frac{N_1 + \gamma N_2}{K} \right) N_1 \tag{5}$$

$$\frac{d}{dt} N_2 = \varepsilon \left(1 - \frac{N_2 + \gamma N_1}{K} \right) N_2 \tag{6}$$

In addition, Equation (4) can be written as $y < 1$. Figure 1 shows the population changes in the two species using Equations (5) and (6), where $K=100$, $y = 1.95$ and $\varepsilon = 0.90$, and species 2 joins the environment 10 seconds after species 1. From the figure, we can observe from this figure that the population of the two species converges quickly to the same value.

We can easily extend Equations (5) and (6) for n species as follows:

$$\frac{d}{dt} N_i = \varepsilon \left(1 - \frac{N_i + \gamma \sum_{j=1, i \neq j}^{n} N_j}{K} \right) N_i \tag{7}$$

Figure 1. Changes in population of two species with the Lotka-Volterra competition model

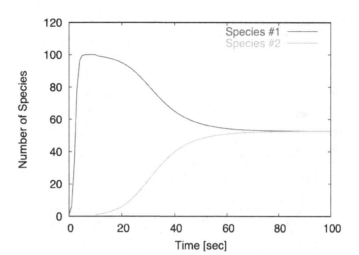

Figure 2 shows the population changes among the ten species when using Equation (7), where $K=100$, $y = 1.95$ and $\varepsilon = 0.90$, where new species join the environment one after another. We can observe that ten species converge in the same manner as two species, as shown in Figure 1. Note that survival and convergence conditions are identical, i.e., $y < 1$. Even when two or more species exist, each independently utilizes Equation (7) to obtain N_i, and the population of the species can converge to the value equally shared among competing species. We consider that the changing population trends of species depicted in Figures 1 and 2 are ideal for controlling the transmission speed of TCP. That is, by using Equation (7) for the congestion control algorithm of TCP, rapid and stable link utilization can be realized, whereas each TCP connection can behave independently as an autonomous distributed system. However, this model cannot be directly applied to the congestion control algorithm of TCP because the model must obtain N_j. This is discussed in the next subsection.

Application to Window Size Control Algorithm

To convert Equation (7) to a window increase/decrease algorithm, we consider N_i as the trans-

mission rate of TCP sender i and K as the physical bandwidth of the bottleneck link. Furthermore, when applying Equation (7) to the congestion control algorithm for connection i, it is necessary for connection i to know the data transmission rates of all other connections that share the same bottleneck link. This assumption is quite unrealistic with respect to the current Internet. Therefore, we use the sum of the data transmission rates of all of the other connections using the physical and available bandwidths as follows:

$$\sum_{j=1, i \neq j}^{n} N_j = K - A_i$$

where A_i is the available bandwidth for connections i. Thus, Equation (7) becomes:

$$\frac{d}{dt} N_i = \varepsilon \left(1 - \frac{N_i + \gamma(K - A_i)}{K} \right) N_i \qquad (8)$$

Here we assume that all connections share the same bottleneck link K in the equation. Note that when each TCP connection has a different physical bandwidth, the proposed mechanism share the bottleneck link bandwidth in a reasonable manner, which we will discuss in Subsection IV-E.

Figure 2. Changes in population of 10 species with the Lotka-Volterra competition model

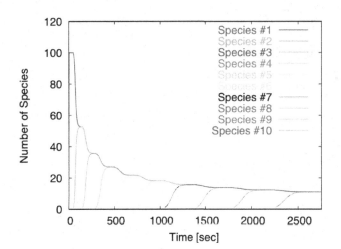

The proposed mechanism requires modifications only with respect to sender-side TCP, and no change in receiver-side TCP is required. A TCP sender controls its data transmission rate by changing its window size. To retain the essential characteristics of TCP and decrease the implementation overhead, we employ window-based congestion control in the proposed TCP by converting Equation (8) to obtain an increasing algorithm of window size in TCP. The window size of connection i, w_i, is calculated from N_i, the transmission rate, using the following equation:

$$w_i = N_i \tau i$$

where τi is the minimum value of the RTTs of connection i, which is assumed to equal the propagation delay without a queuing delay in the intermediate routers between sender and receiver hosts. Next, Equation (8) can be rewritten as follows:

$$\frac{d}{dt} w_i = \varepsilon \left(1 - \frac{w_i + \gamma(K - A_i)\tau_i}{K\tau_i} \right) w_i \qquad (9)$$

Finally, we integrate Equation (9) as follows:

$$w_i(t) = \frac{w_i(0)e^{\varepsilon t\left\{1-\gamma\left(1-\frac{A_i}{K}\right)\right\}}\{K - \gamma(K - A_i)\}\tau_i}{w_i(0)\left(e^{\varepsilon t\left\{1-\gamma\left(1-\frac{A_i}{K}\right)\right\}} - 1\right) + \{K - \gamma(K - A_i)\}\tau_i}$$

$$(10)$$

In Equation (10), when we set the initial value of the window size ($w_i(0)$) and the current time to 0 ($t = 0$), we can directly obtain window size $w_i(t)$ for any time t. We use the above equation for the control algorithm of the window size of TCP connections.

Equation (10) contains the e^x calculation. Generally, exponentiation cannot be operated in the system kernel because of the lack of a library and the processing overhead. Therefore, for function e^x, we give the Taylor polynomial of degree 4 around $x = a$ as follows,

$$e^x \approx e^a \sum_{k=0}^{4} \frac{1}{k!}(x - a)^k$$

where a is the integer part of x (e.g., $a = 0$ when $0 \leq x < 1$). By preparing e^a on a memory table for a limited range of a, we can calculate e^x with minimal processing overhead. In determining the maximum value of a in the proposed mechanism, we consider the following equation:

$$x = \varepsilon t \left\{ 1 - \gamma \left(1 - \frac{A_i}{K} \right) \right\} \leq \varepsilon t$$

That is, when we assume that the maximum RTT of TCP connection is 10 [sec], we can determine the maximum value of a to $\lfloor 10\varepsilon \rfloor$.

Equation (10) requires measurement of the physical and available bandwidths of a network path. Therefore, we utilize the inline network measurement technique in ImTCP (Cao et al, 2004; Cao et al, 2005). In (Cao et al, 2004; Cao et al, 2005), the authors proposed ImTCP, which is an inline network measurement technique for the physical and available bandwidths of network paths between TCP sender and receiver hosts. ImTCP can continuously measure bandwidth by using data and ACK packets of a TCP connection under data transmission. That is, the TCP sender transmits data packets at intervals determined by an inline measurement algorithm and checks the arrival interval times of the corresponding ACK packets to estimate bandwidth. Since ImTCP performs the measurement without transmitting additional probe packets over the network, the effect on other network traffic is negligible. ImTCP can also quickly update the latest changes in bandwidths by frequently performing measurements (one result per 1–4 RTTs) as long as TCP transmits data packets. The authors have also proposed an implementation design of ImTCP, in which the measurement program is located at the bottom of the TCP layer. The proposed implementation design maintains the transmission/arrival intervals of TCP data/ACK packets by introducing a FIFO buffer between the TCP and IP layers. Note that the measurement algorithm has limited effect on TCP's congestion control algorithm (Cao et al, 2004), meaning that the measurement algorithm can be applied to any TCP variant including our method proposed in this paper.

Note that the inline network measurement algorithm can estimate both of the physical and available bandwidths based on the assumption that the narrowest link on the physical bandwidth of the end-to-end network path becomes the tightest link on the available bandwidth. According to the algorithm in (Cao et al, 2005), when such an assumption is not satisfied, that is, when the narrowest link and the tightest link are different in the path, the physical bandwidth cannot be measured exactly, whereas the available bandwidth can be obtained successfully. However, in that case, since the physical bandwidth is likely to be underestimated, this measurement error does not cause a serious problem for the proposed congestion control mechanism, because underestimation of the physical bandwidth does not result in injecting too many packets into the network.

The proposed congestion control algorithm is based on traditional TCP Reno, and we use the same algorithm as TCP Reno for the window updating algorithm until measurement results are obtained through inline network measurements. That is, the slow start phase is used as other TCP congestion control methods. There are two reasons for preserving slow start: if two or more TCP connections were to open large windows at the same time, many packets would be lost, and so probes on the path are still necessary. A more pragmatic reason is that at connection start-up, no information on bandwidth is available, and a measurement method in ImTCP contains some errors for statistical reasons (Cao et al, 2004). Therefore, the slow start phase is utilized during several RTTs for accurate estimation of the bandwidth information. As well, in cases of packet loss, the window size is decreased in a manner identical to that of TCP Reno in both cases of timeout and fast retransmit (Stevens, 1994). When bandwidth information is obtained, the congestion control algorithm adjusts its window size using Equation (10). That is, when the j-th ACK packet is received at the TCP sender, we use Equation (10) to obtain the new value of the congestion window size of the TCP connection by the following calculation: set $w_i(0)$ to the current window size and t to the time duration from the arrival time of the $(j-1)$-th ACK packet to that of the j-th ACK packet.

TCP SYMBIOSIS: BIO-INSPIRED CONGESTION CONTROL MECHANISM

In this section, we analyze various characteristics of the proposed mechanism, such as scalability, convergence, parameter setting issues and fairness against TCP Reno. This analysis illustrates that the proposed mechanism essentially solves the problems inherent in TCP Reno.

Convergence Time and Scalability

Assuming physical bandwidth K and available bandwidth A are constant, the window size converges to a certain value in the proposed mechanism. The converged window size, which is denoted as w^*, can be obtained by setting $dw/dt=0$ in Equation (9):

$$w^* = \{(1-y)K + yA\}\tau \qquad (11)$$

where τ is the round-trip propagation delay the TCP connection. In what follows, we consider the time which is required to increase the window size from $w0$ to ρw^* ($0 < \rho < 1$, $w0 < \rho w^*$). In the proposed mechanism, using Equation (10), the time T becomes as follows:

$$
\begin{aligned}
T &= \frac{1}{\varepsilon\left\{1-\gamma\left(1-\dfrac{A}{K}\right)\right\}} \ln\left(\frac{\rho}{1-\rho}\frac{w^*-w_0}{w_0}\right) \\
&\leq \frac{1}{\varepsilon\left(1-\gamma\right)} \ln\left(\frac{\rho}{1-\rho}\frac{w^*-w_0}{w_0}\right) \\
&= \frac{1}{\varepsilon\left(1-\gamma\right)} \ln\left(\frac{\rho}{1-\rho}\frac{\left((1-\gamma)K+\gamma A\right)\tau-w_0}{w_0}\right)
\end{aligned}
$$

$$(12)$$

because $0 \leq A \leq K$ is satisfied. Note that ε and y are fixed parameters of the proposed mechanism. The issue of setting these parameters will be discussed in the next subsection. This equation indicates that time T of the proposed mechanism increases logarithmically with respect to link bandwidth (K) and propagation delay (τ).

In the case of TCP Reno, we can easily calculate T_{reno}, the time necessary to increase window size from w_0 to w^*, as follows:

$$T_{reno} = (w^* - w_0)\tilde{\tau} = \left[\{(1-\gamma)K + \gamma A\}\tau - w_0\right]\tilde{\tau} \qquad (13)$$

where $\tilde{\tau}$ is the average value of the RTTs of the TCP connection. Here, we ignore the effect of the delayed ACK option (Stevens, 1994) and focus only on the congestion avoidance phase of TCP Reno. In the case of HSTCP, which is essentially based on the AIMD policy as in the case of TCP Reno, T_{hstep} is given by:

$$T_{hstcp} \geq \frac{w^* - w_0}{a_{\max}}\tilde{\tau} = \frac{\{(1-\gamma)K + \gamma A\}\tau - w_0}{a_{\max}}\tilde{\tau} \qquad (14)$$

where a_{max} is a parameter of HSTCP that indicates the maximum window size increase during one RTT (equivalent to $a(W)$ in (Floyd, 2003)). Equations (13) and (14) indicate that the time required to increase the window size is proportional to physical bandwidth K and propagation delay τ. This illustrates that the time required to fully utilize the bandwidth-delay product of the network path is proportional to the bandwidth-delay product. HSTCP was designed as a new congestion control mechanism to resolve problems inherent in TCP Reno for high-speed and long delay networks. However, since the window size control algorithm of HSTCP is essentially based on the AIMD policy, this algorithm suffers from poor scalability to the bandwidth-delay product.

STCP has a window size control algorithm based on Multiplicative Increase Multiplicative

Decrease (MIMD) policy and describes logarithmic increases in time with respect to increases in link bandwidth (Kelly, 2003). We calculate its convergence time T_{step} as follows:

$$T_{stcp} = \frac{1}{a}\left(\ln \frac{w^*}{w_0}\right)\tilde{\tau} = \frac{1}{a}\left(\ln \frac{\{(1-\gamma)K + \gamma A\}\tau}{w_0}\right)\tilde{\tau}$$

$$(15)$$

where a is an STCP parameter that indicates the increase in window size when receiving one ACK packet. In (Kelly, 2003), a=0.01 [packet] is the default value. This equation indicates that STCP has good scalability to network bandwidth: however, STCP has poor scalability to propagation delay.

FAST TCP has the same equilibrium properties as TCP Vegas, and the window size is updated at intervals based on the RTT (Jin et al, 2004). This means that FAST TCP does not have good scalability to the propagation delay of the end-to-end network path, as will be shown in Section IV.

Parameter Settings

The congestion control algorithm of the proposed mechanism has two parameters, y and ε. In this subsection, we discuss the effect of these parameters and present some guidelines for configuring y and ε.

1) y Setting: The parameter y indicates the degree of the influence of the other competing connections that share the same bottleneck link. To converge window size to a positive value despite the physical bandwidth K_i of each connection, it is necessary to satisfy the condition $0 < y < 1$. Furthermore, based on Equations (11) and (12), we need to consider the trade-off between convergence speed and the final number of packets accumulated within the buffer at the bottleneck link. That is, although smaller y leads to faster convergence speed, it increases the queue size of the bottleneck router buffer when the window size is converged. Using Equation (11) we can

easily obtain the sum of the window size of n TCP connections as follows:

$$\sum_{i=1}^{n} w_i = \frac{n}{1 + (n-1)\gamma}K\tau$$

$$(16)$$

where we assume that the physical bandwidth K and the delay τ of each connection are identical. From Equation (16) queue size Q at the bottleneck link is given by:

$$Q = \frac{(n-1)(1-\gamma)}{1 + (n-1)\gamma}K\tau$$

$$(17)$$

This equation shows that iQ increases as n becomes larger. However, as n goes to infinity, we can obtain the following equation:

$$\lim_{n \to \infty} Q = \frac{1-\gamma}{\gamma}K\tau$$

$$(18)$$

That is, there exists an upper bound of the queue size with respect to an increase in the number of concurrent TCP connections. Therefore, if the bottleneck link has a large enough buffer, the proposed mechanism will induce no packet losses regardless of the number of TCP connections. TCP Reno, HSTCP, and STCP, on the other hand, increase their window size until they fully utilize the buffer at the bottleneck link, and as a result, they cannot avoid periodic packet losses.

FAST TCP, which is based on TCP Vegas, has characteristics similar to those of the proposed mechanism, meaning that FAST TCP can avoid the periodic packet losses. We can estimate the total window size of n FAST TCP connections that share the bottleneck link as follows. Just before a FAST TCP connection converges its window size, the window size is updated according to the following equation (Jin et al, 2004):

$$w_i \leftarrow (1-p)w_i + p\left(\frac{\tau}{\tilde{\tau}}w_i + \alpha\right) \qquad (19)$$

where α is a constant that is used in determining the increment degree of the window size and p ($0 < p < 1$) is a smoothing coefficient parameter. From Equation (19), we obtain the following equation for converged window size:

$$w_i = \frac{\alpha\tilde{\tau}}{\tilde{\tau} - \tau} \qquad (20)$$

Since w_i for each connection is independently calculated, the sum of the converged window size of n TCP connections is then calculated as follows:

$$\sum_{i=1}^{n} w_i = n\frac{\alpha\tilde{\tau}}{\tilde{\tau} - \tau} \qquad (21)$$

We observe from Equation (21) that the sum of the window size is proportional to the number of TCP connections. So, in order to avoid packet losses, it is necessary to prepare a bottleneck link buffer based on the number of connections. We therefore conclude that FAST TCP cannot provide scalability to the number of concurrent TCP connections in the network.

2) ε Setting: ε determines convergence speed, as shown in Equation (9). Generally, when we convert Equation (1) into a discrete equation, the population of the species does not converge with $\varepsilon > 2$ (Murray, 2002). In contrast, the window size updating algorithm proposed in Subsection II-B converts Equation (10) into a discrete equation in such a way that it does not cause oscillation. Therefore, in the proposed algorithm, there is no limitation on ε, which means that as ε becomes larger, the window size converges faster. However, an excessively large value of ε causes the TCP sender to transmit numerous packets in bursty fashion, which may reduce the network performance.

3) Delayed Feedback: There is another issue to be considered when setting ε. In the logistic growth model (Equation (1)), on which the proposed mechanism is based, the per capita birth rate is determined according to the current population of the species. In the proposed mechanism, on the other hand, the degree to which the window size is increased is determined using the bandwidth information obtained by ImTCP's inline measurement. Since the measurement algorithm in ImTCP utilizes the arrival time of ACK packets corresponding to the data packets transmitted by the sender host, the obtained measurement results experience some delay. Here, we consider the logistic growth model with delayed feedback described in the following equation:

$$\frac{d}{dt}N(t) = \varepsilon\left(1 - \frac{N(t - \tau_d)}{K}\right)N(t) \qquad (22)$$

where τ_d is the delay of the feedback information. When the population of the species changes with Equation (22), the population does not converge to a certain value even in a continuous-time model, if the following condition is satisfied (Murray, 2002):

$$\tau_d > \frac{\pi}{2\varepsilon}$$

That is, in Equation (22), it is necessary to satisfy $\varepsilon \leq \pi/2\tau_d$ to converge the population. A similar limitation of ε exists in the proposed mechanism. This means that with a delay of the bandwidth information, changing the window size too drastically causes oscillation of the window size.

Due to the nature of ImTCP's bandwidth measurement algorithm, the delay in the proposed mechanism corresponds to the time required for the data (ACK) packets to traverse from the bottleneck link to the sender hosts. Since ImTCP needs up to 4 RTTs to measure the bandwidth information, the delay is approximately 2 RTTs since ImTCP estimates the average values of the physical and available bandwidth for the 4 RTTs. That is, the length of the delay depends on the RTT value of a TCP connection. In other words, by setting ε according to the RTT for each TCP connection, the proposed mechanism can avoid window size oscillation. However, using different values of ε results in different convergence speeds as shown in Equation (9), and short-term unfairness among connections with different RTTs might occur. Therefore, we suggest that the fixed value for ε is used, which is around 2.0 under the rough assumption that the maximum RTT value of a TCP connection is about 500 msec.

Competition with TCP Reno

In this subsection, we investigate the fairness property of the proposed mechanism with respect to competing TCP Reno connections. For this purpose, we compare the throughput of two TCP connections which TCP Reno and the proposed mechanism share a bottleneck link, by analyzing changes in congestion window sizes. Figure 3 depicts the network model for analysis, where K is the physical bandwidth, τ is the minimum round-trip propagation delay, not including the

queuing delay, and B is the size of the output buffer adopting a TailDrop scheme, of the bottleneck link.

As explained above, the proposed mechanism converges its window size to a certain value whereas TCP Reno continues to increase its window size until a packet loss occurs. Hence, even when both TCP connections compete at the bottleneck link bandwidth, periodic packet loss occurs at the buffer. We, therefore, assume that both TCP connections experience packet loss when the buffer becomes fully utilized. Therefore, the window size of the two TCP connections changes cyclically, triggered by packet loss. Figure 4 describes such changes in the window size. Here, we define one cycle as the period between two packet losses and denote the length of the cycle as T. We assume that the received socket buffer of each TCP connection is large enough not to limit the congestion window size evolution.

The proposed mechanism obtains the physical and available bandwidths by inline network measurement. In this analysis, we assume that the sender of the proposed mechanism can obtain precise physical bandwidth information. On the other hand, when several TCP and/or ImTCP connections share the bottleneck link bandwidth, the ImTCP sender cannot obtain the available

Figure 3. Model used for fairness analysis

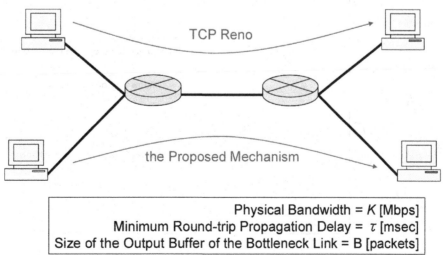

Physical Bandwidth = K [Mbps]
Minimum Round-trip Propagation Delay = τ [msec]
Size of the Output Buffer of the Bottleneck Link = B [packets]

bandwidth as expected, and so the obtained value becomes approximately equal to the available bandwidth for all TCP connections sharing the bottleneck link (Cao et al, 2004). This occurs because a TCP connection tends to transmit bursty data packets (Blanton, 2002), and then packets from each TCP connection traverse the bottleneck link in a back-to-back fashion. Therefore, in this analysis, we assume that the measured available bandwidth A is equivalent to physical bandwidth K. Note that by this assumption we estimate that the available bandwidth for the proposed mechanism is at maximum, meaning that the analysis gives the upper bound throughput of the proposed mechanism.

From Figure 4, by using ρ ($0 < \rho < 1$), the window size of the proposed mechanism just before packet loss occurs is represented as $\rho K\tau$. Since the sum of the window size of both connections is $K\tau+B$ when the buffer becomes full, the window size of TCP Reno connection at that time can be described as $(1-\rho)K\tau+B$. Then, the window size of the proposed mechanism immediately after packet loss occurs becomes decreased to $\rho K\tau /2$, and that of TCP Reno becomes $((1-\rho)K\tau+B)/2$.

Since TCP Reno increases its window size by one packet every RTT, T, which is the duration time of one cycle, can be calculated as follows:

$$T = \frac{(1-\rho)K\tau + B}{2}\tilde{\tau} \qquad (23)$$

where $\tilde{\tau}$ is the average value of the RTTs of the TCP connection. the window size of the proposed mechanism can be obtained from Equation (10) by substituting K for A as follows:

$$w(t) = \frac{w(0)e^{\varepsilon t}K\tau}{w(0)(e^{\varepsilon t}-1)+K\tau} \qquad (24)$$

From Equations (12) and (24), we can calculate T, which is equal to the time required for the window size to increase from $\rho K\tau /2$ to $\rho K\tau$, as follows:

$$T = \frac{1}{\varepsilon}\ln\left(\frac{\rho}{1-\rho}\frac{K\tau - \rho K\tau / 2}{\rho K\tau / 2}\right) = \frac{1}{\varepsilon}\ln\left(\frac{2-\rho}{1-\rho}\right) \qquad (25)$$

Figure 4. Changes in the window sizes of TCP Reno and the proposed mechanism

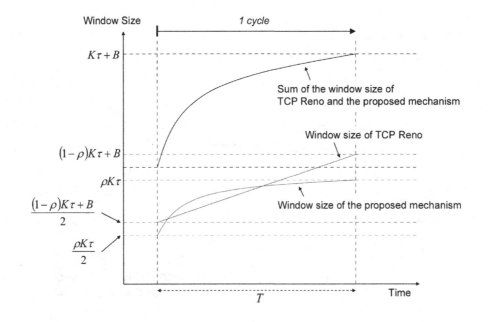

From Equations (23) and (25), we obtain the following equation:

$$\frac{(1-\rho)K\tau + B}{2}\tilde{\tau} = \frac{1}{\varepsilon}\ln\left(\frac{2-\rho}{1-\rho}\right) \qquad (26)$$

Note that the ratio of the throughput of the TCP Reno connection to that of the proposed mechanism is equal to the ratio of areas enclosed by the the x axis and each line, indicating changes in the window size, as depicted in Figure 4. The area for TCP Reno, S_{reno}, is given by:

$$S_{reno} = \frac{3}{4}\left\{(1-\rho)K\tau + B\right\}^2 \tilde{\tau}$$

On the other hand, the area for the proposed mechanism, denoted as $S_{proposed}$, is calculated as follows:

$$S_{proposed} = \int_0^T w(t)dt = \frac{K\tau}{\varepsilon}\ln\frac{2-\rho}{2(1-\rho)}$$

Finally, the average ratio of the throughput of TCP Reno to that of the proposal mechanism is given by:

$$\lambda = \frac{S_{reno}}{S_{proposed}} = \frac{\dfrac{3}{4}\left\{(1-\rho)K\tau + B\right\}^2 \tilde{\tau}}{\dfrac{K\tau}{\varepsilon}\ln\dfrac{2-\rho}{2(1-\rho)}} \qquad (27)$$

Note that ρ is given by solving Equation (26).

From Equations (26) and (27), we can understand the relationship between the variables (ε, K and B) and the ratio of throughput λ. Next, we show some numerical examples of the throughput ratio. Here we ignore the queuing delay and assume $\tilde{\tau} = \tau$. Figure 5 shows changes in the throughput ratio with respect to ε, where we set $K = 10$ [Mbps] and $\tau = 50$ [msec]. The five lines

represent the results when the buffer size B is 1/4, 1/2, 1, 2, and 4 times the bandwidth-delay product (BDP) of the bottleneck link, respectively. In Figure 6, we show the results when we set $\tau = 50$ [msec] and B to 41 [packets] (equals to BDP when $K = 10$ [Mbps]), where the five lines describe the results when $K = 10$, 50, 100, 500, and 1000 [Mbps]. These results show that ε, which realizes fairness between TCP Reno and the proposed mechanism, drastically changes when we modify K and/or B. Furthermore, in some situations, especially when the buffer size is large compared with the bandwidth-delay product, fairness cannot be realized by configuring ε. One reason is that the proposed mechanism converges its window size to $K\tau$, whereas TCP Reno continues increasing its window size until the buffer has been fully used. The primary reason of this unfairness is the characteristics of ImTCP (Cao et al, 2004; Cao et al, 2005) which we deployed in the proposed mechanism for bandwidth measurement: ImTCP estimates an available bandwidth of the end-to-end network path, not a *fair share* of the bottleneck link bandwidth. In other words, if there exists an inline measurement algorithm which can estimate a fair bandwidth share of the network, we can employ it to our proposed congestion control mechanism.

From another point of view, the congestion control algorithm of the proposed mechanism is essentially more conservative than TCP Reno. In contrast, TCP Reno has an aggressive window size control algorithm. Therefore, the unfairness between the proposed mechanism and TCP Reno cannot be avoided when they co-exist in the network. A similar discussion can also be found in the literature regarding TCP Vegas (Hasegawa et al, 2000; Hasegawa et al, 1999), and we believe this is the primary reason that TCP Vegas was not successfully deployed in the Internet. In the case of TCP Reno and its variants using AIMD/MIMD policies, the window size just after packet loss occurs depends on the bottleneck link buffer size.

That is, the throughput of these connections is improved as the buffer size increases. However, as buffer size becomes larger, the packets within the buffer also become larger, which means that the queuing delay is also increased.

Furthermore, due to the difference between the evolution of memory technology and link bandwidth technology, we are unable to prepare enough buffer for TCP connections to retain the utilization of high-speed network links in the near future (Appenzeller et al, 2004). That is, AIMD/MIMD-based congestion control mechanisms will fail to provide sufficient performance for transport layer protocols in the future Internet, and more bandwidth-aware mechanisms will be needed in such situations. We believe that the mechanism proposed herein is the most feasible solution. FAST TCP, originating from TCP Vegas, is also a possible answer since it has a more conservative congestion control mechanism than TCP Reno. However, as described in Subsection III-A, FAST

TCP cannot provide good scalability to the number of connections sharing the bottleneck link.

SIMULATION RESULTS

In this section, we present simulation results by which to evaluate the performance of the congestion control mechanism proposed in Section II.

Simulation Settings

We use ns-2 (The Vint Project, n.d.) for the simulation experiments. Traditional TCP Reno, HighSpeed TCP (HSTCP), Scalable TCP (STCP), and FAST TCP are chosen for performance comparison. We set $\varepsilon = 1.95$ and $y = 0.9$ for the proposed mechanism according to the discussion in Subsections II-A and III-B. Note that we have confirmed that changes in these parameters have a limited effect on the performance of the proposed mechanism, especially on the transient

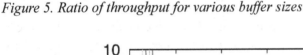

Figure 5. Ratio of throughput for various buffer sizes

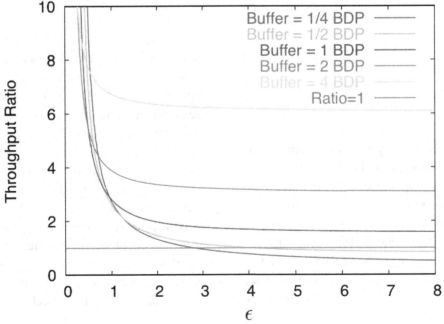

Figure 6. Ratio of throughput for various physical bandwidths

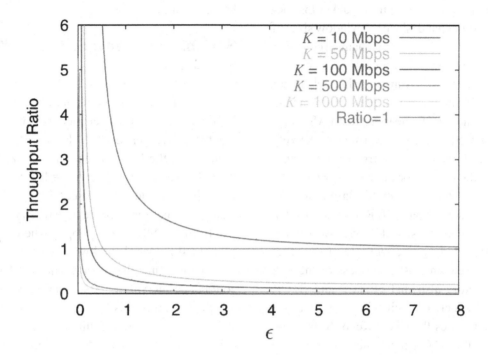

behavior, and that the characteristics of the proposed mechanism shown below do not change. The parameters in HSTCP and STCP are set to the value described in (Floyd, 2003) and (Kelly, 2003), respectively, and SACK option (Mathis, 1996) is enabled for both protocols. FAST TCP has the parameter α, which should be changed according to the link bandwidth. According to the guidelines in (Jin et al, 2003) we set $\alpha = 10, 20, 50, 100, 200, 500,$ and 1000 for link bandwidths K = 10, 20, 50, 100, 200, 500, and 1000 [Mbps], respectively.

The network model used in the simulation is depicted in Figure 7. The model consists of sender/receiver hosts, two routers, and links between the hosts and routers. N_{tcp} TCP connections are established between TCP sender i and TCP receiver i. To create background traffic, we injected UDP packets at a rate of r_{udp} into the network, where the packet size distribution follows the traffic observation results in the Internet (Agilent Technologies, 2004). That is, N_{tcp} TCP connections

and an UDP flow share a bottleneck link between the two routers. The bandwidth of the bottleneck link is denoted as BW, and the propagation delay is τ. The bandwidth and the propagation delay of the access link for TCP sender i are bw_i and τ_i, respectively. We deployed the TailDrop scheme at the router buffer, and the buffer size is set to be equivalent to the bandwidth-delay product between sender and receiver hosts.

Basic Behavior

First, we confirm the fundamental behavior of the proposed mechanism with one TCP connection. Figure 8 shows the changes in window size of TCP Reno, HSTCP, STCP, FAST TCP, and the proposed mechanism, where we set $N_{tcp} = 1$, $BW = 100$ [Mbps], $\tau = 25$ [msec], $bw_i = 200$ [Mbps], and $\tau_i = 5$ [msec]. In this case, we do not inject UDP traffic into the network. The result shows that TCP Reno, HSTCP, and STCP connections experience periodic packet loss due to buffer overflow, because these connections continue increasing the window size until packet loss occurs. On the other hand, since the window sizes of FAST TCP and the proposed mechanism converge quickly to an ideal value, no packet loss occurs. The speed of window size increase is much higher for FAST TCP and the proposed mechanism than for HSTCP and STCP, meaning that FAST TCP and the proposed mechanism can more effectively utilize the link bandwidth. Furthermore, Figure 9 describes the results for the case in which *BW* = 1 [Gbps] and bw_i = 2 [Gbps]. Based on these results, we observe that TCP Reno and HSTCP increase their window size slowly. However, the speed of the window size increase of the other mechanisms remains fast regardless of the link bandwidth. Note also that HSTCP and STCP, which rapidly increase their window size, cause more packet losses than TCP Reno. In the case of Figure 8, the SACK mechanism works well, and the sender host avoids timeouts. However, as shown in Figure 9, many retransmission timeouts occur because the SACK mechanism cannot re-

cover all of the lost packets as the link capacity becomes large.

Scalability to Network Bandwidth and Delay

We next investigate the scalability to the link bandwidth of the proposed mechanism by checking the convergence time, defined as the time required for the TCP connection to utilize 99% of the link bandwidth. We set N_{tcp} = 1, τ_1 = 5 [msec], τ = 25 [msec], and τ_u = 5 [msec]. Figure 10 shows changes in the convergence time when we change *BW* from 10 [Mbps] to 1 [Gbps], where r_{udp} is set to (0.2 *BW*) [Mbps] and bw1 is set to be equal to BW. In the figure, the average values and the 95% confidence intervals for 10 simulation experiments are shown. From this figure, we can see that the TCP Reno connection requires a great deal of time to fully utilize the link bandwidth since the increasing speed of the window size is fixed at a small value, regardless of the link bandwidth. HSTCP dramatically reduces the convergence time, but

Figure 7. Network topology in simulation experiments

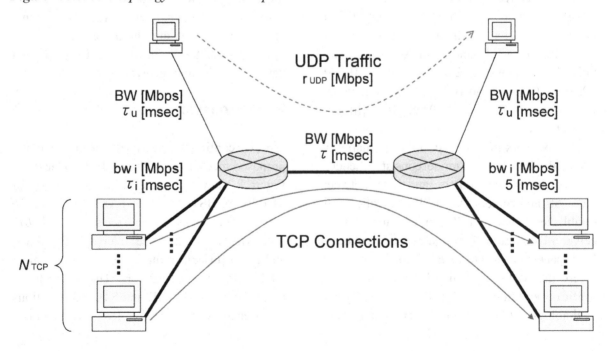

the larger the link bandwidth becomes, the greater the convergence time that is required in order to fill the bottleneck link bandwidth. This means that HSTCP is fundamentally unable to resolve the scalability problem of TCP Reno. In the case of STCP and FAST TCP, the convergence time remains constant regardless of the link bandwidth, which is also confirmed in (Kelly, 2003) and (Jin et al, 2004). The proposed mechanism retains an approximately constant convergence time regard-

less of the link bandwidth, which shows good scalability to network bandwidth.

We also note that the convergence time of the proposed mechanism is a slightly worse than that of FAST TCP, especially in Figure 10. This is because of the choice of the control parameters in both mechanisms. In other words, with a different set of the control parameters for FAST TCP and the proposed mechanism, the opposite results may be obtained. In addition, since the congestion

Figure 8. Changes in window size (BW=100 [Mbps])

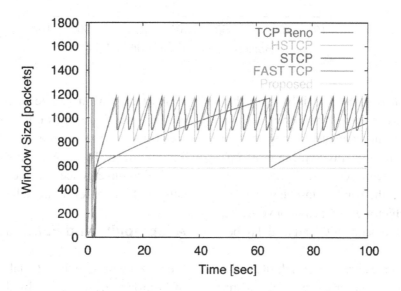

Figure 9. Change in window size (BW=1 [Gbps])

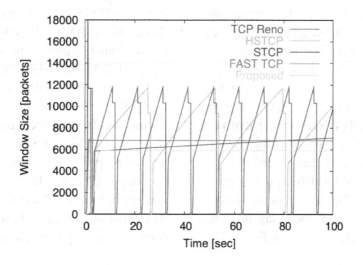

Figure 10. Convergence time with respect to bottleneck link bandwidths

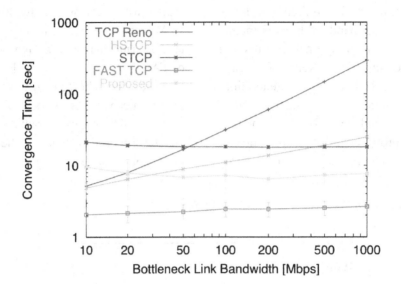

control mechanism of FAST TCP is based on that of TCP Vegas, it is considered that FAST TCP has the same difficluty in parameter setting as TCP Vegas described in [36]. Anyway, the most important characteristics observed in Figures 10 and 11 is scalability to the bandwidth-delay product of the network, which means that the convergence time changes as the bandwidth and/or delay become large.

Moreover, we investigate the scalability to the propagation delay of the proposed mechanism. We set $N_{tcp} = 1$, $BW = 100$ [Mbps], $bw_1 = 200$ [Mbps], $\tau_1 = 5$ [msec], and $r_{udp} = 20$ [Mbps]. Figure 11 shows the changes in the convergence time when we change τ from 10 [msec] to 500 [msec]. This figure shows that the TCP Reno connection requires quite a long time to fully utilize the link bandwidth because it only increases its window size by one packet per RTT. The convergence time of HSTCP and FAST TCP is less than that of TCP Reno. However, the greater the increase in propagation delay, the larger the convergence time becomes. STCP has good scalability to link bandwidth as described in Figure 10, but the convergence time increases when the delay becomes larger because HSTCP, STCP, and FAST TCP

increase their window size when receiving ACK packets, which depends on RTT. The proposed mechanism maintains the best scalability to the network delay, because, as shown in Subsection III-A, the convergence time increases logarithmically with increases in the delay or bandwidth.

Adaptability and Fairness

We also investigate the adaptability and fairness of the proposed mechanism by checking the effect of changes in the number of TCP connections. We set $N_{tcp} = 5$, $BW = 100$ [Mbps], $\tau = 25$ [msec], $bw_i = 100$ [Mbps] ($1 \leq i \leq 5$), and $\tau_i = 5$ [msec]. We do not inject UDP traffic into the network. TCP connections 1–5 join the network at 0, 100, 300, 500, and 700 [sec] and stop sending data packets at 900, 950, 1000, 1050, and 1100 [sec], respectively. Figure 12 shows changes in window size for the five TCP connections with respect to the time for TCP Reno, HSTCP, STCP, FAST TCP, and the proposed mechanism.

Figures 12(a) and 12(b) show that TCP Reno and HSTCP control their window size with the AIMD policy and realize fairness among connections by inducing periodic packet losses. From

Figure 11. Convergence time with respect to bottleneck link delays

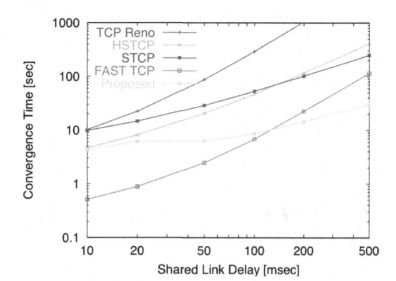

Figure 12(c), we can see that STCP cannot realize fairness among connections because its window size control algorithm is based on the MIMD policy. In Figure 12(d), we can see that the nature of FAST TCP is as follows. Since FAST TCP utilizes queuing delay as a congestion signal, it can adjust its window size without inducing any packet loss when a new TCP connection joins the network. However, FAST TCP cannot achieve fairness among existing connections and a new connection. Although FAST TCP needs RTT information to control the window size, the new connection cannot successfully measure the minimum RTT due to the queuing delay caused by the existing connection. When a connection stops a transmission and exits from the network, the remaining connections enjoy equal throughput because the buffer becomes temporarily empty, and the existing connections can measure the precise values for minimum RTT. On the other hand, Figure 12(e) shows that the proposed mechanism converges the window sizes very quickly, so that no packet loss occurs when a new connection joins the network. Furthermore, when the TCP connection leaves the network, the proposed mechanism connections quickly fill the

unused bandwidth. Borrowing the terminology of biophysics, we say that TCP connections are competitive, but still symbiotic even against the environmental changes.

Adaptability to changes in the available bandwidth is also an important characteristic of the transport layer protocol. To confirm that performance of the proposed mechanism, we set $N_{tcp} = 1$, $BW = 100$ [Mbps], $\tau = 25$ [msec], $bw_l = 100$ [Mbps], $\tau^l = 5$ [msec], and change r_{udp} so that the available bandwidth of the bottleneck link is 80 [Mbps] at 0–50 [sec], 65 [Mbps] at 50–100 [sec], 50 [Mbps] at 100–150 [sec], and 80 [Mbps] at 150–200 [sec]. Figures 13 and 14 present the changes in the throughput of a TCP connection and the queue size of the bottleneck link buffer for TCP Reno, HSTCP, STCP, and the proposed mechanism. The results obviously show the effectiveness of the proposed mechanism, which gives good adaptability to the changes in the available bandwidth. Furthermore, no packet loss occurs even when the available bandwidth suddenly decreases. On the other hand, TCP Reno connections experience packet losses during simulation time, and link utilization is much lower than 100%. Although HSTCP and STCP can

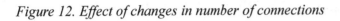

Figure 12. Effect of changes in number of connections

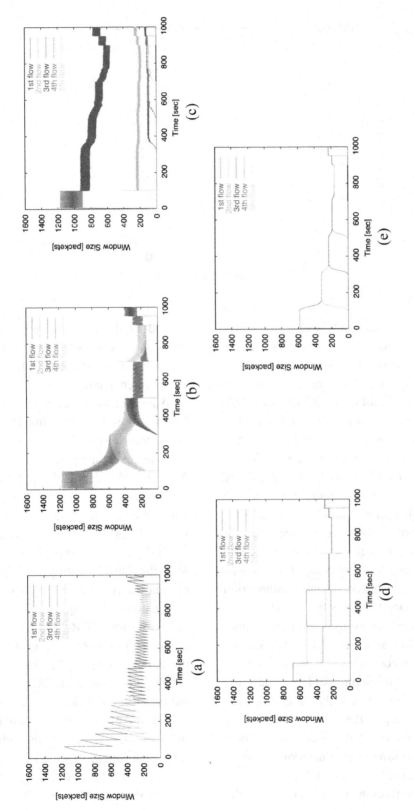

retain their link utilization because of a sufficient buffer, they have largely fluctuating RTTs caused by queuing delays. FAST TCP and the proposed mechanism experience no packet loss and retain their link utilization with small RTTs, but the proposed mechanism has a smaller queue size than FAST TCP. This is one of the advantages of the proposed mechanism, which uses an inline measurement technique, which means that the proposed mechanism is quite robust against environmental changes of the network.

Effect of Heterogeneity in Physical Bandwidth

In the above subsections we demonstrated the effectiveness of the proposed mechanism with respect to various aspects. However, in a sense, these results are expected as a result of the newly developed congestion control mechanism based on the bandwidth measurement technique. A more striking feature of the proposed mechanism is detailed in the following results. Here, we in-

Figure 13. Adaptability to change in available bandwidth (throughput)

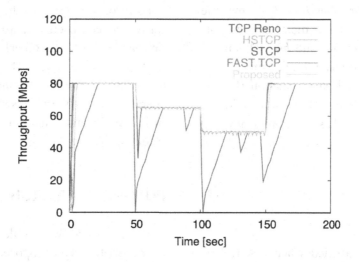

Figure 14. Adaptability to change in available bandwidth (queue size)

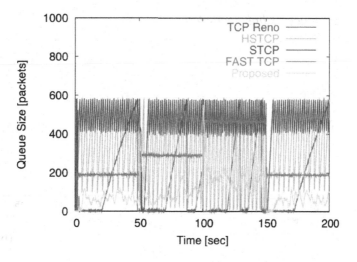

vestigate the effects of the heterogeneity of access networks such as the differences in access link bandwidth. We set $N_{tcp} = 2$, $\tau = 40$ [msec], $bw_1 =$ 10 [Mbps], $bw_2 = 20$ [Mbps], $\tau_1 = \tau_2 = 5$ [msec], and we change BW from 5 [Mbps] to 30 [Mbps]. UDP traffic is not injected into the network. Figure 15 shows the changes in the throughput of the two TCP connections in TCP Reno and the proposed mechanism with respect to BW. The figure shows that TCP Reno shares the bottleneck link bandwidth fairly, regardless of the value of BW. On the other hand, the proposed mechanism shows an interesting characteristic. When $BW < bw_1$, the two TCP connections share bottleneck link bandwidth fairly. However, when $bw_1 < BW < bw_2$, the bottleneck link bandwidth is distributed proportionally to the ratio of bw_1 and bw_2. This property can be explained using the equation of the proposed mechanism. Using Equation (8), the converged transmission rate for connection i, denoted by $\hat{N}_i$, which has a different physical link bandwidth (K_i), can be calculated as follows:

$$\hat{N}_i = \frac{K_i}{\sum_{i=1}^{n} K_i} BW \qquad (28)$$

This equality is satisfied when $y < 1$. This equation means that the bottleneck link bandwidth is shared proportionally to the physical bandwidth of each TCP connection. Since the physical bandwidth of the network path is defined as the bandwidth of the tightest link between TCP hosts (a sender and a receiver), the simulation results shown in Figure 15 agree with Equation (28). We argue that this characteristic is ideal for an Internet congestion control strategy. Throughout the history of the Internet, the ratio of the bandwidth of access networks to backbone networks has been changing over time (Crowcroft et al, 2003). Compared with access networks, the resources of backbone networks are sometimes scarce and sometimes plentiful. We believe that when backbone resources are few, they should be shared fairly between users, regardless of their access link bandwidth. On the other hand, when backbone resources are sufficient, they should be shared according to the access link bandwidth. The characteristics of the proposed mechanism, shown in Figure 15 and Equation (28), realize such a resource sharing strategy.

FUTURE RESEARCH DIRECTIONS

For future work, we should confirm additional characteristics of the proposed mechanism, which include fairness among connections with differ-

Figure 15. Effect of different access link bandwidths

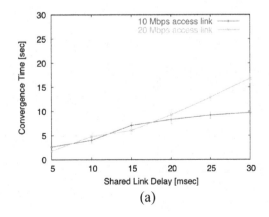

(a)

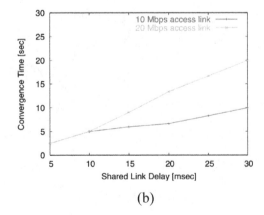

(b)

ent RTTs and the effect of measurement errors on the physical and available bandwidths. The implementation experiments are also needed for confirming the applicability of the proposed mechanism to actual network situations.

We also plan to enhance the congestion control mechanism to to deal with the environmental changes, by adding the noise term to Lotka-Volterra competition model equation and adaptively setting control parameters. The environmental changes include the error and fluctuations on the measurement results of physical capacity and available bandwidth of the network path, and changes in the number of competing connections at the bottleneck. One possible solution is to control the degree of dependence on measured values of congestion indicators. The basic idea for this is to determine how the reliability of the congestion indicators changes based on the accuracy of measurement. Based on these observations, we plan to introduce the dynamic parameter setting mechanism to control the sensitivity of protocol behavior based on the variance of the measurement results of the congestion indicators. Another we also consider adding self-induced oscillations to the data transmission rate to absorb the negative effects of the environmental changes. In general, it is difficult to quickly recognize the sudden changes in the network environment, because the delay in the network measurement cannot be avoided. To avoid this problem, we plan to propose to add some randomness in determining the increase/decrease slope of the data transmission rate.

CONCLUSION

In this chapter, we proposed a new congestion control mechanism of TCP based on inline network measurement. The proposed mechanism obtains information of the physical and available bandwidths from inline network measurement via ImTCP. Using bandwidth information, the proposed mechanism adjusts its window size with an algorithm based on mathematical models borrowed from biophysics. Consequently, the proposed mechanism can converge its window size to an ideal value and avoid the periodic packet loss experienced by TCP Reno.

Through mathematical analysis, we confirmed that the proposed mechanism has good scalability to not only link bandwidth but also propagation delay between the sender and receiver hosts. Other transport layer protocols such as TCP Reno, High-Speed TCP, Scalable TCP, and FAST TCP cannot provide such scalability. Furthermore, based on the mathematical analysis results regarding competition between TCP Reno and the proposed mechanism, although the realization of fairness between them was observed to be difficult, we believed that the proposed mechanism is the only solution for transport layer protocols for future high-speed networks. Furthermore, through extensive simulations, we confirmed that the proposed mechanism exhibits analytically determined characteristics. Therefore, the proposed mechanism is effective regardless of network bandwidth or delay and can solve the many of the problems associated with TCP Reno and its variants.

REFERENCES

Agilent Technologies. (2004). *Mixed packet size throughput*. Retrieved from http://advanced.com-ms.agilent.com/n2x/docs/journal/JTC 003.html

Allman, A., Balakrishnan, H., & Floyd, S. (2001). *Enhancing TCP's loss recovery using limited transmit*. Request for Comments 3042, Jan. 2001.

Appenzeller, G., Keslassy, I., & McKeown, N. (2004). Sizing router buffers. In *Proceedings of ACM SIGCOMM 2004*, Aug. 2004.

Bhandarkar, S., Jain, S., & Reddy, A. L. N. (2005). Improving TCP performance in high bandwidth high RTT links using layered congestion control. In *Proceedings of PFLDnet 2005*, Feb. 2005. Blanton, E., & Allman, M. On making TCP more robust to packet reordering. *ACM Computer Communication Review, 32*(1), 20–30.

Blanton, E., Allman, M., Fall, K., & Wang, L. (2003). *A conservative selective acknowledgment (SACK)-based loss recovery algorithm for TCP.* Request for Comments 3517, Apr. 2003.

Bonabeau, E., Dorigo, M., & Theraulaz, G. (1999). *Swarm intelligence: From natural to artificial systems.* New York, NY: Oxford University Press.

Brakmo, L. S., O'Malley, S. W., & Peterson, L. L. (1994). TCP Vegas: New techniques for congestion detection and avoidance. In *Proceedings of ACM SIGCOMM'94*, Oct. 1994.

Cao, M. L. T., Hasegawa, G., & Murata, M. (2004). Available bandwidth measurement via TCP connection. In *Proceedings of IFIP/IEEE MMNS 2004*, Oct. 2004.

Cao, M. L. T., Hasegawa, G., & Murata, M. (2005). A merged inline measurement method for capacity and available bandwidth. In *Proceedings of NLANR PAM 2005*, Mar. 2005.

Carter, R. L., & Crovella, M. E. (1996). *Measuring bottleneck link speed in packet-switched networks.* Boston University Computer Science Department, (Tech. Rep. BU-CS-96-006), Mar. 1996.

Chiu, D.-M., & Jain, R. (1989). Analysis of the increase and decrease algorithms for congestion avoidance in computer networks. *Journal of Computer Networks and ISDN Systems, 17*, 1–14. doi:10.1016/0169-7552(89)90019-6

Crowcroft, J., Hand, S., Mortier, R., Roscoe, T., & Warfield, A. (2003). QoS's downfall: At the bottom, or not at all! In *Proceedings of ACM SIGCOMM 2003 Workshop on Revisiting IP QoS (RIPQOS)*, Aug. 2003.

Dovrolis, C., Ramanathan, P., & Moore, D. (2001). What do packet dispersion techniques measure? *Proceedings - IEEE INFOCOM*, (Apr): 2001.

Floyd, S. (2003). *HighSpeed TCP for large congestion windows.* Request for Comments 3649, Dec. 2003.

Fu, Z., Zerfos, P., Luo, H., Lu, S., Zhang, L., & Gerla, M. (2003). The impact of multihop wireless channel on TCP throughput and loss. *Proceedings - IEEE INFOCOM*, (Apr): 2003.

Guo, L., & Matta, I. (2001). *The war between mice and elephants.* (Technical Report BU-CS-2001-005).

Hasegawa, G., Kurata, K., & Murata, M. (2000). Analysis and improvement of fairness between TCP Reno and Vegas for deployment of TCP Vegas to the Internet. In *Proceedings of IEEE ICNP 2000*, Nov. 2000.

Hasegawa, G., Murata, M., & Miyahara, H. (1999). Fairness and stability of the congestion control mechanism of TCP. *Proceedings - IEEE INFOCOM, 99*, 1329–1336.

Hoe, J. C. (1996). Improving the start-up behavior of a congestion control scheme of TCP. *ACM SIGCOMM Computer Communication Review, 26*(4), 270–280. doi:10.1145/248157.248180

Jacobson, V. (1997). Pathchar - A tool to infer characteristics of internet paths. Retrieved from http://www.caida.org/tools/utilities/others/pathchar/

Jacobson, V., Braden, R., & Borman, D. (1992). *TCP extensions for high performance.* Request for Comments 1323, May 1992.

Jain, M., & Dovrolis, C. (2002). End-to-end available bandwidth: Measurement methodology, dynamics, and relation with TCP throughput. In *Proceedings of ACM SIGCOMM 2002*, Aug. 2002.

Jin, C., Wei, D. X., & Low, S. H. (2003). *Internet draft: FAST TCP for high-speed long-distance networks.*

Jin, C., Wei, D. X., & Low, S. H. (2004). FAST TCP: Motivation, architecture, algorithms, performance. *Proceedings - IEEE INFOCOM*, (Mar): 2004.

Kelly, T. (2003). Scalable TCP: Improving performance in highspeed wide area networks. In *Proceedings of PFLDnet '03: Workshop for the Purposes of Discussion*, Feb. 2003.

King, R., Baraniuk, R., & Riedi, R. (2005). TCP-Africa: An adaptive and fair rapid increase rule for scalable TCP. *Proceedings - IEEE INFOCOM*, (Mar): 2005.

Mathis, M. (1996). *TCP selective acknowledgement options*. Request for Comments 2018, Oct. 1996.

Melander, B., Bjorkman, M., & Gunningberg, P. (2000). A new end-to-end probing and analysis method for estimating bandwidth bottlenecks. In *Proceedings of IEEE GLOBECOM 2000*, Nov. 2000.

Montresor, A., Meling, H., & Babaoglu, O. (2003). Toward self-organizing, self-repairing and resilient distributed systems [Springer-Verlag.]. *LNCS*, *2584*, 119–124.

Murray, J. D. (2002). *Mathematical Biology I: An introduction*. Springer Verlag.

Postel, J. B. (1981). *Transmission control protocol*. Request for Comments 793, Sept. 1981. Ribeiro, V., Riedi, R., Baraniuk, R., Navratil, J., & Cottrell, L. (2003). PathChirp: Efficient available bandwidth estimation for network paths. In *Proceedings of NLANR PAM2003*, Apr. 2003.

Shenker, S., Zhang, L., & Clark, D. D. (1990). Some observations on the dynamics of a congestion control algorithm. *ACM Computer Communication Review*, *20*(5), 30–39. doi:10.1145/381906.381931

Stevens, W. R. (1994). TCP/IP Illustrated: *Vol. 1. The protocols*. Reading, MA: Addison-Wesley.

The VINT Project. (n.d.). *UCB/LBNL/VINT network simulator - ns* (version 2). Retrieved from http://www.isi.edu/nsnam/ns/

Trinh, T. A., & Molnar, S. (2004). A game-theoretic analysis of TCP Vegas. In *Proceedings of QofIS 2004*, Oct. 2004.

ADDITIONAL READING

R. Braden, "Requirements for Internet hosts – communication layers," Request for Comments 1122, October 1989.

Clark, D. D., Jacobson, V., Romkey, J., & Salwen, H. (1989, June). An analysis of TCP processing overhead. *IEEE Communications Magazine*, *27*, 23–29. doi:10.1109/35.29545

Fall, K., & Floyd, S. (1996, July). Simulation-based comparisons of Tahoe, Reno, and SACK TCP. *ACM SIGCOMM Computer Communication Review*, *26*, 5–21. doi:10.1145/235160.235162

S. Floyd and T. Henderson, "The NewReno modification to TCP's fast recovery algorithm," Request for Comments 2582, April 1999.

Floyd, S., & Jacobson, V. (1995, August). Link-sharing and resource management models for packet networks. *IEEE/ACM Transactions on Networking*, *3*, 365–386. doi:10.1109/90.413212

Ha, S., Rhee, I., & Xu, L. (2008). CUBIC: A new TCP-friendly high-speed TCP variant. *ACM SIGOP Operating Systems Review*, *42*(5), 64–74. doi:10.1145/1400097.1400105

G. Hasegawa, M. Murata, and H. Miyahara, "Fairness and stability of the congestion control mechanism of TCP," in Proceedings of IEEE INFOCOM'99, pp. 1329–1336, March 1999.

Heyman, D. P., Lakshman, T. V., & Neidhardt, L. "A new method for analyzing feedback-based protocols with applications to engineering web traffic over the Internet," in Proceedings of ACM SIGMETRICS'97, pp. 24–38, February 1997.

Hoe, J. "Start-up dynamics of TCP's congestion control and avoidance schemes," Master's thesis, MIT, June 1995.

Hoe, J. C. (1996, October). Improving the start-up behavior of a congestion control scheme of TCP. *ACM SIGCOMM Computer Communication Review*, *26*, 270–280. doi:10.1145/248157.248180

V. Jacobson and R. Braden, "TCP extensions for long-delay paths," Request for Comments 1072, October 1988.

V. Jacobson, R. Braden, and D. Borman, "TCP extensions for high performance," Request for Comments 1323, May 1992.

Kleinrock, L. (1992, April). The latency/bandwidth tradeoff in gigabit networks. *IEEE Communications Magazine*, *30*, 36–41. doi:10.1109/35.135787

Kleinrock, L. (1992, April). The latency/bandwidth tradeoff in gigabit networks. *IEEE Communications Magazine*, *30*, 36–41. doi:10.1109/35.135787

L. S. J. (1989). *M. K. McKusick, M. J. Karels, and J. S. Quarterman, The Design and Implementation of the 4.3BSD UNIX Operating System*. Reading, Massachusetts: Addison-Wesley.

Lakshman, T. V., & Madhow, U. "Performance analysis of window–based flow control using TCP/IP: Effect of high bandwidth–delay product and random loss," in Proceedings of HPN'94, pp. 135–149, June 1994.

T.V. Lakshman, U. Madhow, and B. Suter, "Window-based error recovery and flow control with a slow acknowledgement channel: a study of TCP/IP performance," in Proceedings of IEEE INFOCOM'97, pp. 1201–1211, April 1997.

Mathis, M., Heffner, J., & Reddy, R. (2003, July). Web100: Extended TCP instrumentation for research, education and diagnosis. *ACM Computer Communications Review*, *33*, 69–79. doi:10.1145/956993.957002

Mathis, M., & Mahdavi, J. (1996, October). Forward acknowledgment: Refining TCP congestion control. *ACM SIGCOMM Computer Communication Review*, *26*, 281–291. doi:10.1145/248157.248181

Microsoft Corporation, Microsoft Windows Server 2003 TCP/IP Implementation Details, June 2003.

Paxson, V. "Measurements and analysis of end-to-end Internet dynamics," Ph.D. Thesis, April 1997.

Perloff, M., & Reiss, K. (1995, February). Improvements to TCP performance. *Communications of the ACM*, *38*, 90–100. doi:10.1145/204826.204849

Sarolahti, P., & Kuznetsov, A. "Congestion control in linux TCP," in Proceedings of 2002 USENIX Ammial Tecnical Conference, pp. 49–62, June 2002.

Tan, K., Song, J., Zhang, Q., & Sridharan, M. "Compound TCP: A scalable and TCP-friendly congestion control for high-speed networks," in Proceedings of International Workshop on Protocols for Future, Large-Scale and Diverse Network Transport (PFLDnet 2006), Feb. 2006.

Tanenbaum, A. S. Computer Networks, 3rd edition. Upper Saddle Riverm New Jersey, 07458: Prentice Hall, 1996.

W. chang Feng, D. D. Kandlur, D. Saha, and K. G. Shin, "Understanding TCP dynamics in an integrated services Internet," in Proceedings of The 7th International Workshop on Network and Operating Systems Support for Digital Audio and Video (NOSSDAV'97), pp. 375–385, May 1997.

Z. Wang, "Toward scalable bandwidth allocation on the Internet," On The Internet, pp. 24–32, May/June 1998.

Wang, Z., & Crowcroft, J. (1992, April). Eliminating periodic packet losses in 4.3–Tahoe BSD TCP congestion control. *ACM Computer Communication Review, 22,* 9–16. doi:10.1145/141800.141801

Chapter 7
From Local Growth to Global Optimization in Insect Built Networks

Andrea Perna
Complex Systems Institute of Paris, France & Uppsala University, Sweden

Pascale Kuntz
Site Ecole Polytechnique de l'Université de Nantes, France

Guy Theraulaz
Université de Toulouse, France & CNRS, France

Christian Jost
Université de Toulouse, France & CNRS, France

ABSTRACT

Social insect colonies build large net-like systems: gallery and trail networks. Many such networks appear to show near-optimal performance. Focusing on the network system inside termite nests we address the question how simple agents with probabilistic behaviour can control and optimize the growth of a structure with size several magnitude orders above their perceptual range. We identify two major classes of mechanisms: (i) purely local mechanisms, which involve the arrangement of simple motifs according to predetermined rules of behaviour and (ii) local estimation of global quantities, where sizes, lengths, and numbers are estimated from densities, concentrations, and traffic. Theoretical considerations suggest that purely local mechanisms work better during early network formation and are less likely to fall into local optima. On the contrary, estimation of global properties is only possible on functional networks and is more likely to work through pruning. This latter mechanism may contribute to restore network functionalities following unpredicted changes of external conditions or network topology. An analysis of the network properties of Cubitermes termite nests supports the role of both classes of mechanisms, possibly in interplay with environmental conditions acting as a template.

DOI: 10.4018/978-1-61350-092-7.ch007

ARE INSECT-MADE NET-LIKE STRUCTURES OPTIMAL?

The nests of social insects are among the most impressive objects built by animals, and this for several reasons. First, they can be extremely big: up to several magnitude orders bigger than insects themselves. Second, they usually present a coherent and harmonious global organization even at the larger scale. Third, they are not produced by extremely intelligent animals, but by tiny insects with somewhat noisy, seemingly unpredictable behaviour. These properties make insect nests particularly interesting in a perspective of bio-inspiration.

If these structures optimize some functionality, then we can imagine mimicking insect behaviour to build efficient artificial systems that accomplish similar functionalities.

How do the insects come to build such complex structures?

The question allows for two different interpretations: the first focuses on the evolutionary history of insects while the second focuses on the building mechanisms:

1. By what evolutionary processes social insects have acquired the capability of building complex structures?
2. What building mechanisms and actions at the individual level lead to the formation of the global structure?

Let us illustrate the two interpretations with an example dealing with nest building, if not directly with network like structures. In an emblematic chapter of "The Origin of Species" Charles Darwin (1859, chapter 6) thinks about honeybee combs and states that:

He must be a dull man who can examine the exquisite structure of a comb, so beautifully adapted to its end, without enthusiastic admiration.

We hear from mathematicians that bees have practically solved a recondite problem, and have made their cells of the proper shape to hold the greatest possible amount of honey, with the least possible consumption of precious wax in their construction. (...) it seems at first quite inconceivable how they can make al l the necessary angles and planes, or even perceive when they are correctly made.

Darwin's explanation is in terms of natural selection: in the same chapter he argues that "cells constructed like those of the bee or the wasp gain in strength, and save much in labour and space". It is natural that the instincts of bees must have undergone "numerous, successive, slight modifications" that led to the construction of more and more efficient structures (Darwin, 1859).

An alternative discussion of the very same phenomenon, but this time focusing on building mechanisms is found in D'Arcy Thompson's "On Growth and Form" (Thompson, 1992):

the direct effort of the wasp or bee may be supposed to be limited (...) to the making of little hemispherical cups, as thin as the nature of the material permits, and packing these little round cups as close as possible together. It is then conceivable, and indeed probable, that the symmetrical tensions of the semi-fluid films should suffice (however retarded by viscosity) to bring the whole system into equilibrium, that is to say into the configuration which the comb actually assumes.

For Darwin, bees make combs with minimal surface-volume ratio because this configuration confers the maximum selective advantage; for D'Arcy Thompson, the minimal surfaces appear because this is the configuration naturally assumed by semi-fluid films, be they soap-bubbles, cells of a segmenting egg or honey combs.

In principle there is no contradiction between the two explanations: bees could benefit from having cells with minimum surface to volume ratio and also get this ratio minimized almost for free because this is the minimal energetic configuration. However, these examples illustrate well how difficult is assessing the optimality of insect built structures: when we address the question about evolutionary processes, the surface-volume ratio of honey combs is the objective of optimization, but when we focus on the building process the same minimal surface-volume ratio can be an epiphenomenon of the building mechanism, with no adaptive value. (Incidentally, let us mention that Thompson's explanation is not unique in its kind and a similar "mechanical" explanation had been put forward almost two centuries earlier by Buffon (1753). For Buffon the motor of surface minimization is not the tension of the wax, but the pressure exerted by the body of bees inside the cells. A more recent paper supports the mechanism proposed by D'Arcy Thompson for honeybee combs (Pirk et al., 2004). However, let us say that even if the origin of the hexagonal cells is in physical forces and not in the behaviour of bees, this does not rule out the possibly important role of natural selection. For instance, was could have been selected as a building material because its melting point and viscous properties easily produce the hexagonal pattern).

An additional point that comes out from these examples is that words such as "optimal" and "efficient" do not have the same meaning in biology and in computer science. In biology, the concept of optimality is intrinsically related to the concept of biological fitness (roughly, the ability of an individual to propagate its genes). In other words, it is not sufficient that a biological object maximizes or minimizes a particular function, but the function optimized must also confer a selective advantage to the individuals. For Darwin it is not sufficient that bees build cells with minimal surfaces, it is important that they save "labour" and "costly wax": surface minimization must allow them to save energy that can be reinvested in producing and nourishing a larger offspring.

In practice, the only means to assess the biological efficiency of insect nests would be to measure the reproductive success of the colonies inhabiting them and relate it to measures of nest size, shape and organization, which clearly is extremely difficult. Indeed, most studies of biological optimality do not aim at finding optimality in a biological system, but take the assumption that the system is "optimal" as a starting point to address questions about the constraints and the objectives that have shaped its actual properties (Parker & Smith, 1990).

In the rest of this paper we will not use words such as "efficient" and "optimal" in their biological meaning, but in the sense they usually assume in mathematics and computer science, that is, to indicate how close the solution found by insects is to the optimization of a particular function, without necessarily implying a selective advantage in the biological sense.

In this case, some net-like structures built by insects were shown to optimize different functionalities. In particular, the foraging systems of ants (Acosta et al, 1993; Solé et al., 2000; Buhl et al. 2009) and termites (Lee et al., 2007) tend to maximize food intake for a given total length of the transportation network (galleries and trails) required to collect it. Ant galleries also form efficient transportation networks in terms of distances between destinations and robustness (Buhl et al., 2004a).

In this paper, we focus on the analysis of the gallery system in termite nests. For some species, this complex system forms a 3D network which can be described by a graph G=(V,E): the vertices V represent the chambers and the edges E represent the connections between the chambers (fig. 1).

We have recently shown that the topological structure of the connections in specimens of the genus *Cubitermes* is particularly adapted to fulfil specific functions such as communication efficiency and ease of defence (Perna et al., 2008; Perna et al., 2008a)

Figure 1. A. A Cubitermes nest. The nest is ~ 30 cm high and has the typical mushroom shaped appearance. B. Virtual cast of the same nest. C. Virtual nest cut to show the internal chambers and galleries. Chambers are mapped to network vertices, galleries to edges. D. Detail of the nest, in a similar representation as in B, but here the structure has been thinned to render the paths of interconnections visible. One such path is marked by red dots. E. Graph representation of the same nest. Vertex colours reflect the layer where they are in the nest.

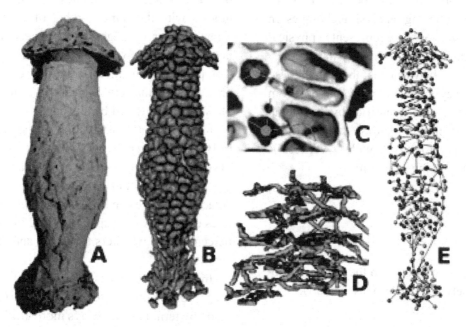

Here, we first complete some results on the communication efficiency: we show that this latter is far better than the one reached in random networks of similar sizes and that this property may be partly explained by the presence of very particular 3D sub-graphs (like "ramps"). The second part of the paper addresses the question of the building mechanisms of such complex structures: how do the insects control and regulate the growth of a structure that is so much bigger than their perception range? In other words, how can global optimization result from local growth rules? We here distinguish two families of processes: (i) local rules which involve the arrangement of very simple motifs, but result in globally efficient structures, and (ii) local estimation of global properties which allows the agents to regulate their own behaviour. We show how these two processes can be involved in the formation of the gallery networks in the termite nests.

Optimization of Global Properties

In order to get quantitative measures of global nest properties, we need a convenient representation for the complex forms of insect nests and trails. Such a representation should describe both the small scale (the one more likely accessible to the perception and action range of insects) and the large scale (the whole structure with the properties it optimizes). This requirement is necessary if we want to explore the relationship between the two scales of representation. For the analysis of termite nests, graphs are particularly well suited. Generally speaking, they are characterized by several measures of the local organization (vertex degree, vertex properties, assortativity or disassortativity between vertices, clustering coefficient etc.), as well as the intermediate (frequency of specific motifs, presence of cycles) and the large scale properties (diameter, average path length, distribution of betweenness and closeness centrality etc.; Boccaletti et al., 2006), as seen in Figure 1.

The termite nests analyzed in this paper have been built by African termites of the genus *Cubitermes*. The nests were imaged with computer tomography and the internal transportation network was extracted with image analysis techniques. In this network, a vertex vi in V represents a physical chamber and an edge *eij = {vi, vj }* in E depicts a physical gallery between chambers *vi* and *vj*.

The efficiency to navigate the network from vertex to vertex is well quantified by its "global topological efficiency"(Latora & Marchiori, 2001), which for a network with N vertices is given by the following equation:

$$L = \frac{1}{N(N-1)} \sum_{\forall v_i, v_j} \frac{1}{d(v_i, v_j)}$$

where *d(vi, vj)* corresponds to the shortest topological path between the vertices *vi* and *vj*.

This quantity is bounded in the interval [0, 1] and is higher for networks where most pairs of vertices are connected with short paths.

Figure 2 reports the average efficiency for five termite nests (black star), compared with the distributions of efficiency for null network models with the same number of vertices, the same number of edges, but connections have been randomly rewired. The rewiring preserves the spatial organization of the network, that is, only vertices that are adjacent in space can be physically connected by an edge.

Red box plots: distribution of the efficiency of 10000 rewired networks with the same number of vertices, the same number of edges and respecting the same spatial constraints (only vertices adjacent in space can be connected). The boundaries of the box correspond to the 25th and 75th percentile; the whiskers to the 5th and 95th percentile.

In spite of differences from one nest to the other (in part due to their different sizes), the networks made by termites are always more efficient than

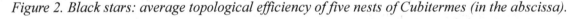

Figure 2. Black stars: average topological efficiency of five nests of Cubitermes (in the abscissa).

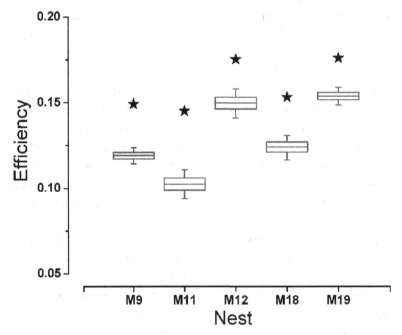

random networks with similar connectivity rules. The higher efficiency of real networks can be explained in part by the presence of long "ramps", or series of connected chambers on the vertical axis, granting fast communication from bottom to top of the nest. One of these ramps is visible in Figure 1-D, where the chambers and galleries of Figure 1-B have been flattened to improve visibility.

Efficient Local Growth Rules

From the point of view of individual insect behavior, some basic mechanisms were already highlighted in the end of the 50's by the French biologist P. P. Grassé, who introduced the concept of stigmergy (Grassé, 1959). Grassé showed that the coordination and regulation of the building activity is controlled by the growing nest structure: the local configuration of the environment and work in progress triggers particular building behaviors in the insects. The insects change their own environment as a result of their actions, and the new configuration of the environment serves as stimulus that triggers the actions of other insects. This very general mechanism explains how large numbers of insects can coordinate their respective activities (Bonabeau et al., 1999). However, this does not explain the link between perception and action of individual insects at a very small scale and harmonious growth of structures three orders of magnitude bigger.

Two broad classes of mechanisms are possible: (i) insects rely on purely local information and local rules of behavior, but these rules have been improved and refined by means of natural selection in such a way that they lead naturally to the appearance of efficient large-scale structures. The other possibility is that (ii) insects make accurate inferences about global structural properties and tune their behavior accordingly. We show in the following how an evaluation of large scale properties is not incompatible with a small perceptual range.

Local Arrangement of Simple Motifs

For layered structures similar to the *Cubitermes* nests, we can imagine simple stigmergic rules relying on local information only, and yet producing efficient large-scale networks.

A simple algorithm based on local decision only could be the following. Let us first consider a chain of a fixed number of vertices positioned on a horizontal straight line (layer 1). Randomly select one vertex $x1$ on the chain. Add a new vertex $x2$ on the layer 2 above $x1$ and connect it to $x1$. On the layer 2, build a chain from $x2$ by successively adding on the right (resp. on the left) new adjacent vertices above those of the previous layer. Stop the chain when there is no vertex below in the previous layer. Repeat the process p times. The resulting graph is a ladder-like tree with a vertical ramp $x1, x2, ..., xp$ (Figure 3-A). This mechanism is only local: at each step the new connections -both vertical and horizontal- are added above the existing ones in a spatial neighborhood. There is no estimation of the global organization of the structure. However, the resulting tree is more efficient than a random spanning tree of the same size. For illustration, let us consider a tree built with this rule composed of 13 layers and 8 vertices per layer. Its topological efficiency is 0.16. By comparison, random spanning trees of an equivalent 2D square lattice with 8 columns and 13 rows have efficiency values around 0.121 with standard error 0.001.

While this example is probably too simplistic to explain the formation of the complex networks observed in *Cubitermes* termite nests, there is some evidence that transportation efficiency can be obtained from similar local mechanisms. Valverde and collaborators (2009) created random lattice networks that matched the distribution of **motifs** of real *Cubitermes* galleries. Motifs are a local network parameter, describing the set of interconnections between small groups of 3, 4 or 5 vertices (Figure 3-B). Here, the only match for global properties was a limit on the total number

Figure 3. **A**. *A simple tree network obtained with no evaluation of global performance. A single vertical ramp connects all the layers (L1, L2, ..., L13).* **B**. *Possible subgraphs of four vertices for undirected graphs. C Global topological efficiency of real Cubitermes networks (dark blue) and of random spatial networks matching the frequencies of four-subgraphs found in the real graphs (yellow). In spite of the fact that the matching involves subgraphs of only four vertices, the model provides a very good approximation to the global efficiency of Cubitermes, at least for nests M12, M18 and M19. (Redrawn from Valverde et al., 2009)*

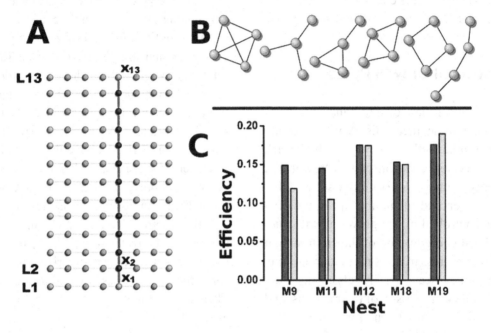

of vertices and on the dimensions of the whole lattice. Yet, the networks produced with this technique matched very well the transportation efficiency of real nests (Figure 3-C). While this was not the main purpose of their study, such results indicate that it is possible to obtain networks with similar global properties only by mixing small-scale features (the motifs) in the correct proportions, a technique that -at least in principle- would also be accessible to termites.

Local Estimation of Global Properties

Purely local mechanisms can possibly explain the formation of efficient large-scale structures. Yet, they might not allow adjusting the organization of a structure in response to environmental changes

or singular unpredictable events. The growth of a colony itself requires that the nest is continuously adapted to fulfill new needs and constraints (see also Deneubourg et al., 1986).

For these reasons, it seems reasonable that optimization of the structures is better achieved if insects have a way to evaluate the efficiency of the current solution and of improving on it based on information about some global parameters of the existing structure.

Assessing the organization and functionality of a large structure typically requires computing measures of distance, of size, of number of elements, both for the whole structure and for its parts. Clearly, insects cannot overcome the limitations imposed by their perceptual range: they cannot directly estimate the volume of the nest, the number of individuals in the colony, the length of the path between remote destinations, at least not when these numbers are much bigger than their own perceptual range and cognitive capacities. However, the ratios between any two such quantities can always be estimated on a local basis and may also provide cues to relevant global properties. For instance, the density of individuals inside the nest carries information about both the total number of individuals and the nest size; the traffic on a foraging trail carries information about both the number of individuals foraging on that trail and the distance of the food source[1]. There is large evidence that similar cues are used by insect colonies. The frequency of intersections of marked paths inside a cavity carries information about the size of the cavity and the total length of marked paths. Observations have proved that this measure is used by ants, at least in the simplest case, where one single ant explores a potential nest site. In this case, the total length of marked paths can be controlled by the ant, and the frequency of intersections gives an accurate estimate of total nest size (Mallon & Franks, 2000). Ants of the species *Leptothorax albipennis* appear to regulate nest size through density, as they are able to maintain a constant ratio such that each adult worker has about 5mm[2] of floor area in the nest (Franks et al., 1992). *Messor sanctus* ants in laboratory conditions dig complex networks of galleries whose size is proportional to the number of individuals in the colony, suggesting that a similar mechanism is in place also for this species (Buhl et al., 2004). Similarly, Argentine ants *Linepithema humile* can find the shortest path from the nest to a source of food, measuring only the local concentration of pheromones or other chemicals laid by nest mates (Goss et al., 1989; Deneubourg et al., 1990). Pheromone concentration depends on the ratio between number of insects on a trail and on the length of the trail, but since the numbers of insects choosing each trail are more or less equivalent in the beginning, all

the information carried by pheromones is about path length.

Can similar mechanism underlie the optimization of transportation efficiency in larger networks such as those made by *Cubitermes* termites?

One mechanism of network optimization based on local estimation of global properties is illustrated on a lattice model in Figure 4. Here, the global parameter to optimize is still network efficiency, and the local quantity estimated is traffic at individual edges. In terms of graphs, the amount of traffic on a vertex or edge is expressed by the betweenness centrality of the vertex or the edge. The betweenness centrality (BC) of the element $\nu \in G$, either a vertex or an edge, is defined as follows:

$$BC(\nu) = \sum_{v_i \neq v_j} \frac{c_{ij}(\nu)}{c(v_i, v_j)}$$

where c_{ij} (ν) is the number of shortest paths from vertex v_i to vertex v_j passing through element ν and $c(v_i, v_j)$ is the total number of shortest paths from v_i to v_j (Anthonisse, 1971).

In the example of Figure 4, starting from a complete lattice, all the edges are marked with their value of betweenness centrality and the edge with lowest betweenness[2] is removed from the network (unless its removal leads to disconnect the network). If the process is iterated until the network becomes a tree, the final network has an efficiency of 0.152 (and almost no variability if the to-be-removed edge is always picked among those with lowest absolute betweenness), only slightly lower than for the purely local growth mechanism tested in the previous section.

This mechanism leads to the appearance of many straight series of connections, that may be reminiscent of the vertical ramps found in the real *Cubitermes* nests.

Could a similar mechanism determine the optimization of termite networks? There is some evidence that young *Cubitermes* nests have more

Figure 4. Network optimization based on local estimation of global properties. At each step the algorithm computes the betweenness centrality of edges and progressively removes from the network the edges with low betweenness, unless their removal triggers disconnections. Betweenness centrality can be estimated at local positions (see text), but it provides indirect information about global network parameters such as network size and path length.

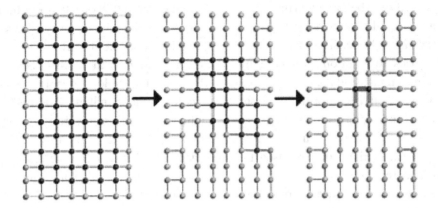

densely connected networks (i.e. networks with higher average vertex degree). This indicates that some edges are removed from the network over time. In a previous work (Perna, 2008) we used the low-betweenness removal algorithm to model *Cubitermes* networks. For each nest we considered the "maximal embedded graph" (MEG), the graph that we would obtain if all adjacent chambers were connected by a corridor. Starting from this nest we iterated the betweenness computation and edge removal procedure till we got a network with the same number of edges as the real termite networks (henceforth a "maximum centrality spanner").

This mechanism leads to networks much more efficient than the real ones (Perna et al., 2008). To make an example, Figure 5 represents a *Cubitermes* network (in B) alongside with two comparison models: a random spanner of the MEG (in A) and a maximum centrality spanner (in C). The maximum centrality spanner has a diameter (as well as other distance measures) much shorter than the other networks. It seems plausible that an implementation of the same algorithm including more noisy edge removal, different initial conditions and possibly additional constraints on the

number of paths that can transit through a single node could lead to the creation of networks more similar to the real termite networks. However, in the present paper we are interested in the general mechanisms of optimization used by social insects and a detailed understanding of the exact factors shaping the form and connectivity of *Cubitermes* nests has little relevance for our present discussion.

We want instead to draw attention to the fact that this class of mechanisms, involving an evaluation of the global properties of a structure, or a network, is only possible if there already is a "global" structure. The structure for which global parameters are evaluated must be an already active and functional one. For this reason we argue that this mechanism of optimization is more likely to work through pruning or reshaping of an existing structure, than concurrently with its primary formation.

CONCLUSION

We have discussed two main classes of mechanisms that underlie optimization in social insect

Figure 5. **B**. *Flattened representation of a Cubitermes network (M11).* **A**. *Random network complying with the same spatial constraints as B (that is, only physically adjacent nodes can be connected), but with randomized connections.* **C**. *"Maximum betweenness" network obtained by iteratively removing low-betweenness edges (see the main text for a more accurate description). The node and edge colouring marks the network diameter in each of the three figures. The diameter contains 44 nodes in A, 23 in B and 17 in C.*

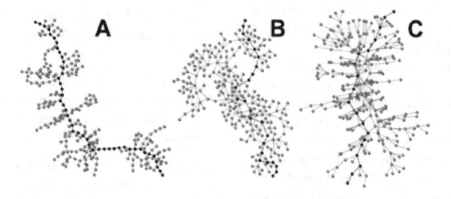

networks: purely local mechanisms, where predetermined rules of behavior lead to the arrangement of simple motifs in an efficient way, and mechanisms involving a distributed estimation of the global form and function of the structure.

Predetermined local rules of behavior can be thought of as genetically determined behavioral modules that have been optimized throughout evolution. The family of networks that can be grown through this class of mechanisms is completely specified by the local rules and their probabilistic range of application. This implies that there is no fine-tuning of parameters during the growth of the individual network or structure and in response to the current performance.

Even if the network gets close to optimal performance at some stage of its growth, this does not affect its subsequent evolution (e.g. trapping the system into a local optimum) for the simple reason that the global performance is not evaluated by this class of mechanisms.

However, purely local mechanisms do not allow for a dynamic optimization or fine tuning of the properties of a structure to fulfill unpredicted requirements, because the family of possible results and their frequency of appearance is predetermined. On the contrary, mechanisms involving an estimation of global properties allow the structure to adapt to new conditions but can only work on already functional structures and are more likely to be important at later stages of network formation.

When the size of a structure is much bigger than the size of insects, insects cannot directly estimate the global properties of their network. We have discussed how some of these properties can be inferred from local properties that correspond to the ratios between two global properties.

Another mechanism that is likely to provide social insects with cues about the shape and size of a structure much bigger than themselves is the exploitation of naturally occurring environmental gradients. Temperature, humidity, irradiation and other physical and chemical quantities are not uniform throughout the environment, but may form spatio-temporal gradients at different scales. The moisture of soil increases with depth, wind speed increases with height above ground, thermal fluctuations decrease when moving deep underground. It seems plausible that these gradients act as cues, e.g. to indicate to the insects the depth of a tunnel, or the height of a nest.

Gradients of temperature and humidity were shown to drive digging activity in ants (Thomé, 1972; Hangartner, 1969), and air currents change the properties of macroscopic spatial structures realized by ants (Jost et al., 2007) e.g. triggering their building behavior (their probability to drop new pellets) (Bollazzi, 2007).

We can speculate that the gradient of humidity, coming from the soil and moistening the nest walls could provide *Cubitermes* termites with information about the current height of their nest. This would explain the fact that, in a small sample of nests, the nests originating from Savannah regions (with higher insulation and desiccation rates) are on average shorter than nests originating from shaded forest regions. However, the data currently available are not sufficient to resolve this issue.

This paper is mostly about biology: we try to understand the mechanisms of network optimization in real insect societies. We hope that our work will be a source of inspiration to computer scientists willing to explore similar mechanisms beyond the biologically plausible.

Often, the models made by biologists do not have to go back "into the jungle", they need not be functional copies of the biological system. On the contrary, bio-inspired systems are usually required to have full functionality. For this reason, we look at bio-inspired systems also as the real "ultimate test" of biological hypotheses.

ACKNOWLEDGMENTS

This work was supported by a research grant from the MESOMORPH project (French National Research Agency ANR-06-BYOS-0008). Andrea Perna would like to acknowledge John Wenzel (Ohio State University) for inspiring discussion. We are grateful to Sergi Valverde for comments to an earlier draft of this paper.

REFERENCES

Acosta, F. J., Lopez, F., & Serrano, J. M. (1993). Branching angles of ant trunk trails as an optimization cue. *Journal of Theoretical Biology, 160*(3), 297–310. doi:10.1006/jtbi.1993.1020

Anthonisse, J. M. (1971). *The rush in a directed graph.* Technical report, Stichting matematisch centrum, Amsterdam.

Boccaletti, S., Latora, V., Moreno, Y., Chavez, M., & Hwang, D. (2006). Complex networks: Structure and dynamics. *Physics Reports – Review Section of Physics Letters, 424*, 175-308.

Bollazzi, M., & Roces, F. (2007). To build or not to build: circulating dry air organizes collective building for climate control in the leaf-cutting ant Acromyrmex ambiguus. *Animal Behaviour, 74*, 1349–1355. doi:10.1016/j.anbehav.2007.02.021

Bonabeau, E., Dorigo, M., & Theraulaz, G. (1999). *Swarm intelligence: From natural to artificial systems.* Oxford University Press.

Buffon, G.-L. L. (1753). *Histoire naturelle générale et particulière avec la description du cabinet du roi*, tome IV. Imprimerie Royale, Paris. Retrieved August 15, 2010, from http://gallica. bnf. fr/ ark:/12148/bpt6k9749f

Buhl, J., Gautrais, J., Deneubourg, J. L., & Theraulaz, G. (2004). Nest excavation in ants: Group size effects on the size and structure of tunneling networks. *Naturwissenschaften, 91*(12), 602–606. doi:10.1007/s00114-004-0577-x

Buhl, J., Gautrais, J., Solé, R., Kuntz, P., Valverde, S., Deneubourg, J. L., & Théraulaz, G. (2004a). Efficiency and robustness in ant networks of galleries. *The European Physical Journal B, 42*, 123–129. doi:10.1140/epjb/e2004-00364-9

Buhl, J., Hicks, K., Miller, E., Persey, S., Alinvi, O., & Sumpter, D. (2009). Shape and efficiency of wood ant foraging networks. *Behavioral Ecology and Sociobiology, 63*, 451–460. doi:10.1007/s00265-008-0680-7

Darwin, C. (1859). *The origin of species by means of natural selection or the preservation of favoured races in the struggle for life*. Retrieved August 15, 2010, from http://www. literature. org/ authors/ darwin-charles/the-origin-of-species-6th-edition/

Deneubourg, J. L., Aron, S., Goss, S., & Pasteels, J. (1990). The self organizing exploratory pattern of the Argentine ant. *Journal of Insect Behavior, 3*, 159–168. doi:10.1007/BF01417909

Deneubourg, J. L., Aron, S., Goss, S., Pasteels, J. M., & Duerinck, G. (1986). Random behaviour, amplification processes and number of participants: How they contribute to the foraging properties of ants. *Physica D. Nonlinear Phenomena, 2*, 176–186. doi:10.1016/0167-2789(86)90239-3

Franks, N. R., Wilby, A., Silverman, B. W., & Tofts, C. (1992). Self-organizing nest construction in ants: Sophisticated building by blind bulldozing. *Animal Behaviour, 44*, 357–375. doi:10.1016/0003-3472(92)90041-7

Goss, S., Aron, S., Deneubourg, J. L., & Pasteels, J. (1989). Self-organized shortcuts in the Argentine ant. *Naturwissenschaften, 76*, 579–581. doi:10.1007/BF00462870

Grassé, P. P. (1959). La reconstruction du nid et les coordinations interindividuelles chez Bellicositermes natalensis et Cubitermes sp. La théorie de la stigmergie: essai d'interprétation du comportement des termites constructeurs. *Insectes Sociaux, 6*, 41–83. doi:10.1007/BF02223791

Hangartner, W. (1969). Carbon dioxide, a releaser for digging behavior in Solenopsis geminata (Hymenoptera: Formicidae). *Psyche, 76*, 58–67. doi:10.1155/1969/58428

Jost, C., Verret, J., Casellas, E., Gautrais, J., Challet, M., & Lluc, J. (2007). The interplay between a self-organized process and an environmental template: Corpse clustering under the influence of air currents in ants. *Journal of the Royal Society, Interface, 4*(12), 107–116. doi:10.1098/rsif.2006.0156

Latora, V., & Marchiori, M. (2001). Efficient behavior of small-world networks. *Physical Review Letters, 87*(19). doi:10.1103/PhysRevLett.87.198701

Lee, S. H., Bardunias, P., & Su, N. Y. (2007). Optimal length distribution of termite tunnel branches for efficient food search and resource transportation. *Bio Systems, 90*, 802–807. doi:10.1016/j.biosystems.2007.04.004

Mallon, E. B., & Franks, N. R. (2000). Ants estimate area using Buffon's needle. *Proceedings. Biological Sciences, 267*, 765–770. doi:10.1098/rspb.2000.1069

Parker, G., & Smith, J. (1990). Optimality theory in evolutionary biology. *Nature, 348*, 27–33. doi:10.1038/348027a0

Perna, A., Jost, C., Valverde, S., Gautrais, J., Theraulaz, G., & Kuntz, P. (2008). The topological fortress of termites. *Bio-Inspired Computing and Communication, LNCS, 5151*, 165–173. doi:10.1007/978-3-540-92191-2_15

Perna, A., Valverde, S., Gautrais, J., Jost, C., Solé R., Kuntz, P., & Theraulaz, G. (2008a). Topological efficiency in three-dimensional gallery networks of termite nests. *Physica A Statistical Mechanics and its Applications, 387*(24), 6235–6244.

Pirk, C. W. W., Hepburn, H. R., Radloff, S. E., & Tautz, J. (2004). Honeybee combs: Construction through a liquid equilibrium process? *Naturwissenschaften, 91*, 350–353. doi:10.1007/s00114-004-0539-3

Solé, R. V., Bonabeau, E., Delgado, J., Fernandez, P., & Marın, J. (2000). Pattern formation and optimization in army ant raids. *Artificial Life, 6*(3), 219–226. doi:10.1162/106454600568843

Thomé, G. (1972). Le nid et le comportement de construction de la fourmi *Messor Ebeninus*, Forel (Hymenoptera, Formicoidea). *Insectes Sociaux, 19*, 95–103. doi:10.1007/BF02224727

Thompson, D. W. (1992). *On growth and form: The complete revised edition*. Dover.

Turner, J. S. (2000). *The extended organism: The physiology of animal-built structures*. Cambridge, MA: Harvard University Press.

Valverde, S., Corominas-Murtra, B., Perna, A., Kuntz, P., Theraulaz, G., & Sole, R. V. (2009). Percolation in insect nest networks: Evidence for optimal wiring. *Physical Review E (Statistical. Nonlinear, and Soft Matter Physics, 79*(6), 066106. doi:10.1103/PhysRevE.79.066106

ENDNOTES

[1] There is an interesting analogy with the thermodynamical notion of extensive and intensive properties. Extensive properties of a system are physical quantities whose value is proportional to the size of the system or the amount of material contained in it: the volume, the mass, the number of molecules. Their value cannot be obtained sampling the system at a particular position. By contrast, intensive properties are scale invariant: they do not depend on the size of the system. These are the pressure, the density etc. The ratio between two extensive quantities is an intensive quantity that can always be estimated on a local basis.

[2] Removing the edge with lowest betweenness is a simplification not completely correct in the context of "local mechanisms". A purely local mechanism could be "remove the edge with lowest betweenness among those in the neighbourhood of a randomly chosen vertex".

Chapter 8
Network Energy Driven Wireless Sensor Networks

Swades De
Indian Institute of Technology Delhi, India

Shouri Chatterjee
Indian Institute of Technology Delhi, India

ABSTRACT

Scarcity of energy in tiny battery-powered wireless sensor nodes have led to a tremendous amount of research thrust at all protocol levels in wireless networks. Despite efficient design of the underlying communication protocols, limited battery energy primarily restricts the usage of nodes and hence the lifetime of the network. As a result, although there has been a lot of promise of pervasive networking via sensors, limited energy of the nodes has been a major bottleneck to deployment feasibility and cost of such a network. With this view, alongside many innovative network communication protocol research to increase nodal as well as network lifetime, there have been significant ongoing efforts on how to impart energy to the depleted batteries on-line. In this chapter, we propose to apply the lessons learnt from our surrounding nature and practices of the living world to realize network energy operated field sensors. We show that, although the regular communicating nodes may not benefit from network energy harvesting, by modifying the carrier sensing principle in a hierarchical network setting, the low power consuming field nodes can extend their lifetimes, or even the scavenged RF energy can be sufficient for the uninterrupted processing and transmission activities of the field nodes.

INTRODUCTION

A common challenge in wireless sensor networks is the limited energy resource of field nodes. Existing techniques on increasing network lifetime aim at efficient processor design and network protocol level solutions, none of which can help replenish the drained battery of a field sensor node. Many

deployment scenarios in hazardous and inaccessible terrains demand that once the sensor nodes are deployed they cannot be physically accessed for replacing the drained batteries. Also, since the field nodes could be hundreds of thousands in number in many cases, once deployed, it is not feasible to physically access all of them for recharging. This restriction puts a huge cost

DOI: 10.4018/978-1-61350-092-7.ch008

of network operation and waste of technology resources, as new nodes need to be redeployed to replace the existing nodes that have drained batteries but are otherwise functionally capable. Even if the energy drained nodes can be collected and recharged, off-line recharging solution adds disruption to the network operation. Certainly, a disruption-free network operation, which requires online recharging of the sensor nodes, would add a significant value to the physical world networking via field sensors.

One technology that serves the purpose of disruption-free operation is energy harvesting -- a process by which energy is derived from an external ambient source. The available online recharging solutions in the research literature propose to use natural energy resources, such as solar (Raghunathan, et al., 2005), vibration (Meninger, et al., 2001; Roundy, et al., 2004), wind (Weimer, et al., 2006), thermal gradient and strain (Starner, 1996; Shenck and Paradiso, 2001; Gonzalez, et al., 2002), etc., as well as a combination of them (Kansal, et al., 2007), (Paradiso and Starner, 2005; the references therein), which are available subject to the specific deployment scenarios. The possibility of charging wireless node batteries from ambient (other than in-network) radio frequency (RF) energy sources is also being investigated via suitable broadband rectenna designs, e.g., (Hagerty, et al., 2004). Since the non-network ambient RF signal can be of any polarization and frequency, the rectenna design has to be adaptive and uniquely designed for wireless recharging only.

Wireless energy transfer from dedicated RF sources is being studied (Paing, et al., 2007) and commercialized (Powercast Corp., 2010; Wild-Charge Technology, 2010; E-coupled technology, 2010). Wild charge technology is based on MIT's wireless electricity technology. E-coupled technology provides wireless energy transfer using electromagnetic induction. The RF technique is also being investigated for solar energy transfer from space to the earth at a mega scale (MIT

Space Solar Power Workshop, 2007). While RF energy transfer technique at a low power domain has been demonstrated to be feasible, in general energy transfer by RF waves involves significant waste of energy due to power law decay of RF signal power with distance. Also, in a remote area deployment setting such an approach to power a large number of spatially dispersed nodes may prove inefficient.

As an alternative and possibly a more generic and cost-effective solution, we propose to harvest the available network RF energy in a field deployment scenario for powering the field sensors. This approach does not require any special antenna design, as the RF energy is available in the same frequency band and with same polarization as the desired information signal. To this end, we use our observations from the surrounding nature and propose to put in effect the learning from practices of the living world.

Motivation: Learning from Nature

The network RF energy harvesting concept is an attempt to build a communication system that mimics thermo-regulation in animals and plants. Animals other than humans regulate and maintain their own body temperature with certain behavioral traits and physiological adjustments. Below, through examples from the living world, the different concepts in a network energy driven sensor network are presented.

- Desert lizards bask in the sun and absorb solar heat. They may also absorb heat by conduction from heated rocks that have stored radiant solar energy. An energy scavenging communication network absorbs ambient RF (or solar, or any other form of ambient energy). This RF energy absorbed could have been transmitted from a super node (analogous to the sun), or from any other node (analogous to reflected heat from rocks.)

- Animals living in extreme cold environments, such as the emperor penguin, maintain their body temperature by preventing heat loss. Their fur is extremely dense to increase the amount of insulation. Emperor penguins also engage in kleptothermy, in which they share or even steal each others body warmth (Jacquet, 2005). An in-network energy scavenging sensor network can be viewed analogous to a community of emperor penguins. At an individual level, the nodes are efficient, with minimized leakage and other losses. At a network level, the RF energy is a shared resource that can be used, and re-absorbed and re-used.

- Sharing of energy among emperor penguins allow them to tolerate extreme cold temperatures of Antarctica (annual average temperature of −50 °C). During extreme snowstorms and blizzards, the emperor penguins huddle together and form a circle. All the penguins within the circle share each others body heat. Heat radiated by one penguin is absorbed by another. Only penguins on the circumference of the ring radiate some of their heat out of the circle. The concept is explained in Figure 1.

- To cope with limited food resources and extreme low temperatures, certain animals and plants hibernate. Certain mammals are known to hibernate in underground burrows and remain in stasis for long periods. Deciduous plants shed all leaves in autumn and stop all activities, awaiting spring (Attenborough, 1995). In an energy scavenging sensor network, in the absence of energy resources, a scavenging node may go into power down (sleep) mode. In the sleep mode, all communication activity is terminated and the sensor node survives, collecting energy from the ambient environment. Once sufficient resources are available, the sensor node wakes up and restarts communication activity.

In essence, the field sensor network can learn significantly from the natural science to adapt its activity with the available resources in the surrounding. While more advances in nodal architecture would be required to achieve such close-to-nature solutions, in this chapter we propose a first step solution to use the conventionally discarded energy that is otherwise available within the system.

Figure 1. Analogy between a community of emperor penguins and an energy scavenging sensor network

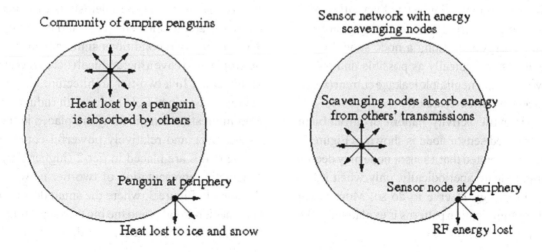

Network Architecture and Access Framework

An on-line recharging process would be truly effective when the energy gain from recharging is at least equal to the loss due to nodal activities and leakage during the sleep mode. Below, we address two major aspects which will have impact on the meaningful network RF energy harvesting process. These are nodal activity pattern, and network architecture.

Nodal Architecture and Activity Pattern

First, each node is assumed equipped with a rectifying circuit associated with the antenna and rechargeable energy storage unit.

In conventional CSMA (carrier-sense multiple access), when a neighboring transmission is detected (i.e., the carrier is sensed busy), to save energy, a node would go to sleep mode during a pre-decided backoff duration. Or, if the communication activity of the nodes are sporadic, a node remains in sleep mode unless it has something to communicate. In contrast to the traditional approaches, in the network energy scavenging principle, whenever a node is not communicating, it should attempt to collect energy from the ongoing neighboring transmissions by directing the received signal power to the rectification and recharging unit.

Since communication related activities consume the most energy, to have energy gain from network energy harvesting a node should communicate as sporadically as possible and has to have very little or negligible leakage current (when its processing circuits are off).

A schematic activity pattern of an ambient RF energy fed sensor node is shown in Figure 2, where it is depicted that a sensor node may decide to communicate aperiodically, only when it has sufficient energy reserve to do so. More about nodal communication patterns is explained in the following subsection.

Network Architecture

Shortcoming of single-tier architecture: One question that appears from Figure 2 is, on one hand higher nodal transmission activities mean availability of more in-network RF energy for harvesting, but at the cost of more energy consumption of the communicating nodes. On the other hand, lesser communication activities (i.e., longer sleep duty cycle) mean more energy saving of the communicating nodes, but at the cost of lesser available RF energy for harvesting. Thus, in a network with a single-tier architecture, these two conditions are contradictory to each other, because if all nodes run with a common principle, say all tend to sleep as long as possible, then the network RF energy will also diminish, thereby reducing the chance of sufficiently recharging the nodes during their sleep periods. Similarly, if the nodes' sleep duty cycle is reduced, the energy loss in the communication cycles cannot be made up by recharging during the shortened sleep cycles. In fact, with an identical set of nodes the only stable condition for achieving perpetual battery life time would be perpetual CPU power down of all nodes (assuming zero leakage during the power down state). Thus, a network consisting of only homogeneous nodes cannot sustain solely from network energy harvesting.

The tiered network architecture: For a sensor node to preserve its energy a longer sleep duration is desirable, and to replenish its lost energy sufficient ambient RF energy would be required. To fulfil the two conditions simultaneously, the network has to have a hierarchical (tiered) network architecture. In a two-tier architecture, the more energy constrained field nodes with rudimentary communication functionality are placed in tier-1 (lower tier), and relatively powerful communication nodes are placed in tier-2 (higher tier). A schematic representation of two-tier network is depicted in Figure 3, where the small dots represent the tier-1 nodes and the big dots represent the tier-2 nodes. Clearly, a tier-1 node's transmission

Figure 2. An illustration of a field node's activity behavior as a function of amount of harvested RF energy

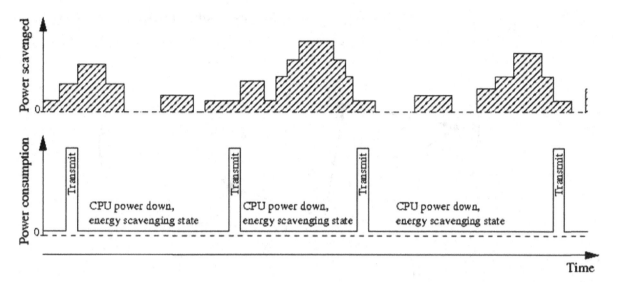

range and sensing coverage has to be about half a tier-2 node's communication range.

The tier-1 field nodes have sensing and very basic communication functionality, namely, the ability to only transmit its data, and are star connected with the router nodes. A field node remains sporadically active and wirelessly transmits (without expecting an acknowledgment) its sensed data to a router to which it is attached, and during its processor inactivity period it is expected to replenish its battery from the network RF energy that is available due to the tier-2 nodes' communication activities. No channel access coordination is done in field nodes' data transmission. The activity of the field nodes being very infrequent and aperiodic, data loss probability due to this uncoordinated communication is expected to be at an acceptable minimum level. While the data loss issue is of interest from network throughput perspective, recharging capability of the field nodes as a function of tier-2 nodes' communication activity is of critical importance with respect to energy availability at the field nodes for their sustained activity.

A tier-2 router node has full-fledged communication capabilities and it can communicate with

any one of the nearby tier-2 nodes to transfer the collected data toward a sink. They form a multihop ad hoc network among themselves in accumulating and forwarding data and contending for channel access. The energy consumption of the tier-2 nodes will be much higher. In this discussion we will assume that they have uninterrupted power supply. In practice uninterrupted tier-2 network operation can be achieved by either introducing nodal mobility (replacing the energy depleted nodes and reconfiguring the network connectivity) or having some kind of recharge capability from other natural energy sources, such as photovoltaic energy. However, our motivation of having a tiered network architecture is to replenish the lost energy of lower tier nodes by network RF energy generated from regular communication activities of higher tier nodes, and achieving operation of lower tier nodes without the constraint of battery lifetime by judicious choice of activity duty cycle as a function of network RF energy.

Note that, even in a two-tier architecture a stable condition for perpetual battery life of field nodes exists where the nodes in both tiers are in power down state. This is a non-working stable solution, however the network can move into or

Figure 3. A two-tier architecture of sensing and wireless ad hoc communication network

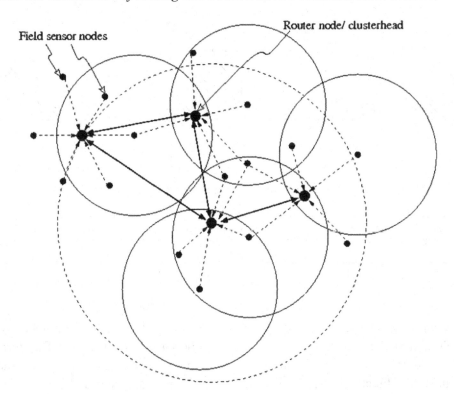

come out of this state as desired, with the help of intelligent tier-2 nodes. In a working stable state of the network, a field node can adjust its duty cycle by the amount of network energy it receives. The tier-2 nodes in turn, can control the activity cycle of tier-1 nodes by adjusting their own communication states (dummy or valid). In a truly battery-less operation of field nodes, when the network wakes up, a field node will first charge itself from the network RF energy, which can be possibly generated by dummy communications among tier-2 nodes. Likewise, when desired, the tier-2 nodes can turn off their own activities to shut down the network.

The proposed solution of network energy driven field sensors is obviously suited for low rate remote telemetry applications, such as structural health monitoring, field crop growth monitoring etc. For faster and real-time applications, however, perpetually network operated solutions may not be feasible – particularly with the current state of

the technology. More will be discussed in Section 5, when we present the case for nodal activity patterns as a function of network energy resource.

It may also be noted that, the router (tier-2) nodes still need to power/recharge themselves from external energy sources. Thus, while the network energy harvesting attempts to utilize the otherwise-unwanted (and unused) network RF energy to recharge the field (tier-1) nodes, this process reduces only to some extent the need for additional energy sources. Nevertheless, since the field nodes are generally much larger in number compared to the router nodes, the network energy harvesting by the field nodes could significantly reduce the cost of network operation. Additionally, reduction of the scale of external powering requirements implies that conventional charging techniques of the router nodes, such as, using non-network unconventional energy sources, mobility based solutions, etc. can be feasibly employed.

Available RF Power at a Field Node

Let us have an estimate of network RF power available for harvesting at a field node. In a two-tier architecture, each field (tier-1) sensor (also called scavenging node) has at least one router (tier-2) node in its one-hop communication range, to which it can be associated with for sending its sensed data. Due to power law decay of signal power with distance, the available power at a field node from a d distance away transmitter is:

$$P_r\left(d\right) = \frac{kP_t}{d^\gamma},$$

where P_t is the power of the transmitted signal, γ is the path loss exponent, and k is a constant which is a function of transmitter and receiver antenna gains, transmitter antenna system losses, and the operating frequency.

If there are n such transmitting router nodes from where a field node can harvest energy, the total available power is the sum of the individual RF signal powers at the field node. The number n can be determined from the knowledge of distance of the nearest transmitter to the field node and the field node's energy reception sensitivity. Also, the total available power at a field node can be calculated if its distances from all simultaneously transmitting neighboring routers are known. However, the distance of neighboring transmitters is a random number that depends on the nodal deployment and activity patterns, and is also governed by the CSMA/CA access mechanism. Therefore, although finding the total power available from all nearby transmitters is an interesting aspect of investigation, its quantification is quite involved. Instead, here we give an intuitive understanding on the order of available power which is sufficient to establish the proof of concept of network energy harvesting.

As depicted in Figure 3, it is most likely that at any time only one transmitting node has the least distance to a field node. Therefore, the power available at a field node due to the nearest transmitter will be the highest, and its energy contribution will likely suppress all other contributions. The nearer the closest transmitter, the further away will be the other neighboring transmitters within the field node's energy sensitivity range, and hence the weaker will be the contribution of other transmitters' power. On the other hand, if the distance from nearest transmitter is large, say, when it is located at the periphery of the field node's communication range, the contribution of other transmitters will not significantly increase the available power, as the highest contribution itself is low. For example, if the highest contribution is –60 dBm, the next highest contribution can make the total available power only up to –57 dBm. Backed with the above observation, the approximate available power at a field node can be estimated as the power due to the nearest node only.

For $\gamma = 2.5$ and with isotropic antennas, the available RF power versus distance from a transmitter is shown in Figure 4 where, for simplicity, the time dependent signal energy fluctuation due to channel uncertainty is discounted. Clearly, for a given leakage power and rectification efficiency, there is a maximum distance from where the field node can harvest RF energy. Beyond this distance the gain from energy harvesting shadowed by the leakage losses of the node. With the same parameter setting, the effect of increased transmission activity of a tier-2 node on the available power at a fixed distance away field node is shown in Figure 5. Although there is an increase in available power with tier-2 nodes' transmission activity, which is intuitive, the gain does not change sharply with transmission probability. Below, we will evaluate how the available power at a field node is translated to its sustainable communication activity.

Network RF Energy Harvesting Versus Field Nodes' Activity Pattern

Energy Requirement of Tier-1 Nodes

Currently available off-the-shelf RFICs have high leakage and active mode consumptions. For example, the leakage current of CC1100 RFIC (Texas Instrument, 2009) is nearly 1 μA, active mode current consumption is about 30 mA, and the lowest operating voltage is 1.8 V. In contrast, specialized sensor nodes with just basic communication capabilities (so called 'reduced function devices') are expected to consume much less communication-related energy, and for network RF energy harvesting to be viable, the leakage consumption should be minimized. To this effect, a recent miniature processor design for sensor network applications (Seok, et al., 2008) has CPU leakage power consumption in the sleep mode only about 30 pW and energy consumption per

activity cycle only 2.8 pJ. In another development, the system-on-chip in (Wong, et al., 2008) for low power transceiver operation runs at about 1 V and consumes a little above 2 mA current during transmit and receive modes.

Let us consider a scenario where the tier-1 (scavenger) nodes are equipped with ultra-low power transceivers (Wong, et al., 2008). To save energy, the communication circuit of such a node is programmed to operate only in 'transmit' mode to send (broadcast) its sensed data to a clusterhead (a tier-2 node) once in a while, without being able to care for its (un)successful delivery. The transceiver operates at a normal voltage $V_{on} = 1.2$ V and utilizes an internal current of $I_{on} = 2.635$ mA for a transmission power output of −7 dBm. Thus, for a transmission of duration T_{on} sec, the energy consumed by a tier-1 node would be: $E_{on} = V_{on}I_{on}T_{on} = 3.162T_{on}$ mJ. During rest of the time T_{sleep} sec, while the node harvests energy, the nodal processor remains in deep sleep mode, which

Figure 4. Available power at a field node versus its distance from a tier-2 transmitter. Transmission probability of a tier-2 node is 0.3. Operating frequency and transmit power are taken as 915 MHz and 5 dBm, respectively.

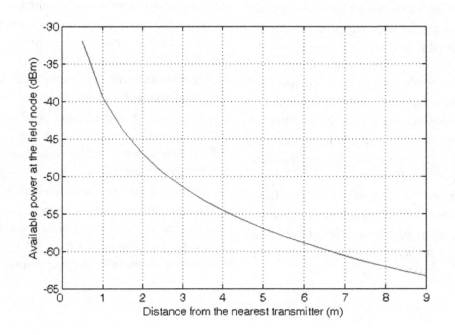

Figure 5. Available power at a field (scavenger) node versus transmission probability of a tier-2 node. Transmitter-to-scavenger distance is 4 m.

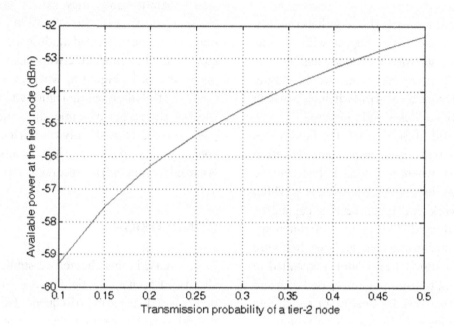

could consume as low as P_{leak} = 30 pW (Seok, et al., 2008). The corresponding energy consumption would be: $E_{leak} = P_{leak} T_{sleep}$ pJ.

Condition of Gain from Network RF Energy Harvesting

If P_a is the available power at a field node and η is the rectification efficiency, the harvested power is $P_{scav} = \eta P_a$. Network energy harvesting gain at a tier-1 node will be positive when the tolerable leakage power is: $P_{leak} < P_{scav}$. Additionally, the condition for network energy powered perpetual operation of sensor nodes is:

$$T_{sleep} = \frac{E_{on}}{P_{scav} - P_{leak}}.$$

To take a look into the effect of P_{leak} and η on the achievable transmission duty cycle of network energy operated tier-1 nodes, we assume data frames are of length 40 Bytes, and the

transmission rate is 250 kbps. It can be easily computed that, if the sleep state consumption of a field node is more than a few nanowatts (as in CC1100), even at a 10% rectification efficiency the field node operation cannot be sustained solely by network RF energy. On the other hand, with about 30% transmission activity at tier-2 nodes and a 30 pW leakage power at a tier-1 node, possible transmission duty cycle of tier-1 field nodes is shown in Figure 6. It shows that, at a lower rectification efficiency, an acceptable distance of network energy operated field nodes around a tier-2 node reduces sharply. For example, at 1% rectification efficiency, a 3 meter away field node can operate by only network energy at a transmit duty cycle of about less than once-a-day. At η = 10%, the transmit duty cycle of a 3 meter away node is however increased to once in every 97 min. Overall it appears that, with the available new ultra-low power processor and transceiver technologies, leakage consumption is not the main bottleneck; rather rectification efficiency sets the operational limit.

Suggested Modification of Transmitter/ Transceiver RF Module

To enable a node for network energy harvesting, a scavenger node should be equipped with conventional signal transmission-reception capabilities as well as the RF energy rectifying circuit, and the node should have a control of switching between the two functionalities at right instants.

As discussed in Section III, the field nodes are equipped with only basic communication functionalities, wherein a node is just capable of transmitting its sensed data once in a while. To add network energy harvesting capability, the suggested modification in a rudimentary communication capable node is shown in Figure 7, where an additional circulator is installed to switch between transmitting the sensed data and receiving the network RF energy for recharging its energy storage unit. The switch connecting the energy unit and the transmitter module is triggered on just when it has sufficient energy to drive the transmitter module.

Although the tier-1 (scavenger) nodes in our discussion are considered having basic transmission capability only, they can in principle be transceivers as well. In case of a scavenging transceiver, the suggested modification of the RF module to accommodate network energy scavenging is shown in Figure 8, wherein a controller (gate) controls the communication and recharging functionalities. For example, the node could be placed in receive mode only when it has sufficient energy to drive the processing circuits and there is a need (command) for receiving a specific data.

CONCLUSION

In summary, in this chapter we studied the possibility of recharging field sensor nodes using otherwise unwanted radio frequency (RF) waves in a wireless ad hoc sensor network. The advantage of this solution is that, the scavenger nodes do not have to rely upon any extraneous energy sources (such as solar, vibration, ambient RF from other

Figure 6. Sustainable transmission duty cycle versus transmitter-to-scavenger distance at various rectification efficiency. A tier-2 node's transmission probability is 0.3, and the leakage power of a tier-1 node is 30 pW.

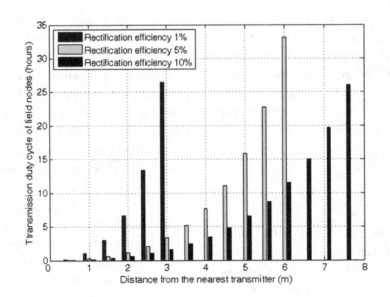

Figure 7. (a) Conventional transmitter; (b) modified transmitter for recharging from network energy.

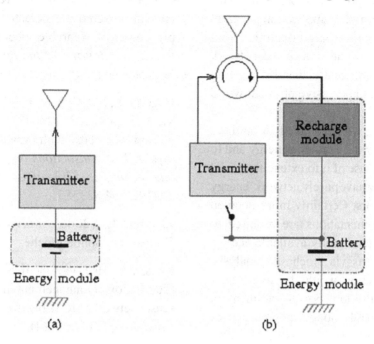

Figure 8. (a) Conventional transceiver; (b) modified transceiver for recharging from network energy.

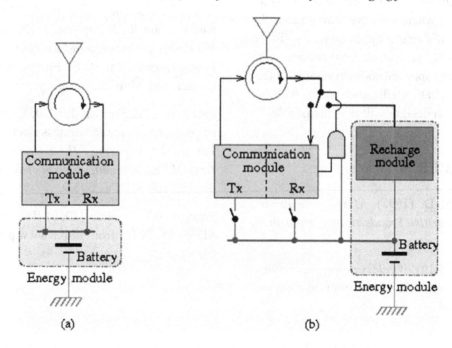

networks, etc.), as proposed in prior art, the availability of which are rather application scenario specific. A feasible online charging solution from network RF energy would reduce the network maintenance cost significantly, thereby reducing the main bottleneck to pervasive physical world networking.

In this discourse, we have taken an intuitive approach to quantify the available energy and to justify how to make use of it to extend the nodal lifetime and possibly have purely network-energy operated field sensors. Certainly more detailed analysis and experimentations are required to quantify and validate the truly available energy. Besides investigations via stochastic analysis, an interesting direction would be to actually deploy a set of ultra-low power rudimentary communication capable nodes in presence of regular router nodes, say wireless LAN access points, and measure the usefulness of the available energy in running rudimentary sensing and transmission applications. Our intuitive analysis has outlined the network and device conditions to ensure rudimentary communication activities of field nodes, where we have extrapolated the rectifier circuit's operation capabilities. To be able to run more practicable applications using network-energy operated nodes, further advancement on rectification efficiency along with the smarter antenna designs will play major roles.

REFERENCES

Attenborough, D. (1995). *Movie: The private life of plants. British Broadcasting Corporation.* UK: BBC.

E-Coupled. (2010). *Wireless power technology.* Retrieved March 28, 2010, from http://www.ecoupled.com/

Gonzalez, J. L., Rubio, A., & Moll, F. (2002). Human powered piezoelectric batteries to supply power of wearable electronic devices. *International Journal of the Society of Materials Engineering for Resources, 10*(1), 34–40.

Hagerty, J., Helmbrecht, F., McCalpin, Q., Zane, V., & Popovic, Z. (2004). Recycling ambient microwave energy with broad-band rectenna arrays. *IEEE Transactions on Microwave Theory and Techniques, 52*(3), 1014–1024. doi:10.1109/TMTT.2004.823585

Jacquet, L. (2005). *Movie: La marche de l'empereur.* Bonne Pioche.

Kansal, A., Hsu, J., Zahedi, S., & Srivastava, M. (2007). Power management in energy harvesting sensor networks. *ACM Transactions on Embedded Computing Systems, 6*(4).

Meninger, S., Mur-Miranda, J., Amirtharajah, R., Chandrakasan, A., & Lang, J. H. (2001). Vibration to electric energy conversion. *IEEE Transactions on VLSI, 9*(1), 64–76. doi:10.1109/92.920820

Paing, T., Morroni, J., Dolgov, A., Shin, J., Brannan, J., Zane, R., & Popovic, Z. (2007, October). *Wirelessly-powered wireless sensor platform.* Paper presented at the IEEE European Microwave Conference, Munich, Germany.

Paradiso, J., & Starner, T. (2005). Energy scavenging for mobile and wireless electronics. *IEEE Pervasive Computing / IEEE Computer Society [and] IEEE Communications Society, 4*(1), 18–27. doi:10.1109/MPRV.2005.9

Powercast Corporation. (2010). *Website.* Retrieved March 28, 2010, from http://www.powercastco.com/

Raghunathan, V., Kansal, A., & Hsu, J. Friedman, J., & Srivastava, M. (2005, April). *Design considerations for solar energy harvesting wireless embedded systems.* Paper presented at the International Symposium of Information Processing in Sensor Networks, Los Angeles, CA.

Roundy, S., Wright, P., & Rabaey, J. (2004). *Energy scavenging for wireless sensor networks with special focus on vibrations.* Kluwer Academic Publishers.

Seok, M., Hanson, S., Lin, Y.-S., Foo, Z., Kim, D., & Lee, Y. … Blaauw, D. (2008, June). *The Phoenix processor: A 30pW platform for sensor applications.* Paper presented at the IEEE Symposium on VLSI Citcuits, Honolulu, HI.

Shenck, N., & Paradiso, J. (2001). Energy scavenging with shoe-mounted piezoelectrics. *IEEE Micro, 21*(3), 30–42. doi:10.1109/40.928763

Space Solar Power Workshop, M. I. T. (2007, May). *Terrestrial energy generation based on space solar power: A feasible concept or fantasy?* Cambridge, MA. Retrieved March 8, 2010, from http://web.mit.edu/space_solar_power/

Starner, T. (1996). Human-powered wearable computing. *IBM Systems Journal, 35*(3-4), 618–629. doi:10.1147/sj.353.0618

Texas Instrument. (2009). *CC1100 data sheet.* Retrieved March 8, 2010, from http://focus.ti.com/lit/ds/symlink/cc1100.pdf

Weimer, M., Paing, T., & Zane, R. (2006, January). *Remote area wind energy harvesting for low-power autonomous sensor.* Paper presented at the IEEE Electronics Specialists Conference, Jeju, South Korea.

WildCharge Technology. (2010). *Website.* Retrieved March 28, 2010, from http://www.wildcharge.com/

Wong, A. C. W., Kathiresan, V., Chan, C. K. T., Eljamaly, O., Omeni, O., & McDonagh, D. (2008). A 1 V wireless transceiver for an ultra-low-powerSoC for biotelemetry applications. *IEEE Journal of Solid-state Circuits, 43*(7), 1511–1521. doi:10.1109/JSSC.2008.923717

Chapter 9
Congestion Control in Wireless Sensor Networks Based on the Lotka Volterra Competition Model

Pavlos Antoniou
University of Cyprus, Cyprus

Andreas Pitsillides
University of Cyprus, Cyprus

ABSTRACT

Next generation communication networks are moving towards autonomous wireless infrastructures, as for example, Wireless Sensor Networks (WSNs) that are capable of working unattended under dynamically changing conditions. Over the last few years, WSNs are being developed towards a large number of multimedia streaming applications, e.g., video surveillance, traffic control systems, health monitoring, and industrial process control. However, WSNs face important limitations in terms of energy, memory and computational power. The uncontrolled use of limited resources in conjunction with the unpredictable nature of WSNs in terms of traffic load injection, wireless link capacity fluctuations and topology modifications (e.g. due to node failures) may lead to congestion. Congestion can cause deterioration of the offered quality of service (QoS). This study proposes a bio-inspired congestion control approach for WSNs streaming applications that necessitate controlled performance with graceful degradation. The proposed approach prevents congestion by regulating the rate of each traffic flow based on the Lotka-Volterra competition model. Performance evaluations reveal that the proposed approach achieves adaptability to changing traffic loads, scalability and fairness among flows, while providing graceful performance degradation as the offered load increases.

DOI: 10.4018/978-1-61350-092-7.ch009

INTRODUCTION

Rapid technological advances and innovations in the area of autonomous systems push the vision of Ambient Intelligence from concept to reality. Networks of autonomous wireless sensor devices offer exciting new possibilities for achieving sensory omnipresence: small, (often) inexpensive, untethered sensor devices can observe and measure various environmental parameters, thereby allowing real-time and fine-grained monitoring of physical spaces around us. Wireless Sensor Networks (Akyildiz, 2002), can be used as platforms for health monitoring, battlefield surveillance, environmental observation, industrial control etc.

Despite the utmost importance of performance control, this issue has not been given enough attention from the research community. One of the main reasons is that research on WSNs has been heavily influenced by military applications in which dense, large-scale networks of sensors are expected to be deployed in a random manner, primarily with a view to tracking objects. However, most of the aforementioned critical applications necessitate small-scale networks with planned deployment of sensors close to selected locations/ objects of interest in order to achieve controlled

performance. The proposed approach is designed on the basis of providing performance control for critical applications in small-scale WSNs.

Typically, WSNs consist of small, cooperative devices (nodes) which may be constrained by computation capability, memory space, communication bandwidth and energy supply. However, with the rapid development of low-cost hardware CMOS cameras and microphones, autonomous sensor devices are becoming capable of ubiquitously retrieving multimedia content such as video and audio streams from the environment. This new and emerging type of sensor network, the so-called Wireless Multimedia Sensor Network (WMSN), has drawn the immediate attention of the research community (Akyildiz, 2007). As shown in Figure 1, a number of nodes that at a particular moment sense an event (grey-shaded nodes), can send streaming data through the network, in a multi-hop manner, to a dedicated sink node. Alternatively, some nodes may be constantly sending streaming data to the sink. The unpredictable nature of traffic load injected into the network as well as the uncontrolled use of the scarce network resources (buffer size, wireless channel capacity) are able to provoke *congestion*. Thus, there is an increased need to design novel congestion control strategies

Figure 1. A WSN for wildlife monitoring

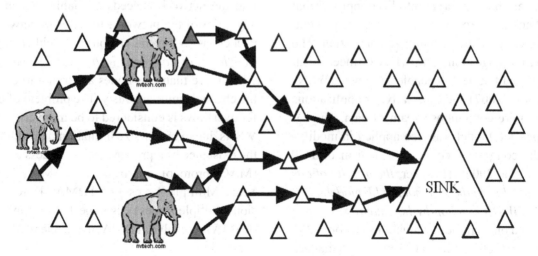

possessing self-* properties like self-adaptability, self-organization as well as scalability, and fairness, which are vital to the mission of dependable multimedia WSNs.

The focal point of this study is to propose a *scalable and self-adaptive bio-inspired congestion control mechanism* targeting streaming applications in WSNs for delivering enhanced application fidelity at the sink (in terms of packet delivery ratio and delay) under varying network conditions. More specifically, the *main objective is to provide efficient and smooth rate allocation and control while maintaining fairness and friendliness with interfering flows*. Biological processes which are embedded in decentralized, self-organizing and adapting environments, provide a desirable basis for computing environments that need to exhibit such properties.

Simple mathematical biology models (Brauer, 2000) which aim at modeling biological processes using analytical techniques and tools are often used to study non-linear systems. Population dynamics has traditionally been the dominant branch of mathematical biology which studies how species populations change in time and space and the processes causing these changes. Information about population dynamics is important for policy making and planning and in our case is used for designing a congestion control policy. This study focuses on the Lotka-Volterra (LV) competition model, and proposes a decentralized approach that regulates the rate of every flow in order to prevent, or at least gracefully minimize congestion. The LV-based congestion control (LVCC) mechanism targets small-scale dependable multimedia WSNs (Akyildiz, 2007) and especially for applications that require continuous stream of data. The LV competition model was also applied in modifying the congestion control mechanism of TCP (Hasegawa, 2006). However, *the novelty of our approach lies in the fact that the LV model is applied to WSNs in a hop-by-hop manner*.

Based on analytical evaluations performed in Antoniou (2007), the LVCC model guarantees that the equilibrium point of the system ensures coexistence of all flows, with stability and fairness among active flows under certain conditions. In this paper, the validity of the analytical results is further investigated by simulating complex scenarios that cannot be formally tested. Performance evaluation results showed that the LVCC approach can provide adaptation to dynamic network conditions as well as scalability, fairness and graceful performance degradation among traffic flows when multiple active nodes are involved.

The remainder of this paper is organized as follows. Section 2 deals with the problem of congestion in WSNs, discusses conventional congestion control techniques for WSNs, and introduces the Lotka-Volterra (LV) competition model. Section 3 presents the analogy between WSNs and ecosystems in nature. Section 4 proposes the LV-based Congestion Control (LVCC) mechanism. Section 5 evaluates the performance of our mechanism in terms of stability, scalability and fairness. Section 6 presents future research directions, while Section 7 draws the conclusion.

BACKGROUND

Congestion in WSNs

Congestion occurs when the traffic load injected into the network exceeds available capacity at any point of the network. In wireless networks, packet losses can be attributed to either *buffer overflows*, or *collisions in the wireless medium* when more than one nodes are trying to access the channel simultaneously. The problem of buffer overflows is considered to be more critical in WSNs due to buffer size limitations. In addition, the existence of a proper medium access control (MAC) protocol, e.g. based on CSMA (Carrier Sense Multiple Access) or TDMA (Time Division Multiple Access), is expected to minimize (CSMA) or resolve (TDMA) the wireless medium contention.

Buffer overflows at a sensor node are caused when the incoming traffic load exceeds the outgoing traffic load. In this case, accumulated packets overwhelm buffer capacity. Even at low traffic rates, buffer overflows can be experienced at some point of the network (usually close to the sink) due to the converging (many-to-one) nature of packets from multiple sending nodes to a single sink node. At the same time, wireless channel contention may cause packet loss. As contention becomes more intensive, the waiting time for obtaining the channel for transmission also increases. As a node waits for the channel, additional traffic may arrive filling up its buffer and further increasing packet delays. The discussion above indicates that congestion may cause multiple packet losses, low link utilization (throughput reduction), increase of queueing delays, leading to the deterioration of the offered quality of service (QoS). Increasingly, congestion in WSNs is responsible for energy waste, decrease of network lifetime and even for the decomposition of network topology in multiple components.

In traditional Internet wired networks, congestion control is usually applied in an end-to-end manner, i.e. only the source-destination pair is involved. However, end-to-end congestion control approaches will not be effective in the error-prone wireless multihop networks because the end-to-end nature may result in reduced responsiveness causing increased latency and high error rates, especially during long periods of congestion. In addition, the end-to-end model is not very effective for WSNs, where delivery of data to the sink, without retransmission of any lost packets, is the normal objective. Due to their severely constrained nature, WSNs necessitate autonomous, decentralized, fast time scale congestion control strategies which promise immediate, effective and efficient relief from congestion. Decentralized approaches are expected to adopt a hop-by-hop model where all nodes along a network path can be involved in the procedure. Each node should make decisions based only on local information

(e.g. buffer load, channel load) since none of them has complete information about the system state. This is a desirable feature as it minimizes the exchange of messages, hence improves both energy and congestion.

Conventional Techniques for Congestion Control in WSNs

Early studies in the area of sensor networks had mainly focused on more fundamental networking problems, e.g. medium access control (MAC), topology, routing, and energy efficiency, and had largely ignored network performance assurances. Lately, with the emergence of mission-critical applications (e.g., health monitoring), there has been increased interest in performance control mechanisms, so as to avoid congestion caused by the uncontrolled use of the scarce network resources.

Various congestion control approaches can be found in WSNs literature based on traffic manipulation (e.g. rate adaptation to network changes CODA (Wan, 2003), Fusion (Hull, 2004), IFRC (Rangwala, 2006), ARC (Woo, 2001), multi-path routing BGR (Popa, 2006), CAR (Kumar, 2006), TADR (He, 2008)), topology control (e.g. clustering formation (Karenos, 2006)), and network resource management (e.g. power control, multiple radio interfaces Siphon (Wan, 2005)). Rate control approaches are considered to be the most appropriate when dealing with streaming applications. Rate control is a common technique for alleviating congestion by throttling the injection of traffic in the network.

Some of the rate-based CC schemes CODA (Wan, 2003), IFRC (Rangwala, 2006), ARC (Woo, 2001) and BGR (Popa, 2006) are based on traditional methodologies and protocols known from the Internet, for example, the Additive Increase Multiplicative Decrease (AIMD) rate control mechanism. AIMD uses packet loss as indication of congestion, i.e. increases rate until packet loss and then decreases rate in a multiplicative way.

However, this model is not very effective in WSNs because it provokes a saw-tooth rate behavior which may violate the QoS requirements (e.g. fidelity of a stream). Also the increase of rate until packet loss seems to be inefficient since it may drive a network into congestion, causing high queueing delays. In addition, AIMD-like mechanisms take a long time for data rates to converge in low-rate wireless links, which would cause significant variation in streaming media quality. The proposed mechanism was found to outperform AIMD (see Section 5), providing smooth rate allocation and control while maintaining friendliness among competing flows.

The Lotka-Volterra Competition Model of Mathematical Biology

Non linear systems are often studied in terms of simple mathematical biology models (Brauer, 2000) which aim at modeling natural and biological processes using analytical techniques. Population dynamics has traditionally been the dominant branch of mathematical biology which studies how populations of species change in time and space as well as the processes that cause these changes. Information about population dynamics is of fundamental importance for policy making and planning as, for example in designing a congestion avoidance policy.

Population dynamics can be modeled with a simple balance equation that describes how the overall population size of a species changes from time to time as a result of species interaction with resources, competitors, mutualists and natural enemies. In particular, mathematical models of competition, mutualism and predator-prey which are among the most studied problems in population dynamics for multiple species can be expressed as a set of parameterized difference or differential equations, or dynamical systems. These mathematical models can be divided into two categories, namely, deterministic and stochastic population models. Deterministic population models play a dominant role in the global behavior investigation of large-scale problems in population dynamics, since they allow much more rigorous and detailed investigation of the model potential compared with stochastic population models.

Deterministic models specify a unique dynamic path of the system called trajectory determined by initial conditions.

The proposed approach is based on *a deterministic competition model which involves interactions among species that are able to coexist, in which the fitness of one species is influenced by the presence of other species that compete for at least one limiting resource*. Competition among members of the same species is known as intra-specific competition, while competition between individuals of different species is known as inter-specific competition. An in depth investigation and modeling of competitive interactions between organisms provides an initial basis for predicting outcomes since they may influence species evolution, the structuring of communities (i.e. which species coexist, which die out), and the distributions of species.

One of the most studied mathematical models of population biology, the Lotka Volterra (LV) competition model (Lotka, 1925), (Volterra, 1931), exhibits this behavior. The generalized form of an *n*-species LV system is expressed by a system of ordinary differential equations:

$$\frac{dx_i}{dt} = r_i x_i \left[1 - \frac{\beta_i}{K_i} x_i - \frac{1}{K_i} \left[\sum_{j=1, j \neq i}^{n} \alpha_{ij} x_j \right] \right],$$

(1)

for $I = 1, \ldots, n$, where $x_i(t)$ is the population size of species i at time t, r_i is the intrinsic growth rate of species i in the absence of all other species, βi and αi_j are the intra-specific and the inter-specific competition coefficients respectively. Also K_i is the carrying capacity of species i i.e., the maximum number of individuals that can be sustained by the biotope in the absence of all other species competing for the same resource. If only one resource exists and all species (having the same carrying capacity K) compete for it, then K can be seen as the resource's capacity. Next we will build on this model to develop our approach.

Previous work on congestion control involving mathematical models of population biology was proposed for the Internet on the basis of either improving the current TCP CC mechanism (Analoui, 2006) or providing a new way of combating congestion (Hasegawa, 2006). The study of Analoui (2006) couples the interaction of Internet entities that involved in CC mechanisms (routers, hosts) with the predator-prey interaction. This model exhibits fairness and acceptable throughput but slow adaptation to traffic demand. Recent work by Hasegawa (2006) focuses on a new TCP CC mechanism based on the LV competition model which is applied to the congestion window updating mechanism of TCP. According to the authors, remarkable results in terms of stability, convergence speed, fairness and scalability are exhibited. However, these approaches are based on the end-to-end model of the Internet, which is completely different from the hop-by-hop nature of WSNs. *The novelty of our approach lies in the fact that the LV model is applied to WSNs in a hop-by-hop manner.*

WIRELESS SENSOR NETWORKS: AN ECOSYSTEM VIEW

A WSN is considered to be analogous to an ecosystem. An ecosystem comprises of multiple species that live together and interact with each other as well as the non-living parts of their surroundings (i.e. resources) to meet their needs for survival and coexist. Similarly, a wireless sensor network involves a number of cooperative nodes. Each node has a buffer in order to store packets and is able to initiate a traffic flow. Traffic flows can be seen as species that compete with each other

for available network resources while traversing a set of intermediate nodes forming a multi-hop path leading to the sink. The number of bytes per traffic flow corresponds to the population size of each traffic flow. In analogy with ecosystems, *the goal is expected to be the coexistence of flows*. In the rest of the paper, the terms flows and species are used interchangeably.

To investigate the decentralized and autonomic nature of the proposed approach, a network is divided into smaller neighborhoods called sub-ecosystems. Each sub-ecosystem involves all nodes that send traffic to a particular one-hop-away node (parent node). *The traffic flows initiated by each node play the role of competing species and the buffer (queue) capacity of the parent node can be seen as the limiting resource within the sub-ecosystem.*

Within a virtual ecosystem, participant nodes may perform different roles. In particular, each node is able to either initiate a traffic flow i.e. is a source node (SN), or serve as a relay node (RN) to forward packets of multiple flows passing through it, or perform both roles being a source-relay node (SRN). Source nodes are mostly located at the edges of a network (e.g. leaf nodes) while relay nodes are internal nodes (e.g. backbone nodes). The proposed approach provides hop-by-hop rate adaptation by regulating the traffic flow rate at each node. *Each node is in charge of self-regulating and self-adapting the rate of its traffic flow i.e., the rate at which it generates or forwards packets. The traffic flows compete for available buffer capacity at their one-hop-away receiving node involved in the path leading to the sink.* As shown in *Figure 2*, the traffic flow 5 (initiated by SRN) is composed of traffic flows *1-4*. Each sending node is expected to regulate its traffic flow rate in a way that limiting buffer capacities at all receiving nodes along the network path towards the sink are able to accommodate all received packets. The sending rate evolution of each flow will be driven by variations in buffer occupancies of relay nodes along the network path towards the sink. Due to the decentralized nature of the proposed approach, thus satisfying the need for low communication overhead, each node will regulate its traffic flow rate using local information (i.e. from one-hop away neighbors). As mentioned before, the number of bytes sent by a node within a given period refers to the population size of its flow. From an ecosystem perspective, the population size of each traffic flow (i.e. of each species) is affected by interactions among competing flows (species) as well as the available resources (buffers) capacities.

The LV-based Congestion Control (LVCC) Approach

This section distinguishes the roles of the different entities (SN, RN, and SRN) involved in the congestion avoidance mechanism along the path towards a sink.

Source Node (SN)

As shown in *Figure 3*, pure source nodes (SNs) are end-entities which are attached to the rest of the network through a downstream node e.g., a relay node (RN), or a source-relay node (SRN) located closer to the sink.

Each SN is expected to initiate a traffic flow when triggered by a specific event. The transmission rate evolution of each flow is calculated by Equation 2 (the solution of Equation 1) that gives the number of bytes sent x_i by flow i. In order to be able to solve Equation 1 for a single node i, it is necessary to be aware of the aggregated number of bytes sent from all other nodes $\sum_{j=1,j\neq i}^{n} x_j$ which compete for the same resource. This quantity is denoted by C_i. In decentralized architectures, the underlying assumption of C_i-awareness is quite unrealistic. However, each SN can indirectly obtain this information through a small periodic backpressure signal sent from its downstream SRN/RN (parent node) containing the total number of bytes sent from all parent's children, denoted by BS. Each node can evaluate its neighbors' contribution C_i by subtracting its own contribution x_i from the total contribution BS as expressed by: $C_i = \sum_{j=1,j\neq i}^{n} x_j = BS - x_i$.
Thus, Equation 1 becomes:

Figure 2. Traffic flows competition in WSNs

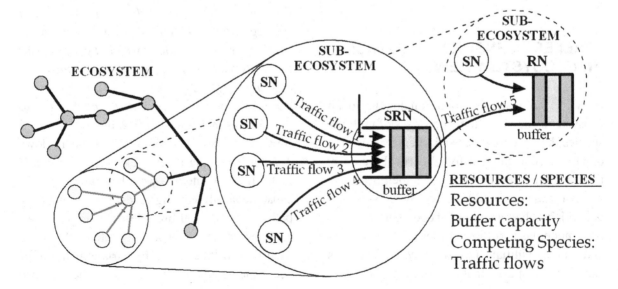

Figure 3. Source nodes competing for a limiting resource at their downstream node

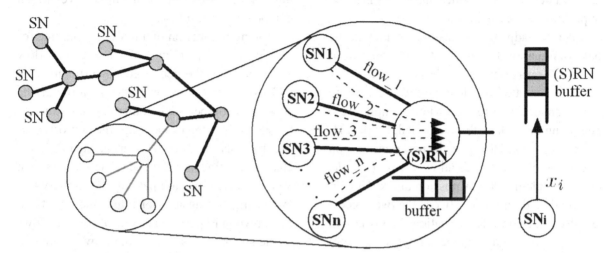

$$\frac{dx_i}{dt} = rx_i \left[1 - \frac{\beta}{K} x_i - \frac{1}{K} C_i \right], \quad i = 1,...,n. \tag{2}$$

Equation 2 is integrated to obtain the calculated transmission rate of each SN, x_i, given by:

$$x_i(t) = \frac{wx_i(0)}{\beta x_i(0) + \left[w - \beta x_i(0) \right] e^{-\frac{wr}{K}t}}, \quad w = K - \alpha C. \tag{3}$$

A recent study by Antoniou (2007) focused on a network (ecosystem) of flows (species) competing for a resource, where the populations of flows (number of bytes sent) are regulated by Equation 3. It was found that such a network has a global non-negative and asymptotically stable equilibrium point when inter-specific competition is weaker than intra-specific competition i.e.,$\beta >$ α and α, $\beta > 0$. Under this condition, the series of values generated by each SN converges to a global and asymptotically stable coexistence solution given by Equation 4. For a detailed proof of this concept refer to \cite{Antoniou}.

$$x_i^* = \frac{K}{\alpha[n-1] + \beta}, \quad i = 1,...n. \tag{4}$$

Furthermore, in order to avoid buffer overflows, it needs to be ensured that when a system of n active nodes converges to the coexistence solution, each node i will be able to send less than or equal to K/n bytes. This is satisfied by Equation 4 when $\alpha[n-1] + \beta > n$ or $\beta-\alpha > \mathbf{n}[1- \alpha$]. *If* we set $\alpha > 1$ a*nd* require $\beta > \alpha$ (*as imp*osed by the equilibrium stability condition), then the aforementioned inequality is always satisfied. Therefore, to ensure both convergence and no buffer overflows the following two conditions must be satisfied:

$$\beta > a, \quad a > 1. \tag{5}$$

The calculated transmission rate of each node, xi(t), $_i$s *i*nitiated by xi(0) a_nd converges to the stable coexistence solution, xi* wit_h *i*n time Tconv. $_{The}$ convergence time, Tconv, $_{can}$ be evaluated by setting xi(Tcon$_v$) $_{= xi}$* (*on t*he basis of Equation 3) and is found to be proportional to parameter α and *in*versely proportional to parameters r. This observation practically means that fast convergence can be achieved using small values of α or large values of r, but further discussion is given in performance evaluations.

Each SN adjusts its transmission rate on the basis of Equation 3. This adjustment is carried out iteratively on a discrete-time basis, projecting the transmission rate from time t to some future time t+T (i.e. over a time period T). For example, at the beginning of the k+1-th time period, t = (k+1)T, Equation 3 is used to obtain the new transmission rate by the following calculation: set (a) xi(0) to the previous calculated transmission rate xi(kT), b) t to the time duration T between the two successive transmission rate evaluations and (c) Ci to Ci(kT) i.e. aggregate number of bytes sent from all competing nodes within the previous period. Therefore, Equation 3 can be expressed in an iterative form as follows:

$$x_i\left((k+1)T\right) = \frac{w\left(kT\right)x_i\left(kT\right)}{\beta x_i\left(kT\right) + \left[w\left(kT\right) - \beta x_i\left(kT\right)\right]e^{-\frac{w(kT)r}{K}T}}$$

$$(6)$$

Equation 6 generates a series of values which correspond to number of bytes sent every period T.

Relay Node (RN)

Pure relay nodes (RNs) are entities which do not generate any packets, but forward packets belong-ing to several flows traversing themselves which compete for their resources.

The main function of a RN is to combine (or multiplex) all incoming flows into a superflow and relay it to the dedicated downstream node (SRN or RN) as shown in *Figure 4*. However, the superflow competes with other flows destined to the same downstream node (e.g., the flow originating from SN in *Figure 4*). Hence, each RN is in charge of acting on behalf of all active upstream nodes whose flows are passing through it when evaluating the transmission rate of the superflow. As shown in *Figure 4*, each one of the four flows of the superflow as well as the flow originating from SN should be allocated equal share of the downstream node's limiting resource. Each RN allocates resources for its active upstream nodes based on a slightly modified expression of Equation 6 as follows:

$$x_{RN}\left((k+1)T\right) = \frac{w\left(kT\right)H\left(kT\right)}{\beta H\left(kT\right) + \left[w\left(kT\right) - \beta x_i\left(kT\right)\right]e^{-\frac{w(kT)r}{K}T}},$$

$$(7)$$

where $H(kT) = x_{RN}(kT)/m$, $w(kT) = K - \alpha C * R_N(kT)$, and m is the total number of active upstream nodes which belong to the tree having RN as root. The number of bytes sent from a superflow within a period kT, xR_N(kT)/, should be equal to the ag-

Figure 4. Relay node creates a superflow which competes for downstream node's buffer

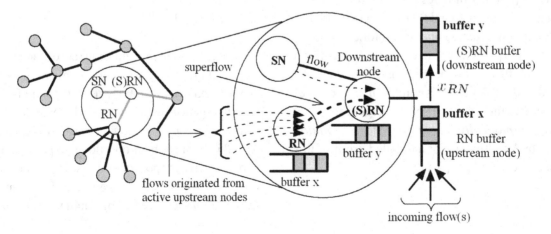

gregated number of bytes sent from m RN's upstream source nodes which compete for RN's buffer. Each RN can calculate the number of its active upstream nodes, m, by examining the source id field of each packet traversing itself. $C*R_{N(}kT)$ reflects the total number of bytes sent ($BS)$ to the downstream node ($(S)RN$ in F*igure 4)* from all its competing children nodes, subtracting the contribution of a single flow belonging to the superflow. $C*R_{N(}kT)$ can be expressed as:

$$C^*_{RN}\left(kT\right) = BS - \frac{x_{RN}\left(kT\right)}{m}. \qquad (8)$$

If the calculated transmission rate of a superflow is less than the aggregated transmission rate of all incoming flows consisting the superflow, a number of packets is expected to be accumulated in buffer x. Thus, the available buffer capacity at buffer x will be progressively decreased causing upstream nodes to decrease their calculated sending rates. In this way, congestion phenomena can be prevented.

Source-Relay Node (SRN)

A source-relay node (SRN) acts as both source and relay node, having both functions concurrently operated as described above.

PERFORMANCE EVALUATION

This section evaluates the performance of the LVCC model and discusses the effectiveness of the model in preventing congestion by mimicking the species competition in nature. More specifically, control system type simulations (through Matlab) and realistic network simulations (using NS2 network simulator) were conducted to show the basic features of the proposed bio-inspired mechanism such as *self-adaptiveness, scalability and fairness*. In addition, evaluation studies investigate how parameters affect the performance of our mechanism in terms of *stability and convergence* and provide effective parameter setting on the basis of congestion-oriented metrics.

Analytical Results: The Basis

Based on analytical results about α and β, the calculated rates of all flows converge to a global and asymptotically stable solution when $\beta > \alpha$, and $\alpha > 1$ for avoiding buffer overflows. There is no upper limitation on β but as it becomes larger, the steady state traffic rate (Equation 4) decreases. In this case, each active node will be limited to transmit data at a lower rate leading to lower quality of the received streams at the sink. As far as r is concerned, the system of Equation 1 has a stable equilibrium point for any value of $r > 0$ (Antoniou, 2007), (Takeuchi, 1980). An upper bound for r is not analytically known, thus will be experimentally explored. The mathematical analysis of our model gives a general understanding of the system's behavior on the basis of stability as function of the parameters α and β. However, the complexity of WSNs necessitates simulation evaluation using plausible scenarios that cannot be formally tested. The analytical study serves as the basis for the simulations.

Simulation Studies: The Step Further

In order to supplement the analytical results, some simulation experiments were conducted both in Matlab (theoretical model analysis scenarios) and in NS2 (realistic network scenarios). We considered a wireless sensor network consisting of *25* wireless nodes which are deployed in a cluster-based topology (*Figure 5*). The proposed LVCC approach can be efficiently and effectively used on top of routing or MAC protocols that create small depth (< 4) cluster/treebased logical topologies over any physical topology. However, a detailed study of such protocols is beyond the scope of the current paper. In this study, a dedicated routing

Figure 5. Evaluation cluster-based topology of 25 nodes (all links are wireless)

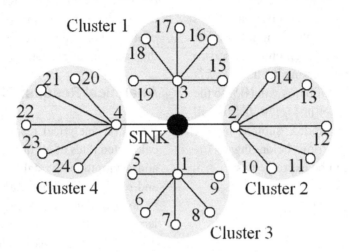

protocol that creates the underlined topology was assumed. We used this type of topology so as to better understand and evaluate the behavior of our LV-based mechanism. The grey-shaded area represents a collision domain. For example, the nodes of cluster 1 (nodes 5, 6, 7, 8, and 9) will perceive each other's transmissions.

Theoretical Model Analysis Using Control System Type Simulations

The validity of analytical results in complex scenarios that could not be formally tested was further investigated in Matlab. It was assumed that nodes *5, 6, 10, 14, 16* and *20* were activated at *1T, 50T, 150T, 300T, 450T, 600T* and *900T* respectively. Node *14* was deactivated at *750T*. Each node buffer size was set to *K=35*KB.

Realistic Network Simulations

In addition, the proposed mechanism was evaluated in a realistic static and failure-free network environment, using a series of representative network operation scenarios under NS2 networking simulator. The two-ray ground radio propagation model was used in all experiments. The buffer

capacity of each node was set to *35*KB. The time period *T* between successive evaluations of the calculated rate of each SN, as well as the time between backpressure control packets was set to *1* sec. The selection of *1* second is guided by the desire to maintain responsiveness to changes in the network state and to avoid overwhelming the network with control packets. The CSMA-based IEEE *802.11* MAC protocol with *1* Mbps transmission rate and an exponential backoff policy was assumed. *Table 1* summarizes all scenarios evaluated in NS2. In each scenario, the different sets of nodes were activated.

Based on the LV competition model, each node is able to calculate its transmission rate i.e., the number of bytes it can send per time unit. In realistic scenarios, we assumed that each node will transmit in one of *5* different levels namely, *1, 2, 4, 6,* and *8* Kbytes per *T=1* second, starting from *1* Kbytes/*T* (i.e. *8* Kbps). Each node can increase its flow (or stream) rate to an upper level rate when the calculated transmission rate (obtained by Equation 6) exceeds the specific upper level rate. Similarly, there should be a transition from the current level rate to a lower level rate when the calculated transmission rate falls below the current level rate but is above the lower level rate.

Table 1. Description of scenarios in NS2

Scenario	No. of active nodes	Active nodes
1	3	5, 6, 10
2	5	5, 6, 10, 13, 14
3	7	5, 6, 10, 12, 13, 14, 21
4	10	5, 6, 10, 11, 12, 13, 14, 18, 21, 24

Performance Measures

Two common performance measures for congestion control approaches were taken into account: the packet delivery ratio (PDR) and the end-to-end delay (EED). Packet delivery ratio is defined as the ratio of the total number of packets received by the sink to the total number of packets transmitted by source nodes. End to end delay is defined as

the time taken for a packet to be transferred from a source node to the sink.

Verification of Stability and Convergence Time Through Control System Type Simulations

Matlab is a technical computing software that can be used for control system type simulations. In these simulations, realistic network conditions such as queueing delays and wireless channel collisions were not considered.

Initially, α and r were set equal to 1 while the value of β varied. *Figures 6-8* illustrate the results obtained using Matlab. *Figure 6* depicts the calculated number of bytes that can be sent per T from each active node when $\beta = 2$. Bear in mind that low α and β values result in high calculated transmission rates at equilibrium, x^*, evaluated by Equation 4. As can be observed, the system

Figure 6. Calculated transmission rate (bytes sent per sec.) when $\alpha = 1$, $\beta = 2$, $r = 1$

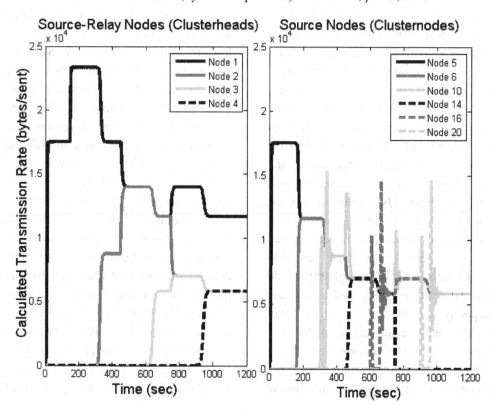

Figure 7. Calculated transmission rate (bytes sent per sec.) when α =1, β = 4, r =1.

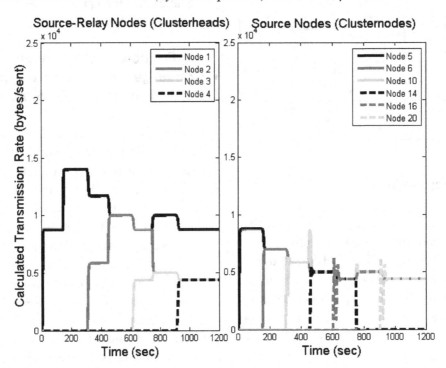

was able to re-converge to a new stable point after a change in network state (node activation). However, some fluctuations in calculated sending rates exhibited by flows initiated from nodes *10, 16* and *20*. This behavior is attributed to the fact that the buffers of nodes involved in the path between active nodes were highly loaded (since traffic flow rates were allowed to converge at high equilibrium values). Thus, with the activation of a new node, the increase of traffic injected into the network could not be smoothly accommodated by network's resources. Also, some fluctuations occurred when the flow of node *14* was deactivated. However, buffer overflows never occurred since the buffer overflow avoidance condition was satisfied. On the other hand, high traffic load injection into the network may lead to wireless channel capacity saturation, a phenomenon that was apparent in realistic network simulations.

When β increased to 4 (*Figure 7*) all flows became almost well-behaved while some very small fluctuations occurred after changes in the

number of active nodes. Recall that the increase of β resulted in convergence of calculated rates at smaller equilibrium values x^*. As a result, the buffers within the network were not highly loaded. Hence, the increase of the traffic injected into the network was conveniently accommodated by network resources, while smooth converging behavior of the calculated transmission rates was preserved. Even though there is no analytical upper bound for β value, as β increases, the incoming traffic load can be conveniently accommodated but the quality of the received data at the sink may be reduced. It can be argued that the best setting for parameter β would be the lowest value that ensures stability and high calculated transmission rates at equilibrium (and thus, high quality), without causing wireless channel capacity saturation. The upper bound for β is further explored in realistic network scenarios.

The role of parameter α is discussed on the basis of *Figure 8*. In this scenario, parameters α and β were set to *3* and *4* respectively. Based on

Figure 8. Calculated transmission rate (bytes sent per sec.) when α =3, β=4, r=1

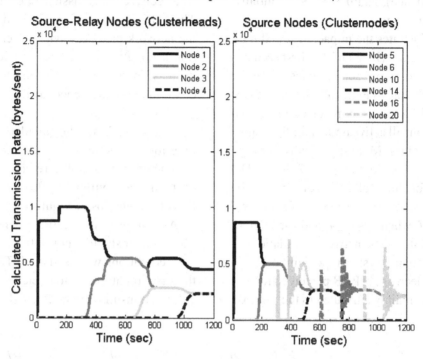

both buffer overflow avoidance and stability conditions, parameter α is lower bounded by *1* and upper bounded by β respectively ($1 < \alpha < \beta$). As can be seen, instability oscillations were observed at source nodes (*Figure 8*(b)) because the system was close to the stability limits. In addition, parameter α was found to be proportional to convergence time. Thus, fast convergence to the stable solution requires α to be close to *1* rather close to β (i.e. far from stability limits). This analytical finding is supported by *Figure 8* which illustrates the slow response of the system towards convergence when α was close β. On the other hand, low α values result in high calculated transmission rates at equilibrium that may not be accommodated by the underlying wireless medium. This issue (that cannot be efficiently simulated in matlab) as well as the influence of α on system performance were further investigated in realistic network scenarios.

In all the previous scenarios, the parameter r was set to *1*. Further matlab simulation studies were carried out in order to study the influence of r on stability. Recall that r was analytically found to be inversely proportional to convergence time, i.e. how fast or slow the system converges to the stable solution. Simulation results showed the value of r cannot grow unboundedly in order to achieve fast convergence. The value of r was tested across quite a large number of combinations of α and β values. Results showed that the calculated flow transmission rates were able to converge for every combination of α and β when $r \leq 2$.

Parameter Setting Based on NS2-based Realistic Network Scenarios

In this section, the impact of parameters α, β and r on a realistic network environment was investigated. A number of scenarios (shown in *Table 1*) were considered. The values of each parameter were chosen to be $4 \leq \beta \leq 7$, $1 \leq \alpha \leq 4$ (in order to satisfy the conditions of stability and buffer overflow avoidance), and $0.5 \leq r \leq 2$. Initially, parameter *r* was set to *1*.

Figure 9 illustrates the impact of α and β on packet delivery ratio (PDR) for the first scenario of operation involving *3* active nodes. It can be observed that the mean PDR for all active nodes was close to *1* (i.e. the sink received almost all packets sent from all active nodes) for the major- ity of β and α values. More specifically, for high values of β as for example $6 \leq \beta \leq 7$, high PDR was achieved for almost all values of α. Similarly, high PDR (close to *1*) was achieved for lower β values $5 \leq \beta \leq 6$ when $2 \leq \alpha \leq 4$, and for $4 \leq \beta \leq 5$ when $2 \leq \alpha \leq 3$. Realistic network simulation re- sults validated control system type simulations. In particular, the decrease in PDR perceived for low values of α was mainly attributed to the increase

in calculated transmission rates at equilibrium. Thus, the increase of traffic load injection into the network provoked wireless channel conten- tion leading to packet loss. In addition, a sharp decrease in PDR was observed when the stability condition was threatened, as for example for $3.5 \leq \alpha \leq 4$ and $\beta = 4$.

Figure 10 shows the calculated transmission rates for the 3 active nodes for 3 combinations of parameter values. Table 2 refers to the validation of stability and buffer overflow avoidance condi- tions for scenarios of Figure 10.

As can be seen in Table 2, when $\alpha = 1$ and $\beta = 0.8$, neither stability nor buffer overflow avoid- ance conditions were satisfied. The violation of the first condition led to cycle instability in cal- culated transmission rates as shown in Figure

Figure 9. Packet Delivery Ratio for the first scenario of Table 1 involving 3 nodes (r=1)

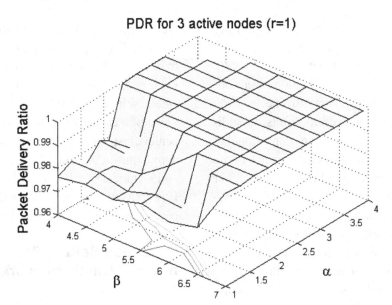

PDR for 3 active nodes (r=1)

Table 2. Validation of stability and buffer overflow avoidance conditions for scenarios of Figure 10

α	β	$\beta > \alpha$	$\alpha[n-1] + \beta \geq n$	x^* (Kbytes/sec) when all active
1.0	0.8	X	2.8≥3 X	–
0.25	0.5	✓	1>3 X	35
3.0	5.0	✓	11>3 ✓	3.18

10(a). In addition, due to the violation of the second condition, the summation of calculated transmission rates of all active nodes was greater than the buffer capacity of each node (35 Kbytes), thus leading to buffer overflows.

As illustrated in Figure 10 (b), when α =0.25 and β =0.5, the stability condition was satisfied whereas the buffer overflow avoidance condition was violated. Figure 10 (b) shows the calculated transmission rates after convergence, x^*, for each active node. As can be seen, the calculated transmission rate of each node is higher than or equal to *35* Kbytes/sec. However, nodes were not transmitting at such high rates but at the highest predefined transmission rate of *8* Kbytes/sec throughout the scenario duration. Even though the buffer capacities within the network could accommodate the generated traffic load, collisions at the wireless channel led to packet loss. As a result, the stream throughput for each active node measured at the sink was fluctuating as shown in Figure 11(a).

On the other hand, as shown in Figure 10 (c), when β =5 and α =3 none of the conditions were violated, while the calculated transmission rates were kept at lower values. Thus, each node was transmitting at the highest allowed predetermined transmission rate (see Figure 11 (b)) without causing packet loss.

It is worth pointing out that due to the low traffic load injected into the network in the presence of *3* active nodes, the mean end-to-end (EED) delay was kept below *4μsec*.

Figure 10. Calculated transmission rates for 3 active nodes scenario

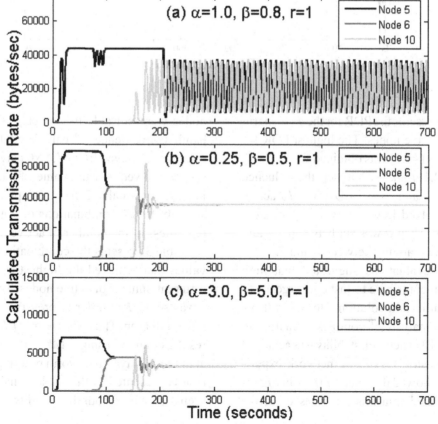

Figure 11. Stream throughput for 3 active nodes scenario measured at the sink

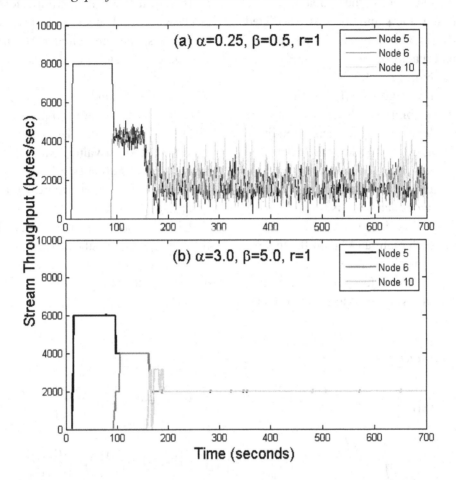

Figure 12 presents the PDR for the *4th* scenario involving *10* active nodes. The highest PDR for *10* active nodes (≈0.9) was obtained for $6 \leq \beta \leq 7$, and $1.8 \leq \alpha \leq 2.1$. *Figure 13* depicts the influence of parameters β and α on EED when *10* active nodes were involved. Low delay values (≈*10μsec*) were achieved when α was set between *1.8* and *2.1*, while β was ranging between *6* and *7*.

Analytical evaluations suggested that high values of *r* can contribute to fast convergence to the stable equilibrium solution. However, theoretical model analysis of complex scenarios in Matlab showed that network stability was achieved for $r \leq 2$. Increasingly, realistic network experiments in NS2 showed that for *r<1* (*r=1* in *Figure 14*),the calculated transmission rates of active

nodes were not able to converge. On the other hand, convergence of calculated transmission rates was achieved for *r=1*. Extensive simulation results showed that the value of *r* must be kept less than or equal to *2* in order to preserve system stability for all combinations of α and β values, regardless of the number of active nodes.

Table 3 presents the combinations of α and β values that achieved the highest mean PDR for different number of active nodes. The parameter *r* was set to *1* in order to preserve smooth flow rate regulation. The last column of *Table 3* shows results obtained using *2* Mbps transmission rate at the MAC layer. It is worth pointing out that the results presented in this table consider only the scenarios where both the stability condition and

Figure 12. Packet Delivery Ratio for the fourth scenario of Table 1 involving 10 active nodes (r=1)

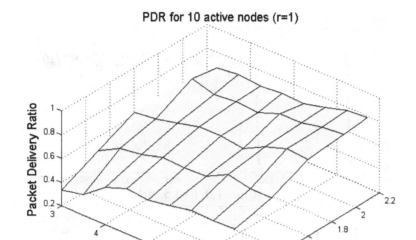

Figure 13. End-to-End Delay for the fourth scenario of Table 1 involving 10 active nodes (r=1)

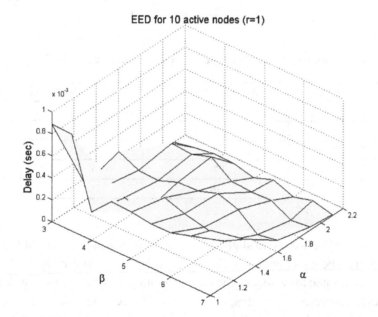

the buffer overflow avoidance condition were satisfied.

Table 3 shows that in all scenarios, α values were significantly lower than β values. The values of α, that achieved the highest mean PDR in each scenario, ranged from *1.6* to *2.1*, while the values of β ranged from *3.3* to *7.0*. Results verified that as the number of active nodes scaled up, stable response of traffic flows and high mean PDR were achieved with the increase of both parameters (i.e. with the decrease of traffic flow transmission rates).

Figure 14. Calculated transmission rates for 5 active nodes scenario when r=0.5 and r=1

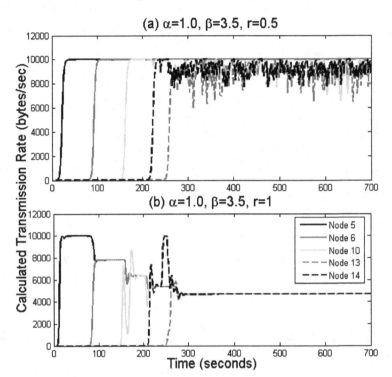

Table 3. Performance evaluations for realistic network conditions using NS2

α	β	No. of active nodes	Mean Packet Delivery Ratio	
			1 Mbps	2 Mbps
1.6	3.3	3	0.981	0.999
1.6	4.3	5	0.993	0.999
1.9	6.5	7	0.961	0.986
2.1	7.0	10	0.892	0.951

In addition, the mean PDR decreased slightly with the increase in the number of active nodes. The decrease of PDR was attributed to the inadequacy of network resources (e.g. wireless channel capacity) to accommodate the traffic load injected from a large number of active nodes. When the MAC transmission rate increased to *2* Mbps, higher PDR values were observed (last column of *Table 3*) as a result of the enhanced channel capacity.

It is beyond any doubt that the values of parameters α, β and r should be chosen to ensure stability of traffic lows as well as buffer overflow avoidance. The parameter r can be set equal to *1* in order to preserve convergence to equilibria as well as smooth flow rate regulation. Based on the evaluation results, the values of parameters α and β depend on the number of active nodes within the network. Therefore, both parameters should be adapted by each sending node according to the number of active nodes as follows:

$$a = \begin{cases} 1.6, & 1 \leq n \leq 5; \\ 2.1, & 6 \leq n \leq 10. \end{cases}$$

$$\beta = \begin{cases} 4.3 & 1 \leq n \leq 5; \\ 7.0 & 6 \leq n \leq 10. \end{cases} \quad (9)$$

The sink node is aware of the total number of active nodes within the network. The sink node can piggyback this number on control packets that are periodically broadcasted within the network. Each node can further spread this information out over the network by means of control packets.

Scalability and Fairness

Taking into consideration all the results presented thus far, the system proved to be adaptable against changing traffic load and achieved scalability by sharing buffer capacity of nodes to their active upstream nodes. For example in *Figure 7*, in the presence of one sender (node *5*) the stable equilibrium point of the system given by Equation 4 was *8750* bytes/*T* (clusterhead node *1* transmitted at the same rate). When node *6* became active, each sender obtained *7000* bytes/*T*, while the downstream node *1* (clusterhead) was able to accommodate both senders by increasing its rate using Equation 7 When the number of senders scaled up, all senders could be supported by the system by diminishing the sending rate per node, thus offering graceful degradation. Fairness was also achieved having the available buffer capacity of each node equally shared among all activated flows.

Comparative Evaluations

The proposed LVCC approach was compared with the traditional AIMD rate adaptation mechanism which is currently involved in recent conges-

tion control protocols for WSNs (Wan, 2003), (Rangwala, 2006), (Woo, 2001) and (Popa, 2006). The values of α, β and r were set to *2.4, 7* and *1* respectively, while scenarios *1* and *3* were considered, involving *3* and *5* active nodes respectively.

As shown in *Figure 15*(a) and (b), the proposed LVCC approach achieved smooth throughput for each active node while maintaining friendliness among competing flows. This controlled behavior is attributed to the powerful LV-based calculated transmission rate evaluation which effectively and efficiently perceives the available network bandwidth, and fairly shares it among active nodes.

On the other hand, as can be seen in *Figure 15*(c) and (d), the AIMD approach displayed a saw-tooth behavior which represents the probe for available bandwidth. The oscillations shown in *Figure 15*(c) and (d) were attributed to multiplicative rate decrease after packet loss events. Therefore, the AIMD rate control policy seems to be ineffective in wireless environments due to the frequent occurrence of packet loss events. In addition, AIMD seems inefficient for streaming applications since the saw-tooth rate behavior may violate the QoS requirements of a stream and can lead to significant variation in streaming media quality. Furthermore, the end-to-end nature of the AIMD mechanism makes it incapable of operating in error-prone wireless multihop networks and results in reduced responsiveness, increased latency and high error rates, especially during long periods of congestion. Contrarily, the LVCC approach operates in a hop-by-hop manner providing fast responsiveness to changing network conditions.

FUTURE RESEARCH DIRECTIONS

Recent technological advancements in low-cost small-scale imaging sensors, CMOS cameras and microphones have fuelled the emergence of novel multimedia applications over WSNs. The so-called Wireless Multimedia Sensor Networks

Figure 15. Throughput comparative evaluations between LVCC and AIMD for 3 and 5 active nodes

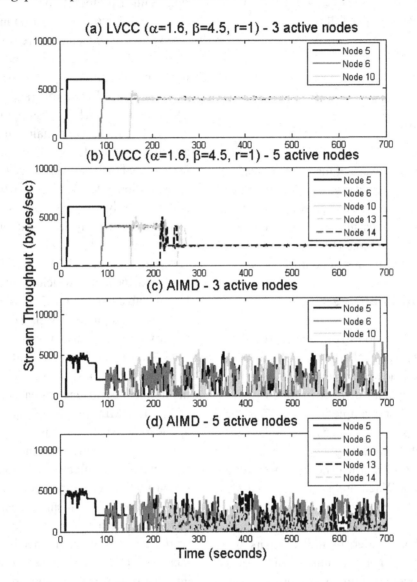

(WMSNs) have drawn the immediate attention of the research community (Akyildiz, 2007) and are expected to boost the capabilities of current wireless sensor networks. WMSNs applications e.g. multimedia surveillance networks, target tracking, environmental monitoring, and traffic management systems, require efficient gathering and transmission of multimedia data in the form of multimedia such as audio, image, and video. Under these circumstances, WMSNs introduce several research challenges for energy-efficient

multimedia processing and communication, primarily related to the delivery of high quality of service (QoS).

In the near future, we can expect to see various applications based on multimedia wireless networks, where many types of sensors such as cameras, audio sensors, vibration sensors, and light sensors will be integrated in the same sensor node. In addition, it is expected that the number of such highly capable sensor nodes in multimedia applications will scale to tenths, hundreds or even thousands (Soro, 2009). Therefore, future protocols designed for WMSNs should be directed toward finding ways to preserve desirable characteristics such as network self-adaptation, scalability and fairness among competing traffic flows, while at the same time coping with the resource-constrained nature of the underlying network as well as the time and bandwidth requirements posed by applications.

This chapter proposes a novel bio-inspired congestion control approach (LVCC) targeting streaming applications in wireless sensor networks. The proposed approach was designed to exhibit the aforementioned characteristics. However, due to the application-dependent nature of WSNs, wireless sensor networks deployed for different applications may require different congestion control approaches. In addition to the challenges for reliable data transport in WSN (e.g. packet loss, delay), there exist additional challenges due to the unique requirements of the multimedia traffic, such as bounded delay and delay variation as well as minimum bandwidth demand. Therefore, a possible area of future work is to assign different priority classes to different kind of flows or different applications, which can be treated in a differentiated way by the congestion control algorithm.

CONCLUSION

This study investigates how a certain biologically inspired model can be employed to prevent congestion in small-scale multimedia WSNs. Inspiration from biological processes was drawn where global properties e.g., self-adaptation, stability, scalability and fairness are achieved collectively without explicitly programming them into individual nodes, using simple computations at the node level.

Motivated by the famous LV competition model, a rate-based, hop-by-hop CC mechanism (LVCC) was proposed, which aims at controlling the traffic flow rate at each sending node. Analytical evaluations and simulations were performed to understand how the variations of the model's parameters influence stability, sensitivity to parameters, scalability and fairness. Control system type simulations in Matlab validated the correctness of analytical results of Antoniou (2007) for plausible scenarios that could not be formally tested and showed that the proposed model achieves stability and smooth network operation under the analytically proposed conditions. Realistic scenarios of network operation and conditions were also taken into consideration for effective parameter setting. Realistic scenarios evaluation suggested certain values for parameters α, β and r that are able to achieve high packet delivery ratio, low end-to-end delay, scalability and fairness among competing flows. Furthermore, the proposed approach was found to outperform AIMD-like rate-based congestion control approaches for WSNs in terms of stability and flow rate smoothness. For future work, it is planned to investigate if and under what conditions parameter values can be analytically optimized using conventional or nature-inspired optimization techniques. In addition, the LVCC approach can be modified to cope with a set of different priority classes (e.g. by means of unequal traffic rates) corresponding to different kind of traffic flows.

ACKNOWLEDGMENT

This work is supported in part by the GINSENG: Performance Control in Wireless Sensor Networks project funded by the 7th Framework Programme under Grant No. ICT-224282 and the MiND2C: Mimicking Nature for Designing Robust Congestion Control Mechanisms in Self-Organized Autonomous Decentralized Networks project funded by the Research Promotion Foundation of Cyprus under Grant No. TPE/EPIKOI/0308(BE)/03.

REFERENCES

Akyildiz, I., Melodia, T., & Chowdhury, K. R. (2007). a survey on wireless multimedia sensor networks. *Computer Networks, 51,* 921–960. doi:10.1016/j.comnet.2006.10.002

Akyildiz, I., Su, W., Sankarasubramaniam, Y., & Cayirci, E. (2002). Wireless sensor networks: A survey. *Computer Networks, 38,* 393–422. doi:10.1016/S1389-1286(01)00302-4

Analoui, M., & Jamali, S. (2006). A conceptual framework for bio-inspired congestion control in communication networks. *Proceedings of the 1st BIMNICS,* (pp. 1–5).

Antoniou, P., & Pitsillides, A. (2007, November). *Towards a scalable and self-adaptable congestion control approach for autonomous decentralized networks.* Nature-Inspired Smart Information Systems Annual Symposium 2007, St Julians, Malta.

Brauer, F., & Chavez, C. C. (2000). *Mathematical models in population biology and epidemiology.* USA: Texts in Applied Mathematics.

Hasegawa, G., & Murata, M. (2006). *TCP symbiosis: Congestion control mechanism of TCP based on Lotka-Volterra competition model.* ACM International Conf. Series 200.

He, T., Ren, F., Lin, C., & Das, S. (2008). *Alleviating congestion using traffic-aware dynamic routing in wireless sensor networks.* 5th Annual IEEE Communications Society Conference on Sensor, Mesh and Ad Hoc Communications and Networks.

Hull, B., Jamieson, K., & Balakrishnan, H. (2004). Mitigating congestion in wireless sensor networks. *Proc. of the 2nd Int. Conf. on Embedded Net. Sensor Systems,* (pp. 134-147).

Karenos, K., Kalogeraki, V., & Krishnamurthy, S. V. (2008). Cluster-based congestion control for sensor networks. *ACM Transactions on Sensor Networks, 4*(1).

Kumar, R., Rowaihy, H., Cao, G., Anjum, F., Yener, A., & La Porta, T. (2006). *Congestion aware routing in sensor networks.* (Tech. Rep. No. 36). Pennsylvania, USA: The Pennsylvania State University, Department of Computer Science and Engineering.

Lotka, A. (1925). *Elements of physical biology.* Baltimore, MD: Williams and Wilkins.

MATLAB. (n.d.). *The language of technical computing.* Retrieved from http:// www. mathworks.com/

NS-2. (n.d.). *Network simulator.* Retrieved from http://www.isi.edu/nsnam/ns/

Popa, L., Raiciu, C., Stoica, I., & Rosenblum, D. S. (2006, November). Reducing congestion effects in wireless networks by multipath routing. *Proceedings of 14th IEEE International Conference on Network Protocols,* (pp. 96-105).

Rangwala, S., Gummadi, R., Govindan, R., & Psounis, K. (2006). Interference-aware fair rate control in wireless sensor networks. *Proceedings of ACM SIGCOMM Symposium on Network Architectures and Protocols.*

Soro, S., & Heinzelman., W. (2009). A survey of visual sensor networks. *Advances in Multimedia.*

Takeuchi, Y., & Adachi, N. (1980). The existence of globally stable equilibria of ecosystems of the generalized Volterra type. [Springer-Verlag.]. *Journal of Mathematical Biology, 10,* 401–415. doi:10.1007/BF00276098

Volterra, V. (1931). *Variations and fluctuations of the numbers of individuals in animal species living together, translation by Chapman, R. Animal Ecology* (pp. 409–448). McGraw Hill.

Vuran, M. C., Gungor, V. C., & Akan, O. B. (2005). On the interdependence of congestion and contention in WSNs. *Proceedings of ICST SenMetrics.*

Wan, C.-Y., Eisenman, S. B., & Campbell, A. T. (2003). CODA: Congestion Detection and avoidance in sensor networks. *Proceedings of the 1ˢᵗ Int. Conf. on Embedded Net. Sensor Systems,* (pp. 266-279).

Wan, C.-Y., Eisenman, S. B., Campbell, A. T., & Crowcroft, J. (2005). Siphon: Overload traffic management using multi-radio virtual sinks in sensor networks. *Proceedings of ACM SenSys.*

Woo, A., & Culler, D. E. (2001). *A transmission control scheme for media access in sensor networks* (pp. 221–235). ACM MobiCom.

Section 3
Biologically Inspired Routing Protocols

Chapter 10
Autonomously Evolving Communication Protocols
The Case of Multi-Hop Broadcast

Endre Sándor Varga
Budapest University of Technology and Economics, Hungary

Bernát Wiandt
Budapest University of Technology and Economics, Hungary

Borbála Katalin Benkő
Budapest University of Technology and Economics, Hungary

Vilmos Simon
Budapest University of Technology and Economics, Hungary

ABSTRACT

While traditional telecommunication still relies on rigid, highly regulated, and highly controlled communication protocols, with the emergence of new forms of networks (mobile ad hoc and delay-tolerant networks, lacking central infrastructure and strict regulations) bio-inspired communication protocols have also found their way to success. In this chapter we introduce a nontraditional way of creating and shaping communication protocols, through an autonomous machine intelligence model, built upon on-line evolutionary methods such as natural selection and genetic programming. Creating a genetic programming language and a selection mechanism for multi-hop broadcast protocols in ad hoc networks, we show that this kind of approach can outperform traditional ones under given circumstances, offering a powerful alternative in the future.

INTRODUCTION

Communication protocols are always of high concern in telecommunication networks, especially in ad hoc networks. While too chatty protocols waste resources such as bandwidth and processing power, unnecessarily tight-lipped communication strategies hinder the flow of information and as a consequence, impede the effective operation of the system. Recent studies indicate that while there is no clear answer for the protocol selection riddle in general, it makes sense to evaluate

DOI: 10.4018/978-1-61350-092-7.ch010

the goodness of communication protocols for a certain problem case (Williams and Camp 2002; Dai and Wu 2004; Cheng, Huang, Li, Wu, and Du 2003; Al Hanbali, Ibrahim, Simon, Varga, and Carreras 2009).

The idea of protocol selection or protocol switching has been present for many years in other areas (e.g. cryptography). Our proposal follows this line, but goes one step further: we do not only select but create and shape the protocols.

Imagine a system where communication protocols are not rigid, pre-deployed parts, instead, the protocol logic itself emerges dynamically and improves flexibly according to the current needs of the communicating parties. What could this idea of evolving protocols mean? As a main advantage, the evolution mechanism removes the burden of designing communication protocols manually. The application of machine intelligence for this task not only reduces costs, but with a suitable model, also guarantees the emergence of successful protocols in the end.

Evolutionary programming comes naturally as an implementation tool for the protocol evolution. However, finding the right representation is non-trivial; it is not just operational parameters what we want to optimize, we aim at optimizing the protocol logic itself.

The objective of the chapter is to elaborate on the idea of autonomously evolving protocols through a concrete example showing how such a model could work. The demonstrative example, the challenge of multi-hop broadcast in ad-hoc networks, is a real problem today. We created a concrete evolutionary model with a pilot implementation for this problem case, and excessive simulation was used, alongside with data mining on the results, in order to explore various aspects.

In our previous work (Simon, Bérces, Varga and Bacsárdi. 2009) we used natural selection to achieve self-adaptation of multi-hop broadcast protocols in ad hoc networks, through automatically selecting the optimal one from a predefined set of protocols. Now we introduce an on-line

Genetic Programming framework that extends our previous ideas: protocol candidates are generated via evolution.

The structure of the chapter is the following. First, we give a short summary on the background of broadcasting in mobile ad-hoc networks – our guinea pig – and the applied toolset such as machine learning, genetic programming and natural selection algorithms. Then, in the main trust of chapters, we discuss the questions and solutions of the evolutionary approach for the multi-hop-broadcast problem. We describe the details of the model, the abstractions, and the genetic programming language itself. Then, various aspects of the model are examined via simulation; a large amount of collected simulation data was analyzed using data mining techniques. Finally, we discuss interesting future directions.

BACKGROUND

It is a common task in ad hoc networks to distribute messages globally to all, or almost all, participants of the network. This is basically an extension of local broadcast, usually referred to as multi-hop broadcast. By nature, this kind of service consumes a significant amount of resources (channel usage, collisions), therefore it is an important objective to optimize the protocol used for multi-hop broadcast.

Various literature sources investigate the possible protocols and their performance characteristics (Williams and Camp 2002; Dai and Wu 2004; Cheng, Huang, Li, Wu, and Du 2003; Al Hanbali, Ibrahim, Simon, Varga, and Carreras 2009), but measurements show that there is no definite winner – the behavior of protocols depend heavily on the parameters of the environment. These parameters include mobility patterns, node speed, node density, transmission technology and traffic models. Selecting the suitable protocol, therefore, requires deep and exact knowledge about the actual environment – which is generally hard to acquire, given the complex factors involved, such as human mobility patterns. Worse, the environment will change over time, by appearing of new nodes, changing technology, or changes in usage practice, therefore any static off-line design results in a compromise. The issues above raise the question whether an automated, on-line, adaptive approach could solve the matter of obtaining the best protocols for a given situation.

The application of machine learning for protocol optimization – fine tuning of parameters – is a known practice, however, the use of machine created models for the protocol logic is less common. Even if they are applied, it usually happens during the manual design phase, not as part of the operation of the actual system. In (Colagrosso 2007) the authors used machine learning algorithms to approximate the behavior of sophisticated broadcast algorithms and found that simple heuristics were able to reproduce their decisions with 87% accuracy. This result indicates that in practice small, but powerful heuristics could provide good approximations instead of sophisticated calculations. Such heuristics are usually hard to find by design, but a genetic programming based system could find them by evolution.

Genetic algorithms are biologically inspired random search algorithms directed towards a global optimum, based on generations of solution candidates (individuals). In each round, the algorithm evaluates individuals with a fitness function; then, the next generation gets produced by applying genetic operators (crossover and mutation) on the selected individuals of the current generation. Genetic programming (GP) is a form of genetic algorithm, where individuals are programs composed of instructions in a particular programming language. When using GP we generally distinguish on-line and off-line approaches. 'Off-line' means that solutions are generated during a design phase, and the result is then used unmodified in the operational phase of the system; while in the 'on-line' case the evolution itself is part of the system and new solution instances are generated continuously, during the system's

normal operation. According to our knowledge, on-line genetic programming has not been applied in the area of multi-hop broadcast communication protocols before.

The variety of challenges present in multi-hop broadcast protocols in mobile ad hoc networks – such as the unpredictability of the position or speed of the mobile node, changing topology and the diversity of devices – makes it an ideal target for genetic programming. Protocols need to cope with numerous and more or less distinct aspects; hence, these aspects can be freely blended by the genetic algorithm so that the blend is still likely to make sense. Human-designed protocols typically have distinct "sweet spots": working best under different conditions. By increasing the diversity of the protocols and enabling them to adapt freely to the current environmental conditions through evolution, it is possible to always maintain a protocol or a family of protocols that works well in the current environment. This approach can also be considered as an automated protocol design tool.

While it provides many benefits, the choice of using GP also has certain design consequences. Fine-tuning the system becomes problematic, as evolution tends to produce individuals that circumvent human imposed rules and design patterns. GP also generates a large amount of individuals, meaning that obtaining insight becomes harder (it is impossible to inspect all the generated individuals manually). However by using data mining techniques, getting an insight into the mapping relations becomes easier, as demonstrated later in this chapter.

The success of any genetic algorithm relies on a carefully designed fitness function. In ad hoc systems the unavailability of global, system-wide data demands a careful approach to fitness calculation, collecting any kind of performance metric may easily result in a prohibitive amount of channel usage.

Our past work revolves around the idea of on-line protocol adaption to get humans out of the loop and avoid costly system maintenance. We concentrated on a self-tuning system that is able to identify the best protocols based on the observed real-life performance indicators. An advantage of this system was that we could sidestep the need for protocol updates, which is a real issue in ad hoc networks considering the potentially large number of participants in such a system. In (Simon, Bérces, Varga, Bacsárdi. 2009) we investigated the use of on-line natural selection among a set of predefined, manually designed protocols to achieve the desired adaptivity. Designing such a system poses several challenges, for example heterogeneous protocols must be able to work with each other in the same network, and the collection of performance indicators for fitness evaluation can become problematic, too.

Our key contribution was the design of a meta-protocol, shared by all protocol instances, and a feed-forward selection mechanism called Inverted Selection that avoids the need for global measurements. Parts of these mechanisms are also used within the genetic programming model; details are described in the section Natural Selection with Inverted Decision.

Using the above principles we attained a scalable and adaptive distributed system with a pre-injected set of algorithms that compete for being selected. However, we also discovered an inherent limitation of this approach: while the need for manually picking one algorithm for the system was sidestepped, the problem of manually selecting the set of possible algorithms still remained. A more severe issue was that the diversity was limited by the size of the initial protocol set; therefore the dynamics of natural selection had only a limited effect. To work effectively, much higher diversity would be needed for the natural selection. With such a low diversity, a simple natural selection scheme could also result in a phenomenon known from Evolutionary Game Theory, namely, that the orbit of the system in the state space of protocol mixtures has no fix point but a limit cycle instead. This situation arises from the fact that many protocols have a "rock-paper-scissors" relation to each other, periodically overturning each other in the network.

The idea described in this chapter is a natural continuation of the self-tuning natural selection system: now we introduce genetic operators – crossover and mutation – over the initial set of protocols to achieve higher diversity among them, and to enable the emergence of inherently novel protocol instances in each new round. This way, we shift from pure natural selection to a broader concept, evolution, that is, survival of the fittest while constantly introducing diversity.

ON-LINE EVOLUTION TO OPTIMIZE MULTI-HOP BROADCAST

The Multi-hop Broadcast Problem

Designing a functional multi-hop broadcast protocol is not a trivial task. Apart from the issue of minimizing channel usage several other problems arise that do not exist in ordinary ad hoc routing protocols. One such phenomenon is the so called Broadcast Storm (Ni, Tseng, Chen, and Sheu 1999) that happens when multiple nodes start forwarding a message simultaneously after they received it from a common previous node. This effect originates from the fact that exponential backoff algorithms were designed for systems where the traffic patterns of neighboring nodes are uncorrelated with each other. In the case of broadcast, several nodes may decide to transmit at the same time, and collide even after several backoff events. To avoid this, all of the broadcast protocols have means to de-correlate traffic of neighbors – usually waiting for a random time before forwarding the message.

Multi-hop broadcast algorithms exploit the local broadcast channel to reduce channel usage and collisions in the system. This way, as one transmission may be overheard by multiple devices, it is possible to drastically reduce the amount of transmissions. The essence of this optimization is the approximation of a Minimal Connected Dominating Set (MCDS) (Guha and Khuller 1996; Dai and Wu 2004). A set $M \subset V$ for a graph $G(V,E)$ is a Connected Dominating Set if:

- M is a connected subgraph of $G(V,E)$
- For every vertex $v \in V$ either $v \in M$ or there exists an edge $e = \{v,w\} \in E$ so that $w \in M$.

A Connected Dominating Set M is an MCDS if $|M|$ is minimal. An additional constraint in multi-hop broadcast is that if B is the set of vertices containing the nodes that initially possess the payload to be broadcasted, then $B \cap M = 0$ must hold. If the vertices V of the graph $G(V,E)$ stand for nodes in the network and an edge $e=\{v,w\}$ represents that v and w are in radio range, then an MCDS gives the smallest set of nodes needed to accomplish a successful global broadcast. Figure 1 illustrates the significance of the MCDS concept.

In practice, deciding if a set of vertices is an MCDS is likely to be NP complete, but even if it was not, detecting MCDSs were not of much help in practice, as the network topology changes faster than we can discover the changes. Instead of dealing with real MCDSs, broadcast protocols typically use some kind of approximations based on simple heuristics and local knowledge. These heuristics range in sophistication from simple counter based solutions to probabilistic methods and complex graph theoretic approximations (Wu and Li 1999, Cheng, Huang, Li, Wu, and Du 2003). These heuristics need to be dependent on the environment; therefore it makes sense to use an abstraction of the local simulation within the heuristics. The implementation of our choice of heuristics is introduced in the following section.

Natural Selection with Inverted Decision

When an autonomous system is equipped with several protocol candidates, in order to select the most suitable protocol, we need to measure the performance of each candidate and push the

Figure 1. An example network with one of the MCDS {c, e, d}. Other possible MCDS are {b, d, e}, {c, e, f}, etc). If the originating node is not in any of the MCDS it is still possible reach all nodes with only one additional transmission, as every node is at most one hop from any MCDS. In this example at most 4 transmissions are needed to reach all 7 nodes.

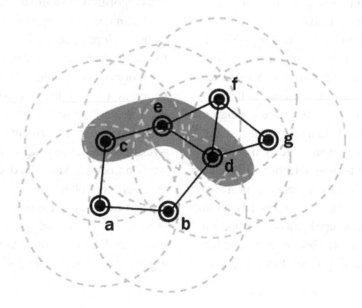

system towards the use of the most efficient one. Designing a performance evaluation criterion in a multi-hop broadcast based ad hoc network is challenging: we need to address conflicting requirements (maximal coverage vs. minimal duplication) as well as the problem of measurability.

The factors we considered here are the following

- Only the sender node is able to reliably measure the real cost of a successful message transmission. Lost messages (by definition) could not be seen by other nodes.

- Only the receiver nodes are able to reliably measure the number of duplicated messages.

- Each receiver node can measure the number of local duplications (i.e. the duplications they personally receive), but they can not measure the number of total duplications in the system.

- In order to collect the measurement results, message forwarding is needed over the same channel the broadcast payloads use.

- Measurement messages may get lost, as well as the acknowledgments for the measurements messages.

Acknowledgement messages use the same channel as broadcast payloads.

The above factors imply (Simon, Bérces, Varga, Bacsárdi. 2009) that implementing a centralized (even locally centralized) protocol selector criterion is impractical, because the reliable collection of performance data is both technically challenging and wasteful in terms of channel usage. Instead, we proposed a feed-forward selection method using stigmergy and natural selection. The idea of natural selection in ad hoc network protocol selection is not new, in (Alouf, Carreras, Miorandi and Neglia 2007) authors applied a form of natural selection for parameter optimization, using explicit feedback from neighboring nodes. In their system,

the local collection of performance indicators was suitable because the protocol was of a specialized class. Our approach is different; it does not require feedback mechanisms and works with arbitrary broadcast protocols.

The solution is based on the idea of *decision inversion*. The naive way of natural selection could be that a sender collects its performance metrics from the surrounding receivers and chooses its next protocol according to this measurement. As we explained earlier, this can not be efficiently implemented in general. Instead of trying to select locally at the sender, we planted the ability of decision making into the receivers, because they are in an optimal position to observe the performance of a protocol. To make this possible, receivers must know the protocol that generated a given payload message. This is achieved by senders attaching a protocol code to every payload. Such compound packets act as a virtual seeds where the nutritional part of the seed is the payload and the genetic material is the code of the sender protocol.

Nodes (as receivers) collect seeds from surrounding nodes and assign scores to the protocol instances they carry. Every payload that is useful to the receiver node means a score for the sender protocol. Every unnecessary message (duplicate) means a negative score to the sender protocol. This algorithm is summarized in Figure 2.

The main advantage of the inverted selection is that performance results don't need to get back to the sender: instead, the receiver will utilize them during the creation of its own next protocol generation (so, in the next round, the sender may meet the offsprings of its own good protocol). This way, the measurement overhead is minimal – result container messages are not needed–, and, we don't need to keep the operation of the nodes in synchron, either.

In order to keep the number of messages sent out by a protocol under control, we assigned a *cost* to each transmission. As the selection of new algorithms happens at the receiver it is impossible to implement explicit cost calculation without expensive control overhead. To avoid this, we adopted a stigmergic solution: by assigning a limited transmission budget to each protocol instance, protocols are forced to make good use of channel resources. Any lost or duplicate message is a lost opportunity for reproduction, therefore transmission has an implicit cost function, even if it is not expressed directly. Similarly, we added a timer, that upon firing, removes the current protocol, and replaces it with a new generation forcing protocols to use the available time efficiently.

A GENETIC PROGRAMMING LANGUAGE FOR MULTI-HOP BROADCAST PROTOCOLS

In the previous section we introduced the idea of Inverted Selection that implements a feed-forward, natural selection based approach to the problem of distributed protocol evaluation and selection. While this method shows how protocols are selected, it does not answer the question which

protocols are to be selected from. This leads us to the second half of the puzzle: introducing new protocols, and thus diversity to the network. Our answer is to use Genetic Programming on existing protocol instances to achieve new, and over time, better performing algorithms. In order to make Genetic Programming and evolution possible, the representation of protocols needs careful consideration. As the protocols in the system are no longer engineered by humans, a lightweight, flexible and robust formal description is needed which suits genetic operators.

Using a general purpose programming language as protocol representation would be problematic because applying genetic operators could result in frequent syntactic errors and un-interpretable code. To avoid these issues several GP specific languages were designed.. A promising family of GP languages is based on artificial chemistries (Dittrich, Ziegler and Banzhaf 2001), as they provide great resilience against harmful random modifications. A good example of such a language is Fraglets (Tschudin 2003), which was used to conduct experiments in protocol

Figure 2. Inverted Selection based protocol selection to implement Natural Selection. Algorithm B is running on the current node while a message from a node running algorithm A arrives.

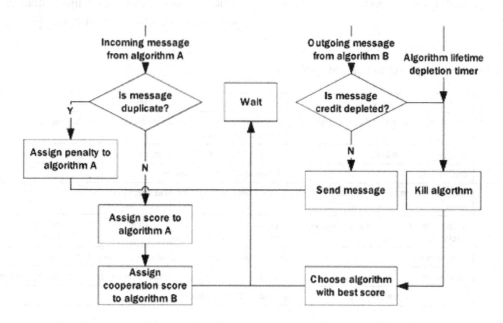

evolution in (Yamamoto, Schreckling and Meyer 2007). While these languages may have great possibilities, in our approach we followed a more conservative – but not less promising – approach, and selected the well-known Push3 language (Spector and Robinson 2002) as a starting point for the design of our own language, called GPDISS. The rationale is that evolved protocols are already notoriously difficult to analyze for humans and artificial chemistries tend to produce even more complicated programs.

By design, the focus of our language is to describe multi-hop broadcast protocols, and to enable the efficient use of genetic operators through a flexible, mutation friendly syntax. Most of these features are inherited from the parent language Push3 but several new aspects were introduced that are specific to our problem domain. GP-DISS extends the original PUSH language with a custom instruction set. The data structures and the instruction set consist of primitive building blocks inspired by the common ideas in several well-known multi hop broadcast protocols. The abstraction level of the instruction set was chosen carefully to find a balance between granularity and expressiveness. Table 1 shows some of the instructions in the language (like in Push3, instructions are associated with typed stacks).

An interesting example of the custom instructions and types is the introduction of relation types. We created relation types and the accompanying instructions to enable the efficient calculations on graph structures, tabular data, or trees, as they are common in broadcast protocols. On the relation stack ordered, typed pairs of objects could be stored. Relations can be imagined as two column tables, the first column being the key, and the second column being the value. The key and the value columns are typed, which means they receive their elements from the appropriate typed stack. Relations give a new dimension to stored data by describing relationships between the objects on the stacks. Relations are immutable: every operation creates a new instance on the relation stack. With the help of the operations defined on relations we can do sophisticated data manipulations, such as filtering by key or value, intersecting, joining, subtracting or creating the union of two relations. The code snippet below (Figure 3) creates a new relation containing our 2-hop neighbors. Suppose we have a neighbor map on top of our relation stack. A neighbor map is a node-node relation.

Instead of using monolithic programs, our language defines several hooks – event handlers – that protocols can use to implement different behavioral directions. Therefore, the code of a

Table 1. Most important instructions in GPDISS

Stack	Instruction	Description
*	dup, drop, swap, rotate, hold, release, ...	Common instructions available on all stacks. They are ideal for common stack handling tasks.
number	add, div, mult, random, ...	Simple floating point arithmetic and random number generation
bool	and, or, not, ...	Boolean logic for control flow.
list	additem, nth, remove_first, delete_duplicates, ...	Typed list handling. Common operations are available.
relation	addpair, union, join, remove_first, invert, intersect, ...	Typed relations are like two column tables. They can be filtered, joined, intersected, etc.
messages*	send, sender, ...	Common instructions for handling all types of messages.
timer	id, start_timer, ...	Timers can be used to schedule different tasks at different points in time.
-	if, else, endif, do, while, return, ...	Control flow constructs.

protocol is a list of assembly-like instructions grouped into event handlers. Each message type has its own event handler which gets activated when a message of that type arrives.

Below the layer of event handlers there is a shared meta-protocol: a behavioral segment, uniformly present in all possible protocol instances, that is performed before the event reaches the handler. Please note that the handlers themselves are not bound to use the effect of a meta-protocol, e.g. they can freely ignore any of the received messages. The possible most basic meta-protocol simply defines the structure of a payload packet and the actions that must be taken when such a packet arrives (take the message from the channel). In a very simple system, the payloads may simply be received by the Virtual Machine (VM) itself, and passed to the upper layer. In our GPDISS language we extended the previous meta-protocol with the format of several control messages that are processed by the VM before being passed to the protocol instance. Again, this reflects our conservative approach to GP, restricting the protocols to use primitives we already know and consider to be useful. It is currently impossible for protocols to "grow" their own control messages. It is important to note, however, that the meta-protocols do not restrict the order of messages nor do they enforce messages to get processed, therefore, there is still a large degree of freedom for protocols to explore.

Event handlers are also the basic units of genetic operators: the crossover operator mixes the instructions of two event handlers, while the mutation operator modifies the instructions of a single handler. Implementing a protocol via event handlers is a natural choice because it enables the genetic operators to modify certain parts of a protocol's behavior by mixing code snippets of similar task or extending protocols by adding new event handlers (or removing ones). This is a somewhat conservative design, as it narrows the search space of genetic programming, but these restrictions may be lifted in the future.

The available event handlers are summarized in Table 2.

Although syntax is maintained, the semantic correctness of a program can not be guaranteed after the application of genetic operators. If an instruction is impossible to execute (such as pop on an empty stack), it defaults to a no-op instruction – which does nothing – and the execution of the code continues undisturbed. This results in a quasi-linear (Brameier and Banzhaf 2007) genetic programming language.

To demonstrate our language we show the implementation of a basic flood algorithm, the Adaptive Periodic Flood (APF). APF is a controlled flooding protocol, which achieves better performance than blind flood without the use of control messages. An APF node periodically transmits all the messages it possesses to all neighbors

Figure 3. Code snippet: Looking up our two-hop neighbors from the known neighbor relations

```
relation.dup // Pushes a copy of the relation to the relation stack (for Step1)
relation.dup // Pushes a copy of the relation to the relation stack (for Step2)

node.self // Pushes the identifier of the node to the node stack

// Step1: look up my direct neighbors
relation.filter_key eq //Filters the top element of the relation stack by key, leaving only those
rows whoose key column equals to the node

// Step2: look up neighbors of the neighbors
relation.join // Joins the two relations (filtered one and the original), so finding our neighbor's neighbors in the
original map
```

Table 2. Event handlers in GPDISS

Message type	Event handler description
data	The common wrapper for all data messages in the system. Data messages are useful messages originating from a node with the goal of reaching all nodes in the system.
neighbor	Neighbor messages contain other nodes' neighbor maps. We can use it to further increase the precision of our predictions in other event handlers.
timer	Internal event handler. A protocol receives a timer event when one of its timers finished. One can use it to implement features such as Random Assessment Delay (a transmission delay used in broadcast protocols)
init	Internal event handler. Protocols receive this event once upon initialization, before the first message arrives to them.

it encounters. However, when it detects that there is another node sending similar messages, it increases the period of broadcasting, to reduce the total channel usage. In our example (see Figure 4), the event handler uses two lists storing data messages. The list on the top of the global stack is called "to_send" and contains the messages we are about to send when the timer we started earlier fires. The next list is the "seen" list and contains the data messages we have seen so far. This list is used to detect duplicate incoming messages and reduce the rate of periodic transmissions.

EVALUATION

We used simulation to shed light to various interesting aspects of the model. This subsection describes the examinations and the most important results.

Test Setting

We used our custom discrete-event simulator, written in the Scala programming language (Cremet 2006), to collect data about the behavior of protocols over time. We modeled the behavior of 100 nodes in a 50m x 50m area using the Random Direction Mobility Model to generate the movement pattern of nodes. During 7000s of simulated time new payload messages were injected in every 20 seconds with the average length of 250 bytes. These messages were then broadcasted by one of the initial protocols, Blind Flood, APF or

MMSBA (Hanbali, Ibrahim, Simon, Varga and Carreras 2009), or one of their offsprings, obtained by Genetic Programming. Table 3 sums up the parameters used for the simulation.

Execution

Each VM (node) executes its own, independent protocol evolution; as each has its own generation of protocols. Individuals of the current generation are scheduled using the round robin algorithm, so, each protocol instance is given a transfer and runtime quota. If the transfer quota is exhausted, the protocol can no longer send messages but remains an executed one. If the remaining runtime quota of a protocol is zero, the virtual machine switches to the next protocol from the current generation. If there is no more protocol left in the current generation, a new generation gets created.

Selection

For the new generation, we use the previous local generation and those non-local protocols that sent a message to us in the last round. (Man, Tang, Kwong 1996) We use SUS (Stochastic Universal Sampling) to obtain a new generation of protocol candidates after the death of all protocols, with a score function that gives priority to better performing individuals. This selection algorithm provides zero bias and minimum spread, which means that the actual and expected probabilities of selecting an individual are equal and the range

Figure 4. Code snippet: AFP, first in pseudo code then as a GPDISS event handler

```
<!-- Program logic in pseudo code
  On receive (data: DataMessage) {
    delta := 2
      if contains(seen, data) then
        period := period + delta  // Increases the broadcast period
      else
        to_send := to_send + data  // Adds the recieved message to the list of messages to send
        seen := seen + data  // Saves the message to the seen list
  }
-->

handler data {  // If a new message arrives
  // Data between event handlers is shared via a global stack
  number.popglobal  // Gets the sending period from the global stack
  list.popglobal  // Gets the to_send list from the global stack
  list.popglobal  // Gets the seen list from the global stack

  data.dup  // Makes a copy of the data message

  list.inlist  // Checks if the data message (top of the data stack) is in the seen list (top of
the list stack), and puts the result to the bool stack. (Note: the lists are typed.)


  // Condition comes from the bool stack
  if  // If we already saw this message
    number(2)  // Instantiates a new number with value=2 (delta)
    number.add  // Increases sending period with delta
  else  // If the message is new
    data.dup  // Duplicates the message so that it can be added to two lists
    list.additem  // Adds the message to the seen list
    list.swap  // Swapts the to_send and seen lists
    list.additem  // Add the message to to_send list
    list.swap
  endif

  number.pushglobal  // Puts the sending period to the global stack
  list.pushglobal  // Puts the to_send list to the global stack
  list.pushglobal  // Puts the seen list to the global stack
}
```

in the possible number of trials that an individual can achieve is minimal.

SUS is a variant of the roulette wheel selection. The steps are as follows.

1. Order the individuals by their fitness values in non-increasing order
2. Allocate slices on the wheel proportional to the fitness of the individuals
3. Choose a starting point on the wheel: for example if we want to select *n* elements we choose a random point between 0 and *(sum of fitness values)/n* and we have chosen our first individual
4. The rest of the new generation can be selected by stepping around the wheel by *(sum*

of fitness values/n) steps and choosing the individual assigned to the slice we are in.

Selecting an individual means making a copy of it and adding that copy to the new generation. The new generation is then shuffled and for each pair the crossover and mutation operators are applied.

Genetic Operators

On every pair of protocols A and B we used a modified one-point crossover:

1. Choose an event handler from A randomly
2. If the chosen handler is present in B then

Table 3. Main parameters of the test setting

Parameter	Value
Node count	100
Simulated area	50m x 50m
Simulated time	7000 s
Mobility model	Random Direction
Movement speed	1m/s
Transmission Range	5m
Interference Range	7m
Transmission bandwidth	1Mb/s
Injected traffic	New message in every 20 s
Avg. payload	250 byte
Avg. length of instructions	4 byte
Starting set of protocols	Blind Flood, APF, MMSBA
Maximum lifetime of protocol instances	7s
Maximum message quota of protocol instances	5000 byte

a. A crossover point is selected for each handler (A and B)

b. Event handlers are cut along the crossover points giving two fragments --- a head and tail for each handler

c. With 1/2 probability we exchange the order of the head and tail that we are about to attach.

d. Handler fragments are glued together such that the event handler's tail chosen from A is attached to the event handlers head chosen from B.

e. The same procedure is applied to the tail from B and the head from A

For safety reasons we had to limit the size of the event handlers to protect the event handlers from growing indefinitely.

Measurements

During the simulation we collected various metrics about the protocol instances that appeared in the system. Table 4 summarizes our metrics which can be categorized as:

- Static protocol code metrics (INST, HANDLER, DTAHAND, HLOHAND, INIHAND, TMRHAND, TPGHAND)
- Dynamic code and behavioral metrics collected during the execution of the protocol (USDHAND, NOP, QUOTA)
- Global quality metrics for the protocol (GBLUFL, GBLDUP, GBLSCR)
- Averages and other aggregates of local quality metrics (AVGUFL, GBLUFL, AVGSCR, MINSCR, MAXSCR, SCRDEV)
- Metrics about the environment of the executing node (NEIGH, EPOCH)
- Evolutionary success metrics of the protocol (WINS, WINRATE)

Dependence of Local and the Global Scores

In the first round of analysis the correlation of global and local parameters was examined with the goal to find out more about the relationship of locally available and globally aggregated values.

We used three correlation metrics to get a detailed picture about the level and nature of dependence (Kendall and Stuart 1973, Rodgers and Nicewander 1988):

- *Pearson's* product-momentum correlation coefficient indicates the level of linear dependence between two series.
- *Kendall's* correlation coefficient describes the level of association between them based on the order of ranked pairs.
- *Spearman's* correlation coefficient is a measure of statistical dependence.

In all three cases '+1' means perfect correlation, '0' means no correlation, and '-1' indicates perfect inverse relationship.

Table 4. Measured metrics in the test setting

Metric	Description
INST	Number of instructions in the protocol instance
HANDLER	Number of handlers that are present in the protocol instance
USDHAND	Number of actually executed handlers during the life of the protocol instance
DTAHAND	Length of the DATA handler, 0 if not used
HLOHAND	Length of the HELLO handler, 0 if not used
INIHAND	Length of the INIT handler, 0 if not used
TMRHAND	Length of the TIMER handler, 0 if not used
TPGHAND	Length of the TOPOLOGY CHANGE handler, 0 if not used
NOP	Number of instructions executed as NOP during the life of the protocol instance
QUOTA	Remaining message quota at the death of the protocol instance
GBLDUP	Total number of duplicate messages generated by the protocol instance
GBLUFL	Total number of useful (non-duplicate) messages generated by the protocol instance
GBLSCR	Total score for the protocol instance using global metrics. This metric is used as reference, as the global value is not practically computable in a real environment.
AVGDUP	Average number of received duplicate messages among the neighbor nodes
AVGUFL	Average number of received useful messages among the neighbor nodes
AVGSCR	Average score given to the protocol instance by its neighbors
MINSCR	Minimum score given to the protocol instance by its neighbors
MAXSCR	Maximum score given to the protocol instance by its neighbors
SCRDEV	The difference between MAXSCR and MINSCR
NEIGH	Number of neighbors of the protocol instance during its lifetime
WINS	Number of neighbors selecting the protocol instance for the new generation
WINRATE	The ratio between WINS and NEIGH (WINS/NEIGH). This metric could be larger than one, as a selected protocol may be used to generate several offsprings.
EPOCH	Epoch ID. The simulation time was divided into three equally long epochs designated by 1, 2 and 3.

Result 1.1. In the analysis of GBLSCR and AVGSCR all three coefficients indicate very high level of correlation which means that *global and local scores are linearly dependent and strongly associated throughout the experiment.* (Table 5)

Result 1.2. In the analysis of GBLSCR and AVGSCR per epoch all three coefficients indicate very high level of correlation meaning that *global and local scores are linearly dependent and strongly associated in each epoch locally.* (Table 6)

The conclusion of Result 1.1 and 1.2 is that the dependence between local and global scores is not only high but also deep and stable. The relationship is clearly present on both examined levels (per epoch and globally), and the values measured on different levels do not vary significantly. Such a strong relationship indicates that global and local scores are interchangeable, so *it is a reasonable alternative to use local scores instead of global ones within the evolutionary selection phase*. In other words, the use of local scores will not cause notable loss of information or significant disturbance of other nature.

Result 1.3. Global and local UFL and DEP values show very high correlation, meaning that global/local useful messages and global/local duplication levels are both linearly dependent and

Table 5. Correlation of global and local score throughout the experiment

Type	corr(GBLSCR, AVGSCR)
Pearson	0.97
Kendall	0.91
Spearman	0.95

Table 6. Correlation of global and local scores per epoch

	Epoch1	Epoch2	Epoch3
Pearson	0.97	0.97	0.96
Kendall	0.91	0.92	0.91
Spearman	0.94	0.96	0.96

Table 7. Correlation of global and local useful messages, duplicates

	corr(GBLUFL, AVGUFL)	corr(GBLDUP, AVGDUP)
Pearson.	0.930	0.987
Kendall	0.964	0.996
Spearman	0.991	1.000

strongly associated. (Table 7) This relationship is also present on the epoch level.

Result 1.3 extends the previous findings with a new aspect: the dependence between local and global measures is not limited to the score values but is also true for the other two other measured variables, the useful messages and duplicates.

Information Content of Data Sets

In the second experiment the information content of various data sets were examined. The goal of the analysis was to determine the level of information – directly or indirectly – present in these metrics, as well as the descriptive power of these sets. For example, what is the information content of locally available raw metrics compared to the global score, or how much do those metrics help that are not strictly available locally but may be acquired from the neighborhood (e.g. winning rate).

Model

The information content was modeled in form of regressive potential: if a set of variables can reliably predict a target value than its information content is considered the same. In means of tools, we used machine learning models, Support Vector Machines (Drucker, Burges, Kaufman, Smola, and Vapnik 1997) and Generalized Linear Models (McCullagh and Nelder 1989) to predict the target value from the data set, then examined the goodness and confidence of the model and the nature of errors. 60% of the data was used for training and the remaining 40% for evaluation. Practically, SVMs slightly but consequently outperformed GLMs so we are using the results gathered from the SVMs here. Learning and evaluation were performed in Oracle data Miner (Tamayo, Berger, Campos, Yarmus, Milenova, Mozes, Taft, Hornick, Krishnan, Thomas, Kelly, Mukhin, Haberstroh, Stephens and Myczkowski 2005).

The goodness of the model was evaluated along the following lines:

- *Mean actual value* and *Mean predicted value*: the difference between these values indicates how near the mass center of the predicted and the actual target series fall to each other.
- *Mean absolute error* and *Root mean square error* describe the size of the prediction error.
- The *Predictive confidence* of a learning model measures how good the model is compared to naïve regression. (A naïve model always returns the average of the train data as prediction.) For example, 15% predictive confidence means that the model is 15% better than the naïve model.

We used Oracle's intuitive categorization: 60% or higher predictive confidence means a reliable model.

- *Residual plots* were created to visualize the difference between the actual and the predicted data. These graphs show the actual value (X axis) and the prediction error (Y axis) as an XY scatter chart.

Please note that our analysis method gives lower estimation for the information content: we show that there exists a predictive model with the given reliability but we do not state that it is the best possible one.

Examined Sets

The information content of four different measure sets was examined, probed against the global score.

- Set 1. Local Scores (AVGSCR, MINSCR, MAXSCR, SRCDEV). Although we already know that local and global scores are highly connected, it is interesting to analyze their relationship from the point of view of information content. The properties of this model also serve as a reference.
- Set 2. Raw local measures (AVGDUP, AVGUFL, DTAHAND, HANDLER, HLOHAND, INIHAND, INST, NOP, QUOTA, TMRHAND, TPGHAND, USDHAND). These measures represent the most basic set of raw information avail-

able locally. The riddle is: do they contain as much information as the scores (Set 1.)?

- Set 3. Local scores + Local raw measures (AVGSCR, MINSCR, MAXSCR, SRCDEV, AVGDUP, AVGUFL, DTAHAND, HANDLER, HLOHAND, INIHAND, INST, NOP, QUOTA, TMRHAND, TPGHAND, USDHAND). The goal with this measure set was to find out if raw measures can increase the quality of the model, thus, contribute with additional or clearer information.
- Set 4. Local scores + Local raw measures + Quasi-local measures (AVGSCR, MINSCR, MAXSCR, SRCDEV, AVGDUP, AVGUFL, DTAHAND, HANDLER, HLOHAND, INIHAND, INST, NOP, QUOTA, TMRHAND, TPGHAND, USDHAND, NEIGH, WIN, WINRATE). This set contains all locally or quasi-locally available items of information. Again, the question is if the information content of this set exceeds that of the local scores.

Results

Table 8 summarizes the prediction metrics of each data set, while Figure 5, Figure 6, Figure 7, and Figure 8 visualize the residual plot, respectively.

Result 2.1. (Set 1) The information content of local scores is clearly very similar to the global ones content. The prediction error is tiny and the

Table 8. Main descriptors of the best predictive models for each measure set

	Local scores	Raw local	Local scores +Raw local	Local scores +Raw local +Quasi-local
Mean actual value	-6.68	-6.68	-6.68	-6.68
Mean predicted value	-6.69	-6.23	-7.24	-7
Mean absolute error	1.63	5.62	3.98	1.21
Root mean square error	4.67	8.41	2.51	1.78
Predictive confidence	Naïve+85.49%	Naïve+73.89%	Naïve+87.6%	Naïve+94.44%

Figure 5. Local scores

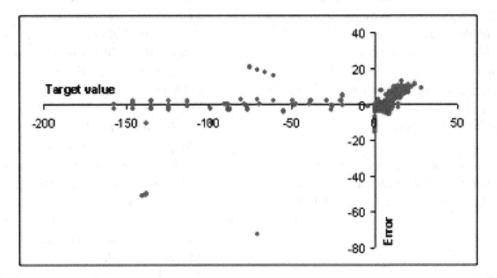

Figure 6. Raw local variables

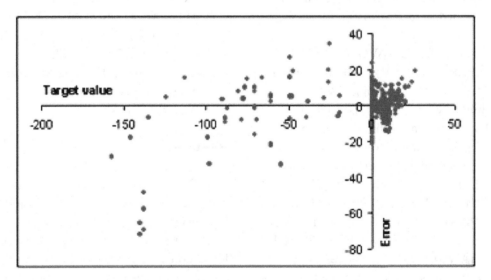

mass centers of the predicted and actual series nearly overlap. The residual plot shows that large errors are very rare, and the performance is highly homogeneous, except for the [0;20] X range where the mass center of the error is slightly above zero, indicating that the predictor tends to underestimate the global score in this range.

Result 2.2. (Set 2) In case of raw local measures, the most important result is that their information content approaches the level of the previous model (Set 1). The difference in the error size and distribution is clear, but as a magnitude, the difference is not so significant. Clearly, this model is worse in means of some details than Set 1 (e.g. larger errors are more common, as shown in the residual plot), but, in means of other aspects, it

Figure 7. Local scores+Raw local

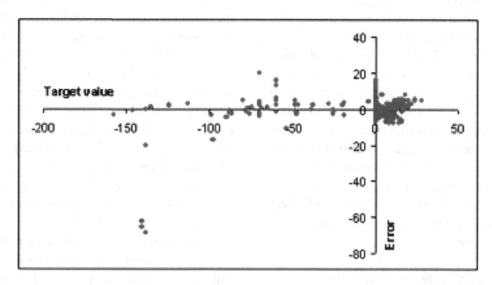

Figure 8. Local scores+Raw local+Quasi-local

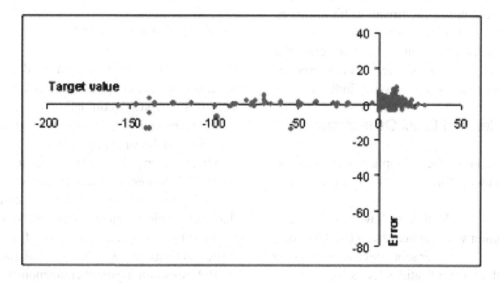

is maybe more stable (e.g. the mass center of the error is more around zero in the 0-20 range, too).

Result 2.3. (Set 3) In case of Set 3 (local scores + raw), the advantages of the two previous models seem to get combined. Even though the slightly worse error size, the predictive confidence improved, and the error is more balanced in the critical [0-20] region. The consequence is that the information content of the score values may be

improved when considering other local variables in addition.

Result 2.4. (Set 4) In case of all available measures, including quasi-local ones (Set 4), the performance of the model becomes significantly better. The improvement is visible not only in the confidence level (94%, so plus 9% which very high at this goodness) but also in the size of errors (1.21 and 1.78). The residual plot confirms that the error is balanced, larger errors are rare, and the maximal error size is remarkably smaller than in case of Set 1 (15 instead of 73).

The results indicate that locally and quasi-locally available measures provide the same information content and quality as the global score. While the *local score itself is a very good approximator already*, the consideration of raw local measures and of quasi-local measures may even increase the information content. *The combination of all locally and quasi locally available measures has such a high predictive quality that its information content practically coincides with the global score.*

Relationship Between Measures

The last round of analysis focused on unveiling interesting relationships and trends within measures. We set up and analyzed correlation matrices per epoch and globally, identified extreme elements, trends and notable differences. This subsection summarizes the most expressive findings.

Duplicates and Local Overestimations

The nature and effect of duplicates is well characterizes by the following observations.

- Result 3.1. SCRDEV shows very high correlation with duplicates (global 0.95, local 0.97), i.e. higher score deviations co-occur with high duplications levels.
- Result 3.2. MINSCR shows very high correlation with the scores (local 0.98, global 0.97), while MAXSCR does not tend to have this relationship so clearly (0.41). In other words, the minimum score tends to move together with the average, while the maximum score tends to result outliers from time to time.
- Result 3.3. AVGSCR shows high negative correlation with the score deviation (-0.88), i.e. higher scores have smaller deviations.

The above observations can be explained by the situation where most neighbors of the sender already possess a certain message, while a small minority does not. In this case, when the sender broadcasts the information, most neighbors will consider it as duplicate and decrease the score; while the few interested nodes will appreciate the message and will assign high values to the sender (local overvaluation). This clearly explains that high duplication levels co-occur with high score differences; and, that maximal scores may step away from the collective opinion upwards. Result 3.3. is a consequence: since it is unlikely to have too many duplicates when the score is high (the correlation of scores and duplicates is -0.98 locally and -0.99 globally), there is not much chance to fall in the trap of local over-valuation, hence, individual scores will not deviate much.

NOPs and the Evolution

Result 3.4. The only significant trend in the correlation matrix over epochs occurred in relation with of NOPs. NOP's correlation with the unused quota decreases significantly over epochs: the original weak linear dependence (0.24) turns first into linear independence (0.07), then into a weak negative dependence (-0.24). Hence, while in the beginning the presence of NOPs was contraproductive (remaining quota), in the end NOPs seem to occur more frequently in successful protocol instances (instances with less unused quota).

Before examining the phenomenon, the nature and significance of NOPs must be understood. NOPs are not real operators, they are a failover mechanism for invalid operations. We must note that the presence of NOPs is an unnecessary but sufficient indicator for evolutionary protocols: manually designed protocols will not produce NOPs, so a protocol with a NOP is guaranteed to originate from evolution. Another important property of NOPs is that they do not harm other parts of the protocol, so the presence of a NOP is not fatal when the protocol is good otherwise.

The phenomenon in the first epoch indicates that NOPs tend to be a bad sign: a protocol with NOPs is likely to perform poorly, which is not surprising in case of random combinations and mutations. While the majority of these NOP-containing protocols is ineffective, there are a few exceptions where the combination/mutation is beneficial otherwise. As the evolution proceeds, weak instances become extinct, and NOPs tend to be present in successful, useful protocols (obviously, NOPs do not help but do not make harm either). The final correlation value clearly means that some evolutionary protocols – the presence of NOPS indicates that they have evolved – perform very well. *In other words, the correlation trend of NOPs is evidence that the evolutionary mechanisms work; with time, evolved protocols are clearly present among the surviving and successful instances.*

FUTURE RESEARCH DIRECTIONS

Albeit most of the details were described through the example of the multi-hop broadcast problem, the idea behind is quite general, and can be utilized for some other telecommunication problems too (for instance broadcast in sensor networks). When used on a different problem case, the points that need to be fine-tuned are the fitness metrics and the genetic language itself, alongside with the initial protocol instances. In general, the fitness function should depict the requirements of the actual problem case. Domain-specific measures should be applied. Although GPDISS was intended to be general enough, it may make sense to extend the language with further elements to match the requirements of the specific problem case more smoothly. In general, adding new operations or even a new stack type is in conformance with the basic idea of the language.

The initial protocol instances have a strong influence on the short-term performance of the system (evolution guarantees the long-term con-vergence, but a good starting point is of great help on the short term). It is advised to start the evolution from protocol instances that make sense for the specific problem, and, besides that, show high enough diversity. Diversity is a key factor in the effectiveness of the evolution, and without initial diversity, mutation is the only tool that brings in this factor (which is enough if we can afford waiting).

The cardinal element of protocol evolution is the selection mechanism that drives the adaptation of protocols and pushes evolution in the right direction. Currently our understanding about selecting an appropriate score function is limited. For example, in our present work, we used a linear score function, however, we do not know yet, what are the limitations of such a form. Even if linear functions turn out to be appropriate, finding the best parameters for a given global performance score is important. An important future question is how different scoring functions influence the quality of the service provided by the evolved protocols, especially the duplicate/useful ratio.

In our current work we did not examine the code of the resulted protocol instances directly. Analysis of the resulting protocols presents a difficult problem as the number of different programs produced by evolution could be huge. Even the manual analysis of one program is pretty hard; therefore efficient data mining techniques are required to cope with the large amount of available data. Insight into common code patterns could help us to improve our selection mechanisms, crossover strategies and the GPDISS language itself. Efficient evolved protocols could also give interesting ideas for non-adaptive systems as well. In this study, our idea of Inverted Selection was used for the particular problem of multi hop broadcast. In the future we want to extend this framework and apply it for other, similar systems. In the future we will investigate the various mathematical methods that will allow faithful modeling of Inverted Selection and its consequences

CONCLUSION

This chapter revealed that – after decades of rigid and overregulated telecommunication protocols – the demands of the rapidly appearing new forms of networking infrastructure (like opportunistic networking) can be addressed by bio-inspired solutions. The focus was on presenting an evolutionary mechanism for the family of multi-hop broadcast protocols in ad hoc networks, where recent studies have shown that there is no absolute candidate for the most suitable message forwarding protocol, as the winner always depends on the actual environment and application conditions.

We have introduced a novel way of thinking in this field: instead of predefined protocols, autonomous evolutionary methods are applied to achieve the dynamic emergence of protocols, according to the current needs of the communicating nodes. For this purpose we have presented mechanisms like natural selection together with a novel genetic programming language, the GP-DISS, by shifting from pure natural selection to a broader concept, evolution, that is, survival of the fittest while constantly introducing diversity. The GPDISS language introduces novel concepts: relations and event handlers, and with the help of these concepts we showed with simulation that the evolution of protocols is feasible.

Results suggest that the proposed model of evolving protocols is applicable to the multi-hop broadcast problem in ad-hoc networks, as with time, evolution results in better performance than the initial – manually engineered – protocols. The fitness function can be defined using local (or quasi-local) input sources only, so the model is feasible for fully distributed cases such as ad-hoc sensor networks. With purely local fitness functions, the evolutional selection phase does not require the existence of any central entity. The process is carried out in an online manner,

meaning, that the evolution of protocols happens during the normal operation of the system, i.e. the evolution does not impede the system's normal goals.

The limitation of the model is that – as being based on random search – it cannot provide guarantees of any kind on the short term; for example, it cannot claim that the next protocol will not be worse than the current one. However, if the guarantee is not intended on any specific message or protocol instance but on the performance of the system as a whole (especially for a longer time windows) then probabilistic guarantees are possible.

According to our knowledge, there have not been similar initiatives – researching the automatic creation of protocol logics in an online manner, using nature-inspired autonomic techniques. The idea may be of interest to others for theoretic and practical reasons. Practically, as the approach works, it may help solving other similar problems, especially in the area of ad-hoc, sensor and peer-to-peer networks. Theoretically, the idea is a promising subject for further research, and we hope that numerous interesting aspects and derivations will be unveiled.

REFERENCES

Al Hanbali, A., Ibrahim, M., Simon, V., Varga, E., & Carreras, I. (2009). A survey of message delivery protocols in mobile ad hoc networks. In *Proc. of Inter-Perf 2008*, Athens, Greece, October 20-24, 2008.

Alouf, S., Carreras, I., Miorandi, D., & Neglia, G. (2007). Embedding evolution in epidemic style forwarding. In *Proc. of IEEE International Conference on Mobile Adhoc and Sensor Systems (MASS 2007)*, Pisa, Italy.

Brameier, M., & Banzhaf, W. (2007). *Linear genetic programming. Series: Genetic and Evolutionary Computation, XVI.* New York, NY: Springer.

Cheng, X., Huang, X., Li, D., Wu, D., & Du, D. Z. (2003). Polynomial-time approximation scheme for minimum connected dominating set in ad hoc wireless networks. *Networks, 42*(4), 202–208. doi:10.1002/net.10097

Colagrosso, M. D. (2007). Intelligent broadcasting in mobile ad hoc networks: Three classes of adaptive protocols. *EURASIP Journal on Wireless Communications and Networking, 1*, 16.

Cremet, V. (2006). *Foundations for SCALA: Semantics and proof of virtual types.* Unpublished doctoral thesis. EPFL, Lausanne, Switzerland

Dai, F., & Wu, J. (2004). Performance analysis of broadcast protocols in ad hoc networks based on self-pruning. *IEEE Transactions on Parallel and Distributed Systems, 15*, 1027–1040. doi:10.1109/TPDS.2004.69

Dittrich, P., Ziegler, J., & Banzhaf, W. (2001). Artificial chemistries – A review. *Artificial Life, 7*(3), 225–275. doi:10.1162/106454601753238636

Drucker, H., Burges, C. J. C., Kaufman, L., Smola, A., & Vapnik, V. (1997). Support vector regression machines. [MIT Press.]. *Advances in Neural Information Processing Systems, 9*, 155–161.

Guha, S., & Khuller, S. (1996). Approximation algorithms for connected dominating sets. *Algorithmica, 20*, 374–387. doi:10.1007/PL00009201

Kendall, M. G., & Stuart, A. (1973). *The advanced theory of statistics, volume 2: Inference and relationship.* Griffin.

Man, K. F., Tang, K. S., & Kwong, S. (1996). Genetic algorithms: Concepts and applications (in engineering design). *IEEE Transactions on Industrial Electronics, 43*(5), 519–534. doi:10.1109/41.538609

McCullagh, P., & Nelder, J. (1989). *Generalized linear models* (2nd ed.). Boca Raton, FL: Chapman and Hall/CRC.

Ni, S. Y., Tseng, Y. C., Chen, Y. S., & Sheu, J. P. (1999). The broadcast storm problem in a mobile ad hoc network. In *Proceedings of the 5th Annual ACM/IEEE International Conference on Mobile Computing and Networking, MobiCom '99*, Seattle, Washington, United States.

Rodgers, J. L., & Nicewander, W. A. (1988). Thirteen ways to look at the correlation coefficient. *The American Statistician, 42*(1), 59–66. doi:10.2307/2685263

Simon, V., Bérces, M., Varga, E., & Bacsárdi, L. (2009). Natural selection of message forwarding algorithms in multihop wireless networks. In *Proceedings of IEEE WiOpt*, Seoul, Korea.

Spector, L., & Robinson, A. (2002). Genetic programming and autoconstructive evolution with the push programming language. *Genetic Programming and Evolvable Machines, 3*(1), 7–40. doi:10.1023/A:1014538503543

Tamayo, P., Berger, C., Campos, M., Yarmus, J., Milenova, B., & Mozes, A. … Myczkowski, J. (2006). Oracle data mining. In O. Maimon & L. Rokach (Eds.), *Data mining and knowledge discovery handbook* (pp 1315-1329). United States: Springer.

Tschudin, C. (2003). Fraglets – A metabolistic execution model for communication protocols. In *Proc. 2nd Annual Symposium on Autonomous Intelligent Networks and Systems (AINS)*, Menlo Park, USA.

Williams, B., & Camp, T. (2002). Comparison of broadcasting techniques for mobile ad hoc networks. In *Proc. of the 3rd ACM International Symposium on Mobile Ad Hoc Networking & Computing, MOBIHOC '02*, Lausanne, Switzerland.

Wu, J., & Li, H. (1999). On calculating connected dominating set for efficient routing in ad hoc wireless networks. In *Proceedings of the Third International Workshop on Discrete Algorithms and Methods for Mobile Computing and Communications (DiaLM)*, Seattle, Washington, United States.

Yamamoto, L., Schreckling, D., & Meyer, T. (2007). *Self-replicating and self modifying programs in fraglets*. Budapest, Hungary: In BIONETICS.

Chapter 11
Application of Genetic Algorithms for Optimization of Anycast Routing in Delay and Disruption Tolerant Networks

Éderson R. Silva
Federal University of Uberlândia, Brazil

Paulo R. Guardieiro
Federal University of Uberlândia, Brazil

ABSTRACT

Delay and disruption tolerant networks (DTNs) have the capacity of providing data communication to remote and rural areas where current networking technology does not work well. In such challenging areas characterized by long duration partition, routing is a common problem. Anycast routing can be used for many applications in DTNs, and it is useful when nodes wish to send messages to at least one, and preferably only one, of the members in an anycast destination group. In this chapter, an anycast routing algorithm for DTNs based on genetic algorithms (GAs) is presented and analyzed. The GA is applied to find the appropriate combination of each path to comply with the delivery needs of the group of anycast sessions simultaneously. The routing algorithm based on GAs under consideration uses the concept of subpopulation to produce the next generation of the population, a limited number of solutions to be evaluated, and yields minimum delay in achieving a specified rate of delivery. Simulation results show that the studied GA-based anycast routing algorithm can produce good results.

INTRODUCTION

It has been awhile since the Internet has become very popular due to its flexibility, capacity, and robustness offered by the success of protocols used, such as TCP/IP. However, as the Internet is used more and more for communication, new challenges and working groups interested in proposing solutions arise. In this sense, there is a growing effort to allow communications in networks whose scenarios involve frequent disruption and/ or long and uncertain delays, thus requiring new

DOI: 10.4018/978-1-61350-092-7.ch011

techniques and protocols. This general networking problem can be called delay and disruption tolerant networking (DTN) (Farrell & Cahill, 2006).

It turns out that there are many applications that can make use of DTNs. The DTNs have the potential to interconnect devices and areas of the world that are underserved by traditional networks. The development of these networks can lead to the revolution of technology information for the population in developing countries that lack infrastructure, especially in remote and rural regions. DTNs have been investigated by the DTN research group (DTNRG), which is currently the main open venue for work on the DTN architecture (Cerf et al., 2007) and protocols. Many of the principles of DTN architecture are reviewed by Fall and Farrell (2008). More information about DTN can be found in a book on this subject (Farrell & Cahill, 2006).

One of the main challenges that arises in the design of DTNs that handle long/variable delays and frequent disconnections is routing. Zhang (2006) reviewed some of the routing protocols and categorized them as deterministic and stochastic, depending on the information available about the network. Deterministic protocols use information that nodes obtain about connectivity and network conditions to make efficient forwarding decisions. On the other hand, stochastic protocols address ways in which several copies of the messages can be disseminated among several carriers. The DTN architecture (Cerf et al., 2007) specified by the DTNRG offers a framework where a variety of routing protocols can be used, but it does not define any particular routing protocol. This way, routing is an open issue in DTNs and new proposals can contribute to the effective implementation of DTNs.

In order to operate efficiently in the vast diversity of environments in which the node may find itself, a number of routing algorithms that explore particular features are seen. In this chapter, the network is modeled for the problem of providing data communication to remote and rural areas.

These regions, possibly disconnected, can use a car, bus, motorbike, and/or truck, equipped with a storage device, to act as a carrier (mobile nodes that exploit device mobility are used to enable the communication) to deliver messages. Based on this network model, a routing algorithm for DTNs in scenarios where the network topology may be known ahead of time is presented.

The routing for anycast delivery is a useful service in DTNs and it has not been very well explored yet. Anycast routing is aimed at networks where some client nodes require a route to any member from a certain group of service nodes. Anycast can be used for many applications in DTNs such as disaster rescue field (people may want to find a doctor or fireman without knowing their location and specific IDs), long distance education (students may want to get an article from any one of the libraries), battle fields (a command center may want to deliver a particular message to any soldier in a group) etc. Therefore, efficient anycast services are necessary for supporting these applications.

A critical issue in DTN routing is to find the appropriate combination of routes taking into account the node storage constraint and the network traffic dynamics (this problem is NP-complete). Thus, an anycast routing algorithm for DTNs making use of genetic algorithms (GAs) is analyzed, because GAs have the ability to solve complex optimization problems. Moreover, the DTNs can tolerate longer delays than the elaboration time required for GAs to converge toward the optimal solution. Hence, DTNs can be a good application field for GAs. To improve the performance of the GA-based algorithms, strategies, such as the concept of subpopulation (the next generation population is produced using four subpopulations) and a reduction of the number of solutions to be evaluated, are used.

The anycast routing algorithm based on GAs is studied and compared with other strategies. Through the results based on modeling and simulation, it can be determined if each approach used in the algorithm is efficient and effective. Clearly, the routing algorithm is designed to optimize the network performance metrics, i.e. it distributes the message traffic properly in the network, providing a high rate of delivery and limited delay.

PRELIMINARIES

Routing in DTNs

Routing is an active area of research and development in DTNs. Zhang (2006) reviewed some routing algorithms for DTNs and most works address the unicast delivery. However, in this case, the destination is fixed and is determined when the message is generated. On the other hand, the anycast service is appropriate to take the opportunity to send messages to only one destination, possibly the one that provides the best communication opportunities among the nodes in a destination group, allowing communication in scenarios where the unicast service would be impracticable.

Multicasting is analyzed in DTNs (Abdulla & Simon, 2006; Zhao, Ammar, & Zegura, 2005) using several multicast routing schemes. It is important to note that when the multicast service is used, mobile nodes responsible for assisting in the delivery of messages (bundles), store the messages until there is confirmation that all members of the destination group have already received the messages. In the anycast case, mobile nodes responsible for bringing the messages to a member of the anycast group need to store them until they are delivered to only one member of the anycast group, which leads to a substantial saving in storage of mobile devices that relay the messages to a destination group.

Gong et al. (2006) analyzed the anycast semantic for DTNs and presented a metric named expected multi-destination delay for anycast (EMDDA). The authors assumed that nodes in the network are stationary. The connectivity among the nodes is established by the mobile devices that act as carriers to deliver messages to the nodes. Also the moving patterns of these mobile devices can be obtained. In this chapter, this same DTN model (Gong et al., 2006) is used, but the routing performed by Gong et al. (2006) is categorized as stochastic and the routing under consideration is deterministic.

Though Gong et al. (2006) presented three types of anycast semantics that allow the source to explicitly specify the destination of a message, the network traffic during the selection of routing and the storage constraint of mobile devices are not considered. The anycast routing scheme under study is designed to incorporate both node storage constraint and network traffic dynamics.

Genetic Algorithms in Routing

GA-based approaches have been used to address the problem of shortest path (SP) routing. Different chromosome representations can be employed for encoding the problem, e.g. Inagaki, Haseyama, and Kitajima (1999) proposed an algorithm that employs fixed length chromosomes while Ahn and Ramakrishna (2002) employed variable length chromosomes. The length of the chromosome used by the studied anycast routing algorithm based on GAs is fixed.

There are several GAs that address the problem of multicast (Leung, Li, & Xu, 1998; Randaccio & Atzori, 2007). However, those approaches are beyond the scope of this chapter.

The main differences in these previous works are in the different chromosome representations, routing objectives, problems based on constraints, characteristics of the networks and methods to improve the algorithm convergence. In this chapter, GAs are applied to optimize anycast routing in DTNs. To do this, some of the concepts addressed in the previous works are used (each strategy used is described along with the routing algorithm based on GAs) to find the appropriate combination of routes of each anycast session with optimized rate of delivery and delay. The use of GAs in DTNs was introduced in (Silva & Guardieiro, 2008) and it was shown that GAs can optimize the delivery probability (*DP*) and delay *D* when compared to SP algorithm based on hop count. Moreover, it was shown that when the number of sessions and the traffic increases a lot, the performance of the proposed GA is reduced. In order to make the proposal more attractive in terms of time required to converge, the concept of subpopulation and a limited number of potential solutions in isolation are used. The combination of both ideas is proposed by Silva and Guardieiro (2010). A more detailed analysis of this GA-based solution and each strategy used are described in this chapter.

SYSTEM MODEL

Anycast Semantics

If messages can be sent to only one node, the delivery semantic is unicast and therefore the destination group contains one node. When referring to a group size greater than one, the delivery semantics may be of either the anycast (messages are sent to any one of a group of nodes) or multicast (messages are sent to all in a group of nodes).

As stated earlier, DTNs are characterized by long delivery delay. In this situation, the group membership may change during a message transfer, introducing ambiguity in anycast semantics. Consequently, new anycast semantic models should be developed. To do this, the intended receivers should be clearly defined for a message as group membership changes when nodes join and leave the group. Gong et al. (2006) presented three anycast semantic models that allow the message sender to explicitly specify the intended receivers of a message:

- Current membership model (CM): the receiver of the message should be a member of the destination group at the time of message delivery;
- Temporal interval membership model (TIM): a message includes a temporal interval that specifies the period during which the intended receiver must be a member of the destination group;
- Temporal point membership model (TPM): the intended receiver should be at least a member of the destination group at some time during the membership interval.

These models can be used according to the needs of the application (other models are possible and further experience with DTN applications will help clarify which semantics are most useful). The algorithm developed in this chapter can be easily applied to these three models. In the following sections, the intended receivers are defined when the message is generated. This is, in particular, the case of the TIM model, where the temporal interval is the instant of the message generation. After that, the anycast routing algorithm chooses the route, and consequently the message can be delivered to one of the intended receivers.

Network Model

As the network is modeled for the problem of providing data communication to remote and rural areas using a car, bus, motorbike, and/or truck, equipped with a storage device to act as carriers to deliver messages, the network model used by Gong et al. (2006) is more suitable than that used by Jain, Patra, and Fall (2004). The DTN is represented by an evolving graph and the link capacities are time-dependent. A notion of evolving graphs is introduced by Ferreira (2004).

According to the model used, the DTN graph is a directed graph G = (V, E), where V represents the nodes and E is the set of edges. An edge between node *1* and *2* (Figure 1) means that some mobile device moving from the initial node *1* to the terminal node *2* exists. Every mobile device has a moving delay $md(1,2)$ denoting the time spent by the mobile device from the node *1* to the node *2*, and a leaving time $w(1,2)$ representing the time in which a mobile device leaves from node *1* to node *2*. $b(1)$ and $b(2)$ represents the storage capacity (buffer size) of node *1* and node *2*, respectively. $c(1,2)$ is the storage capacity of the mobile device.

Moreover, the nodes in the network (remote and rural areas) are stationary and generate messages. On the other hand, mobile devices (a car, bus, motorbike, and/or truck) move from one node to another and do not generate messages by themselves. The routing algorithm determines each mobile device in the network through which the message should be forwarded in order to reach its destination. As the network model used considers that information about the network topology is known in advance, proactive fragmentation is used in the source, i.e. only the source can fragment the message. In order to support DTN fragmentation, the ability to reassemble fragments at the destination is required.

PROPOSED GA-BASED ANYCAST ROUTING ALGORITHM

GAs provide robust and efficient search in complex spaces based on the mechanics of natural selection and natural genetics (Goldberg, 1989). To exploit all the advantages of GAs, there are some components that need to be carefully addressed: genetic representation, i.e. encoding potential

solutions into chromosomes; the generation of an initial population; an evaluation function that can evaluate the fitness of the chromosome; the genetic operators; and setting the control parameters. Figure 2 shows a flowchart of the proposed GA-based routing algorithm and each step is detailed in the following sections.

The GAs are applied to find out an appropriate (sub-optimal) combination of anycast paths to route the messages generated by every anycast source. The proposed GA-based anycast routing algorithm uses two main steps: a) finding a set of possible solutions for each session in isolation; b) evaluating the combinations of these sets. These two steps can also be seen in (Randaccio & Atzori, 2007). However, the proposed GA uses a different and optimized way to compute potential solutions in isolation.

Potential Solutions in Isolation

For each anycast session z, a source node S_z can send messages to destination group $K_{z,l}$, where l is the number of possible intended receivers for each anycast session.

The set of potential solutions for the anycast routing is found by combining unicast paths connecting every source-destination couple in a session using the graph that represents the DTN. These potential solutions are found by applying Dijkstra's algorithm to compute the paths with the least number of hops between each source-destination couple in an isolated way. Each route is computed using the matrix h_{ij}, which has value one if the nodes n_i and n_j are connected. Otherwise it has value zero. Next, the Dijkstra's algorithm is applied again, and additional paths (adding to

Figure 1. Edge in a DTN graph

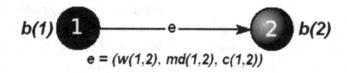

$$e = (w(1,2), md(1,2), c(1,2))$$

Figure 2. Flowchart of the proposed GA-based anycast routing algorithm

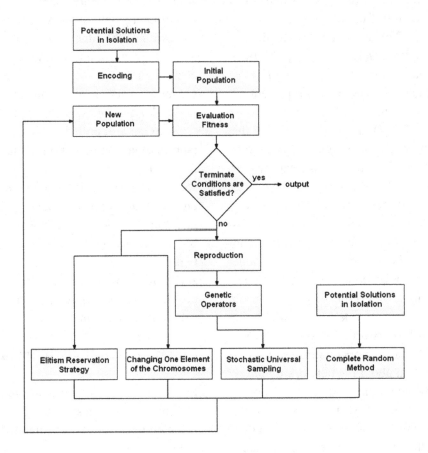

the solutions already computed) for the source-destination couple are obtained. For each anycast session a set of potential solutions in isolation can be obtained.

The potential solutions in isolation are clarified by the simple example in Figure 3. Consider the source node n_1 wants to send messages to the intended receivers n_5, n_8, and n_9, i.e. only one anycast session. Using the matrix h_{ij}, and applying Dijkstra's algorithm, F having the set of potential solutions in isolation is obtained. The zeros appear to maintain the same length of rows in F. In the next section, it is shown that this feature is useful for encoding the potential solutions into chromosomes.

Since the set of potential solutions in isolation is used as input to the routing algorithm, and for each anycast session z an array F_z is created, the

combination of all paths represents the search space. To understand the dimension of the search space, assuming a network with 20 anycast sessions, and each of these with in average 10 potential solutions in isolation, the total number of combinations is 10^{20}. As a result, the complexity of finding the solution with the optimal combination of routes grows with the number of sessions and potential solutions in isolation, requiring a search and optimization algorithm for solving this complex problem. Since GAs are suitable for finding solutions in complex spaces, the anycast routing algorithm under study makes use of GAs.

A large number of potential solutions can be obtained depending on the number of nodes, sessions, edge density, and intended receivers. The number of potential solutions to be computed can be limited using two approaches: limiting

Figure 3. Example of network topology used to compute potential solutions in isolation

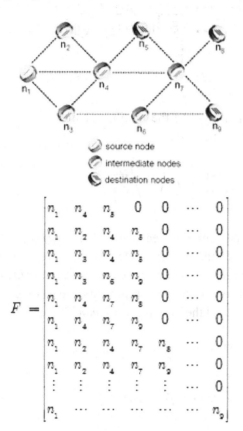

- ○ source node
- ◑ intermediate nodes
- ◐ destination nodes

$$F = \begin{bmatrix} n_1 & n_4 & n_8 & 0 & 0 & \cdots & 0 \\ n_1 & n_2 & n_4 & n_8 & 0 & \cdots & 0 \\ n_1 & n_3 & n_4 & n_8 & 0 & \cdots & 0 \\ n_1 & n_3 & n_6 & n_9 & 0 & \cdots & 0 \\ n_1 & n_4 & n_7 & n_8 & 0 & \cdots & 0 \\ n_1 & n_4 & n_7 & n_9 & 0 & \cdots & 0 \\ n_1 & n_2 & n_4 & n_7 & n_8 & \cdots & 0 \\ n_1 & n_2 & n_4 & n_7 & n_9 & \cdots & 0 \\ \vdots & \vdots & \vdots & \vdots & \vdots & \cdots & 0 \\ n_1 & \cdots & \cdots & \cdots & \cdots & \cdots & n_9 \end{bmatrix}$$

the number of columns (i.e. the number of hops) or limiting the number of rows (i.e. the number of potential solutions in isolation). The question, if limiting the number of potential solutions to be considered by the GA-based algorithms is a good approach or not, is analyzed in this chapter.

Genetic Representation and Population Initialization

At first, it is assumed that a certain set of possible routes for each couple source-destination (potential solutions in isolation) is available. The adopted representation scheme is based on associating each gene to each node forming the route between source-destination. The chromosome is essentially a list of nodes along the path for all sessions. The length of the chromosome is then proportional to the number of anycast sessions (z). Figure 4 shows an individual representation, where s_z (with $z = 1, 2, ..., z$) are the source nodes, the n_x (with $x = i, j, ..., o$) are the intermediate nodes and the $k_{z,l}$ (with $z = 1, 2, ..., z$ and l = number of intended receivers) represent the destinations chosen. The zeros (0) appear to maintain the constant length of the chromosome. This explains the placement of zeros in F (potential solutions in isolation). Each anycast session has its source node position represented by sp (constant for all individuals). The length of the path for each anycast session is based on the number of columns (defined by the last potential solution computed) of the array F.

GAs work from a rich database of solutions simultaneously (population) reducing the probability of finding a false peak. To generate the initial population, a route for each couple source-destination is randomly chosen using the set of potential solutions in isolation, i.e. a random initialization is adopted.

Fitness Function

It is necessary to define an evaluation function that can evaluate the fitness of the chromosome: the performance metrics DP (1) and delay D (5) are considered, as shown in the following equations:

$$DP = \sum_{a=1}^{z} m_k(a) / m_s(a, f) \qquad (1)$$

where

$$m_k(z) = \sum_{f=1}^{N_f} m_s(z, f) \qquad (2)$$

subject to

$$\sum_{(i,j) \subset F_z} x_{ij} m_s(z, f) < c(i, j) \qquad (3)$$

Figure 4. Genotype coding

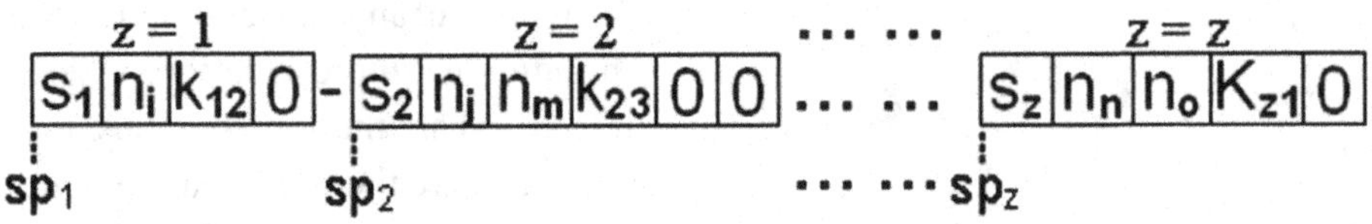

$$\sum_{(i,j)\subset F_z} x_{ij}\left[md\left(i,j\right)+w\left(i,j\right)\right]<t_{toal} \qquad (4)$$

Where:

$m_k(z)$: estimated anycast messages received by an anycast group member from each anycast session z;

$m_s(z,f)$: fragmented messages transmitted by each source node.

F: indicates the fragments (in our approach only the source can fragment messages);

N_f: total number of fragments;

F_z: array containing potential solutions in isolation;

$c(i,j)$: storage capacity of mobile devices;

$md(i,j)$: moving delay of mobile devices;

$w(i,j)$: leaving time of mobile devices;

t_{total}: total simulation time;

x_{ij}: 1 if edge (i,j) is selected, otherwise 0.

The DP (1) is proportional to the estimated number of unique anycast messages received by an anycast group member $m_k(z)$ (2) divided by the number of messages transmitted by each anycast source $m_s(z,f)$. Equation (3) guarantees that the number of messages relayed does not exceed the storage capacity of mobile devices, and (4) guarantees that the time of message delivery does not exceed the total simulation time (acting as a lifetime).

To represent the delay for all traffic (time spent by messages in traveling between their source and destination nodes), the weighted mean delay or delay D (5) is defined, where f is the number of fragments and w_i is the weight of each fragment proportional to the number of messages in the current fragment.

$$D=\sum_{i=1}^{f}\left[w_i\cdot D_z\left(f\right)\right]\Big/\sum_{i=1}^{f}w_i \qquad (5)$$

The delay for each fragment $D_z(f)$ (6) is the sum of the average delay $d(i,j)$ from each hop forming the route source-destination. $d(i,j)$ (7) will consist of two components, the waiting time $w(i,j)$ and the moving delay $md(i,j)$.

$$D_z\left(f\right)=\sum_{s_z\leq i\leq k_z-1,s_z+1\leq k_z} d\left(i,j\right) \qquad (6)$$

$$d\left(i,j\right)=w\left(i,j\right)+md\left(i,j\right) \qquad (7)$$

The fitness of chromosomes is sorted using the following strategy (the proposed GA-based algorithm searches routes with DP above a threshold, i.e. above a minimum delivery probability DP_{min}, and with the least delay):

```
for every individual in the popula-
tion at current generation do
    sort the individuals in descend-
ing order of delivery probability
    if the current individuals have
delivery probability above DP_min
        for the individuals with
delivery probability above DP_min do
            sort the individuals
in ascending order of delay D
        end
    end
end
```

A large number of different DTN applications can be found. As the values of DP_{min} can be adjusted according to application needs, it is clear that different values can be used for DP_{min}. In this chapter, the intention is to show that the proposed algorithm is able to meet a minimum delivery probability. Some studies guaranteeing a minimum data delivery probability are found in the literature. A large number of these works (Sudhaakar et al., 2009; Wang & Wu, 2007) have been published with DP_{min} between 0.9 and 0.95.

Next Generation Population

After sorting the individuals according to their fitness, the termination conditions are checked. The number of generations is used as terminate condition. If this condition is satisfied, the GA is finished. Otherwise, the next generation population (new population) must be formed. The concept of subpopulation is used, i.e. the next generation population is the mixing of four subpopulations (this method is efficient and effective (Lo & Chang, 2000)):

1. Elitism reservation strategy: the chromosomes with the best fitness survive and are carried into the next generation;
2. Change of one element of the chromosomes: replaces one route in the chromosomes with best fitness to form a new individual;
3. The stochastic universal sampling: the spin of a roulette wheel. This subpopulation uses the offspring resulting from crossover and mutation;
4. Complete random method: population is generated randomly using the potential solutions in isolation.

There are two competing factors in the selection procedure: selection pressure and population diversity. Ahn and Ramakrishna (2002) define selection pressure "as the ratio of the probability of selection of the best chromosome in the popula-

tion to that of an average chromosome" (p. 569). An increase of selection pressure decreases the diversity of the population, and vice versa. When these four subpopulations are used, different selection pressures are seen. On the one hand, the stochastic universal sampling method increases selection pressure. On the other hand, the complete random method decreases selection pressure.

The new population is constituted by the four subpopulations as shown in Table 1. These values are used to increase the diversity in the new population (e.g. complete random method representing 60%).

Reproduction

The selection operator employed for reproduction is the pairwise tournament selection without replacement, i.e. two chromosomes are picked and the one with higher fitness values is selected for reproduction.

The genetic operators used are: one point crossover and mutation. To produce only regular individuals, the genetic operators use the source node positions represented by sp_{1-z} (constant for all individuals) as a cross point. Figure 5 shows an example of one point crossover and mutation. Suppose two individuals X1 and X2 (clearly letters are used as a generic representation, since the chromosomes are represented by the nodes in the network and, when necessary, they are filled with zeros). For one point crossover, one source node position sp_{1-z} is chosen randomly, e.g. the individuals Y1 and Y2 are generated by the crossover between X1 and X2 at point sp_3. Mutation is performed by replacement of one route (this route is obtained using the potential solutions in isolation). The individual X' is generated by the mutation of the second route of the individual X1. Therefore, it is not necessary to repair or impose a penalty to deal with infeasible chromosomes.

Table 1. New population distribution

	Subpopulation	Size of each subpopulation
1	Elitism reservation strategy	10%
2	Changing one element of the chromosomes	10%
3	The stochastic universal sampling	20%
4	Complete random method	60%

Genetic Algorithm Based Approaches

Finally, the control parameters are set up, e.g., population size (50 individuals) and the probability of applying the genetic operators (crossover probability P_c: 0.8 and mutation probability P_m: 0.03). The influence of P_c and P_m on the total population is reduced because they are only applied in the third subpopulation. The proposed GA is controlled by the number of generations (terminate condition).

The performance of five routing approaches is compared. First, the SP algorithm that computes the path with the least number of hops between the source and the destination is considered. Second, the earliest delivery (ED) algorithm that computes the path in which each edge has a cost proportional to delay ($md(i,j)$ and $w(i,j)$) is studied. Next, a GA-based approach (GA1) that considers only the elitism reservation strategy is analyzed. Then a GA-based approach (GA2) that uses the elitism reservation strategy and a limited number of potential solutions in isolation (limited to 15% of the number of nodes in the network) is studied. Finally, a GA-based approach (GA3) that uses the concept of subpopulation and a limited number of potential solutions in isolation is proposed. GA-based approaches are summarized in Table 2.

MODELING AND SIMULATION

In this section, a computational study is carried out to compare the algorithms. In the simulation,

it is employed the Waxman Network Topology Generator (Waxman, 1988) to generate a random graph over a square coordinate grid. The probability of having an edge between nodes i and j is given by function $P(i,j) = \alpha.\exp(-dist(i,j)/\beta.L)$, where $dist(i,j)$ is the Cartesian distance from i to j, L is the maximum distance between any two nodes, and the parameters α and β are real numbers in the range (0,1]. These parameters can be adjusted to obtain the desired characteristics in the resulting graph. In our simulation, α is set to 0.4 (an intermediate density of short edges relative to longer ones), and β to 0.25 (graphs with lower edge densities) for 40 nodes.

To simulate the behaviors of DTNs, a mobile device replaces each edge generated by the Waxman generator, as a carrier. The leaving times $w(i,j)$ of mobile devices on each edge are random numbers from the Poisson distribution with mean interval time selected randomly from 600 to 6000 seconds. The moving delay $md(i,j)$ is a number selected randomly between 60 and 600 seconds, which is multiplied by the distance $dist(i,j)$ between the nodes. The storage capacity $c(i,j)$ of each mobile device may vary from 500 to 800 messages. For the nodes, the capacity $b(node)$ may vary between 600 and 1000 messages.

Each anycast session (only anycast traffic is considered in our simulation) can have between 2 and 5 possible destinations ($2 \leq l \leq 5$). A node is randomly picked as the anycast source, and each source node can send between 300 and 500 messages. A message is split only at source and different fragments are routed along the same paths.

Figure 5. Example of the genetic operators used

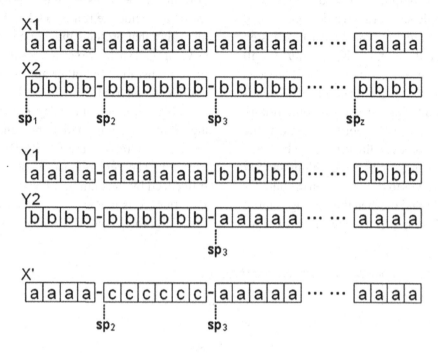

Table 2. GA-based approaches

Algorithm	Limited number of potential solutions	Elitism reservation strategy	Concept of subpopulation
GA1	No	Yes	No
GA2	Yes	Yes	No
GA3	Yes	Yes	Yes

It is important to analyze the computational time. The SP and ED algorithms answer comes almost immediately. On the other hand, for the GA-based routing algorithms the mean simulation time ($t_{simtime}$) that they take until good routes are found is computed:

$$t_{simtime} = \frac{t_{total} \cdot g_{toconverge}}{g_{total}} \qquad (8)$$

where t_{total} is the total time taken by the algorithm until it achieves the termination condition of the GA, i.e. the total number of generations (g_{total}). $g_{toconverge}$ is the total number of generations spent until the algorithm finds good or sub-optimal routes.

PERFORMANCE EVALUATION

Test Analysis

To compare the algorithms, statistics about *DP*, delay *D*, and average number of hops and generations were collected. The results are the average over 10 runs with different random seeds and network topologies. For *DP* (Figure 6), the 95% confidence interval (plotted using a scale of 1:2) on the mean is computed based on the sample mean and sample standard deviation. GA-based algorithms use a $DP_{min} = 94\%$ (this can be adjusted according to application needs). The DP for all algorithms decreases when the number of sessions increases. This is because with more traffic, nodes will need to wait more time for an opportunity to transmit. SP and ED algorithms present the worst results. Moreover, the difference between the performance of GA-based algorithms and SP/ED algorithms tends to increase when the number of sessions is high, i.e. when the routing is more challenging. This is because the SP and ED al-

gorithms do not consider the combination of the traffic to decide the route. GA2 is the GA-based algorithm that presents the worst results for DP. GA1 and GA3 achieve similar results and they are more robust than the other approaches (smaller confidence interval).

Table 3 presents the delay D for the routing algorithms. It is important to note that the results presented in Table 3 are for the DP obtained in Figure 6. The performance of the algorithms is influenced by the number of sessions. However, its influence is higher for DP than for delay D, especially for SP and ED algorithms.

Figure 6. Delivery probability for different numbers of sessions

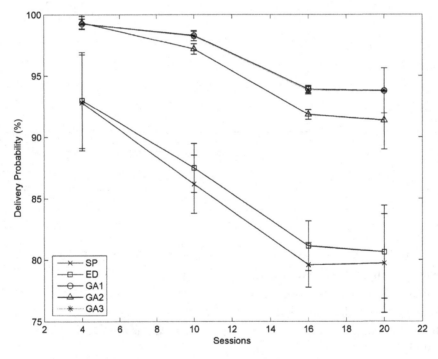

Table 3. Delay D (seconds) for different numbers of sessions

Algorithm	4 sessions	10 sessions	16 sessions	20 sessions
SP	16111 s	20834 s	19119 s	19848 s
ED	15991 s	20120 s	19087 s	19180 s
GA1	16846 s	19779 s	19841 s	21386 s
GA2	17199 s	20458 s	20540 s	20891 s
GA3	16847 s	19871 s	20515 s	20798 s

Figure 7 depicts the average number of hops used by each routing algorithm. SP algorithm uses the least number of hops because it computes paths with the least number of hops. ED algorithm finds routes with a number of hops slightly larger than SP. GA-based routing algorithms use more hops than the SP and ED algorithms, consequently distributing the traffic in the network better. Moreover, the difference between the number of hops used by the GA-based algorithms and the SP/ED algorithms tends to increase when the traffic is high. This is because, when the time waiting for an opportunity to transmit is high, i.e. the number of sessions increases, the GA-based algorithms need to avoid a large number of messages passing through the same edge, i.e. they search alternative routes to distribute the traffic in the network better.

Figure 8 shows the average number of generations that the GA-based routing algorithms require to converge. The number of generations for every GA-based algorithm increases when the number of sessions is high. This is because with more sessions, the chromosome length is higher and there is a large number of combinations to be evaluated by the GA-based algorithms. GA2 and GA3 use almost the same number of generations. On the other hand, the number of generations that GA1 takes to converge increases meaningly.

Figure 9 shows the mean simulation time ($t_{simtime}$) that the GA-based algorithms take to converge and this ($t_{simtime}$) follows the behavior of the average number of generations. As a result, GA1 takes large amounts of computational time to converge. For the most challenging simulated scenario (20 anycast sessions), GA3 spent on average 786.3 seconds, against 2063.0 seconds for GA1 to converge. If this is compared with the leaving time $w(i,j)$, this time shows that GA3 is a better solution.

The results show that GA1 and GA3 present the best performance for message delivery. Besides, GA3 gets these results using a smaller number of generations than GA1. This way, when the number of potential solutions in isolation is limited, the GA-based algorithms converge

Figure 7. Average number of hops used by each routing algorithm

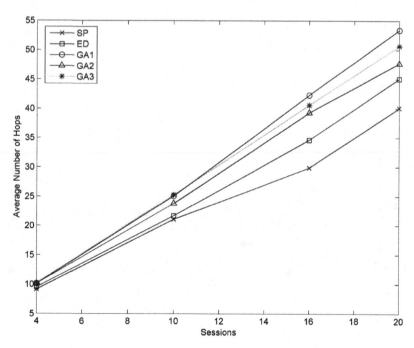

Figure 8. Average number of generations for GA-based routing algorithms

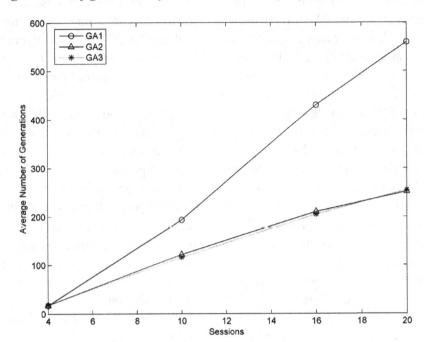

Figure 9. Mean simulation time ($t_{simtime}$) for GA-based routing algorithms

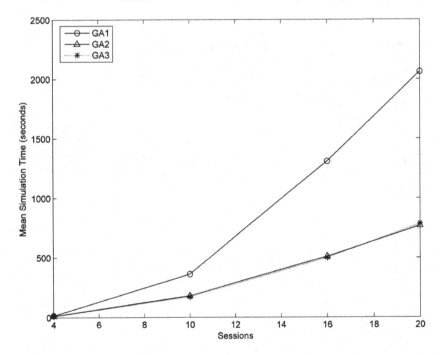

faster, and when the concept of subpopulation is used, the GA-based algorithms search solutions more efficiently.

Complexity

Beyond the mean simulation time ($t_{simtime}$) that the GA-based algorithms take to converge, computed for the anycast routing algorithms based on GAs, it is possible to see how the running time grows as the volume of data provided as input to the algorithms increases. For this, the big O notation that defines the running time in terms of key functions is used, eliminating constants and other functions. The resulting time complexity of the GA-based algorithms is expressed by:

$$O(GA) = O\left(n\_ger \cdot n\_pop \cdot z \cdot N^2\right)$$

where n_ger represents the number of generations, n_pop the size of the population and z the number of anycast sessions. Moreover, an array NxN is considered as the worst case, i.e. N potential solutions in isolation containing all the N nodes.

Analyzing the running time found, it is clear that this time is dependent on the dimensions of the array of potential solutions in isolation, hence the convergence time of GA-based algorithms is reduced when the number of potential solutions in isolation is limited. On the other hand, when these potential solutions are limited, some routes that could be part of better solutions are lost. The results found in the last section show that limiting the number of potential solutions in isolation reduces the time complexity of the algorithm considerably (Figure 9), with results very close to those found when the number of potential solutions is unlimited. Therefore, limiting the number of potential solutions in isolation is a good approach to reduce the average running time to the routing algorithms based on GAs until they converge. This way, limiting the number of potential solutions in isolation is a good approach, especially in cases where time constraints are found.

DISCUSSION

The results in the previous sections suggest that when the network resources are scarce, the improvement obtained by GA-based algorithms is higher if compared with SP and ED algorithms. This is because the SP algorithm considers only the number of hops for route decision and the ED algorithm takes into account information about moving delay and leaving time. On the other hand, the routing algorithms based on GAs consider the combination of the traffic to decide the route. This suggests that with few resources, more complex routing algorithms are necessary to achieve a good performance, and available information can be used to optimize the performance. Moreover, the good results obtained by the GA-based algorithms can be explained by the main characteristic of the algorithm: it searches for the combination of routes above a DP_{min} and having the shortest delay. This DP_{min} can be adjusted according to the application needs.

It is noted that when the number of potential solutions in isolation is limited, the GA-based algorithms converge faster. This is because the search space of the GA-based algorithms is reduced and the number of generations required by the GA-based algorithms to converge decreases. This is in contrast when the number of potential solutions in isolation is unlimited, where solutions containing large quantities of hops, which most possibly will not be part of the optimal solution, are combined by the GA-based algorithms, requiring a large number of generations.

Finally, it is observed that when the concept of subpopulation is used, the GA-based algorithms search for solutions more efficiently. Simulation results indicate that the mix method is a reasonable approach and it permits the new population to be generated according to the four subpopulations using different selection pressures.

FUTURE RESEARCH DIRECTIONS

A few real-world deployments of the DTN architecture have been tested successfully. As a possible future research direction, an extension of this research is to set up a testbed using real mobile devices. This way, the proposed anycast routing algorithm based on GAs can be tested in environments that are more realistic. Moreover, GAs allow the use of various techniques and approaches to improve their performance, as studied for the anycast routing algorithm based on GAs proposed in this chapter. Thus, new and/or different strategies can emerge and be investigated in order to improve the anycast routing algorithm based on GAs.

CONCLUSION

DTNs have the potential of providing data communication to scenarios involving frequent disconnection and variable delays, allowing communication in areas that are underserved by traditional networks. As routing is one of the main challenges that arises and the anycast service can be used for many applications in DTNs, a GA-based solution to the anycast routing in deterministic DTNs has been analyzed in this chapter. The proposed algorithm has the advantage of computing good routes above a minimum delivery probability and with the least delay. To do this, it searches for the appropriate anycast traffic combination in the group of anycast sessions. Simulation results have shown that the performance of the proposed GA-based anycast routing algorithm (GA3) is only slightly smaller than GA-based

approach (GA1) with unlimited number of routes, against the significant decrease in the number of generations required. Moreover, it is shown that the concept of subpopulation improves the performance of the algorithm, and the proposed GA-based routing algorithm, using all approaches described, requires an acceptable time to converge for the simulated scenarios. Hence, DTNs can be a good application field for GAs and, as routing is an open issue in DTNs, the proposed anycast routing algorithm based on GAs can contribute to the effective implementation of the DTNs. Finally, future research directions were mentioned in the previous section in order to improve the GA-based solution analyzed in this chapter.

REFERENCES

Abdulla, M., & Simon, R. (2006). A simulation analysis of multicasting in delay tolerant networks. *Proceedings of the Winter Simulation Conference – WSC*, (pp. 2234-2241).

Ahn, C. W., & Ramakrishna, R. S. (2002). A genetic algorithm for shortest path routing problem and the sizing of populations. *IEEE Transactions on Evolutionary Computation*, 6(6), 566–579. doi:10.1109/TEVC.2002.804323

Cerf, V., Burleigh, S., Hooke, A., Torgerson, L., Durst, R., Scott, K., … Weiss, H. (2007). *Delay-tolerant networking architecture*. (IETF RFC 4838).

Fall, K., & Farrell, S. (2008). DTN: An architectural retrospective. *IEEE Journal on Selected Areas in Communications*, 26(5), 828–836. doi:10.1109/JSAC.2008.080609

Farrell, S., & Cahill, V. (2006). *Delay- and disruption-tolerant networking*. Norwood, MA: Artech House.

Ferreira, A. (2004). Building a reference combinatorial model for MANETs. *IEEE Network*, *18*(5), 24–29. doi:10.1109/MNET.2004.1337732

Goldberg, D. E. (1989). *Genetic algorithms in search, optimization and machine learning.* Boston, MA: Addison-Wesley.

Gong, Y., Xiong, Y., Zhang, Q., Zhang, Z., Wang, W., & Xu, Z. (2006). *Anycast routing in delay tolerant networks.* IEEE Global Telecommunications Conference (*GLOBECOM*), (pp. 1-5).

Inagaki, J., Haseyama, M., & Kitajima, H. (1999). A genetic algorithm for determining multiple routes and its applications. *Proceedings of the IEEE International Symposium on Circuits and Systems*, (pp. 137-140).

Jain, S., Patra, R., & Fall, K. (2004). Routing in a delay tolerant network. *Proceedings of the 2004 Conference on Applications, Technologies, Architectures, and Protocols for Computer Communications*, (pp. 145-158).

Leung, Y., Li, G., & Xu, Z. B. (1998). A genetic algorithm for the multiple destination routing problems. *IEEE Transactions on Evolutionary Computation*, *2*(4), 150–161. doi:10.1109/4235.738982

Lo, C. C., & Chang, W. H. (2000). A multiobjective hybrid genetic algorithm for the capacitated multipoint network design problem. *IEEE Transactions on Systems, Man, and Cybernetics*, *30*(3), 461–470. doi:10.1109/3477.846234

Randaccio, L. S., & Atzori, L. (2007). Group multicast routing problem: A genetic algorithms based approach. *Computer Networks*, *51*(14), 3989–4004. doi:10.1016/j.comnet.2007.04.008

Silva, E. R., & Guardieiro, P. R. (2008). *Anycast routing in delay tolerant networks using genetic algorithms for route decision.* 11th International Conference on Computer and Information Technology, (pp. 65-71).

Silva, E. R., & Guardieiro, P. R. (2010). An efficient genetic algorithm for anycast routing in delay/disruption tolerant networks. *IEEE Communications Letters*, *14*(4), 315–317. doi:10.1109/LCOMM.2010.04.092066

Sudhaakar, R. S., Yoon, S., Zhao, J., & Qiao, C. (2009). A novel Qos-aware MAC scheme using optimal retransmission for wireless networks. *IEEE Transactions on Wireless Communications*, *8*(5), 2230–2235. doi:10.1109/TWC.2009.080294

Wang, Y., & Wu, H. (2007). Delay/fault-tolerant mobile sensor network (DFT-MSN): A new paradigm for pervasive information gathering. *IEEE Transactions on Mobile Computing*, *6*(9), 1021–1034. doi:10.1109/TMC.2007.1006

Waxman, B. M. (1988). Routing of multipoint connection. *IEEE Journal on Selected Areas in Communications*, *6*(9), 1617–1622. doi:10.1109/49.12889

Zhang, Z. (2006). Routing in intermittently connected mobile ad hoc networks and delay tolerant networks: Overview and challenges. *IEEE Communications Surveys & Tutorials*, *8*(1), 24–37. doi:10.1109/COMST.2006.323440

Zhao, W., Ammar, M., & Zegura, E. (2005). Multicast routing in delay tolerant networks: Semantic models and routing algorithms. *Proceedings of the ACM SIGCOMM Workshop on Delay-Tolerant Networking*, (pp. 268-275).

KEY TERMS AND DEFINITIONS

Routing: A decision of paths through which the messages generated by the source nodes should be forwarded in order to reach its destinations.

Anycast: A network scheme whereby messages are sent to any one of a group of destination nodes.

Delay and Disruption Tolerant Networking (DTN): General networking problem to allow communications in networks whose scenarios involving frequent disruption and long and/or variable delays.

Genetic Algorithms: A kind of evolutionary algorithm based on the mechanics of natural selection and natural genetics.

Subpopulation: Subset of a larger population defined by the way that each subset is formed.

Chapter 12

Data Highways:
An Activator–Inhibitor–Based Approach for Autonomic Data Dissemination in Ad Hoc Wireless Networks[1]

Karina Mabell Gomez
CREATE–NET, Italy

Daniele Miorandi
CREATE–NET, Italy

David Lowe
University of Technology, Sydney, Australia

ABSTRACT

The design of efficient routing algorithms is an important issue in dense ad hoc wireless networks. Previous theoretical work has shown that benefits can be achieved through the creation of a set of data "highways" that carry packets across the network, from source(s) to sink(s). Current approaches to the design of these highways however require a–priori knowledge of the global network topology, with consequent communications burden and scalability issues, particularly with regard to reconfiguration after node failures. In this chapter, we describe a bio–inspired approach to generating these data highways through a distributed reaction–diffusion model that uses localized convolution with activation–inhibition filters. The result is the distributed emergence of data highways that can be tuned to provide appropriate highway separation and connection to data sinks. In this chapter, we present the underlying models, algorithms, and protocols for generating data highways in a dense wireless sensor network. The proposed methods are validated through extensive simulations performed using OMNeT++.

DOI: 10.4018/978-1-61350-092-7.ch012

INTRODUCTION

An activator-inhibitor model is a special case of a reaction-diffusion system where two chemicals interact in an antagonistic way, resulting in Turing patterns in space (Turing, 1952), such as spots and stripes on the skin of animals (e.g. leopard, zebra). Activator-inhibitor models are customarily used to study the process of morphogenesis. They offer an abstract model to explain many different morphogenetic phenomena, including the regular spacing of cactus thorns and bird feathers, shape regeneration after damage, the production of sequences of repeated elements such as insect body segments, the assembly of photoreceptor cells in insect eyes, and the positioning of leaves in growing plants (Bar-Yam, 2003 ; Koch & Meinhardt, 1994). They have also been used as inspiration for algorithms to produce textures and landscapes in computer graphics, and for autonomous, decentralized, distributed coordination algorithms, for instance in amorphous computing (Abelson, 2000), wireless and sensor networks (Durvy & Thiran, 2005), and autonomous surveillance systems (Yoshida, Aoki & Araki, 2005; Hyodo, Wakamiya & Murata, 2007).

In several works, authors proposed the use of bio-inspired approaches in order to face the design of an efficient routing protocol, which is the major challenge in ad hoc wireless network research. An ad hoc wireless network is a decentralized wireless network, where each node can communicate with every other node within communication range. In ad hoc wireless networks, the specific algorithm used for conveying traffic through the network from a data source to a destination can have a major impact on the power efficiency, communication latency and robustness of the network (Yu & Chong, 2005; Erciyes, 2007). Previous work (Franceschetti, Dousse, Tse & Thiran, 2007) showed that the creation of a set of wireless "backbones" or data highways that carry packets across the network, from sources to sink, can provide a communication capacity in networks with randomly located nodes that is comparable to that which can be achieved in networks with arbitrarily placed nodes. The highways are constructed such that every source node is within range of at least one highway (implying it can access it in a single hop). The highways then drain packets to the sinks along a series of much shorter length hops, with correspondingly lower power requirements and hence a lower interference footprint. Every sink is at most one hop from the highway.

In previous work, approaches such as percolation theory were used to identify the existence of highways (Franceschetti, Dousse, Tse & Thiran, 2007). This has the disadvantage that it requires an a-priori analysis of the entire network structure, with the consequence that the approaches cannot readily accommodate randomly placed nodes unless there is a mechanism for determining and communicating node location— a constraint that adds a layer of complexity and a performance burden. It also typically makes the network less robust, as any change (such as a failure or location change of a highway node) requires a global recalculation of the routing pathways.

In this chapter, we discuss a bio-inspired approach to addressing this problem through distributed construction and optimization of the data highways based on an activation-inhibition diffusion that generates optimal highway separation. We argue that this bio-inspired approach represents a significant contribution, insofar as it will improve robustness and allow localized self-healing of the data highways — an important characteristic of dense networks with randomly placed nodes.

The remainder of this chapter is organized as follows. In Section 2, we briefly describe the bio-inspired approach pursued to build data highways in a fully distributed fashion. In Section 3, we describe the algorithms used to build the data highways and to route packets from any node to the closet sink. Then, Section 4 presents simulation results and analysis showing the performance of the bio-inspired approach. Finally, we present our conclusions in Section 5.

Box 1.

$$u(k, t+1) = g\left[\phi_s u(k,t) + \sum_{j \in R_i} \phi_i(j) u(k+j,t) + \sum_{j \in Ra} \phi_a(j) u(k+j,t)\right] \qquad (1)$$

A BIO–INSPIRED APPROACH TO DATA HIGHWAYS FORMATION

Highway Generation

As outlined above, we wish to develop self–organizing processes that lead to the natural emergence of data highways in a wireless network. We assume that there is a set of nodes (of limited cardinality), which we can data sinks, that shall gather the information generated by other nodes. These highways should be optimally spaced such that all nodes are within range of a highway (using a single hop), but the highways themselves utilize short–range hops to transport messages to any data sink. Further, the highways should be built only through local interactions among nodes. In order to explain clearly our bio–inspired approach, we focus our attention on wireless sensor networks (WSNs) (Akyildiz, Su, Sankarasubramaniam & Cayirci, 2002). A WSN is a wireless network used in order to monitor environmental or physical conditions, for example temperature, humidity, luminosity, sound and others. WSN is composed of nodes and data sinks. Nodes are used to sense physical phenomena and are usually battery-operated. Data sinks are used to collect data from the nodes and are usually connected to a power line. From a communication perspective, traffic patterns in WSNs are of the many–to–one or many–to–some type, depending on the presence of one or multiple data sinks (Soro & Heinzelman, 2009). Data sinks can be either gateway nodes, through which the sensed information, appropriately processed, can be accessed by remote machines, or actuators (e.g., programmable logic controller PLCs), where

control decisions are taken based on the physical phenomena monitored by the WSN.

In developing an approach to this problem, we took inspiration from mechanisms that utilize activation–inhibition reaction diffusion techniques (Bar–Yam, 2003; Durvy & Thiran, 2005; Neglia & Reina, 2007). These mechanisms describe how field strengths or substance concentrations vary in space and time under a pair of competing influences – a short–range positive activation region within which the field is strengthened, and a longer range negative inhibition region within which the field is retarded — with the resultant emergence of specific patterns when the effects are diffused through the network. The resultant models have been widely used to describe behaviours in biological and physical processes (see Deutsch & Dormann, 2005) for a discussion.

Several mathematical models have been developed to study the behaviour of reaction-diffusion systems. Most of them are based on a system of coupled partial differential equations (Murray, 2003; Meinhardt, 1982). Cellular neural networks (CNNs) represent a discrete model for locally-coupled identical dynamical systems (cells). CNNs, first introduced in (Chua & Yang, 1988) found a variety of applications in the distributed computing domain. CNNs can be used to engineer activation– inhibition patterns. The simplest formulation of this model, using a single field variable, can be written as shown in Box 1.

Where R_i is the region over which the inhibition function φi is applied, Ra is the region over which the activation function φa ,s applied, and g() is a limiting function. The activation functions are time–invariant, and applied uniformly across the sensor field. Note that this is equivalent to the convolution of u(*t*) with the sum of φi, φa and the self–activation value φs — which collectively form a convolution filter. Note also that, in general, it is assumed that φi takes negative values, while φa and φ_s take positive values.

Recent work has adapted reaction–diffusion models to the design and/or configuration of wireless networks. As an example, Neglia and Reina (2007) have used activator–inhibitor diffusion to select active nodes within a dense WSN. The nodes have deeply overlapping sensing fields, and hence only a small number of nodes are required to be active in order to adequately provide full data on the region to be sensed.

In order to show the operation of equation (1) in a real scenario of WSN, Figure 1 depicts some results obtained varying the values of the coefficients φi, φa, φs and radius. A random dense WSN (Figure 1.a) is repeatedly convolved with a symmetric 2–dimensional diffusion filter (Figure 1.b). The resultant field strength after 20 iterations of a filter (Figure 1.d) is then analyzed to determine local maxima (Figure 1.e) — which represent the nodes to be activated. All other nodes can be switched to a low–power non–sensing state. The filter used in this case presented a central self–activation strength φs = 2 a flat activation ring of strength φa = 1 and radius 1, and a flat inhibition ring of strength φi = -0.01 and radius 6. The result is a distributed process for identifying a subset of nodes to be activated, such the nodes are suitably distributed.

The solution is based on changing the nature of the diffusion filter. Previous work on wireless networks has used symmetric filters, leading to the emergence of patterns that have isolated peaks in the sensor activation field. Work in other areas (e.g. Deutsch & Dormann (2005) has shown that changing the nature of the diffusion filter can lead to changes in the patterns that emerge in the activation field. As an example, consider the bottom row of Figure 1. In this case, the random dense WSN is repeatedly convolved with a rotationally asymmetric filter that has a dominant horizontal activation axis, whilst inhibiting along the vertical axis (Figure 1.c). The resultant field strength pattern after 20 iterations of a filter that has this structure is shown in (Figure 1.f). This has developed a striped pattern of ridges and troughs, with the orientation controlled by the orientation of the activation axis in the filter and the separation determined by the range of the filter inhibition. The ridges in this pattern can then be used to determine local ridge maxima (Figure 1.g) — giving the potential data highways that we are seeking. Nodes at ridge maxima become highway nodes, and all other nodes communicate with the highways in order to deliver data to desired sinks. By tuning the filter parameters appropriately, we can control the separation between the highways, and thereby ensure that all non–highway nodes are within a single hop of a highway.

The repeated filter convolution causes the emergence of the ridge peaks in the activation field by activating localised regions that align with the filter axis, whilst inhibiting the off–axis areas between these regions. The width of the filter's inhibition zone controls the separation of the resultant ridge peaks. It is therefore possible to select filter parameters to achieve desired ridge separations.

Further, by appropriately adapting the direction of the axis throughout the network, it is possible to change the ridge orientation in different locations within the network. If this is done appropriately then the ridges can be controlled to converge on specific locations — i.e. the data sinks within the network. If we have multiple data sinks then the filter orientation, and hence the ridge orientation, can be derived based on a gravitational attraction model. In other words, the direction of the diffusion filter at node ni can be given by the vector di:

$$d_i = \frac{\sum_{sj \in S} \left(n_i - s_j \right) \left| n_i - s_j \right|^{-2}}{\sum_{sj \in S} \left| n_i - s_j \right|^{-2}} \qquad (2)$$

Figure 1. Sensor activation/inhibition: (a) the sensor field; (b) symmetric filter; (c) rotationally asymmetric filter; (d) activation field resulting from symmetric diffusion filter; (e) detected peaks in field; (f) activation field resulting from asymmetric diffusion filter; (g) detected ridges in field

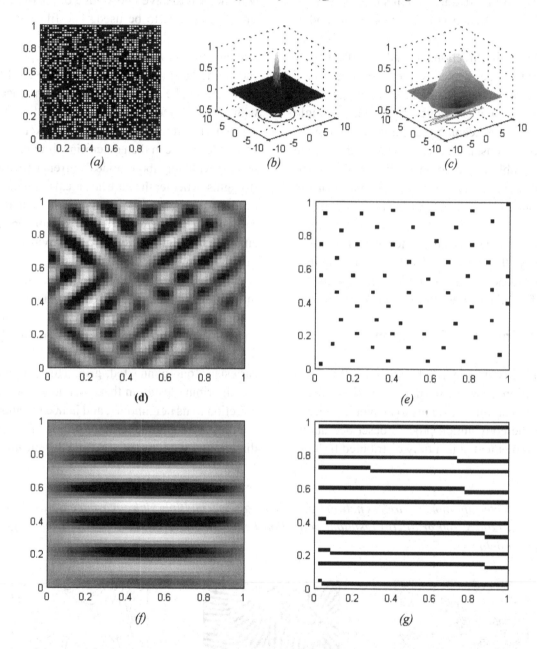

where S is *t*he set of sink nodes.

Having obtained the desired ridges it is then possible to use the ridge peaks (i.e. nodes that are in a local maxima orthogonal to the filter axis) to select those nodes to become highway nodes.

Because the ridges converge on the data sinks, the resultant highways will converge as well. An example simulation result of this process is shown in Figure 2. Figure 2a shows a sample 200x200 wireless node grid, with three sink nodes at (25,140),

(120,180), and (175,25). The resultant activation field after 20 iterations of a directional convolution is shown in Figure 2b. From this it is possible to see clearly the pattern of ridges that form, and in particular, the way in which the mechanism for calculating the directionality of the diffusion filter has led to ridges that converge on the data sinks. In numerous cases, as the ridges converge on the sinks, two or more ridges merge into a single ridge, thereby keeping the spatial separation of the ridges constant. From the ridge patterns, we are then able to extract local ridge maxima and then post–process these ridge maxima to ensure full connectivity is achieved. The result of this is shown in Figure 2.c. As can be seen from this figure, we have a connected network of localised highways that can carry data to one or more data sinks. No non–highway node is further than 5 units from the nearest highway node, as desired.

Limitations and Extensions

The bio–inspired approach outlined in the previous section, based on the use of polarized filters, required certain constraints to be met in order to allow the convolution process described above to be implemented in a fully distributed fashion,

leading to active node selection with no network–wide oversight. The simplest of these was that each node needed to have knowledge of the diffusion filter parameters to be used. The filter used in the activation-inhibition diffusion can be readily implemented in a distributed fashion, provided each node has knowledge of the diffusion filter parameters to be used. Each node communicates with its neighbours their resultant activation field, and acts to either strengthen or weaken them. The nodes also can then determine through comparison with neighbour nodes' current activation strengths, whether they are at a local maxima and hence should be activated. This requirement is not particularly problematic, as the parameters can either be built into the system, or provided by an initial system–wide broadcast.

The remaining two constraints are, however, much more significant and represent major limitations. The first of these relates to the activation and inhibition process. The network used in the bio–inspired approach described above is a cartesian, four–connected, grid. This simplified the algorithm design in that each node knew the direction to its neighbours, and hence whether or not they were aligned with, or orthogonal to, the direction of the filter axis. Whilst this meant that

Figure 2. Determination of wireless network data highways in a multiple sink environment: (a) Example node field (200 x 200 grid); (b) resultant activation field; (c) derived data highways from ridges in activation field

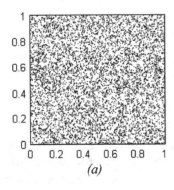
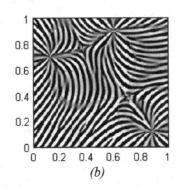
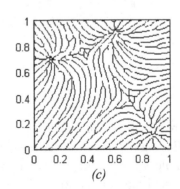

(a)   *(b)*   *(c)*

the process of determining whether neighbouring nodes should be activated or inhibited was greatly simplified, a simple grid model of a network is not realistic in most applications.

The second significant constraint was that each node was required to know the distance and direction (i.e. the vector) to each of the sinks in the network. This allowed each node to perform the calculation given in Equation (2) and hence to determine the orientation of the convolution filter used in the diffusion process. Whilst some networks will contain nodes that are location aware (and hence able to meet this requirement) this is typically not the case in many applications, and hence an alternative approach to orient the diffusion filter must be found.

Neither of the above two major constraints are realistic in the context of most practical ad hoc WSNs deployments. However, we have a single approach to addressing both the limitations described above — the use of an initial beacon broadcast from each sink that propagates through the network (using the fixed minimum–power connections between nodes) and allows each node to thereby determine how many hops it is from each sink. As we shall outline below, this information can then be used to generate an effective approximation of the diffusion process. Following the bio-inspired approach, we designed a set of algorithms in order to implement the proposed method. In the following section, we present the description of these algorithms.

ROUTING FRAMEWORK DESCRIPTION

This section reports the data structures and algorithms needed for constructing highways and routing packets along them in a graph setting. Table 1 shows the notation used in the following sections in order to explain the proposed method.

Firstly, we assume the following:

- Nodes are assigned a unique identifier;
- Nodes can tune dynamically their transmission power level P_{tx} in the range $[P_{min}, P_{max}]$;
- The network is connected when all nodes use $P_{tx} = P_{min}$;
- Nodes transmit at P_{min} unless otherwise specified.

There are two important parameters involved in the highway construction process. The first one, *filterRadius*, denotes the maximum distance (in number of hops) of nodes which can influence the actual activation level. The second one, *neighbRadius*, is used for activating highway nodes, and denotes the maximum distance (in hops) of nodes to which it is possible to connect directly (through a single –yet possibly high–power–hop). In general, *neighbRadius* ≤ *filterRadius*. We set *neighbRadius=ceil[d_{max}/d_{min}]* where ceil(.) represent the ceiling function. This is a conservative choice, in reality it might be possible to reach through single–hop communications at high

Table 1. Notation used in the routing framework description

Notation	Description
P_{tx}	Transmission power radiated by the node
P_{min}	Minimum transmission power
P_{max}	Maximum transmission power
d_{max}	Communication range when transmitting at the minimum power level
d_{min}	Communication range when transmitting at the maximum power level

power nodes located further. However, as such parameter defines the maximal distance (in hops when transmitting at the minimal power) between any node and the highway, it ensures correctness of the protocol.

Data Structures

Each node maintains two databases: *sinkDB* and *nodeDB*.

- **sinkDB:** includes information about the data sinks in the network. Entries are of the type <*sinkID, distance*>. Where:
  - ◦ *sinkID* is the ID of a sink node;
  - ◦ *distance* is the distance (in hops) from *sinkID*.
- **nodeDB:** includes information about nodes in the neighborhood. The neighborhood is defined in terms of number of hops. Nodes at a distance less than or equal to *filterRadius* hops are considered to be part of the neighborhood. Entries are of the type: <*nodeID, nodeDist, state, hwSta-*

tus, connStatus, nextHop, nearestSinkDist, sinkDB>. Where:
- ◦ *nodeID* is the ID of the node;
- ◦ *nodeDist* is the distance (in hops) along the shortest path;
- ◦ *state* is the activation level of the node (expressed as a double precision real number);
- ◦ *hwStatus* is a boolean field describing whether the node is on a highway or not.
- ◦ *connStatus* is a boolean field describing whether the node is connected (i.e., has a valid nextHop field value that leads towards a sink);
- ◦ *nextHop* is the ID of the next–hop node, if it exists, otherwise it is empty by default;
- ◦ *nearestSinkDist* is the distance (in hops) to the nearest sink;
- ◦ *sinkDB* is the data structure described above.

Figure 3 shows a graphical representation of the sinkDB and nodeDB databases. Initially each

Figure 3. Graphical representation of the NodeDB and SinkDB database (* see Figure 4)

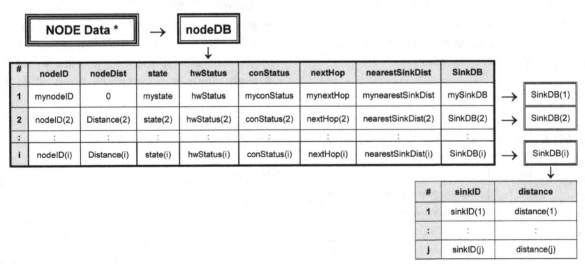

node stores its own data in the nodeDB database, adding data from its neighborhood nodes as they get collected. The number of elements in the nodeDB database corresponds to the number of nodes within the neighbRadius. The number of elements in the sinkDB database corresponds to the number of sinks in the network.

Sequence of the Algorithms

In order to ensure proper construction of the highway ridges, the proposed method has a specific sequence of processes. In Figure 4, a work-flow–like representation of the operations of the whole **routing** framework is reported, specifying the sequence and timing of the operations of the protocol. Our goal is to define a specific schedule of operations of nodes and sinks in order to build highway ridges.

The sink and nodes have different role in the system. The algorithm, for nodes and sink, works according to the following steps:

i. **Sink announcement:** each sink broadcasts a beacon, called "SinkBeacon" message, with its ID (referred to as BROADCAST BEACON in Figure 4). Nodes receiving such a beacon update the distance field and re–broadcast it (referred to as SINK INFORMATION COLLECTION in Figure 4). In such a way, each node will eventually have knowledge of all sinks and its distance from them. The sink repeats the broadcast beaconing algorithm each *timer1* seconds. This iterative process allows nodes to: (i) update the data in case of changes in the network (i.e., one node runs out of power) and (ii) monitor the presence of the sink (i.e., there are two sinks in the network one of those has experienced a fault, the node does not receive the beacon anymore, therefore it finds a path to another sink).

ii. **Neighbourhood discovery:** Firstly, in order to ensure correct completion of the opera-

tions, nodes *must have knowledge of at least one sink present in the network*. Secondly, after *timer2* each node broadcasts a message, called "NodeQuery" message, to its one–hop neighbours, asking for information about them (including activation state) and about nodes which are at most $(R-1)$ hops from them (referred to as BROADCAST NODE QUERY in Figure 4). Nodes reply to the NodeQuery message with an "ACKNodeQuery" message, it contained the information asked by its neighbours (this process is referred to as NodeDB UPDATE in Figure 4). In such a way, each node may acquire (by means of a gossiping mechanism) information on nodes that are within its 'neighbourhood' (at most R hops away).

iii. **Filter construction and activation level update:** based on the information gathered, each node constructs its local filter and updates its activation level. Let us now consider the specific algorithm for performing the activation–inhibition convolution within each node. Firstly, given that we are assuming that the nodes *do not* know their own spatial location nor that of the sinks, the convolution filter cannot be oriented using Equation (2). We can however obtain an estimate of the direction to the sink from a given source node based on the sink hop count of the neighbouring nodes, and in particular whether or not they are on the shortest path to the sink. If a neighbouring node is n hops from the selected node ($n \leq R$, where R is *the size of the neighbourhood expressed in hops*), and either n hops closer to, or n hops further away from, the sink node, then the neighbour will be on the shortest path to/from the sink – and hence can be viewed as being along the filter alignment axis, and should therefore be an activator for the selected node. Conversely, a node that is n hops from the selected node, and not n hops closer to, or n hops further away from sink, will not

Figure 4. Workflow–like representation of the operations of the whole routing framework (values for duration of timeouts are indicative and have been derived for the network sizes considered in this chapter)

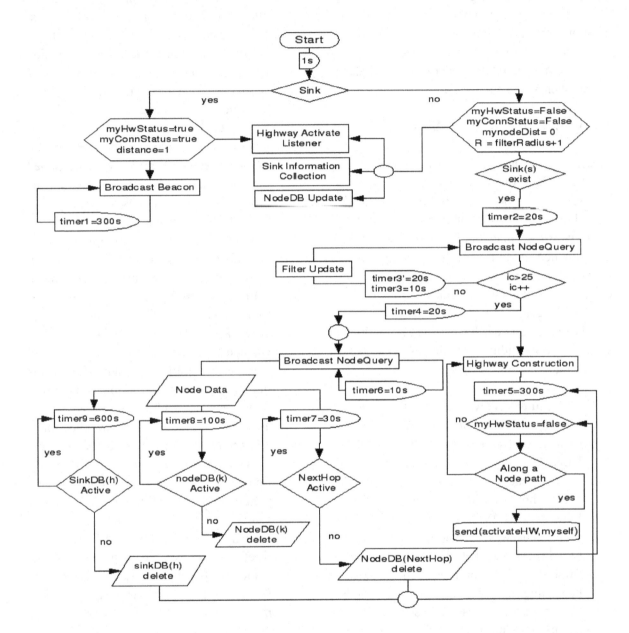

be on the shortest path, and can therefore be considered to be orthogonal to the filter axis, and will therefore be an inhibitor for the selected node. One additional implication to the algorithm is that rather than determining the weighted direction to all sinks, given that

each node knows the distance to all sinks, we apply the filter convolution separately for each sink, and hence determine a set of independent ridges for each sink (this process is referred to as FILTER UPDATE in Figure 4). The highways are then only generated at each node using the ridge data for the closest sink. *Steps (ii) and (iii) are repeated each timer3 seconds for a number of times, 25 in this case, in order to achieve a stable spatial pattern.*

iv. **Ridge detection and tracing:** each node, after *timer4* seconds, runs a procedure for deciding whether it should act as highway node, by checking whether it is in range of an already existing highway (in which case it just connects to it) or whether it is a local peak, and should therefore activate (i.e., turn into a highway node). If a node is activated, it starts a tracing process by identifying which node shall represent the next hop on the way to the closest sink. Then the node sends a message, called "HwActive", to that node (referred to as HIGHWAY CONSTRUCTION in Figure 4). When a node receives a HwActive message became activates and it *repeats the steps (iv) in order to continue the* construction of highway paths toward the sink (referred to as HIGHWAY ACTIVATE LISTENER in Figure 4). Highway links (i.e., a link between two highway nodes) are always set at minimum transmission power and non–highway links (i.e., a link between a highway node and a non–highway node) are set depending on the distance between them.

v. **Ridge optimization and maintenance:** Each node rebuilds its highway path each *timer5* seconds in order to optimize the path toward the sink. *In parallel, nodes repeat Steps (ii), every timer6 seconds, in order to inform nodes about changes in the neighbourhood.* Finally, each node checks frequently its databases (each *timer7, timer8* and *timer9* seconds respectively) and runs processes in order to maintain and guarantee a valid route to the sink. These processes allow the nodes to (i) recover highway paths when the link to the next–hop is broken and (ii) find a highway path toward a new sink when the previous one is broken.

In order to ensure the proper construction of data highways, the value of the timers should be fixed considering the following (i) the number of nodes and data sinks in the network and (ii) the average of data traffic across the network. These are critical values because in a dense WSN the interference between nodes and high data traffic could cause delays in the network and packet loss. Therefore, the value of the timers should be sufficiently large in order to ensure the diffusion of the broadcast beacon from sink(s) towards the nodes in the network and allow the exchange of data between nodes within the neighbourhood. At the same time, the value of the timers should be sufficiently small in order to guarantee the fault detection and allow the construction of data highways as soon as possible. Moreover, the value of the timers has an impact on the overhead, caused by the protocol, and bootstrapping time. We will discuss each of these points separately in the following section.

SIMULATIONS AND NUMERICAL RESULTS

In this section, we report the outcomes of a set of experiments carried out using a freely available simulation tool, OMNeT++ (http://www.omnetpp. org). We have implemented the architecture and protocols described in the previous sections, and run simulations in order to (i) validate the correctness of the proposed protocols (ii) evaluate the performance of the system in terms of time necessary to bootstrap the system, robustness and overhead related to the data highway construction process.

Implementation Details and Simulation Settings

We developed the proposed method in OMNeT++ using the Mobility Framework. OMNeT++ has a set of packages implementing standard network protocols, mobility models and traffic models.

The Mobility Framework is a network simulation framework that supports wireless and mobile simulations within OMNeT++.

The simulations setting used are reported in Table 2. The first part of the table contains the parameters used for the simulation scenario. In particular, we were interested in assessing the ability of the proposed bio–inspired approach to scale to large network deployments. In order to do so, we ran a set of experiments varying the number of nodes in the network from 10 to 1500. For scaling the system in a consistent way, wc used a fixed node density (set to 0.1429 nodes m², corresponding to an average neighbourhood size equal to 7 when transmitting at the minimum power). The larger the number of nodes, the larger the playground size on which they were placed. Nodes were placed according to a uniform random distribution. We used one single sink, located at (1,1) for all simulations. The maximum and minimum communication distance were setup considering, in the absence of interference, a power transmission range of (–25, 0) dBm, a signal attenuation threshold of –120 dBm and a path loss coefficient of 2. No data traffic was injected in the network. The scenarios were evaluated over 10 runs of the duration of 3600 seconds each one. The second part of the table contains the parameters used to setting our proposed method. The maximum and minimum communication distances were fixed to 4 and 12 meters respectively and the neighbourhood size was set to 4 hops. The value of the coefficients φi, φa and φs were setting to use, see Section 2, a linear version of the filter.

Results

In order to evaluate the performance of the proposed method, we preliminarily focused on some specific graphs and metrics. From the simulations with OMNeT++, logs were obtained and successively *Matlab* (MATLAB is a commercial numerical computing environment and programming language) was used to elaborate the logs and plot various results. The first set of graphs is about the stages of the highway paths construction. In order to provide insight into the patterns arising in the network as a consequence of the activator–inhibitor mechanism, we report in Figure 5 the following graphs, related to the case with 750 nodes:

a. Physical location of the nodes in the network;
b. Connectivity graph among nodes when transmitting at minimum transmission power;
c. Contour plot (distance in hops) of resulting distance from the sink when the notes are transmitting at minimum power;
d. Resulting activation field after 25 iterations of convolution with the activation–inhibition filter;
e. Data highways resulting from tracing activation field ridges to the sink;
f. Representation of the level of transmission power, to each node, in the network;

As it can be seen, highways tend to arise where dense clusters of nodes are present; the ridge tracing process ensures then the ability to reach back to the sink. The control of the distance among highways is achieved by appropriately selecting the neighbourhood size for the activation filter. Figure 6 shows the data highways resulting from tracing activation field ridges to the sink whilst varying the number of nodes in the network, from 50 up to 1,500 nodes. In all simulation runs our protocol was able to build valid routes, i.e., all nodes had a valid nextHop field, highways were connected to the sink and nodes not on highways were within the maximum communication distance of 12 m from a highway node.

The second set of graphs is about three specific metrics. The first metric is the time needed by a node in the network to achieve a valid path to the sink node. This corresponds to the time needed to bootstrap a WSN. Before getting a

Table 2. Calibrated OMNeT++ simulation parameters

Parameter	Unit	Value
Network Parameters		
Duration of each run	s	3,600
Number of runs	–	10.0
Playground SizeX	m	8.5/18.7/26.5/118.5/59/72.5/84/102.5
Playground SizeY	m	8.5/18.7/26.5/118.5/59/72.5/84/102.5
Playground area	m²	70/350/700/1,400/3,500/5,250/7,000/10,500
Number of Hosts N		10/50/100/200/500/750/1,000/1,500
Carrier Frequency	GHz	2.4
Maximum transmission power	dBm	0.0
Minimum transmission power	dBm	−25.0
Signal attenuation threshold	dBm	−120.0
Path loss coefficient $\propto$	–	2.0
MAC–address of the sink	–	0
MAC–address of the nodes	–	[1..N]
Position sinkX	m	1.0
Position sinkY	m	1.0
Position nodeX	m	Uniform random distribution
Position nodeY	m	Uniform random distribution
Proposed method Parameters		
Maximum communication distance	m	12.0
Minimum communication distance	m	4.0
Neighbourhood size	hops	4.0
Self–activation coefficient ϕ_s	–	2.0
Activation coefficient ϕ_a	–	1.0
Inhibition coefficient ϕ_i	–	−0.1

Figure 5. Application of the proposed protocol to a network with 750 nodes and one data sink. The most important states to the highway ridges and paths construction.

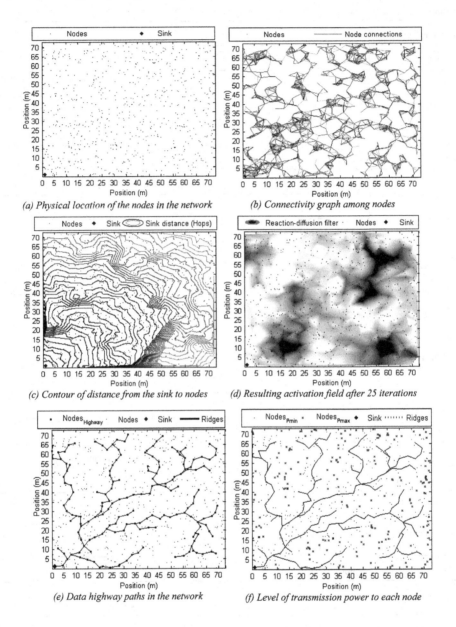

(a) *Physical location of the nodes in the network*

(b) *Connectivity graph among nodes*

(c) *Contour of distance from the sink to nodes*

(d) *Resulting activation field after 25 iterations*

(e) *Data highway paths in the network*

(f) *Level of transmission power to each node*

valid next–hop address, each node runs the processes to build the highways ridges. The time needed by nodes to get a valid next–hop address is reported in Figure 7. We considered the minimum, average and maximum value attained for any node over 10 runs with their respective confidence intervals. The confidence interval is used to indicate the reliability of each estimate and was calculated with a confidence level of 95%. Both the minimum and average number turns out to be only slightly sensitive to the number of nodes in the system. This is because the time needed to construct routing paths, from any node to the sink, turns out to be dominated by the values of some

Figure 6. Data highways resulting varying the number of nodes in the network. Each point in the graph represents a node while each line represents the link between two highway nodes (x and y-axes measured in meters).

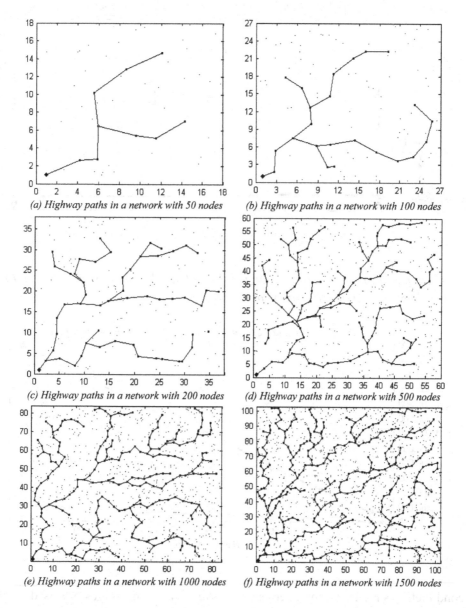

(a) Highway paths in a network with 50 nodes

(b) Highway paths in a network with 100 nodes

(c) Highway paths in a network with 200 nodes

(d) Highway paths in a network with 500 nodes

(e) Highway paths in a network with 1000 nodes

(f) Highway paths in a network with 1500 nodes

timers. These timers are part of the routing framework (see Figure 4). Following the routing framework, the value of the minimum time, needed by node to get a valid next–hop address, calculated in an ideal scenario is 311 seconds. The case of 10 nodes shows significantly better performance, due to the simple topology achieved (in most runs all nodes were directly connected to the sink). The maximum value increased as a function of the number of nodes. A more detailed analysis revealed that this was due to problems related to interference, which prevented some nodes from correctly decoding messages destined for them, causing therefore a delay in the setup time.

Figure 7. Bootstrapping time (s) as a function of the network size

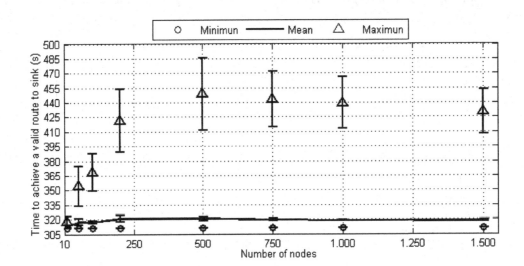

Figure 8. Number of control messages (exchanged throughout the whole simulation and until a valid route to sink is achieved) as a function of the network size

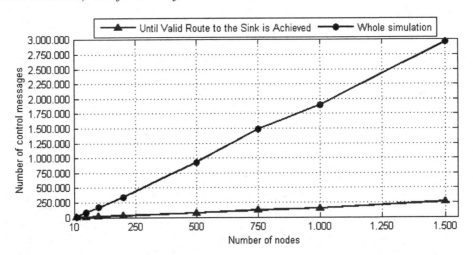

The second metric is related to the overhead induced by the protocol in terms of the number of messages exchanged until a valid route to sink is achieved and throughout the whole simulation run. Figure 8 depicts this metric. The proposed method involved four different types of control messages in order to build and maintain the highway paths to the sink. These messages are: *Sink-Beacon, NodeQuery, ACKNodeQuery* and *HwActive*. Each type of message plays a different role:

SinkBeacon messages are used to generate the sinkDB database; *NodeQuery* and *ACKNodeQuery* messages are used to generate the nodeDB database and *HwActive* is used to generate the highway paths. The number of such messages scales (slightly) superlinearly with the number of nodes. A more detailed analysis, based on the different types of messages involved in the routing protocol, revealed that all messages except sink beacons grow linearly with the number of

Table 3. Percentage of node with highway and non–highway role in the network

Number of nodes	Area (m2)	Fraction of Highway nodes (%)	Fraction of Non–highway nodes (%)
10	70	20	80
50	350	18	82
100	700	23	77
200	1400	26	74
500	3500	25.4	74.6
750	5250	22.5	77.5
1500	10500	24.4	75.6

nodes. The number of sink beacon messages tends on the other hand to grow in a superlinear fashion (actually exponentially), which explains the behavior observed in our experiments.

Finally, the last metric is about the statistical distribution of highway and non–highway nodes. Table 3 reports the fraction of highway and non–highway nodes. Both percentages turned out to be rather insensitive to the total of nodes in the network. The percentages of highway nodes are less than 30% while non–highway nodes are bigger than 70% in all scenarios. Hence, the proposed method behaves invariable to change of the number of nodes in the network. We explained previously that: (i) the power consumption of each link depend of the distance (in hops) to highway nodes, (ii) the highway link is always set at minimum power and (iii) the node computes next hop destination choosing the nearest highway node, so 1 hop distance. Hence, the proposed method is always looking to create 1–hop links thus minimize the maximum transmission power assigned to each node reducing the interference levels for other links and saving battery life.

CONCLUSION

The design of efficient routing algorithms is a key issue in ad hoc wireless networks. In this chapter, we have described a bio–inspired approach to the distributed design of data highways for use in routing data within dense WSNs. The algorithms developed allow these data highways to emerge naturally from localized processing in the network, without requiring network–wide knowledge or oversight, while still ensuring that design criteria are met. In particular, the highways will converge to the data sinks and ensure a maximum highway separation that allows all non–highway nodes to be within a desired maximum distance of a data highway.

We expect this bio–inspired approach to lead naturally to self–healing of the network – in terms of regeneration of the highways in the event of a sink failure, localized recalculation of highway routes in the event of the failure of a highway node, and reconnection of source nodes to the highways when necessary. Ongoing work will explore these self–healing characteristics.

Other questions that remain open, and represent ongoing research, relate to refining the mechanisms for performing the local diffusion (alleviating the signaling burden related to the knowledge necessary to build activation filters) and on considering the impacts of the sink locations on the structure of the data highways. In particular, it may be possible to selectively position the sinks in order to allow the highways to be tuned, and the data loads across the highways to be optimally balanced.

REFERENCES

Abelson, H. (2000). Amorphous computing. *Communications of the ACM*, 43.

Akyildiz, I. F., Su, W., Sankarasubramaniam, Y., & Cayirci, E. (2002). Wireless sensor networks: A survey. *Computer Networks*, *38*(4), 393–422. doi:10.1016/S1389-1286(01)00302-4

Bar-Yam, Y. (2003). *Dynamics of complex systems*. Westview Press.

Chua, L., & Yang, L. (1988). Cellular neural networks: Theory. *IEEE Transactions on Circuits and Systems*, *44*(2).

Deutsch, A., & Dormann, S. (2005). *Cellular automaton modeling of biological pattern formation: Characterization, applications, and analysis*. Birkhauser.

Durvy, M., & Thiran, P. (2005). *Reaction–diffusion based transmission patterns for ad hoc networks*. Paper presented at IEEE INFOCOM, Miami, USA.

Erciyes, K. (2007). Graph theoretic clustering algorithms in mobile ad hoc networks and wireless sensor networks. *Application Computing Mathematical*, *6*, 162–180.

Franceschetti, M., Dousse, O., Tse, D., & Thiran, P. (2007). Closing the gap in the capacity of wireless networks via percolation theory. *IEEE Transactions on Information Theory*, *53*(3), 1009–1018. doi:10.1109/TIT.2006.890791

Hyodo, K., Wakamiya, N., & Murata, M. (2007). *Reaction-diffusion based autonomous control of camera sensor networks*. Paper presented at Bionetics, Budapest, Hungary.

Koch, A. J., & Meinhardt, H. (1994). Biological pattern formation: From basic mechanisms to complex structures. *Reviews of Modern Physics*, *66*(4). doi:10.1103/RevModPhys.66.1481

Lowe, D., Miorandi, D., & Gomez, K. M. (2009). *Activation-inhibition-based data highways for wireless sensor networks*. Paper presented at Bionetics, Avignon, France.

Lowe, D., & Miorandi, M. (2009). *All roads lead to Rome: Data highways for dense wireless sensor networks*. Paper presented at S-Cube 2009: The first International Conference on Sensor Systems and Software, Pisa, Italy.

Meinhardt, H. (1982). *Models of biological pattern formation*. London, UK: Academic Press.

Murray, J. D. (2003). *Mathematical biology: Spatial models and biomedical applications*. Springer, volume 2 of Mathematical Biology.

Neglia, G., & Reina, G. (2007). *Evaluating activator–inhibitor mechanisms for sensors coordination*. Paper presented at Bionetics, Budapest, Hungary. ICST.

Soro, S., & Heinzelman, W. B. (2009). Cluster head election techniques for coverage preservation in wireless sensor networks. *Ad Hoc Networks*, *7*, 955–972. doi:10.1016/j.adhoc.2008.08.006

Turing, A. M. (1952). The chemical basis of morphogenesis. *Philosophical Transactions of the Royal Society of London. Series B, Biological Sciences*, *327*, 37–72. doi:10.1098/rstb.1952.0012

Yoshida, A., Aoki, K., & Araki, S. (2005). Cooperative control based on reaction-diffusion equation for surveillance system. *Proceedings of KES International Conferences in Knowledge-Based and Intelligent Engineering & Information Systems*, *3*, 533–539. doi:10.1007/11553939_76

Yu, J. Y., & Chong, P. H. J. (2005). A survey of clustering schemes for mobile ad hoc networks. *IEEE Communications Surveys and Tutorials*, *7*, 32–48. doi:10.1109/COMST.2005.1423333

KEY TERMS AND DEFINITIONS

Activation–Inhibition: Activation is the act or process of rendering active and inhibition is the arrest or restraint of a process.

Ad hoc Wireless Network: A decentralized wireless network. A wireless ad-hoc network is a computer network in which the communication links are wireless. The network is ad hoc because each node is willing to forward data for other nodes, and so the determination of which nodes forward data is made dynamically based on the network connectivity.

Convolution: A mathematical operation way of combining two signals, f and g, to form a third signal.

Data Highway: A path of devices used for the transfer of digitized information through a network.

Reaction–Diffusion Systems: Mathematical models, which explain how the concentration of one or more substances distributed in space changes under the influence of two processes: local chemical reactions in which the substances are transformed into each other, and diffusion, which causes the substances to spread out over a surface in space. In a figurative sense, the reaction–diffusion systems can be applied on artificial system in order to model a specific behavior of the system.

Routing: The process of selecting paths in a network along which to send network traffic from source to destination.

Self–Healing: A phrase applied to the process of recovery (generally from psychological disturbances, trauma, etc.), motivated by and directed by the patient, guided often only by instinct. In a figurative sense, self-healing properties can be ascribed to systems or processes, which by nature or design tend to correct any disturbances brought into them.

Wireless Sensor Networks: A wireless network consisting of spatially distributed autonomous devices using sensors to cooperatively monitor physical or environmental conditions, such as temperature, sound, vibration, pressure, motion or pollutants, at different locations. A sensor network normally constitutes a wireless ad-hoc network, meaning that each sensor supports a multi-hop routing algorithm.

ENDNOTES

[1] Part of this work appeared in the Proceedings of S-Cube 2009 (Lowe & Miorandi, 2009) and BIONETICS 2009 (Lowe, Miorandi & Gomez, 2009).

Chapter 13
Scented Node Protocol for MANET Routing

Song Luo
Intelligent Automation Inc., USA

Yalin E. Sagduyu
Intelligent Automation Inc., USA

Jason H. Li
Intelligent Automation Inc., USA

ABSTRACT

Ant Colony Optimization (ACO) for biologically inspired networking introduces performance gains over classical routing solutions for Mobile Ad Hoc Networks (MANETs). However, the current ACO protocols involve significant amount of overhead and do not fully reflect the wireless interference effects in routing decisions. In ant routing, sources send out ant-based control packets for route discovery and path maintenance. Destinations can assist ant packets by disseminating scent messages to provide better guidance for route discovery and thus effectively reduce the protocol overhead. For that purpose, Scented Node Protocol (SNP) is introduced for interference-aware routing with novel scent diffusion and reinforcement mechanisms. The wireless link rates are measured by identifying the node pairs that are the most impacted by wireless interference, and network flows are routed to avoid severe interference effects among concurrent wireless transmissions. The throughput and overhead performance of SNP is evaluated through extensive realistic simulations for dynamic MANET environment. The resulting amount of overhead for scent and ant packets is also evaluated through the asymptotic analysis of scaling laws, as the network size grows, and through the dynamic analysis of the finite overhead constraint, by discussing the possible effects of local network coding on scent dissemination between neighbor nodes. Our results verify the throughput and overhead gains of biologically inspired SNP in wireless networks over the existing ACO and MANET routing protocols.

DOI: 10.4018/978-1-61350-092-7.ch013

INTRODUCTION

Swarm Intelligence (SI) is based on the notion that "swarms" or large collections of simple interacting entities acting in some cooperative fashion can solve complex problems. A popular example is the large *ant colonies*, which can, with apparently low level of intelligence, limited functionality and information processing capability or minimal information exchange, perform collective tasks, efficiently allocate resources or flexibly implement division of labor among workers in the colony.

As an adaptive, decentralized, and robust system, an ant colony solves the *shortest path problem* to find sources of food through the use of chemical substances known as *pheromones*, which have a scent that decays over time through the process of evaporation (Bonabeau, Dorigo, & Thraulaz, 1999). Ants first set out in search of a food source by (apparently randomly) choosing several different paths. Along the way they leave traces of pheromone. Once ants find a food source, they retrace their path back to their colony (and in so doing inform other ants in the colony) by following their scent back to their point of origin. Since many ants go out from their colony in search of food, the ants that return first are presumably those that have found the food source closest to the colony or at least have found a source that is in some way more accessible. In this way, an ant colony can identify the shortest or "best" path to the most desirable food source.

Ants simply follow the path that has the strongest pheromone traces, again the one associated with the shortest path. This leads more ants to go along this path that further strengthens the pheromone trail and thereby reinforces the shortest path to the food source – hence is a form of *reinforcement learning* (Kaelbling, Littman, & Moore, 1996). If, for instance, a shortest path is somehow obstructed, then the second best shortest path will, at some later point in time, attain the strongest pheromone, hence will induce ants to traverse it and thereby will strengthen it. The decay in the pheromone level allows for redundancy and robustness of the emergent solution as well as dynamic adaptation.

Such reinforcement learning methods are known in the SI literature as *ant colony optimization* (ACO) (Dorigo & Stutzle, 2004), or simply, *ant algorithms* and have been used to provide heuristics for a number of difficult combinatorial optimization problems such as the Traveling Salesman Problem (Dorigo & Stutzle, 2004), Job-shop Scheduling Problem (Colorni, Dorigo, Maniezzo, & Trubian, 1994), Graph Coloring Problem (Cost & Hertz, 1997), Vehicle Routing Problem (Bullnheimer, Hartl, & Strauss, 1999), and Quadratic Assignment Problem (Maniezzo, 1999). In many cases, ACO algorithms are competitive with, if not superior to, well-established heuristics.

In the search of food sources, ants and many other insects are not just guided by pheromones, but also attracted by the *scent* emanated by the food sources (Edmund, Mark, & Ryohei, 1993), as illustrated in Figure 1. The food scent increases relatively, as insects approach the food source, and it exhibits a decreasing gradient as they move farther away from it. In particular, insects wander until they pick up the slightest hint of this scent, and then very quickly follow the scent gradient toward the source. This scent-based mechanism is intended to interact with and *enhance* any of the ACO algorithms, which typically use only pheromones.

The use of pheromones along with food scent forms the basis of what amounts to a clever information storage and retrieval system. The fact that pheromone and food scent strengths or intensities decay over time suggest that they are very simple information processing mechanisms that can also implement a form of positive and negative feedback. This "processing" capability is illustrated in the simplicity of how ants utilize and respond to pheromones and food scent.

In this book chapter, the *Scented Node Protocol* (SNP) is introduced to enhance ant routing

Figure 1. Food (destination) scent attracts ants (ant packets)

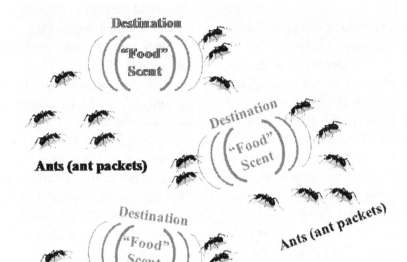

for Mobile Ad Hoc Networks (MANETs). SNP is inspired by the odor localization and tracking in insect colonies. A wide variety of insects use plumes of pheromone (odor) to locate prey, mates and other sources of interest (Edmund, Mark, & Ryohei, 1993). Insects themselves follow a route to regions of higher pheromone concentration by means of olfactory sensing, since this represents a higher order of relevance in finding the designated odor source.

SNP is specifically designed for mobile *wireless* networks. The key innovation is to introduce scent-based guidance for ant packets to efficiently discover and maintain routes. Different biologically inspired routing algorithms, e.g. AntHocNet (Di Caro, Ducatelle, & Gambardella, 2005), have been proposed to improve the performance and robustness of the classical MANET routing protocols such as Ad hoc On-Demand Distance Vector (AODV) routing protocol (Perkins & Royer, 1999).

However, there are two key issues that have not been solved yet for ACO routing algorithms: (*i*) The protocol *overhead* requirement is very large, (*ii*) the crucial "wireless" network properties, such as the *interference* effects, are not taken into account in the routing protocol design.

The traditional wireless ACO algorithms are hybrid protocols in the sense that they incorporate both a reactive route setup and a proactive route improvement or maintenance. Such design incurs significantly more control overhead (namely, the number of control packets) than traditional MANET protocols. In addition, ACO algorithms usually do not consider the destructive wireless interference effects when routing packets from sources to destinations. These two drawbacks make ACO routing protocols (e.g., AntHocNet) less applicable to heavy-loaded wireless networking environments, although experimental results showed that they generally achieve higher throughput and shorter packet delay when compared against traditional MANET routing protocols.

The key contributions of SNP are (*i*) to improve the throughput performance under realistic wireless network assumptions, in particular mobility and wireless interference effects, (*ii*) to maintain low level of overhead. In that sense, SNP can assist the current ACO and other traditional MANET algorithms to improve the robustness against wireless interference and reduce the overhead thereby improving the end-to-end throughput performance. The building blocks of SNP are illustrated in Figure 2. SNP uses interference-aware routing metric assisted by scent messages in form of location updates and boosts reliable network information to limit the number of necessary control packets for network inference.

BACKGROUND

The most relevant ACO algorithm for MANET routing is AntHocNet (Di Caro, Ducatelle, & Gambardella, 2005), where ants, i.e. control packets, lay and reinforce pheromones to be used for route discovery and maintenance. Nodes relate each route with a pheromone value in terms of the accumulative cost to the destination. Then, the probability of forwarding packets over a route is proportional to the route's pheromone value. Two kinds of ants are used in AntHocNet, reactive ants for route establishment and proactive ants for path maintenance. Compared with MANET routing protocols like AODV, AntHocNet shows significant performance improvement in terms of packet delivery ratio and end-to-end latency. However, the overhead requirement of AntHocNet limits its practical use compared with AODV. Experimental results in (Ducatelle, Di Caro, & Gambardella, 2006) indicate the importance of reflecting the wireless interference effects into the link cost when tuning AntHocNet for MANET environment. The interference metric of this experiment is based on the achievable signal-to-noise-ratios, which vary with the user traffic and may cause route fluctuations. Therefore, there is a need for a more reliable, accurate, and stable metric to reflect the wireless interference effects.

Swarm Intelligent Odor Based Routing (SWOB) is proposed in (Ghataoura, Yang, Matich, & Galileo, 2009), where a virtual Gaussian odor plume technique is used to describe the odor dispersion effects found in nature, allowing information agents in a distributed manner to be

Figure 2. Overview of scented node protocol (SNP)

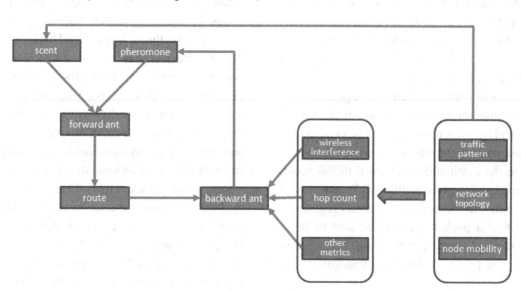

guided towards the region of interest effectively. This work mimics the natural pheromone/odor plume driven by wind and the odor concentration at any given point is determined by a Gaussian function. The routing decisions are guided by the odor concentration within the plume and thus can avoid simple flooding. However, SWOB relies on GPS devices on each node to provide geographic coordinates to calculate the plume and the locations of the source and also the sink of a data session must be known *a priori*. These two properties limit the practical use of SWOB in dynamic MANET environment.

Similar to AntHocNet, Ant-Colony-Based Routing Algorithm (ARA) (Gunes, Sorges, & Bouazizi, 2002) uses forward and backward ants to discover paths and lay pheromone traces. In addition, data packets can also lay pheromone and thus maintain the active path. However, ant/data packets lay fixed amount of pheromone, while pheromone values in AntHocNet depend on both the end-to-end delay and number of hops. In general, ARA is a simpler ACO algorithm than AntHocNet. However, since it does not use proactive approach to maintain the active path, its adaptation to network dynamics is limited compared with AntHocNet.

Probabilistic Emergent Routing Algorithm (PERA) (Baras & Mehta, 2003) is derived from AntNet (Di Caro & Dorigo, 1998), which is designed for wireline networks. However, PERA utilizes wireless broadcast to transmit forward ants instead of using several unicasts in AntNet. To avoid stagnation problem (an optimal route may become non-optimal because of changes in traffic and network dynamics), PERA uses a new type ant, namely the uniform ant, to explore new paths to the destination. However, PERA nodes proactively and periodically send out forward ants to randomly chosen destinations regardless of whether a packet needs to be sent to those destinations. Therefore, there is still a significant overhead requirement for control packets.

Overview of Scented Node Protocol

In SNP, each node can be assigned as the destination of a data session. Therefore, we imagine that *food* is deposited on each node, and releases scent to attract ants (ant packets). When forward ants are sent out for a specific destination (namely, for the food deposited on that node), they are guided by the scent of the destination instead of blind broadcast. If the destination scent is unavailable, ants simply follow the pheromone (and other existing routing mechanisms). As in AntHocNet, routing decisions are based on pheromone values, which are updated by backward ants returning from destinations.

In a mobile environment, destination scent provides a *robust* mechanism to guide the existing route discovery algorithms. For example, when working together with ACO, ants can be guided by scents to find paths quickly and with less overhead, but only ants can confirm the validity and cost of a path to the destination. This is because the scent is spread through hello messages, which could be a long process depending on the network size and does not necessarily reflect the most recent network dynamics.

Initially, each node is assigned a default scent value (under the assumption that each node is equally interesting to users/applications). Then, nodes start exchanging their knowledge of scents of other nodes through periodical hello messages. To limit the overhead, there is a maximum number (N) of scents a node can forward through its hello message. Besides its own scent, a node can forward at most N-1 other strongest scents. Like the natural scent, node scents decay both over *time* and *distance* (after transmission). The spatial decay of the scent is proportional to the link cost. Once a node receives a scent from a neighbor, it checks the emission time of the scent which was first set by its originator, and sets up an expiration timer. If the node has not received any further update of the scent when the timer goes off, the scent expires and it is removed from the node's memory.

Scent Diffusion Mechanism

SNP relies on periodic information exchange to spread the scents of (destination) nodes. Such periodic information exchange is usually carried out by hello messages. To minimize the overhead, SNP can reuse the existing mechanism of hello messages that is a typical core part of MANET protocols. In each hello packet, a node broadcasts its current scent value to its neighbors, and the scent values for up to N-1 other nodes. Let S_i^j denote the scent value of i at node j. At any time t, the neighbor k of node j decreases the scent value received from node j according to the link cost function c_{jk} between nodes j and k:

$$S_i^k(t+1) = S_i^j(t) \ (1 - c_{jk}), \qquad (1)$$

where $c_{jk} < 1$. It is possible that a node receives the scent of a particular destination from different neighbors, which implies the existence of multiple paths to the destination with different costs. The receiving node keeps all the entries of the same destination in its scent table. When the node prepares the next hello message, it uses only the strongest value of each destination to declare the scent in its hello message.

Each time when a node emits its own scent, it generates a unique sequence number for this emission. A node can accept the scent values with the same sequence number from different neighbors, but not the scent with the same or lower sequence number from the same neighbor. When a node receives a scent update with a new higher sequence number, it removes all the entries (from different neighbors) of this scent with the older sequence number, and replaces them with the new scent values. The sequence number of scent values guarantees that the network will be updated with the most recent information and the old scents will be eventually removed.

SNP Example

Consider the network topology shown in Figure 3. Node A periodically broadcasts hello packets to all neighbors, B, C, and D, within the transmission range. Nodes E and F are out of transmission range. In hello packets, node A sends the corresponding node ID and the scent value. The value of scent *originated* at node A is 10 and we denote this by "A = 10". On the receiving side, nodes B, C, and D all learn that the scent value of node A is 10 and they decrease this scent value in proportion to their link costs from node A.

After adjusting the scent of node A, each of nodes B, C, and D has two scents: The new scent of A, and its own scent. Nodes D, B, C receive the cost-adjusted scent of A (Aa = 7, Aa = 5, Aa = 3) and have their own scents D = 10, B = 10, C = 10, respectively. Then, each node tries to propagate these two scents (i.e., its own scent and the scent from A) by using the hello packets.

Node D then broadcasts its own hello packet with the two scents D = 10 and Aa = 7 to node E. Node E now has the cost-adjusted scent of A, sent by D (Ad = 3), the cost-adjusted scent of D, sent by D (Dd = 8), and its own scent E = 10.

Node E then broadcasts its hello packet H(E,A,D) with its own scent E = 10 and the new scents Ad = 3, and Dd = 8. These scents become weaker at node C and the cost-adjusted values are Ee = 5, Ae = 0, and De = 2. Note that node C already has C = 10 and Aa = 3. The scent of A sent directly by A (Aa = 3) is larger than the scent of A sent by E (Ae = 0), so node C removes scent Ae = 0 from the memory.

Node F receives H(C,E,D,A) from node C's hello message, and now it has scents F = 10, Bb = 8, Ab = 0 (which was removed), Cc = 8, Ac = 0 (to be removed), as well as Ec = 1 and Dc = 0 (to be removed).

Figure 3. An example scenario for scent propagation mechanism

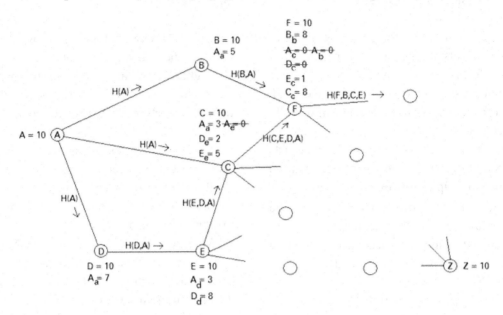

Key Advantages of SNP for MANET

Scent Reinforcement Mechanism and Hot Spot Formation

In traditional ACO algorithms, ants follow the path that has the strongest pheromone associated with the shortest path. This leads more ants to travel on the same path that strengthens the pheromone trail and reinforces the shortest path to the food source. Similar to pheromone reinforcement, a scent reinforcement mechanism based on *hot spot* formation is introduced to guide more ants to the popular food sources (destinations).

In SNP, all nodes start with a common scent value, which ensures that each node has the same capability to attract ants under the symmetric network model (i.e., same link costs, same congestion levels, etc.). When an ant from a random source finds a destination for the first time, the level of interest in that particular destination increases, i.e., it is likely that other sources would request the same destination. This scenario of multiple sources being interested in the same destination can be modeled as a *hot spot* effect. Figure 4 il-

lustrates the formation of a hot spot. When more traffic is destined to node A, it becomes a hot spot thereby increasing its scent value propagated over a larger area.

SNP takes advantage of the hot spot situations by allowing popular destinations to increase their scent values and propagating their scents to a broader range. On the other hand, the scent value gradually decreases over time when fewer ants use it as a destination, until it eventually decreases to the initial value.

Mobility Adaptation Capability

SNP is equipped with powerful mechanisms to handle node *mobility* and dynamic topology changes. For that purpose, nodes utilize their hello messages to notify their existence to their neighbors. Figure 5 illustrates the format of the hello message. Nodes put their hello intervals into their hello messages, so the one-hop neighbors learn when to expect the next hello message, and can use this information to set up a timer, which is fired off when a node is lost.

Figure 4. Hot spot formation during scent propagation

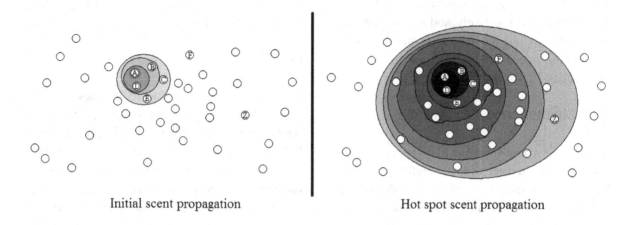

Initial scent propagation   Hot spot scent propagation

Figure 5. Hello message and scent entries format

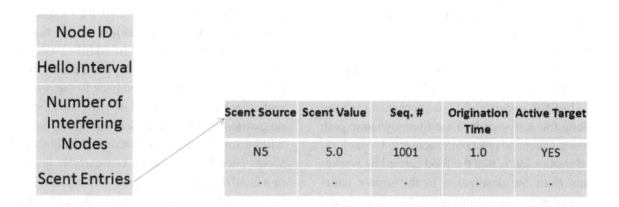

Scent Source	Scent Value	Seq. #	Origination Time	Active Target
N5	5.0	1001	1.0	YES
.	.	.	.	.

Hello Message Format   Scent Entries Format

Stationary nodes send out hello messages at the default hello intervals. However, when nodes are moving, they increase the frequency of hello messages by decreasing their hello intervals. The reason is that moving nodes need to update their location information more frequently so their neighbors can quickly detect the topology changes.

This dynamic mechanism is useful specifically for nodes moving on the path of an active data session. When a node is moving out of the transmission range, its neighbors can quickly start the link failure mechanism to minimize the data packet loss. However, the hello interval cannot be decreased arbitrarily from the practical implementation point of view. SNP uses the following expression to control how the hello interval varies with the node speed:

$$T(s) = T_{default} - \left[\frac{1 - e^{-bs}}{1 + e^{bs}} \right] \left(T_{default} - T_{min} \right),$$

(2)

where $T(s)$ is the hello interval of a node with speed s, $T_{default}$ and T_{min} are the default and minimum hello intervals, respectively, and b is a parameter to control how fast the hello interval drops with the moving speed. Then, $T(s)$ decays fast and approaches T_{min}, as speed s increases.

Path Maintenance

Wireless networks are prone to higher error rates compared to wired networks. Therefore, the wireless routing protocols need to find alternative paths quickly so as to minimize the packet loss during the link recovery phase. For example, to reduce the link recovery time, AntHocNet sends periodical proactive ants from the source to the destination along the path when the data session is active. To explore alternative routes, proactive ants also randomly change into broadcast mode. These random broadcasts increase the chance that the link failures can be fixed locally at the price of additional control overhead.

In SNP, a scent diffusion mechanism is used along the active path to facilitate dynamic path maintenance and link failure recovery. The biological inspiration is that the food carried by worker ants from the destination to the source emits limited scent (compared with the food source) to other locations near the path. The proposed scent diffusion mechanism is similar to the one used for the destination scents. However, the *path scent* is diffused along the path and not centered on the destination. The path scent is spread only to nodes that are close to the active path (a few hops away) through hello messages. These two diffusion mechanisms complement each other. This mechanism has the advantages of (*i*) reducing the scent transmission cost, and (*ii*) using only local repair to find a detour near the original path, when a link fails.

Figure 6 demonstrates the scent diffusion along the path for the scenario, where nodes are deployed in each cell of a 10x10 grid with the destination located at cell (10, 10) and the source at (0, 10).

The scent intensity is not a standard cone, but with higher scent values along the straight path from (0, 10) to (10, 10).

Link Failure Recovery

We consider two possible techniques to cope with link failures: Sending local repair ant and introducing active target. First, in the case of a link failure, the upstream node of the failed link sends out a local repair ant to find a detour. To guarantee that the detour is near the original path, we can set a limit on the maximum number of broadcasts that any local repair ant must have. Because of the path diffusion, nodes near the path have kept the destination's scent, and we can expect that within a few hops, the local repair ant is able to find the scent of the destination and change to unicast mode, just like the normal route discovery operation. In addition, because the scent is diffused from the path, the local repair ant is eventually guided back to the original path, reaching the destination. However, there is no guarantee that such a local repair mechanism will be always successful because the number of scents each hello message can carry is limited, or a local detour may not exist. If the local repair fails, a link failure notice is sent to the source node of the data session, where a new path discovery can be triggered.

Another optional technique to tackle the link failure caused by network dynamics is to introduce the concept of *active target*. An active target is a destination node having active data sessions. For routing, the most critical information of a data flow is the current location of the destination. The sooner other nodes receive the updated location of the destination, the more accurate the route would be. The idea is to propagate scents of active targets as soon as possible thereby reducing the session abruption to the minimum level. When an active target emits its own scent, it marks the Boolean field "Active Target" as true for its scent entry in the hello message. After the hello

Figure 6. Scent diffusion along the path of an active data session

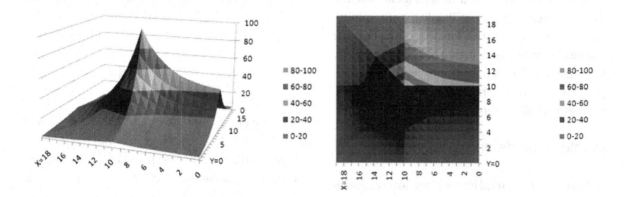

message reaches a neighbor, and if this scent is one of the N strongest scents (after decaying with the link cost), the node cancels the current hello timer and sends out the next hello message immediately. Note that the protocol will generate more hello messages this way, and the overhead may increase significantly when there are many data sessions. The technique should be applied only to data sessions with high priority, such as the ones with high QoS requirements, or to long flows in a heavy-tailed traffic scenario.

Wireless Interference-Aware Routing Mechanism in SNP

DB Pair and Link Cost Measurement

The dominant factor in wireless network performance is the wireless *interference*. Therefore, there is a strong need for interference-aware routing, which is not effectively represented in the previous ACO algorithms. SNP is equipped with the interference-aware routing metrics motivated by the interesting phenomenon of *Deaf and Bottleneck (DB) pair* in wireless networks. The DB Pair concept is used to measure the link cost in the SNP design. "Deaf" node is the one not able to respond to its neighbors' transmissions because

of the heavy interference, and "Bottleneck" node is the one with the most packet drops. The deaf and bottleneck nodes usually occur in pairs, one node with the most severe wireless interference and its next upstream node, which is the actual bottleneck for the traffic flow.

Figure 7 illustrates the DB pair concept for nodes placed in a hexagon grid with 6 neighbors. Nodes that are within two hops away interfere with each other. The top left corner of each node marks the number of interfering nodes. Two traffic flows are generated, from node 1 to 21, and from node 2 to 22. For flow 1, the deaf node (with the highest interference) is node 5 and the bottleneck node (with most packet drops) is node 1, because its downstream neighbor, node 5, experiences heavy interference and cannot send timely MAC (Medium Access Control) acknowledgements for the packets received from node 1. Thus, the interface queue of node 1 is quickly filled up by packets waiting for the MAC acknowledgements and this forces node 1 to drop packets in its queue. For flow 2, the deaf node is node 6 and the bottleneck is node 2. This is because node 6 lies upstream, and its non-responsive behavior causes node 2 to drop packets and thus shapes the traffic. DB pair is unique for wireless networks using CSMA/CA MAC (IEEE 802.11) and has the important implication on routing and network performance tuning.

Once the DB pair of a flow is identified and the interference degree of the deaf node is measured, the existence or the location of the DB pair can be controlled by changing the path of the flow to reduce the flow's overall interference and improve the network performance, e.g., the end-to-end network throughput.

Wireless Interference Metric in SNP

DB pair concept is used in workload-aware routing algorithm for wireless networks. To achieve the maximum path rate, the optimal route for a flow should have the minimal intra-flow and inter-flow wireless interference, which can be measured by the number of interfering neighbors of the deaf node. The routing algorithm needs to collect the interference information on multiple paths before it actually assigns a path to a new flow. The algorithm then compares the interference degrees of the deaf nodes on different paths and chooses the path that includes the deaf node with the least interference degree.

When measuring the interference degree (number of interfering neighbors) of a deaf node, it is practical to use only long flows under the heavy-tailed traffic condition. For a single flow on path $(x_1, x_2, ..., x_f)$, the path rate is given by

$$R\left(x_1, x_2, ..., x_f\right) = \min_{k \in \{1, ..., f-1\}} r\left(x_k, x_{k+1}\right), \qquad (3)$$

where $r\left(x_k, x_{k+1}\right)$ is the rate of link (x_k, x_{k+1}). Let $N_{CS}\left(x_k\right)$ denote the number of nodes having long flows in the carrier sense range of x_k. For a shared baseband channel in IEEE 802.11, the link rate is assumed to be

$$r\left(x_k, x_{k+1}\right) = \frac{B}{N_{CS}(x_k) - 1}, \qquad (4)$$

where $B > 0$ is the physical bandwidth. Hence, the deaf node is the first node with the largest value of $N_{CS}\left(x_k\right) > 1$. Note that the above formulation ignores the PHY layer diversity, packet capture effects, and dynamical systems properties of ad hoc wireless networks that can significantly influence the performance results in realistic network applications. When applied in the ACO

Figure 7. Nodes 5 and 6 are deaf nodes and nodes 1 and 2 are bottlenecks

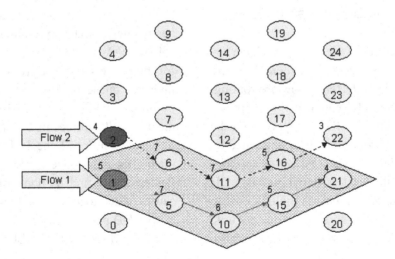

algorithms, the ants should be able to collect long flow interference information at each node along the path. This requires that each node tracks the long messages. In addition to the scent value, each node also indicates whether it is running a long flow in its hello message, and this information is forwarded by its one-hop neighbors. However, long flow information can only reach at most two-hop neighbors of the originating node, because the carrier sensing range is typically twice of the transmission distance.

After computing the long-flow-interference at each node, this information can be used in scent/pheromone diffusion. The scent decays more from a node with higher interference than from a node with lower interference. Thus, scent-guided ants tend to take the path with lower interference towards a destination. Then, the path rate formulation in Equations (3)-(4) can be used to define the pheromone, which directly affects how data packets are dispatched.

Protocol Implementation

The format of the basic data structures used by SNP is described as follows.

Hello Message

Hello message includes four components as illustrated in Figure 5:

1. **Node ID:** a string which is also the ID to indicate the originator of this hello message.
2. **Hello interval:** a positive real number which indicates the time period from the current time to the next hello message from the same originator.
3. **Number of interfering nodes:** a non-negative integer which indicates how many nodes in its capture sensing range, including itself, are interfering with its transmissions. SNP only counts nodes with active long flows.

4. **Scent entries:** a list of up to N scents stored by the originator node.

Each scent entry has the following fields:

1. **Scent source:** a string which indicates the source of this scent.
2. **Scent value:** a non-negative real number.
3. **Sequence number:** a non-negative integer which is unique for an emission of this source node.
4. **Origination time:** the time when the scent is emitted by the originator.
5. **Active target:** a Boolean variable which indicates whether or not the scent source is being used by a data session.

Scent Table

Each node keeps a scent table which contains all fresh scents it learns from the hello messages. The scent table has the following fields:

1. **Scent source/destination:** a string which indicates the originator of the scent. For routing protocols, this is the routing table.
2. **Sender:** a string which indicates the direct neighbor which forwards this scent.
3. **Scent value:** a non-negative real number which indicates the strength of the scent.
4. **Sequence number:** a non-negative integer. It is the same sequence number, which is assigned by the originator when it sends out this scent.
5. **Expiration time:** the time when this scent should be outdated.

Simulation Results for Throughput and Overhead

In this session, we show the performance gains of SNP through simulations and verify the advantage of SNP over other ACO and MANET routing protocols. We choose AODV and AntHocNet

(AHN) as the reference protocols, because AODV is one of the most popular MANET protocols, and AntHocNet is a well-known bio-inspired routing protocol based on ACO algorithm.

We use in-house network simulator CCNS (Cross-layer Composable Network Simulator) of Intelligent Automation, Inc. for experiments. Simulations are configured as follows: All nodes are uniformly randomly placed in a 50m x 50m rectangular area. The transmission range of each node is 15m. All nodes employ 802.11 as the MAC protocol and use the same communication channel. In each simulation experiment, multiple data connections are generated with randomly selected source and destination pairs from the existing nodes. The data type is CBR (Constant Bit Rate) using UDP (User Datagram Protocol), the transmission rate is 10 packets/second, and each packet contains 1024 byte application data. The connections arrive according to a Poisson process, and its mean interarrival time equals to the whole simulation time divided by the total number of connections.

To reflect the heavy-tailed nature of packet traffic, 80% of connections have a short lifetime (2 seconds) and 20% of connections have long lifetime (40 seconds). To mimic the hot spot phenomenon, 80% of total connections are destined to the same group of nodes, which account for 20% of total nodes. Node mobility is generated using a waypoint model, in which a node goes to a randomly selected point at a fixed speed, and rests for a random time, and then heads to the next point. In our experiments, we varied values of four parameters: node number, connection number, node moving speed, and node resting time. Figure 8 shows the node placement of one sample simulation experiment.

We compare the protocol performance under different networking conditions, and we vary the values of the following simulation parameters:

- **Number of Nodes:** varies from 10, 15, 20, 25, to 30, default value = 20.

- **Number of Connections:** varies from 10, 25, 50, 75, to 100, default value = 50.
- **Node Moving Speed:** varies from 0.05, 0.5, 1, 1.5, to 2 m/s, default value = 0.5 m/s.
- **Node Resting Time:** varies from 10, 20, 30, 40, to 50 sec, default value = 30 sec.

When we change values of one parameter, we set the other three parameters to their default values. For each parameter combination, we run five passes of simulation with different random effects of topology, mobility and traffic, and compute the mean throughput and overhead of these five passes. The throughput is measured as the total number of successfully delivered packets, and the overhead is measured as the total transmissions of non-data packets by all nodes in the simulation. For example, after a source node sends out a route request, this request is forwarded by five other nodes, and then the overhead is six transmissions. On the other hand, when a data packet travels through multiple hops and reaches the destination, it is considered as only one packet delivery when we measure the throughput. Next, we illustrate the simulation results (throughput and overhead) for different network parameters.

Figure 9 shows the throughput and overhead performance of the three protocols when we randomly place different number of nodes into the network topology. Note that we set three other parameters to their default values such that these simulations run 50 data connections, all nodes are moving at 0.5m/s, and the node rest time is 30 seconds. All three protocols achieve almost the same throughput when the node number is very small (=10). AODV has the worst throughput among the three protocols when the node number becomes larger. AHN generally has higher throughput than the other two protocols when the node number is low (<=15). But SNP has the best throughput performance when more nodes (>15) are placed in the same simulation setup. On the other hand,

Figure 8. Sample network topology for simulations

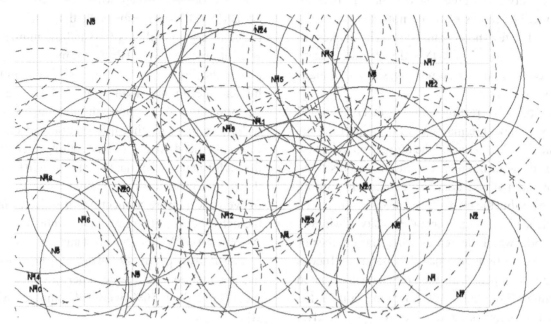

Figure 9. Throughput and overhead with different node numbers

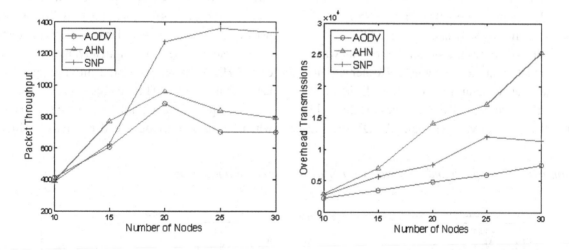

SNP requires much less control overhead than AHN, but more than AODV.

Both AHN and SNP achieve higher or the same throughput rates than AODV because the ant and pheromone mechanisms enable them to have quicker and more accurate response to the network dynamics. For example, nodes in AHN or SNP keep multiple next-hop entries for the same des-tination in their routing tables. When one next-hop becomes less reliable, the next entry will emerge as the best one and is used by the succeeding data packets. This takes place without waiting for extra route repair or rediscovery like AODV does. The three protocols achieve almost the same throughput performance when the number of nodes in the network is small. In this case, the routes between sources and destinations become simple, i.e., routes either do not exist or consist only of a few hops. This simplicity makes all advanced features of AHN and SNP unnecessary. Therefore, all protocols result in similar throughput performance.

Another interesting feature is that AODV and AHN achieve the maximum throughput performance for 20 nodes and the throughput decrease when the node number continues to increase. The throughput of SNP does not decrease after hitting 20 nodes, but the increase rate drops sharply. This result is related to the general capacity of wireless network, which decreases when the number of nodes over a finite area increases, because all nodes have to compete with each other for the shared medium. From the result shown in Figure 9, the network becomes saturated for AODV and AHN when the node number reaches 20, but SNP does not saturate the network until the node number is 25. This is because SNP incurs less overhead than AHN (see Figure 10) and also SNP is better adapted to network dynamics than AODV.

Figure 10 shows the simulation results when the connection number changes and other parameters are set to default values. For all different connection numbers, SNP improves the throughput at least 20% over AHN, and AODV has the lowest throughput except when connection number is 10. AODV performs better than AHN when the connection number is 10 (smallest number in simulations), because AHN has the most broadcast among the three protocols and experiences much higher interference than AODV. Again, SNP performs the best in terms of throughput, because it delivers more routing information and incurs lower overhead. In terms of the routing overhead, the performance is similar to that shown in Figure 9. All three protocols incur an increasing amount of overhead as more connections are injected into the network. For all connection numbers tested, AHN and AODV incur the most and least amount of overhead, respectively. On the other hand, SNP has the intermediate overhead performance, and incurs only about 50% overhead compared with AHN.

Figure 11 shows the simulation results for different node moving speeds. Generally, the throughput decreases for all protocols when nodes move faster, and SNP still has the best throughput performance in most cases. However, it is interesting to note that the throughput advantage of SNP over AHN narrows when the moving speed is larger than 1.0 m/s. This suggests that SNP does not have a particular advantage compared to AHN when the node moving speed is relatively high

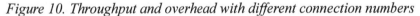

Figure 10. Throughput and overhead with different connection numbers

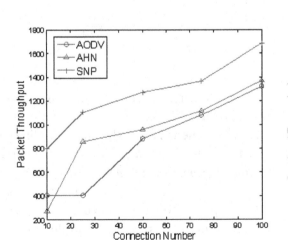
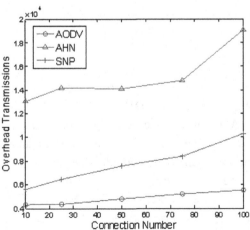

with respect to the chosen transmission range. This is because the scent dissemination in SNP relies on hello messages to propagate, and on the average it requires a time interval that is given by the hello period multiplied by the number of hops to reach a particular remote node. By the time when a forward ant picks up the scent at this remote node, it might already be stale if nodes are moving fast.

However, in AHN, forward ants always use the broadcast to flood the network to find a destination. Although it causes larger overhead, it is the most reliable routing approach when nodes are moving fast. The overhead analysis shows that both AHN and SNP incur more overhead when the node moving speed increases. SNP requires only around 50% of overhead compared with AHN. Note that unlike previous experiments, the overhead of AODV is almost constant for different values of moving speed, which conforms to its protocol design.

Node rest time is another aspect of network mobility. In a waypoint mobility model, after a node moves to a destination point, it stops for the rest time, and then starts to move to the next destination. So, network mobility is higher while the rest time is shorter. From Figure 12, all three protocols achieve higher throughput when the

rest time becomes longer, because the overall network mobility decreases, and it benefits all the three protocols. SNP still achieves the highest throughput and as expected, AODV has the worst throughput performance. On the other hand, AODV has the lowest overhead, which is almost independent of the node rest time, and AHN has the highest overhead in all cases. The overhead of SNP and AHN both decrease when the node rest time is longer, which means both protocols perform less route repair and rediscovery.

From the simulation results, we can conclude that, compared with AHN, SNP reduces the routing overhead significantly, and consequently achieves higher throughput in most instances of the simulation experiments. The throughput gain comes from (*i*) nodes have opportunities to maintain the scent information of potential destinations, especially hot spots, and this saves routing overhead; (*ii*) the wireless interference factor in scent or pheromone's decay expression allows SNP to avoid nodes with heavy interference, and thus mitigates the potential network congestion. Therefore, SNP has the best performance in dense wireless networks, where the interference between nodes is severe. However, because the scent information travels with hello messages, it is rather slow to reach nodes far away. In a network

Figure 11. Throughput and overhead with different node moving speeds

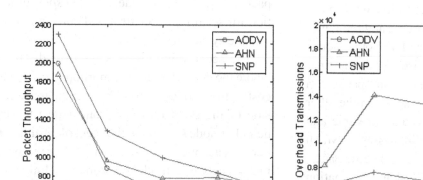

Figure 12. Throughput and overhead with different node rest times

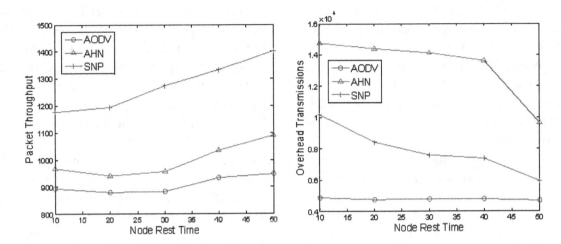

where nodes move very fast, the scent information may quickly become stale, and this may be very inefficient in terms of guiding routing ants towards destinations. Because AHN uses flooding mechanism to find routes, it is more accurate for a network with high-speed nodes. Therefore, a more reliable mechanism with less overhead than flooding is needed to improve the performance of SNP in highly mobile networks.

Overhead Analysis of SNP

Next, we analyze the overhead requirement of SNP. A general network is assumed with n nodes randomly distributed over a fixed finite area. Each node generates packet traffic with rate λ (packets per second) as the source and randomly addresses each packet to one of $n-1$ other nodes as the destination. Sources discover the destinations of their packets by sending ant packets in form of location request messages. On the other hand, each destination holds a scent value and disseminates it in form of hello messages, which would correspond to the location update messages.

The scent value (strength) of any destination decays both over time and distance. A slotted time system is assumed, where the scent value decays every time slot with linear factor $c_{time} < 1$. When-

ever a location request message arrives at a destination (which occurs with total rate λ), the popularity of the destination increases along with the value of scent it releases. Let $n_i(t)$ denote the number of the location update messages arriving at node i at slotted time t. In Equation (1), S_i^k denotes the scent value of destination i at node k. The value S_i^i that destination i holds for its own scent evolves over time as

$$S_i^i(t+1) = c_{time}\ S_i^i(t) + \sigma\ n_i(t), \qquad (5)$$

where σ is a positive constant that represents the linear scent increase with every incoming ant packet. Equation (5) models the *hot spot* formation for scent reinforcement and corresponds to a stable system for $c_{time} < 1$.

The scent value also decays over distance, where the decay factor is proportional to the link cost c_{jk} from node j to node k. After the transmission of the scent message from node j to any neighbor node k at time t, the scent of destination i decays according to Equation (1). For the symmetric network model, a common link cost $c_{jk} = c_{link} < 1$ is assumed for any link (j,k), where c_{link} includes both spatial and temporal decay factors.

Global Asymptotic Analysis of SNP Overhead

First, we evaluate the scaling laws for SNP overhead, as the number of nodes, n, grows to infinity. A circular model is assumed for the communication ranges and the scent strength disappears, when its ratio to the initial value drops below a finite threshold $0 < \varepsilon < 1$. The maximum number of hops that the scent of any node can travel before it expires is defined as the scent radius k_{max}, and it is computed from Equation (1) as

$$k_{max} < \frac{\log(1/\varepsilon)}{\tilde{c}_{link}} + 1, \tag{6}$$

where $\log(.)$ is the natural logarithm and $\tilde{c}_{link} = -\log\left(1 - c_{link}\right)$.

Before the scent expires, it can diffuse over the maximum area of $\pi \, k_{max}^2 r^2(n)$, where $r(n)$ is the common communication range. Given two functions $f(n)$ and $g(n)$, we say $f(n) = O(g(n))$, if and only if $\sup_n \left(f(n)/g(n)\right) < \infty$, we say $f(n) = \Omega(g(n))$, if and only if $g(n) = O(f(n))$, and we say $f(n) = \Theta(g(n))$, if and only if $f(n) = O(g(n))$ and $f(n) = \Omega(g(n))$. Since n nodes are randomly distributed over a fixed area, the maximum number of nodes, n_{max}, which can be reached by any scent (before its strength disappears), is bounded as

$$n_{max} = O\left(\frac{n \, r^2(n)}{\tilde{c}_{link}^2}\right). \tag{7}$$

For the global network connectivity such that no node is isolated in the network, the minimum transmission range (Gupta & Kumar, 2000) must satisfy

$$r(n) = \Theta\left(\sqrt{\frac{\log(n)}{n}}\right). \tag{8}$$

The hello messages (corresponding to the destination scents) are flooded to n_{max} nodes over a minimum spanning tree (MST). Then, each hello message travels on the average the distance of $d_{max} = O\left(\sqrt{n_{max}}\right)$ hops over the MST (Steel, 1988). Scent messages are transmitted from each of n nodes at rate λ (with new ant packet arrivals). There are n potential destinations each generating hello messages with rate λ. Then, each hello message travels the average distance of d_{max} hops, and each hello message consists of m bits. Therefore, the total overhead is given by $n\lambda d_{max} m$ and it is computed from Equations (7) and (8) as

$$N_{scent} = O\left(\frac{n\lambda\sqrt{\log(n)}m}{\tilde{c}_{link}}\right). \tag{9}$$

The hello message contains the ID information and location information of the corresponding destination. To identify the originator of the scent, $\log(n)$ bits are sufficient. If the network is divided into square cells with the quantization level of $cr(n) \times cr(n)$ for some constant $c > 0$, the approximated node locations can be described in one of $O(n/\log(n))$ cells with $O(\log(n))$ bits (La & Seo, 2008). Combining the overhead terms to describe node IDs and node locations, $m = O(\log(n))$ bits are sufficient to represent each scent message. Then, the total scent overhead generated for the entire network to carry is given by

$$N_{scent} = O\left(\frac{n\lambda\log^{3/2}(n)}{\tilde{c}_{link}}\right). \tag{10}$$

The total SNP overhead should also reflect the overhead requirement for ant routing. To deliver each ant packet (location request message), MST is constructed with the average distance of $O\left(\sqrt{n}\right)$. This yields the total overhead $O\left(n\,\lambda\sqrt{n}\,m\right)$ for the location request messages, where m is the bit length of an ant packet. Then, total of $\log(n)$

bits are sufficient to identify the ID of each of n destinations, i.e., we have $m = \log(n)$. On the other hand, the location reply messages from any destination are not flooded but sent on a single path with the average distance of $O(1)$. Since $O(\log(n))$ bits are sufficient to inform the source of the location of the requested destination, the total overhead for ant routing (La & Seo, 2008) is given by

$$N_{\text{ant}} = O\left(n^{3/2}\lambda \log(n)\right). \tag{11}$$

Both scent and ant messages are carried in the network concurrently. From Equations. (10) and (11), the scent overhead does not increase the order of total overhead beyond ant routing, if and only if

$$\tilde{c}_{link} = \Omega\left(\sqrt{\frac{\log(n)}{n}}\right), , \tag{12}$$

i.e., if the exponential link cost factor for scent decay over one hop is chosen at least proportional to the hop distance $r(n)$. Since $\tilde{c}_{link} = -\log\left(1 - c_{link}\right)$, the linear decay factor must satisfy $c_{link} = \Omega\left(1 - \exp\left(-\sqrt{\log(n)/n}\right)\right)$, which approaches $c_{link} = \Omega\left(r(n)\right)$, as n grows to infinity.

As a result, it is possible to operate both scent and ant-based routing schemes jointly with the same overhead order of $O\left(n\sqrt{\log(n)}\right)$. Note that the maximum rate λ_{max} that a random network can carry is achieved for the minimum communication range given by (8) (Gupta & Kumar, 2000) and it is computed as

$$\lambda_{\text{max}} = \Theta\left(\frac{1}{\sqrt{n \log(n)}}\right). \tag{13}$$

For the worst-case overhead, each source sends out a new ant packet for the destination discovery whenever it generates a new data packet. Then, the maximum possible scent overhead is given by

$$N_{\text{scent}} \tag{14}$$

which is the same as the overhead for ant routing provided that c_{link} is chosen according to (12).

Local Dynamic Analysis of SNP Overhead

Next, we evaluate the effects of *finite overhead* on scent dissemination. Hello messages of different destinations compete with each other in the form of dynamic information exchange. Then, the finite overhead limits the scent radius because of the *avalanche* effect of the scent dissemination. In SNP, each relay node keeps the strongest N scents of different destinations (including one for its own scent), and discards the other weak scents. Let d denote the vertex degree of each node (i.e., one-hop neighbors that can be reached by any broadcast transmission) in a symmetric network, and let λ_0 denote the rate at which ant packets reach a given target destination.

The hello message of any node i must include (a) the scent of i provided that at least one location request message arrives in the previous time slot, (b) the scents of the one-hop neighbors provided that they received location request messages in the previous time slot, (c) the scents relayed by the neighbors (i.e., the scents of nodes that are two or more hops away) in the previous time slot. Then, the average scent overhead N of any node satisfies

$$N = \lambda_0 + d\lambda_0 + d\left(N - 2\lambda_0\right)\delta. \tag{15}$$

The first term λ_0 in Equation (15) corresponds to the individual scent of the node under consideration, the second term $\lambda_0 d$ corresponds to the scents of neighboring nodes, which must be kept in the hello messages because they have scent values greater than the ones already stored at the node, and the third term $(N - 2\lambda_0) d\delta$ corresponds to the scents that are incoming from the neighboring nodes and are relayed by the node (Each node forwards only δ portion of the scents relayed from each neighbor node). The third term excludes the individual scent of the node and the scents of the neighbors, since a node always drops its own scent value that is returned back by the neighbor node and always forwards new scents of the neighboring nodes. In general, δ is a topology-dependent parameter, and in particular it depends on k_{max} and d, where k_{max} is the maximum number of nodes a scent can reach and d is the node degree.

A minimum spanning tree is used to flood the hello messages. The parameter δ can be analytically computed as a function of k_{max} and d as follows. Scent messages incoming from any neighbor node i to node j consists of four parts: (*a*) Scents of nodes in group G_1 (nodes that are closer in hop-distance to i than j and are k_{max} hops away from j), (*b*) Scents of nodes in group G_2 (nodes that are closer to j than i and are $k_{max} - 2$ hops away from j), (*c*) Scent of node i, and (*d*) Scent of node j. The computation of δ excludes scents of node i and j. From the rest of scents

incoming from i, node j does not forward scents of group G_2, because j already has received these scents before they reach i, and does not forward scents from group G_1 that are k_{max} hops away from j, because they expire when they arrive at j. Therefore, node j relays only scents from group G_3, which contains nodes from group G_1 that are at most $k_{max} - 1$ hops away from j and $k_{max} - 2$ hops away from i. Groups G_1, G_2, and G_3 are illustrated in Figure 13.

We can express $\delta = G_3 / (G_1 + G_2)$, where

$$G_1 = \sum_{j=1}^{k_{max}-1} (d-1)^j$$

and $G_2 = G_3 = \sum_{j=1}^{k_{max}-2} (d-1)^j$

such that the parameter δ can be computed as a function of $k_{max} > 2$ and d:

$$\delta(d, k_{max}) = \frac{\sum_{j=1}^{k_{max}-2} (d-1)^j}{\sum_{j=1}^{k_{max}-1} (d-1)^j + \sum_{j=1}^{k_{max}-2} (d-1)^j}. \tag{16}$$

Then, from Equations (15)-(16) the average scent overhead, N, can be computed as

Figure 13. Illustration of the parameter δ to quantify the effect of network topology on overhead N for tree networks with d = 3 and k_{max} = 4. In this example, δ = 0.3

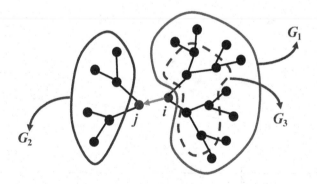

$$N = \begin{cases} \lambda_0, & k_{\max} = 1, \\ (1+d)\lambda_0, & k_{\max} = 2, \\ \left[\left(\dfrac{1 + d(1 - 2\,\delta(d, k_{\max}))}{1 - d\,\delta(d, k_{\max})}\right)\right]\lambda_0, & k_{\max} > 2. \end{cases}$$

$$(17)$$

The overhead N increases with node degree d and scent radius $k_{\max}$. To avoid the avalanche effect of scent dissemination, the scent radius k_{max} should be kept small, which can be realized by increasing the link cost c_{link}. Figure 14 evaluates the overhead term (17) for $\lambda_0 = 0.1$.

The scent range, i.e., the number of nodes any scent can reach (excluding the scent origin), is given by

$$n_{\max}(d, k_{\max}) = d \sum_{j=0}^{k_{\max}-1} (d-1)^j \qquad (18)$$

for the minimum spanning tree constructed for scent message dissemination.

The overhead is evaluated in Figure 15 as a function of scent range $n_{\max}(d, k_{\max})$, where

k_{max} is fixed and d is changed from 2 to 10. The scent range shows polynomial increase with the overhead that is necessary to support the scent message distribution.

Benefits of Network Coding

SNP overhead increases fast with node degree d and scent radius k_{max}, and causes a bottleneck for the scent message exchange between neighboring nodes. We discuss next the potential use of *network coding* to improve the local exchange of scent messages at a single node with node degree d. Network coding is a novel networking paradigm that extends store-and-forward-based routing and allows intermediate nodes to code over the incoming packet traffic (Ahlswede, Cai, Li, & Yeung, 2000). Network coding provides significant throughput gains over routing at the cost of additional coding complexity and overhead, which would increase with the network size. Here, network coding is applied only *locally* to reduce the SNP overhead, i.e., network coding is applied for the exchange of scent messages between neighboring nodes rather than for delivering data packets (that is carried out by ant routing).

Figure 14. Overhead N as a function of scent radius k_{max} and node degree d

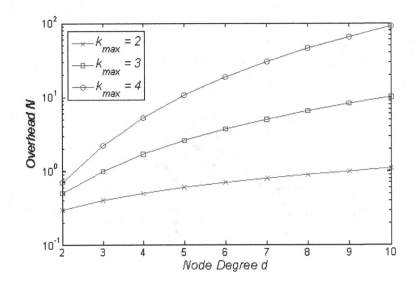

Figure 15. Overhead N as a function of scent range n_{max}

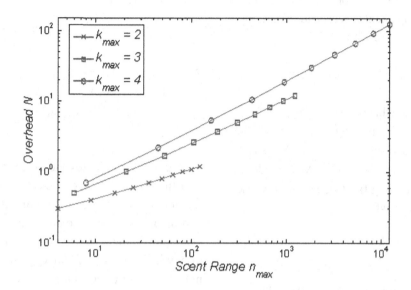

The scent message at any node i consists of two parts: (*a*) Individual scent of node i, (*b*) Scent messages incoming from the neighboring nodes that need to be relayed. The content of any scent message is partitioned into two terms $X^{(a)}$ for case (*a*) and $\underline{X}^{(b)}$ for case (*b*):

$$\underline{X} = [X^{(a)} \ , \ \underline{X}^{(b)}].\tag{19}$$

Accordingly, we partition N in Equation (19) into two terms: $N^{(a)}$ and $N^{(b)}$, where

$$N^{(a)} = \lambda_0, \qquad N^{(b)} = \lambda_0 \ + (N - 2\lambda_0) \ \delta \tag{20}$$

such that $N = N^{(a)} + d \ N^{(b)}$. Coding $X^{(a)}$ with any element of $\underline{X}^{(b)}$ would not reduce the length of scent message, because neighbor nodes do not have $X^{(a)}$ and cannot decode unless one degree of freedom (one innovative packet) for $X^{(a)}$ is received. Therefore, we assume that only elements of $\underline{X}^{(b)}$ are network-coded (with linear coding matrix G) such that the total scent message trans-

mitted by any node has the common format given by

$$\underline{Y} = [X^{(a)} \ , \ G\underline{X}^{(b)}].\tag{21}$$

The goal is to find the coding matrix G with the minimum number of rows such that all d neighboring nodes can decode $\underline{X}$ from $\underline{Y}$. We assume that (in addition to its own scent) each neighboring node already has η scents from $\underline{X}$ with the most current scent values. For instance, this may model the case that multiple paths exist or nodes overhear each other's omnidirectional transmissions. Then, each neighboring node needs at least $(d - 1 - \eta) \ N^{(b)}$ degrees of freedom to decode the scent messages $\underline{X}$.

This problem is similar to wireless broadcast exchange with network coding over relay nodes (Sagduyu, Guo, & Berry, 2008) and here we can refer to the same code construction scheme such that there exists $(d - 1 - \eta) \ N^{(b)} \times d \ N^{(b)}$ matrix G and all neighboring nodes can decode the messages in $\underline{X}$ from $\underline{Y}$. In general, Maximum Distance Separable (MDS) codes (MacWilliams & Sloane,

1977) can be used to solve this broadcast problem with $\eta +1$ packets of side information (one individual scent and η scents overheard from the other neighbors). The result is a

$$(d - 1 - \eta)\ N^{(b)} \times d\ N^{(b)}$$

generator matrix such that whenever $(\eta + 1)\ N^{(b)}$ columns are removed, the remaining matrix is full-rank, i.e., it has rank $(d - 1 - \eta)\ N^{(b)}$. The existence of $[d\ N^{(b)}, (\eta + 1)\ N^{(b)}]$ MDS code is guaranteed, if the coding field size q for network coding operations satisfies

$$q > d(\lambda_0\ + (N - 2\lambda_0)\ \delta). \tag{22}$$

With network coding for local scent exchange, Equation (17) for the scent overhead N is changed to

$$N = \lambda_0 + (\lambda_0\ + (N - 2\lambda_0)\ \delta)\ (d - 1 - \eta). \tag{23}$$

Then, from Equation (23) the scent overhead N is computed as

$$N = \begin{cases} 1, & k_{max} = 1, \\ 1 + d - 1 - \eta, & k_{max} = 2, \\ \dfrac{1 + (d - 1 - \eta)\ (1 - 2\ \delta(d, k_{max}))}{1 - (d - 1 - \eta)\ \delta(d, k_{max})}, & k_{max} > 2. \end{cases} \tag{24}$$

Figure 16 evaluates the protocol overhead N as a function of node degree d with and without network coding for scent dissemination. Network coding provides significant reduction in the overhead requirement and slows down the increase in N with respect to d and k_{max}. In particular, the network coding gain increases with the amount of side information (on scent messages) available at neighbor nodes.

FUTURE RESEARCH DIRECTIONS

The main focus of our approach was to improve the throughput and overhead properties of bio-

Figure 16. Benefits of network coding to reduce protocol overhead (shown for $k_{max} = 3$)

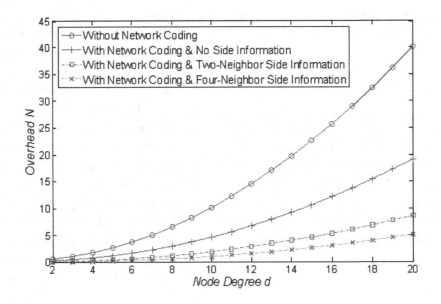

logically inspired routing protocols compared to the state-of-the-art ACO and traditional MANET routing protocols. There are additional important performance metrics, including *energy efficiency* and *packet delay*, which typically involve interesting tradeoffs with the throughput and overhead measures. Future work should evaluate these tradeoffs with realistic models of energy and delay in wireless networks. Note that energy may be consumed for both processing and transmission, whereas the total delay includes both service and queueing delay for stochastically varying packet traffic.

Our primary interest in this book chapter was the *average* network performance, where we simulate and analyze the performance of the average throughput and overhead. Another point of interest is to analyze the reactive performance of SNP to dynamic changes beyond mobility effects, which we extensively simulated for the average performance. Those effects include node or link malfunctions such as the case when nodes run out of battery, or we could also incorporate malicious user activities, when some nodes intentionally generate interference to the other nodes or drop packets from the other nodes to degrade the total system performance in the form of Denial of Service (DoS) attacks. For those cases, it is crucial to evaluate the *robustness* of SNP compared to the other ACO and traditional MANET routing protocols. A suitable performance measure to assess robustness is the convergence time, namely the duration of time from the start of any network malfunction or DoS attack until the network recovers from these particular effects and converges again to the next level of stationary performance.

SNP is a novel routing protocol and it is designed to operate seamlessly with the other layer operations. In particular, one of the key features in SNP is taking into account the *wireless interference* effects for routing decisions. This aspect strongly depends on how the physical channel and MAC layers are modeled. It is crucial to evaluate the physical channel and MAC effects

beyond IEEE 802.11. This may involve enhancing the mechanisms to measure and incorporate the interference effects in wireless link costs, although the main structure of SNP remains oblivious to the underlying network tasks. Similarly, *congestion control* can be built upon SNP for end-to-end network resilience. The interactions of different Transmission Control Protocols with SNP and other biologically inspired routing protocols should be further addressed.

CONCLUSION

As a novel biologically inspired MANET routing protocol, we introduced the Scented Node Protocol (SNP) to enhance the reliability of ant routing while achieving high throughput and low overhead objectives. The key innovation of SNP is that destinations release scent messages to guide the route discovery and maintenance in ant routing instead of blind broadcast. The major advantages of SNP are that it takes into account realistic wireless network properties such as mobility and wireless interference effects in routing decisions, and it operates with low overhead while maintaining high throughput rates. SNP is based on scent reinforcement at destinations with ant packet arrivals to model the hot spot formation, and it includes novel mechanisms for dynamic adaptation to mobility, path maintenance, and link failure recovery.

Extensive simulations for dynamic MANET environment show that SNP with its interference-aware routing metric improves the average throughput and overhead over the existing ACO and traditional MANET routing algorithms, namely AntHocNet and AODV, respectively. Then, analytical results are presented to evaluate the SNP overhead for scent message dissemination. For the model where the node density grows, SNP overhead does not increase the order of overhead for ant routing provided that the link cost is chosen at least proportional to the transmission range.

Then, the dynamic behavior of scent message exchange among neighboring nodes is evaluated to show how the finite overhead constraint limits the scent range. Finally, the benefits of local network coding are discussed to improve the rate of disseminating scent messages thereby reducing the overall requirement of protocol overhead.

ACKNOWLEDGMENT

This material is based upon work supported by U.S. Army RDECOM ACQ CTR under SBIR Contract W911QX-09-C-0055. Any opinions, findings and conclusions or recommendations expressed in this material are those of the authors and do not necessarily reflect the views of the U.S. Army.

REFERENCES

Ahlswede, R., Cai, N., Li, S.-Y., & Yeung, R. W. (2000). Network information flow. *IEEE Transactions on Information Theory, 46*(4), 1204–1216. doi:10.1109/18.850663

Baras, J. S., & Mehta, H. (2003). A probabilistic emergent routing algorithm for mobile ad hoc networks. *Proc. Workshop on Modeling and Optimization in Mobile, Ad Hoc and Wireless Networks.*

Bonabeau, E., Dorigo, M., & Thraulaz, G. (1999). *Swarm intelligence: From natural to artificial systems.* Oxford, UK: Sante Fe Institute Studies in the Sciences of Complexity, Oxford University Press.

Bullnheimer, B., Hartl, R. F., & Strauss, C. (1999). Applying the ant system to the vehicle routing problem. In *Meta-heuristics: Advances and trends in local search paradigms for optimization* (pp. 285–296). Dordrecht, The Netherlands: Kluwer Academic Publishers. doi:10.1007/978-1-4615-5775-3_20

Colorni, A., Dorigo, M., Maniezzo, V., & Trubian, M. (1994). Ant system for job-shop scheduling. *JORBEL Belgian Journal of Operations Research. Statistics and Computer Science, 34*(1), 39–53.

Cost, D., & Hertz, A. (1997). Ants can colour graphs. *The Journal of the Operational Research Society, 48,* 295–305.

Di Caro, G., & Dorigo, M. (1998). AntNet: Distributed stigmergetic control for communications networks. *Journal of Artificial Intelligence Research, 9,* 317–365.

Di Caro, G., Ducatelle, F., & Gambardella, L. M. (2005). AntHocNet: An adaptive nature-inspired algorithm for routing in mobile ad hoc networks. *European Transactions on Telecommunications, 16*(5), 443–455. doi:10.1002/ett.1062

Dorigo, M., & Stutzle, T. (2004). *Ant colony optimization.* Cambridge, MA: The MIT Press.

Ducatelle, F., Di Caro, G., & Gambardella, L. M. (2006). An analysis of the different components of the AntHocNet routing algorithm. *Lecture Notes in Computer Science, 4150,* 37. doi:10.1007/11839088_4

Edmund, A. A., Mark, A., & Ryohei, K. (1993). Organization of goal oriented locomotion: Pheromone-modulated flight behavior of moths. *Proc. Workshop on "Locomotion Control in Legged Invertebrates" on Bilogical Neural Networks in Invertebrate Neuroethology and Robotics.*

Ghataoura, D. S., Yang, Y., Matich, G., & Galileo, S. (2009). SWOB: Swarm intelligent odour based routing for geographic wireless sensor network applications. *Proc. IEEE Military Communications Conference.*

Gunes, M., Sorges, U., & Bouazizi, I. (2002). ARA-the ant-colony based routing algorithm for MANETs. *Proc. the International Workshop on Ad Hoc Networking.*

Gupta, P., & Kumar, P. R. (2000). The capacity of wireless networks. *IEEE Transactions on Information Theory, 46*(2), 388–404. doi:10.1109/18.825799

Kaelbling, L. P., Littman, M. L., & Moore, A. W. (1996). Reinforcement learning: A survey. *Journal of Artifical Intelligence, 4*, 237–285.

La, R. J., & Seo, E. (2008Submitted to). *Expected routing overhead in mobile ad-hoc networks with flat geographic routing.* IEEE Tansactions on Mobile Computing.

MacWilliams, F. J., & Sloane, N. J. (1977). *The theory of error-correcting codes.* Amsterdam, The Netherlands: North-Holland.

Maniezzo, V. (1999). Exact and approximate nondeterministic tree-search procedures for the quadratic assignment problem. *INFORMS Journal on Computing, 11*(4), 358–369. doi:10.1287/ijoc.11.4.358

Perkins, C. E., & Royer, E. M. (1999). Ad hoc on-demand distance vector routing. *Proc. 2nd IEEE Workshop on Mobile Computing Systems and Applications,* (pp. 90-100). New Orleans, LA.

Sagduyu, Y. E., Guo, D., & Berry, R. (2008). On the delay and throughput of digital and analog network coding for wireless broadcast. *Proc. Conference on Information Sciences and Systems, CISS.* Princeton, NJ.

Steel, J. M. (1988). Growth rates of Euclidean minimal spanning trees with power weighted edges. *Annals of Probability, 16*(4), 1767–1787. doi:10.1214/aop/1176991596

Compilation of References

Abdulla, M., & Simon, R. (2006). A simulation analysis of multicasting in delay tolerant networks. *Proceedings of the Winter Simulation Conference – WSC*, (pp. 2234-2241).

Abelson, H. (2000). Amorphous computing. *Communications of the ACM*, 43.

Abrash, H. I. (1986). Studies concerning affinity. *Journal of Chemical Education, 63*, 1044–1047. English translation of the original paper by Waage and Guldberg (1864).

Acosta, F. J., Lopez, F., & Serrano, J. M. (1993). Branching angles of ant trunk trails as an optimization cue. *Journal of Theoretical Biology, 160*(3), 297–310. doi:10.1006/jtbi.1993.1020

Aggarwal, A., Savage, S., & Anderson, T. (2000). Understanding the performance of TCP pacing. In *Proceedings of the 9th Annual Joint Conference of the IEEE Computation and Communication Societies (INFOCOM 2000)* (pp. 1157–1165).

Agilent Technologies. (2004). *Mixed packet size throughput.* Retrieved from http://advanced.comms.agilent.com/n2x/docs/journal/JTC 003.html

Ahlswede, R., Cai, N., Li, S.-Y., & Yeung, R. W. (2000). Network information flow. *IEEE Transactions on Information Theory, 46*(4), 1204–1216. doi:10.1109/18.850663

Ahn, C. W., & Ramakrishna, R. S. (2002). A genetic algorithm for shortest path routing problem and the sizing of populations. *IEEE Transactions on Evolutionary Computation, 6*(6), 566–579. doi:10.1109/TEVC.2002.804323

Akyildiz, I., Melodia, T., & Chowdhury, K. R. (2007). a survey on wireless multimedia sensor networks. *Computer Networks, 51*, 921–960. doi:10.1016/j.comnet.2006.10.002

Akyildiz, I., Su, W., Sankarasubramaniam, Y., & Cayirci, E. (2002). Wireless sensor networks: A survey. *Computer Networks, 38*, 393–422. doi:10.1016/S1389-1286(01)00302-4

Akyildiz, I. F., Su, W., Sankarasubramaniam, Y., & Cayirci, E. (2002). Wireless sensor networks: A survey. *Computer Networks, 38*(4), 393–422. doi:10.1016/S1389-1286(01)00302-4

Al Hanbali, A., Ibrahim, M., Simon, V., Varga, E., & Carreras, I. (2009). A survey of message delivery protocols in mobile ad hoc networks. In *Proc. of Inter-Perf 2008*, Athens, Greece, October 20-24, 2008.

Al-Hammadi, Y., Aickelin, U., & Greensmith, J. (2008). DCA for bot detection. In *Proceedings of the IEEE World Congress on Computational Intelligence* (WCCI 2008. Bejtlich, R. (2005). *The Tao of network security monitoring: Beyond intrusion detection.* Pearson Education.

Allen, C., & Stevens, C. F. (1994). An evaluation of causes for unreliability of synaptic transmission. *Proceedings of the National Academy of Sciences (PNAS) USA, vol. 91*, (pp. 10380–10383).

Allman, A., Balakrishnan, H., & Floyd, S. (2001). *Enhancing TCP's loss recovery using limited transmit.* Request for Comments 3042, Jan. 2001.

Alouf, S., Carreras, I., Miorandi, D., & Neglia, G. (2007). Embedding evolution in epidemic style forwarding. In *Proc. of IEEE International Conference on Mobile Adhoc and Sensor Systems (MASS 2007)*, Pisa, Italy.

Analoui, M., & Jamali, S. (2006). A conceptual framework for bio-inspired congestion control in communication networks. *Proceedings of the 1st BIMNICS*, (pp. 1–5).

Andrianantoandro, E., Basu, S., Karig, D. K., & Weiss, R. (2006). Synthetic biology: New engineering rules for an emerging discipline. *Molecular Systems Biology, 2,* E1–E14. doi:10.1038/msb4100073

Anthonisse, J. M. (1971). *The rush in a directed graph.* Technical report, Stichting matematisch centrum, Amsterdam.

Antoniou, P., & Pitsillides, A. (2007, November). *Towards a scalable and self-adaptable congestion control approach for autonomous decentralized networks.* Nature-Inspired Smart Information Systems Annual Symposium 2007, St Julians, Malta.

Appenzeller, G., Keslassy, I., & McKeown, N. (2004). Sizing router buffers. In *Proceedings of ACM SIGCOMM 2004,* Aug. 2004.

Atakan, B., & Akan, O. B. (2008). *On molecular multiple-access, broadcast, and relay channels in nanonetworks.* In International Conference on Bio-Inspired Models of Network, Information, and Computing Systems, 16.

Attenborough, D. (1995). *Movie: The private life of plants. British Broadcasting Corporation.* UK: BBC.

Banâtre, J. P., Fradet, P., & Radenac, Y. (2006). A generalized higher-order chemical computation model. *Electronic Notes in Theoretical Computer Science, 135*(3), 3–13. doi:10.1016/j.entcs.2005.09.016

Bandyopadhyay, S., Hasuike, K., Horisawa, S., & Tawara, S. (2001). An adaptive MAC and bidirectional routing protocol for ad hoc wireless network using ESPAR antenna. In N. H. Vaidya, M. S. Corson, & S. R. Das (Eds.), *MobiHoc '01: Proceedings of the 2nd ACM International Symposium on Mobile ad hoc Networking & Computing,* (pp. 243–246). New York, NY: ACM.

Baras, J. S., & Mehta, H. (2003). A probabilistic emergent routing algorithm for mobile ad hoc networks. *Proc. Workshop on Modeling and Optimization in Mobile, Ad Hoc and Wireless Networks.*

Bar-Yam, Y. (2003). *Dynamics of complex systems.* Westview Press.

Bernstein, L. E. (1989). Independent or dependent feature evaluation: A question of stimulus characterization. *The Behavioral and Brain Sciences, 12,* 756–757. doi:10.1017/S0140525X00025632

Bhandarkar, S., Jain, S., & Reddy, A. L. N. (2005). Improving TCP performance in high bandwidth high RTT links using layered congestion control. In *Proceedings of PFLDnet 2005,* Feb. 2005. Blanton, E., & Allman, M. On making TCP more robust to packet reordering. *ACM Computer Communication Review, 32*(1), 20–30.

Bi, G. Q., & Poo, M. M. (1998). Synaptic modifications in cultured hippocampal neurons: Dependence on spike timing, synaptic strength and postsynaptic cell type. *The Journal of Neuroscience, 18,* 10464–10472.

Blake, C. L., Hettich, S., & Merz, C. J. (1998). *UCI repository of machine learning databases.*

Blanton, E., Allman, M., Fall, K., & Wang, L. (2003). *A conservative selective acknowledgment (SACK)-based loss recovery algorithm for TCP.* Request for Comments 3517, Apr. 2003.

Boccaletti, S., Latora, V., Moreno, Y., Chavez, M., & Hwang, D. (2006). Complex networks: Structure and dynamics. *Physics Reports – Review Section of Physics Letters, 424,* 175-308.

Bollazzi, M., & Roces, F. (2007). To build or not to build: circulating dry air organizes collective building for climate control in the leaf-cutting ant Acromyrmex ambiguus. *Animal Behaviour, 74,* 1349–1355. doi:10.1016/j.anbehav.2007.02.021

Bonabeau, E., Dorigo, M., & Theraulaz, G. (1999). *Swarm intelligence: From natural to artificial systems.* Oxford University Press.

Boyan, J. A., & Littman, M. L. (1994). Packet routing in dynamically changing networks: A reinforcement learning approach. [Morgan Kaufmann Publishers, Massachusetts, US.]. *Advances in Neural Information Processing Systems, 6,* 671–678.

Brakmo, L. S., O'Malley, S. W., & Peterson, L. L. (1994). TCP Vegas: New techniques for congestion detection and avoidance. In *Proceedings of ACM SIGCOMM '94,* Oct. 1994.

Brameier, M., & Banzhaf, W. (2007). *Linear genetic programming. Series: Genetic and Evolutionary Computation, XVI.* New York, NY: Springer.

Brauer, F., & Chavez, C. C. (2000). *Mathematical models in population biology and epidemiology*. USA: Texts in Applied Mathematics.

Brunel, N., & Lavigne, F. (2009). Semantic priming in a cortical network model. *Journal of Cognitive Neuroscience, 21*(12), 2300–2319. .doi:10.1162/jocn.2008.21156

Buffon, G.-L. L. (1753). *Histoire naturelle générale et particulière avec la description du cabinet du roi*, tome IV. Imprimerie Royale, Paris. Retrieved August 15, 2010, from http://gallica. bnf. fr/ ark:/12148/bpt6k9749f

Buhl, J., Gautrais, J., Deneubourg, J. L., & Theraulaz, G. (2004). Nest excavation in ants: Group size effects on the size and structure of tunneling networks. *Naturwissenschaften, 91*(12), 602–606. doi:10.1007/s00114-004-0577-x

Buhl, J., Gautrais, J., Solé, R., Kuntz, P., Valverde, S., Deneubourg, J. L., & Théraulaz, G. (2004a). Efficiency and robustness in ant networks of galleries. *The European Physical Journal B, 42*, 123–129. doi:10.1140/epjb/e2004-00364-9

Buhl, J., Hicks, K., Miller, E., Persey, S., Alinvi, O., & Sumpter, D. (2009). Shape and efficiency of wood ant foraging networks. *Behavioral Ecology and Sociobiology, 63*, 451–460. doi:10.1007/s00265-008-0680-7

Bullnheimer, B., Hartl, R. F., & Strauss, C. (1999). Applying the ant system to the vehicle routing problem. In *Meta-heuristics: Advances and trends in local search paradigms for optimization* (pp. 285–296). Dordrecht, The Netherlands: Kluwer Academic Publishers. doi:10.1007/978-1-4615-5775-3_20

Calude, C. S., & Paun, G. (2001). *Computing with cells and atoms: An introduction to quantum, DNA and membrane computing*. Bristol, PA: Taylor & Francis/Hemisphere.

Campbell, S., Chancelier, J.-P., & Nikoukhah, R. (2006). *Modeling and simulation in Scilab/Scicos*. New York, NY: Springer.

Cao, M. L. T., Hasegawa, G., & Murata, M. (2004). Available bandwidth measurement via TCP connection. In *Proceedings of IFIP/IEEE MMNS 2004*, Oct. 2004.

Cao, M. L. T., Hasegawa, G., & Murata, M. (2005). A merged inline measurement method for capacity and available bandwidth. In *Proceedings of NLANR PAM 2005*, Mar. 2005.

Caporale, N., & Dan, Y. (2008). Spike timing–dependent plasticity: A Hebbian learning rule. *Annual Review of Neuroscience, 31*(1), 25–46. doi:10.1146/annurev.neuro.31.060407.125639

Carr, C. E. (1993). Processing of temporal information in the brain. *Annual Review of Neuroscience, 16*, 223–243. doi:10.1146/annurev.ne.16.030193.001255

Carter, R. L., & Crovella, M. E. (1996). *Measuring bottleneck link speed in packet switched networks*. Boston University Computer Science Department, (Tech. Rep. BU-CS-96-006), Mar. 1996.

Casillas, J., Carse, B., & Bull, L. (2004). *Fuzzy XCS: An accuracy-based fuzzy classifier system*. Paper presented at XII Congreso Espanol sobre Tecnologia y Logica Fuzzy (ESTYLF 2004), September 2004, Universidad de Jaen, ES.

Cerf, V., Burleigh, S., Hooke, A., Torgerson, L., Durst, R., Scott, K., … Weiss, H. (2007). *Delay-tolerant networking architecture*. (IETF RFC 4838).

Chakrapani, L. N., Korkmaz, P., Akgul, B. E. S., & Palem, K. V. (2007). Probabilistic system-on-a-chip architectures. *ACM Transactions on Design Automation of Electronic Systems, 12*(3), 1–28. doi:10.1145/1255456.1255466

Cheng, X., Huang, X., Li, D., Wu, D., & Du, D. Z. (2003). Polynomial-time approximation scheme for minimum connected dominating set in ad hoc wireless networks. *Networks, 42*(4), 202–208. doi:10.1002/net.10097

Chiu, D.-M., & Jain, R. (1989). Analysis of the increase and decrease algorithms for congestion avoidance in computer networks. *Journal of Computer Networks and ISDN Systems, 17*, 1–14. doi:10.1016/0169-7552(89)90019-6

Chua, L., & Yang, L. (1988). Cellular neural networks: Theory. *IEEE Transactions on Circuits and Systems, 44*(2).

Cohen, R. I. (2004). *Tending Adam's garden: Evolving the cognitive immune self*. Paperback edition. Elsevier Academic Press.

Cohen, R. I. (2007). Real and artificial immune systems: Computing the state of the body. *Nature Reviews. Immunology, 7*, 569–574. doi:10.1038/nri2102

Cohen, B. (2003). *Incentives build robustness in BitTorrent*. Paper presented at the 1st Workshop on Economics of Peer-to-Peer Systems, May 2003, Berkeley, US.

Coico, R., Sunshine, G., & Benjamini, E. (2003). *Immunology: A short course*. John Wiley & Sons.

Colagrosso, M. D. (2007). Intelligent broadcasting in mobile ad hoc networks: Three classes of adaptive protocols. *EURASIP Journal on Wireless Communications and Networking, 1*, 16.

Collier, N. (1997). Convergence time characteristics of an associative memory for natural language processing. *Proceedings of Fifteenth International Joint Conference on Artificial Intelligence*, (pp. 1106-1113).

Colorni, A., Dorigo, M., Maniezzo, V., & Trubian, M. (1994). Ant system for job-shop scheduling. *JORBEL Belgian Journal of Operations Research. Statistics and Computer Science, 34*(1), 39–53.

Cost, D., & Hertz, A. (1997). Ants can colour graphs. *The Journal of the Operational Research Society, 48*, 295–305.

Cremet, V. (2006). *Foundations for SCALA: Semantics and proof of virtual types*. Unpublished doctoral thesis. EPFL, Lausanne, Switzerland

Crick, F. (1989). The recent excitement about neural networks. *Nature, 337*, 129–132. doi:10.1038/337129a0

Crowcroft, J., Hand, S., Mortier, R., Roscoe, T., & Warfield, A. (2003). QoS's downfall: At the bottom, or not at all! In *Proceedings of ACM SIGCOMM 2003 Workshop on Revisiting IP QoS* (RIPQOS), Aug. 2003.

Dai, F., & Wu, J. (2004). Performance analysis of broadcast protocols in ad hoc networks based on self-pruning. *IEEE Transactions on Parallel and Distributed Systems, 15*, 1027–1040. doi:10.1109/TPDS.2004.69

Darwin, C. (1859). *The origin of species by means of natural selection or the preservation of favoured races in the struggle for life*. Retrieved August 15, 2010, from http://www. literature. org/ authors/ darwin-charles/the-origin-of-species-6th-edition/

de Castro, L. N., & Timmis, J. (2003). *Artificial immune systems: A new computational intelligence approach*. Springer-Verlag.

de Castro, L. N., & Von Zuben, F. J. (2000). *The clonal selection algorithm with engineering applications*. In Genetic and Evolutionary Computation Conference (GECCO) (pp. 36-37). Las Vegas, USA.

Deco, G., & Obradovic, D. (1996). *An information-theoretic approach to neural computing*. Heidelberg, Germany: Springer.

Deneubourg, J. L., Aron, S., Goss, S., & Pasteels, J. (1990). The self organizing exploratory pattern of the Argentine ant. *Journal of Insect Behavior, 3*, 159–168. doi:10.1007/BF01417909

Deneubourg, J. L., Aron, S., Goss, S., Pasteels, J. M., & Duerinck, G. (1986). Random behaviour, amplification processes and number of participants: How they contribute to the foraging properties of ants. *Physica D. Nonlinear Phenomena, 2*, 176–186. doi:10.1016/0167-2789(86)90239-3

Deutsch, A., & Dormann, S. (2005). *Cellular automaton modeling of biological pattern formation: Characterization, applications, and analysis*. Birkhauser.

Di Caro, G., & Dorigo, M. (1998). AntNet: Distributed stigmergetic control for communications networks. *Journal of Artificial Intelligence Research, 9*, 317–365.

Di Caro, G., Ducatelle, F., & Gambardella, L. M. (2005). AntHocNet: An adaptive nature-inspired algorithm for routing in mobile ad hoc networks. *European Transactions on Telecommunications, 16*(5), 443–455. doi:10.1002/ett.1062

Dittrich, P., & Banzhaf, W. (1998). Self-evolution in a constructive binary string system. *Artificial Life, 4*, 203–220. doi:10.1162/106454698568521

Dittrich, P., & Speroni di Fenizio, P. (2007). Chemical organization theory. *Bulletin of Mathematical Biology, 69*, 1199–1231. doi:10.1007/s11538-006-9130-8

Dittrich, P., Ziegler, J., & Banzhaf, W. (2001). Artificial chemistries – A review. *Artificial Life, 7*(3), 225–275. doi:10.1162/106454601753238636

Dittrich, P. (2005). Chemical computing. In J.-P. Banâtre, P. Fradet, J.-L. Giavitto, & O. Michel (Eds.), *Unconventional programming paradigms, Vol. 3566. Lecture notes in computer science* (pp. 19–32). Berlin / Heidelberg, Germany: Springer.

Dorigo, M., & Stutzle, T. (2004). *Ant colony optimization.* Cambridge, MA: The MIT Press.

Dovrolis, C., Ramanathan, P., & Moore, D. (2001). What do packet dispersion techniques measure? *Proceedings - IEEE INFOCOM*, (Apr): 2001.

Drucker, H., Burges, C. J. C., Kaufman, L., Smola, A., & Vapnik, V. (1997). Support vector regression machines. [MIT Press.]. *Advances in Neural Information Processing Systems*, *9*, 155–161.

Ducatelle, F., Di Caro, G., & Gambardella, L. M. (2006). An analysis of the different components of the AntHocNet routing algorithm. *Lecture Notes in Computer Science*, *4150*, 37. doi:10.1007/11839088_4

Dunbar, K., & MacLeod, C. M. (1984). A horse race of a different color: Stroop Interference patterns with transformed words. *Journal of Experimental Psychology. Human Perception and Performance*, *10*, 622–639. doi:10.1037/0096-1523.10.5.622

Durvy, M., & Thiran, P. (2005). *Reaction–diffusion based transmission patterns for ad hoc networks.* Paper presented at IEEE INFOCOM, Miami, USA.

Easwaran, Y., & Labrador, M. (2004). Evaluation and application of available bandwidth estimation techniques to improve TCP performance. In *Proceedings of the 29th annual IEEE international conference on local computing networks*, (pp. 268–275).

Eckford, A. (2007). *Nanoscale communication with Brownian motion.* In 41st Annual Conference on Information Sciences and Systems, (pp. 160-165).

E-Coupled. (2010). *Wireless power technology.* Retrieved March 28, 2010, from http://www.ecoupled.com/

Edmund, A. A., Mark, A., & Ryohei, K. (1993). Organization of goal oriented locomotion: Pheromone-modulated flight behavior of moths. *Proc. Workshop on "Locomotion Control in Legged Invertebrates" on Bilogical Neural Networks in Invertebrate Neuroethology and Robotics.*

Eger, K. (2009). *Simulation of BitTorrent peer-to-peer networks in ns-2.* Retrieved from http://www.tuharburg.de/et6/research/bittorrentsim/index.html

Eiben, A. E., & Smith, J. E. (2003). *Introduction to evolutionary computing. Natural Computing Series* (*Vol. 2*). Berlin, Germany: Springer Verlag.

Eigen, M., & Schuster, P. (1979). *The hypercycle: A principle of natural self-organization.* Berlin, Germany: Springer.

Ellis, H. C., & Hunt, R. R. (1993). *Fundamentals of cognitive psychology.* Boston, MA: McGraw-Hill.

Ellis, R., & Humphreys, G. (1999). *Connectionist psychology* (pp. 23–30). UK: Psychology Press.

Elman, J. L. (1990). Finding structure in time. *Cognitive Science*, *14*, 179–211. doi:10.1207/s15516709cog1402_1

Enomoto, A., Moore, M., Nakano, T., Egashira, R., Suda, T., & Kojima, H. … Oiwa, K. (2006). *A molecular communication system using a network of cytoskeletal filaments.* In 2006 NSTI Nanotechnology Conference, vol. 1, (pp. 725-728).

Erciyes, K. (2007). Graph theoretic clustering algorithms in mobile ad hoc networks and wireless sensor networks. *Application Computing Mathematical*, *6*, 162–180.

Erickson, C. A., & Desimone, R. (1999). Responses of Macaque Perirhinal neurons during and after visual stimulus association learning. *The Journal of Neuroscience*, *19*(23), 10404–10416.

Fall, K., & Farrell, S. (2008). DTN: An architectural retrospective. *IEEE Journal on Selected Areas in Communications*, *26*(5), 828–836. doi:10.1109/JSAC.2008.080609

Fall, K. (1999). *Network emulation in the Vint/NS simulator.* Paper presented at the Fourth IEEE Symposium on Computers and Communications, Washington, DC, US.

Farago, A., Myers, A. D., Syrotiuk, V. R., & Zaruba, G. V. (2000). Meta-MAC protocols: Automatic combination of MAC protocols to optimize performance for unknown conditions. *IEEE Journal on Selected Areas in Communications*, *18*(9), 1670–1681. doi:10.1109/49.872955

Farmer, J. D., Packard, N. H., & Perelson, A. S. (1986). The immune learning, adaptation, and machine learning. [Elsevier.]. *Physica D. Nonlinear Phenomena, 4*, 187–204. doi:10.1016/0167-2789(86)90240-X

Farrell, S., & Cahill, V. (2006). *Delay- and disruption-tolerant networking*. Norwood, MA: Artech House.

Fernando, C., & Rowe, J. (2007). Natural selection in chemical evolution. *Journal of Theoretical Biology, 247*, 152–167. doi:10.1016/j.jtbi.2007.01.028

Ferreira, A. (2004). Building a reference combinatorial model for MANETs. *IEEE Network, 18*(5), 24–29. doi:10.1109/MNET.2004.1337732

Fisher, C. G. (1968). Confusions among visually perceived consonants. *Journal of Speech and Hearing Research, 11*, 796–804.

Floyd, S. (2003). *HighSpeed TCP for large congestion windows*. Request for Comments 3649, Dec. 2003.

Folk, C. L., Remington, R. W., & Johnston, J. C. (1992). Involuntary covert orienting is contingent on attentional control settings. *Journal of Experimental Psychology. Human Perception and Performance, 18*, 1030–1044. doi:10.1037/0096-1523.18.4.1030

Fontana, W., & Buss, L. W. (1994). The arrival of the fittest: Toward a theory of biological organization. *Bulletin of Mathematical Biology, 56*, 1–64.

Franceschetti, M., Dousse, O., Tse, D., & Thiran, P. (2007). Closing the gap in the capacity of wireless networks via percolation theory. *IEEE Transactions on Information Theory, 53*(3), 1009–1018. doi:10.1109/TIT.2006.890791

Franks, N. R., Wilby, A., Silverman, B. W., & Tofts, C. (1992). Self-organizing nest construction in ants: Sophisticated building by blind bulldozing. *Animal Behaviour, 44*, 357–375. doi:10.1016/0003-3472(92)90041-7

Freitas, R. A., Jr., & Merkle, R. C. (2004). *Kinematic self-replicating machines*. Georgetown, TX: Landes Bioscience. Retrieved June 22, 2010, from http://www.molecularassembler.com/KSRM.htm

Fu, Z., Zerfos, P., Luo, H., Lu, S., Zhang, L., & Gerla, M. (2003). The impact of multihop wireless channel on TCP throughput and loss. *Proceedings - IEEE INFOCOM*, (Apr): 2003.

Garthwaite, P. H., Jolliffe, I. T., & Jones, B. (2006). *Statistical inference* (2nd ed.). Oxford Science Publications.

Georganopoulos, N., & Lewis, T. (2007). *A framework for dynamic link and network layer protocol optimisation*. Paper presented at the 16th IST Mobile and Wireless Communications Summit, July 2007, Budapest, HU.

Gerstner, W., Kempter, R., Leo van Hemmen, J., & Wagner, H. (1996). A neuronal learning rule for sub-millisecond temporal coding. *Nature, 383*, 76–78. doi:10.1038/383076a0

Gerstner, W., & Kistler, W. (2002). *Spiking neuron models: Single neurons, populations, plasiticity*. Cambridge, UK: Cambridge University Press.

Ghataoura, D. S., Yang, Y., Matich, G., & Galileo, S. (2009). SWOB: Swarm intelligent odour based routing for geographic wireless sensor network applications. *Proc. IEEE Military Communications Conference.*

Gibson, M. A., & Bruck, J. (2000). Efficient exact stochastic simulation of chemical systems with many species and many channels. *The Journal of Physical Chemistry A, 104*, 1876–1889. doi:10.1021/jp993732q

Gillespie, D. T. (1977). Exact stochastic simulation of coupled chemical reactions. *Journal of Physical Chemistry, 81*, 2340–2361. doi:10.1021/j100540a008

Gillespie, D. T. (2007). Stochastic simulation of chemical kinetics. *Annual Review of Physical Chemistry, 58*, 35–55. doi:10.1146/annurev.physchem.58.032806.104637

Gillespie, D. T. (1992). A rigorous derivation of the chemical master equation. *Physica A: Statistical Mechanics and its Applications, 188*, 404–425.

Goldberg, D. E. (1989). *Genetic algorithms in search, optimization and machine learning*. Boston, MA: Addison-Wesley.

Gong, Y., Xiong, Y., Zhang, Q., Zhang, Z., Wang, W., & Xu, Z. (2006). *Anycast routing in delay tolerant networks*. IEEE Global Telecommunications Conference (*GLOBECOM*), (pp. 1-5).

Gonzalez, J. L., Rubio, A., & Moll, F. (2002). Human powered piezoelectric batteries to supply power of wearable electronic devices. *International Journal of the Society of Materials Engineering for Resources, 10*(1), 34–40.

González, F. A., & Dasgupta, D. (2003). Anomaly detection using real-valued negative selection. [Springer.]. *Genetic Programming and Evolvable Machines*, *4*, 383–403. doi:10.1023/A:1026195112518

Goss, S., Aron, S., Deneubourg, J. L., & Pasteels, J. (1989). Self-organized shortcuts in the Argentine ant. *Naturwissenschaften*, *76*, 579–581. doi:10.1007/BF00462870

Goyal, P., Vin, H. M., Sheny, C., & Shenoy, P. J. (1995). *A reliable, adaptive network protocol for video transport.* In IEEE INFOCOM'96 - The Conference on Computer Communications Fifteenth Annual Joint Conference of the IEEE Computer and Communications Societies - Networking the Next Generation, (pp. 1080–1090). IEEE, Los Alamitos, US.

Grassé, P. P. (1959). La reconstruction du nid et les coordinations interindividuelles chez Bellicositermes natalensis et Cubitermes sp. La théorie de la stigmergie: essai d'interprétation du comportement des termites constructeurs. *Insectes Sociaux*, *6*, 41–83. doi:10.1007/BF02223791

Gray, F. (1953). *Pulse code communication.* (U.S. Patent 2,632,058, March, 1953).

Green, K. P., & Miller, J. L. (1985). On the role of visual rate information in phonetic perception. *Perception & Psychophysics*, *38*, 269–276. doi:10.3758/BF03207154

Greensmith, J., Feyereisl, J., & Aickelin, U. (2008). The DCA-SOMe comparison: A comparative study between two biologically-inspired algorithms. *Evolutionary Intelligence*, *1*(2), 85–112. doi:10.1007/s12065-008-0008-6

Greensmith, J. (2007). *The dendritic cell algorithm*, PhD Thesis, University of Nottingham, UK.

Greensmith, J., Aickelin, U., & Cayzer, S. (2005). Introducing dendritic cells as a novel immune-inspired algorithm for anomaly detection. In *Proceedings of the 4th International Conference on Artificial Immune Systems (ICARIS), LNCS 3627*, (pp. 153-167). Springer.

Greensmith, J., Aickelin, U., & Twycross, J. (2006). Articulation and clarification of the dendritic cell algorithm. In *Proceedings of the 5th International Conference on Artificial Immune Systems (ICARIS), LNCS 4163*, (pp. 404-417). Springer, Greensmith, J., & Aickelin, U. (2007). Dendritic cells for SYN scan detection. In *Proceedings of the Genetic and Evolutionary Computation Conference (GECCO)* (pp. 49-56). London, UK.

Gu, Q. (2002). Neuromodulatory transmitter systems in the cortex and their role in cortical plasticity. *Neuroscience*, *111*(4), 815–835. doi:10.1016/S0306-4522(02)00026-X

Gu, F., Greensmith, J., & Aickelin, U. (2008). Further exploration of the dendritic cell algorithm: Antigen multiplier and moving windows. In *Proceedings of 7th International Conference on Artificial Immune Systems (ICARIS 2008)*, (pp. 54-66).

Gu, F., Greensmith, J., & Aickelin, U. (2009). Integrating real-time analysis with the dendritic cell algorithm through segmentation. In *Proceedings of the Genetic and Evolutionary Computation Conference (GECCO)*, (pp. 1203–1210).

Gu, F., Greensmith, J., Oates, R., & Aickelin, U. (2009). PCA 4 DCA: The application of principal component analysis to the dendritic cell algorithm. In *Proceedings of the 9th Annual Workshop on Computational Intelligence (UKCI)*.

Guha, S., & Khuller, S. (1996). Approximation algorithms for connected dominating sets. *Algorithmica*, *20*, 374–387. doi:10.1007/PL00009201

Gunes, M., Sorges, U., & Bouazizi, I. (2002). ARA-the ant-colony based routing algorithm for MANETs. *Proc. the International Workshop on Ad Hoc Networking.*

Guo, L., & Matta, I. (2001). *The war between mice and elephants.* (Technical Report BU-CS-2001-005).

Gupta, P., & Kumar, P. R. (2000). The capacity of wireless networks. *IEEE Transactions on Information Theory*, *46*(2), 388–404. doi:10.1109/18.825799

Hagerty, J., Helmbrecht, F., McCalpin, Q., Zane, V., & Popovic, Z. (2004). Recycling ambient microwave energy with broad-band rectenna arrays. *IEEE Transactions on Microwave Theory and Techniques*, *52*(3), 1014–1024. doi:10.1109/TMTT.2004.823585

Hand, D. J., Manila, H., & Smyth, P. (2001). *Principles of data mining*. Cambridge, MA: The MIT Press.

Hangartner, W. (1969). Carbon dioxide, a releaser for digging behavior in Solenopsis geminata (Hymenoptera: Formicidae). *Psyche, 76*, 58–67. doi:10.1155/1969/58428

Harel, D. (2003). *Computers Ltd.: What they really can't do. Revised paperback edition*. Oxford University Press.

Harel, D., & Feldman, Y. (2004). *Algorithmics: The spirit of computing* (3rd ed.). Addison Wesley.

Harris, K. D. (2008). Stability of the fittest: Organizing learning through retroaxonal signals. *Trends in Neurosciences, 31*(3), 130–136. doi:10.1016/j.tins.2007.12.002

Hart, E., & Timmis, J. (2008). Application areas of AIS: The past, the present and the future. *Applied Soft Computing, 8*, 191–201. doi:10.1016/j.asoc.2006.12.004

Hasegawa, G., Murata, M., & Miyahara, H. (1999). Fairness and stability of the congestion control mechanism of TCP. *Proceedings - IEEE INFOCOM, 99*, 1329–1336.

Hasegawa, G., & Murata, M. (2006). *TCP symbiosis: Congestion control mechanism of TCP based on Lotka-Volterra competition model*. ACM International Conf. Series 200.

Hasegawa, G., Kurata, K., & Murata, M. (2000). Analysis and improvement of fairness between TCP Reno and Vegas for deployment of TCP Vegas to the Internet. In *Proceedings of IEEE ICNP 2000*, Nov. 2000.

He, T., Ren, F., Lin, C., & Das, S. (2008). *Alleviating congestion using traffic-aware dynamic routing in wireless sensor networks*. 5th Annual IEEE Communications Society Conference on Sensor, Mesh and Ad Hoc Communications and Networks.

Hebb, D. O. (1949). *The organization of behavior*. New York, NY: Wiley.

Heinzelman, W. B. (2000). *Application-specific protocol architectures for wireless networks*. PhD thesis, Massachusetts Institute of Technology, US.

Hettich, S., & Bay, S. D. (1999). *The UCI KDD archive. Technical report*. Irvine, CA: University of California, Department of Information and Computer Science.

Hiltunen, M. A., Schlichting, R. D., Ugarte, C. A., & Wong, G. T. (2000). *Survivability through customization and adaptability: The Cactus approach*. Paper presented at DISCEX'00: DARPA Information Survivability Conference and Exposition, 2000, vol. 1, (pp. 294–307). January 2000, Hilton Head, US.

Hiyama, S., Inoue, T., Shima, T., Moritani, Y., Suda, T., & Sutoh, K. (2008). Autonomous loading, transport and unloading of specified cargoes by using DNA hybridization and biological motor-based motility. *Small, 4*(4), 410–415. doi:10.1002/smll.200700528

Hiyama, S., Moritani, Y., Suda, T., Egashira, R., Enomoto, A., Moore, M., & Nakano, T. (2005). *Molecular communication*. In 2005 NSTI Nanotechnology Conference, vol. 3 (pp. 392-395).

Hoe, J. C. (1996). Improving the start-up behavior of a congestion control scheme of TCP. *ACM SIGCOMM Computer Communication Review, 26*(4), 270–280. doi:10.1145/248157.248180

Hofmeyr, S. A., & Forrest, S. (1999). Immunity by design: An artificial immune system. In *Proceedings of Genetic and Evolutionary Computation Conference (GECCO1999)* (pp. 1289-1296). Orlando, USA.

Hofstadter, D. (1979). *Gödel, Escher, Bach: An eternal golden braid*. New York, NY: Basic Books.

Holland, J. H. (1992). *Adaptation in natural and artificial systems*. Cambridge, MA: MIT Press.

Hopcroft, J. E., & Ullmann, J. D. (1979). *Introduction to automata theory, languages, and computation*. Mass.: Addison-Wesley.

Hopfield, J. J. (1982). Neural networks and physical systems with emergent collective computational abilities. *Proceedings of the National Academy of Sciences of the United States of America, 79*, 2554–2558. doi:10.1073/pnas.79.8.2554

Huang, K. C., Jing, X., & Raychaudhuri, D. (2009). *MAC protocol adaptation in cognitive radio networks: An experimental study*. Paper presented at the International Conference on Computer Communications and Networks, August 2009, San Francisco, US.

Hull, B., Jamieson, K., & Balakrishnan, H. (2004). Mitigating congestion in wireless sensor networks. *Proc. of the 2nd Int. Conf. on Embedded Net. Sensor Systems*, (pp. 134-147).

Hutton, T. J. (2002). Evolvable self-replicating molecules in an artificial chemistry. *Artificial Life, 8*, 341–356. doi:10.1162/106454602321202417

Hyodo, K., Wakamiya, N., & Murata, M. (2007). *Reaction-diffusion based autonomous control of camera sensor networks*. Paper presented at Bionetics, Budapest, Hungary.

Inagaki, J., Haseyama, M., & Kitajima, H. (1999). A genetic algorithm for determining multiple routes and its applications. *Proceedings of the IEEE International Symposium on Circuits and Systems*, (pp. 137-140).

International Phonetic Association. (1999). *Handbook of the International Phonetic Association: A guide to the use of the international phonetic alphabet*. Cambridge, UK: Cambridge University Press.

Izhikevich, E. M. (2003). Simple model of spiking neurons. *IEEE Transactions on Neural Networks, 14*(6), 1569–1572. doi:10.1109/TNN.2003.820440

Jacobson, V. (1988). Congestion avoidance and control. In *Applications, technologies, architectures, and protocols for computer communication: Symposium proceedings on communications architectures and protocols*, (pp. 314–329), New York, NY: ACM.

Jacobson, V. (1997). Pathchar - A tool to infer characteristics of internet paths. Retrieved from http://www.caida.org/tools/utilities/others/pathchar/

Jacobson, V., Braden, R., & Borman, D. (1992). *TCP extensions for high performance*. Request for Comments 1323, May 1992.

Jacquet, L. (2005). *Movie: La marche de l'empereur*. Bonne Pioche.

Jain, M., & Dovrolis, C. (2002). End-to-end available bandwidth: Measurement methodology, dynamics, and relation with TCP throughput. In *Proceedings of ACM SIGCOMM 2002*, Aug. 2002.

Jain, S., Patra, R., & Fall, K. (2004). Routing in a delay tolerant network. *Proceedings of the 2004 Conference on Applications, Technologies, Architectures, and Protocols for Computer Communications*, (pp. 145-158).

Jerne, N. K. (1974). Towards a network theory of the immune system. *Ann. Immunol. (Inst. Pasteur), 125C*, 373-389.

Ji, Z., & Dasgupta, D. (2006). Applicability issues of the real-valued negative selection algorithms. In *Proceedings of Genetic and Evolutionary Computation Conference (GECCO2006)* (pp. 111-118). Washington, USA.

Jin, C., Wei, D. X., & Low, S. H. (2004). FAST TCP: Motivation, architecture, algorithms, performance. *Proceedings - IEEE INFOCOM*, (Mar): 2004.

Jin, C., Wei, D. X., & Low, S. H. (2003). *Internet draft: FAST TCP for high-speed long-distance networks*.

Johnson, B. W. (1996). An introduction to the design and analysis of fault-tolerant systems. In *Fault-tolerant computer system design* (pp. 1–87). Upper Saddle River, NJ: Prentice-Hall, Inc.

Jost, J. (2005). *Dynamical systems – Examples of complex behavior*. Springer.

Jost, C., Verret, J., Casellas, E., Gautrais, J., Challet, M., & Lluc, J. (2007). The interplay between a self-organized process and an environmental template: Corpse clustering under the influence of air currents in ants. *Journal of the Royal Society, Interface, 4*(12), 107–116. doi:10.1098/rsif.2006.0156

Kaelbling, L. P., Littman, M. L., & Moore, A. W. (1996). Reinforcement learning: A survey. *Journal of Artifical Intelligence, 4*, 237–285.

Kansal, A., Hsu, J., Zahedi, S., & Srivastava, M. (2007). Power management in energy harvesting sensor networks. *ACM Transactions on Embedded Computing Systems, 6*(4).

Karenos, K., Kalogeraki, V., & Krishnamurthy, S. V. (2008). Cluster-based congestion control for sensor networks. *ACM Transactions on Sensor Networks, 4*(1).

Kelly, T. (2003). Scalable TCP: Improving performance in highspeed wide area networks. In *Proceedings of PFLDnet '03: Workshop for the Purposes of Discussion*, Feb. 2003.

Kempter, R., Gerstner, W., & van Hemman, J. L. (1999). Hebbian learning and spiking neurals. *Physical Review E: Statistical Physics, Plasmas, Fluids, and Related Interdisciplinary Topics, 59*(4), 4498–4514. doi:10.1103/PhysRevE.59.4498

Kendall, M. G., & Stuart, A. (1973). *The advanced theory of statistics, volume 2: Inference and relationship.* Griffin.

Kephart, J. O., & Chess, D. M. (2003). The vision of autonomic computing. [IEEE.]. *IEEE Computer, 1*(36), 41–50.

Kilian, J., & Siegelmann, H. T. (1996). The dynamic universality of sigmoidal neural networks. *Information and Computation, 128*, 48–56. doi:10.1006/inco.1996.0062

Kim, J. W., Bentley, P., Aickelin, U., Greensmith, J., Tedesco, G., & Twycross, J. (2007). Immune system approaches to intrusion detection - A review. *Natural Computing, 6*, 413–466. doi:10.1007/s11047-006-9026-4

Kim, J. W. (2002). *Integrating artificial immune algorithms for intrusion detection.* PhD Thesis. University College London.

King, R., Baraniuk, R., & Riedi, R. (2005). TCP-Africa: An adaptive and fair rapid increase rule for scalable TCP. *Proceedings - IEEE INFOCOM*, (Mar): 2005.

Kleene, S. C. (1938). On notation for ordinal numbers. *Journal of Symbolic Logic, 3*, 150–155. doi:10.2307/2267778

Koch, A. J., & Meinhardt, H. (1994). Biological pattern formation: From basic mechanisms to complex structures. *Reviews of Modern Physics, 66*(4). doi:10.1103/RevModPhys.66.1481

Kornek, B., Storch, M. K., Weissert, R., Wallstroem, E., Stefferl, A., & Olsson, T. (2000). Multiple sclerosis and chronic autoimmune encephalomyelitis: A comparative quantitative study of axonal injury in active, inactive, and remyelinated lesions. *American Journal of Pathology, 157*, 267–276. doi:10.1016/S0002-9440(10)64537-3

Kumar, R., Rowaihy, H., Cao, G., Anjum, F., Yener, A., & La Porta, T. (2006). *Congestion aware routing in sensor networks.* (Tech. Rep. No. 36). Pennsylvania, USA: The Pennsylvania State University, Department of Computer Science and Engineering.

Kunz, T. (2003). *Reliable multicasting in MANETs.* PhD thesis, Carleton University, CA.

La, R. J., & Seo, E. (2008 Submitted to). *Expected routing overhead in mobile ad-hoc networks with flat geographic routing.* IEEE Tansactions on Mobile Computing.

Langton, C. G. (1984). Self-reproduction in cellular automata. *Physica D. Nonlinear Phenomena, 10*, 135–144. doi:10.1016/0167-2789(84)90256-2

Latora, V., & Marchiori, M. (2001). Efficient behavior of small-world networks. *Physical Review Letters, 87*(19). doi:10.1103/PhysRevLett.87.198701

Lee, S. H., Bardunias, P., & Su, N. Y. (2007). Optimal length distribution of termite tunnel branches for efficient food search and resource transportation. *Bio Systems, 90*, 802–807. doi:10.1016/j.biosystems.2007.04.004

Legenstein, R., Naeger, C., & Maass, W. (2005). What can a neuron learn with spike-timing-dependent plasticity? *Neural Computation, 17*(11), 2337–2382. doi:10.1162/0899766054796888

Leung, Y., Li, G., & Xu, Z. B. (1998). A genetic algorithm for the multiple destination routing problems. *IEEE Transactions on Evolutionary Computation, 2*(4), 150–161. doi:10.1109/4235.738982

Lo, C. C., & Chang, W. H. (2000). A multiobjective hybrid genetic algorithm for the capacitated multipoint network design problem. *IEEE Transactions on Systems, Man, and Cybernetics, 30*(3), 461–470. doi:10.1109/3477.846234

Lotka, A. (1925). *Elements of physical biology.* Baltimore, MD: Williams and Wilkins.

Lowe, D., & Miorandi, M. (2009). *All roads lead to Rome: Data highways for dense wireless sensor networks.* Paper presented at S-Cube 2009: The first International Conference on Sensor Systems and Software, Pisa, Italy.

Lowe, D., Miorandi, D., & Gomez, K. M. (2009). *Activation-inhibition-based data highways for wireless sensor networks.* Paper presented at Bionetics, Avignon, France.

Luke, S., Cioffi-Revilla, C., Panait, L., & Sullivan, K. (2004). *MASON: A new multi-agent simulation toolkit.* Paper presented at The 2004 Swarmfest Workshop, May 2004, University of Michigan, US.

Lutz, M. B., & Schuler, G. (2002). Immature, semi-mature and fully mature dendritic cells: Which signals induce tolerance or immunity? *Trends in Immunology, 23*, 445–449. doi:10.1016/S1471-4906(02)02281-0

Maass, W., Natschlger, T., & Markram, H. (2002). Real-time computing without stable states: A new framework for neural computation based on perturbations. *Neural Computation, 14*(11), 2531–2560. doi:10.1162/089976602760407955

Macdonald, J., & McGurk, H. (1978). Visual Influences on speech perception process. *Perception & Psychophysics, 24*, 253–257. doi:10.3758/BF03206096

MacWilliams, F. J., & Sloane, N. J. (1977). *The theory of error-correcting codes*. Amsterdam, The Netherlands: North-Holland.

Mallon, E. B., & Franks, N. R. (2000). Ants estimate area using Buffon's needle. *Proceedings. Biological Sciences, 267*, 765–770. doi:10.1098/rspb.2000.1069

Man, K. F., Tang, K. S., & Kwong, S. (1996). Genetic algorithms: Concepts and applications (in engineering design). *IEEE Transactions on Industrial Electronics, 43*(5), 519–534. doi:10.1109/41.538609

Maniezzo, V. (1999). Exact and approximate nondeterministic tree-search procedures for the quadratic assignment problem. *INFORMS Journal on Computing, 11*(4), 358–369. doi:10.1287/ijoc.11.4.358

Markram, H. (2006). The blue brain project. *Nature Reviews. Neuroscience, 7*(2), 153–160. doi:10.1038/nrn1848

Markram, H., Lübke, J., Frotscher, M., & Sakmann, B. (1997). Regulation of synaptic efficacy by coincidence of postsynaptic APS and EPSPS. *Science, 275*(5297), 213–215. doi:10.1126/science.275.5297.213

Massaro, D. W., & Stork, D. G. (1998). Speech recognition and sensory integration. *American Scientist, 86*, 236–244.

Mathis, M. (1996). *TCP selective acknowledgement options*. Request for Comments 2018, Oct. 1996.

MATLAB. (n.d.). *The language of technical computing*. Retrieved from http:// www. mathworks.com/

Matzinger, P. (2002). Danger model: A renewed sense of self. *Science, 296*, 301–305. doi:10.1126/science.1071059

McClelland, J. L., & Rumelhart, D. E. (1985). Distributed memory and the representation of general and specific information. *Journal of Experimental Psychology. General, 114*, 159–197. doi:10.1037/0096-3445.114.2.159

McCullagh, P., & Nelder, J. (1989). *Generalized linear models* (2nd ed.). Boca Raton, FL: Chapman and Hall/CRC.

McGurk, H., & Macdonald, J. (1976). Hearing lips and seeing voices. *Nature, 264*, 746–748. doi:10.1038/264746a0

Meinhardt, H. (1982). *Models of biological pattern formation*. London, UK: Academic Press.

Melander, B., Bjorkman, M., & Gunningberg, P. (2000). A new end-to-end probing and analysis method for estimating bandwidth bottlenecks. In *Proceedings of IEEE GLOBECOM 2000*, Nov. 2000.

Meninger, S., Mur-Miranda, J., Amirtharajah, R., Chandrakasan, A., & Lang, J. H. (2001). Vibration to electric energy conversion. *IEEE Transactions on VLSI, 9*(1), 64–76. doi:10.1109/92.920820

Meyer, T., Yamamoto, L., & Tschudin, C. (2008). A self-healing multipath routing protocol. In *Proceedings of the 3rd International Conference on Bio-Inspired Models Of Network, Information and Computing Systems (BIONET-ICS '08)* (pp. 1–8). Brussels, Belgium: ICST.

Mines, M. A., Hanson, B. F., & Shoup, J. E. (1978). Frequency of occurrence of phonemes in conversational English. *Language and Speech, 21*(3), 221–241.

Miranda, H., Pinto, A., & Rodrigues, L. (2001). Appia: A flexible protocol kernel supporting multiple coordinated channels. In *Proceedings of the 21st International Conference on Distributed Computing Systems* (ICDCS 2001), April 16-19, 2001, Phoenix, Arizona, USA, (pp. 707–710). IEEE Computer Society, Los Alamitos, US.

MIT Lincoln Lab Information System Technology Group. (1998). *The 1998 intrusion detection off-line evaluation plan*. Retrieved from http://www.ll.mit.edu/IST/ideval/data/1998/

Mitchell, T. M. (1997). *Machine learning*. McGraw-Hill.

Mokhtar, M., Bi, R., Timmis, T., & Tyrrell, A. M. (2009). A modified dendritic cell algorithm for on-line error detection in robotic systems. In *Proceedings of the 11th IEEE Congress on Evolutionary Computation* (CEC), (pp. 2055–2062).

Mongillo, G., Amit, D. J., & Brunel, N. (2003). Retrospective and prospective persistent activity induced by Hebbian learning in a recurrent cortical network. *The European Journal of Neuroscience*, *18*, 2011–2024. doi:10.1046/j.1460-9568.2003.02908.x

Montana, D., & Redi, J. (2005). Optimizing parameters of a mobile ad hoc network protocol with a genetic algorithm. In H.-G. Beyer, & U.-M. O'Reilly (Eds.), *Genetic and Evolutionary Computation Conference, GECCO 2005, Proceedings*, Washington DC, USA, June 25-29, 2005, ACM, New York, US.

Montresor, A., Meling, H., & Babaoglu, O. (2003). Toward self-organizing, self-repairing and resilient distributed systems [Springer-Verlag.]. *LNCS*, *2584*, 119–124.

Moore, M., Suda, T., & Oiwa, K. (2009). Molecular communication: Modeling noise effects on information rate. *IEEE Transactions on Nanobioscience*, *8*(2), 169–180. doi:10.1109/TNB.2009.2025039

Moritani, Y., Hiyama, S., & Suda, T. (2006). *Molecular communication among nanomachines using vesicles*. In 2006 NSTI Nanotechnology Conference.

Mukai, M., Maruo, K., Kikuchi, J., Sasaki, Y., Hiyama, S., Moritani, Y., & Suda, T. (2009). Propagation and amplification of molecular information using a photo-responsive molecular switch. *Supramolecular Chemistry*, *21*(3-4), 284–291. doi:10.1080/10610270802468439

Müller, B., Reinhardt, J., & Strickland, M. T. (1990). *Neural networks*. Springer.

Murray, J. D. (2002). *Mathematical Biology I: An introduction*. Springer Verlag.

Murray, J. D. (2003). *Mathematical biology: Spatial models and biomedical applications*. Springer, volume 2 of Mathematical Biology.

Nakano, T., Koujin, T., Suda, T., Hiraoka, Y., & Haraguchi, T. (2009). A locally induced increase in intracellular Ca^{2+} propagates cell-to-cell in the presence of plasma membrane ATPase inhibitors in non-excitable cells. *FEBS Letters*, *583*(22), 3593–3599. doi:10.1016/j.febslet.2009.10.032

Nakano, T., Hsu, Y. H., Tang, W. C., Suda, T., Lin, D., & Koujin, T. … Hiraoka, Y. (2008). *Microplatform for intercellular communication*. In Third Annual IEEE International Conference on Nano/Micro Engineered and Molecular Systems (pp. 476-479).

Naya, Y., Yoshida, M., & Miyashita, Y. (2001). Backward spreading of memory-retrieval signal in the primate temporal cortex. *Science*, *291*, 661–664. doi:10.1126/science.291.5504.661

Naya, Y., Yoshida, M., & Miyashita, Y. (2003). Forward processing of long term associative memory in monkey inferotemporal cortex. *The Journal of Neuroscience*, *23*, 2861–2871.

Neglia, G., & Reina, G. (2007). *Evaluating activator–inhibitor mechanisms for sensors coordination*. Paper presented at Bionetics, Budapest, Hungary. ICST.

Neuts, M. F. (1981). *Matrix-geometric solutions in stochastic models*. New York, NY: Dover Publications Inc.

Ni, S. Y., Tseng, Y. C., Chen, Y. S., & Sheu, J. P. (1999). The broadcast storm problem in a mobile ad hoc network. In *Proceedings of the 5th Annual ACM/IEEE International Conference on Mobile Computing and Networking, MobiCom '99*, Seattle, Washington, United States.

NIST. (2001). *Intrusion detection systems*. NIST Computer Science Special Reports SP 800–31, November 2001.

Normand, E. (1996). Single event upset at ground level. *IEEE Transactions on Nuclear Science*, *43*, 2742–2750. doi:10.1109/23.556861

NS-2. (n.d.). *Network simulator*. Retrieved from http://www.isi.edu/nsnam/ns/

Oates, R., Greensmith, J., Aickelin, U., Garibaldi, J., & Kendall, G. (2007). The application of a dendritic cell algorithm to a robotic classifier. In *Proceedings of the 6th International Conference on Artificial Immune* (ICARIS), (pp. 204–215).

Oates, R., Kendall, G., & Garibaldi, J. (2008). Frequency analysis for dendritic cell population tuning: Decimating the dendritic cell. *Evolutionary Intelligence, 1*(2).

Pahlavan, K., & Krishnamurthy, P. (2001). *Principles of wireless networks: A unified approach*. Upper Saddle River, NJ: Prentice Hall PTR.

Paing, T., Morroni, J., Dolgov, A., Shin, J., Brannan, J., Zane, R., & Popovic, Z. (2007, October). *Wirelessly-powered wireless sensor platform*. Paper presented at the IEEE European Microwave Conference, Munich, Germany.

Paradiso, J., & Starner, T. (2005). Energy scavenging for mobile and wireless electronics. *IEEE Pervasive Computing/IEEE Computer Society [and] IEEE Communications Society, 4*(1), 18–27. doi:10.1109/MPRV.2005.9

Parker, G., & Smith, J. (1990). Optimality theory in evolutionary biology. *Nature, 348*, 27–33. doi:10.1038/348027a0

Paugam-Moisy, H., Martinez, R., & Bengio, S. (2008). Delay learning and polychnization for reservoir computing. *Neurocomputing, 71*(7-9), 1143–1158. doi:10.1016/j.neucom.2007.12.027

Paun, G. (2000). Computing with membranes. *Journal of Computer and System Sciences, 61*, 108–143. doi:10.1006/jcss.1999.1693

Perkins, C. E., & Royer, E. M. (1999). Ad hoc on-demand distance vector routing. *Proc. 2nd IEEE Workshop on Mobile Computing Systems and Applications*, (pp. 90-100). New Orleans, LA.

Perna, A., Jost, C., Valverde, S., Gautrais, J., Theraulaz, G., & Kuntz, P. (2008). The topological fortress of termites. *Bio-Inspired Computing and Communication, LNCS, 5151*, 165–173. doi:10.1007/978-3-540-92191-2_15

Perna, A., Valverde, S., Gautrais, J., Jost, C., Solé R., Kuntz, P., & Theraulaz, G. (2008a). Topological efficiency in three-dimensional gallery networks of termite nests. *Physica A Statistical Mechanics and its Applications, 387*(24), 6235–6244.

Perrier, J.-Y., Sipper, M., & Zahnd, J. (1996). Toward a viable, self-reproducing universal computer. *Physica D. Nonlinear Phenomena, 97*, 335–352. doi:10.1016/0167-2789(96)00091-7

Pirk, C. W. W., Hepburn, H. R., Radloff, S. E., & Tautz, J. (2004). Honeybee combs: Construction through a liquid equilibrium process? *Naturwissenschaften, 91*, 350–353. doi:10.1007/s00114-004-0539-3

Popa, L., Raiciu, C., Stoica, I., & Rosenblum, D. S. (2006, November). Reducing congestion effects in wireless networks by multipath routing. *Proceedings of 14th IEEE International Conference on Network Protocols*, (pp. 96-105).

Popoviciu, N., & Boncut, M. (2005). On the Hopfield algorithm: Foundations and examples. *General Mathematics, 13*(2), 35–50.

Postel, J. B. (1981). *Transmission control protocol*. Request for Comments 793, Sept. 1981. Ribeiro, V., Riedi, R., Baraniuk, R., Navratil, J., & Cottrell, L. (2003). PathChirp: Efficient available bandwidth estimation for network paths. In *Proceedings of NLANR PAM2003*, Apr. 2003.

Pouwelse, J. A., Garbacki, P., Epema, D. H. J., & Sips, H. J. (2005). The BitTorrent P2P file-sharing system: Measurements and analysis. In M. Castro & R. van Renesse (Eds.), *Peer-to-Peer Systems IV, 4th International Workshop, LNCS 3640*, (pp. 205-216). Springer Verlag.

Powercast Corporation. (2010). *Website*. Retrieved March 28, 2010, from http://www.powercastco.com/

Pradhan, D. K. (1996). *Fault-tolerant computer system design*. Upper Saddle River, NJ: Prentice-Hall, Inc.

Prothmann, H., Branke, J., Schmeck, H., Tomforde, S., Rochner, F., Hähner, J., & Müller-Schloer, C. (2009). Organic traffic light control for urban road networks. In [Inderscience Publishers.]. *International Journal of Autonomous and Adaptive Communications Systems, 2*, 203–225. doi:10.1504/IJAACS.2009.026783

Raghunathan, V., Kansal, A., & Hsu, J. Friedman, J., & Srivastava, M. (2005, April). *Design considerations for solar energy harvesting wireless embedded systems*. Paper presented at the International Symposium of Information Processing in Sensor Networks, Los Angeles, CA.

Rajewsky, K. (1996). Clonal selection and learning in the antibody system. *Nature, 381*, 751–758. doi:10.1038/381751a0

Randaccio, L. S., & Atzori, L. (2007). Group multicast routing problem: A genetic algorithms based approach. *Computer Networks, 51*(14), 3989–4004. doi:10.1016/j.comnet.2007.04.008

Rangwala, S., Gummadi, R., Govindan, R., & Psounis, K. (2006). Interference-aware fair rate control in wireless sensor networks. *Proceedings of ACM SIGCOMM Symposium on Network Architectures and Protocols.*

Rodgers, J. L., & Nicewander, W. A. (1988). Thirteen ways to look at the correlation coefficient. *The American Statistician, 42*(1), 59–66. doi:10.2307/2685263

Rojas, R. (1996). *Theorie der neuronalen Netze: Eine systematischen Einfhrung.* Berlin, Germany: Springer.

Rosa, L., Rodrigues, L., & Lopes, A. (2007). *Appia to R-Appia: Refactoring a protocol composition framework for dynamic reconfiguration* (Tech. Rep. No. 1). University of Lisbon, Department of Informatics.

Roundy, S., Wright, P., & Rabaey, J. (2004). *Energy scavenging for wireless sensor networks with special focus on vibrations.* Kluwer Academic Publishers.

Sagduyu, Y. E., Guo, D., & Berry, R. (2008). On the delay and throughput of digital and analog network coding for wireless broadcast. *Proc. Conference on Information Sciences and Systems, CISS.* Princeton, NJ.

Sakai, K., & Miyashita, Y. (1991). Neural organization for the long term memory of paired associates. *Nature, 354,* 152–155. doi:10.1038/354152a0

Schmeck, H. (2005). *Organic computing - A new vision for distributed embedded systems.* Paper presented at the Eighth IEEE International Symposium on Object-Oriented Real-Time Distributed Computing (ISORC 2005), 18-20 May 2005, Seattle, WA, USA.

Schmeck, H., & Müller-Schloer, C. (2007). A characterization of key properties of environment-mediated multiagent systems. In D. Weyns, S. Brueckner, & Y. Demazeau (Eds.), *Engineering Environment-Mediated Multi-Agent Systems, International Workshop, EEMMAS 2007,* (pp. 17–38). Berlin/Heidelberg, Germany: Springer Verlag.

Schneidman, E., Freedman, B., & Segev, I. (1998). Ion channel stochasticity may be critical in determining the reliability and precision of spike timing. *Neural Computation, 10,* 1679–1703. doi:10.1162/089976698300017089

Schöler, T., & Müller-Schloer, C. (2005). An observer/controller architecture for adaptive reconfigurable stacks. In M. Beigl & P. Lukowisz (Eds.), *Systems Aspects in Organic and Pervasive Computing - Proceedings of the 18th International Conference on Architecture of Computing Systems* (ARCS'05). Berlin, Germany: Springer Verlag.

Sekiyama, K., & Tohkura, Y. (1991). McGurk effect in non-English listeners: Few visual effects for Japanese subjects hearing Japanese syllables of high auditory intelligibility. *The Journal of the Acoustical Society of America, 90,* 1797–1805. doi:10.1121/1.401660

Seok, M., Hanson, S., Lin, Y.-S., Foo, Z., Kim, D., & Lee, Y. ... Blaauw, D. (2008, June). *The Phoenix processor: A 30pW platform for sensor applications.* Paper presented at the IEEE Symposium on VLSI Citcuits, Honolulu, HI.

Shenck, N., & Paradiso, J. (2001). Energy scavenging with shoe-mounted piezoelectrics. *IEEE Micro, 21*(3), 30–42. doi:10.1109/40.928763

Shenker, S., Zhang, L., & Clark, D. D. (1990). Some observations on the dynamics of a congestion control algorithm. *ACM Computer Communication Review, 20*(5), 30–39. doi:10.1145/381906.381931

Shepherd, G. M. (1994). *Neurobiology.* Oxford University Press.

Silva, E. R., & Guardieiro, P. R. (2010). An efficient genetic algorithm for anycast routing in delay/disruption tolerant networks. *IEEE Communications Letters, 14*(4), 315–317. doi:10.1109/LCOMM.2010.04.092066

Silva, E. R., & Guardieiro, P. R. (2008). *Anycast routing in delay tolerant networks using genetic algorithms for route decision.* 11th International Conference on Computer and Information Technology, (pp. 65-71).

Simon, V., Bérces, M., Varga, E., & Bacsárdi, L. (2009). Natural selection of message forwarding algorithms in multihop wireless networks. In *Proceedings of IEEE WiOpt,* Seoul, Korea.

Sipper, M. (1998). Fifty years of research on self-replication: An overview. *Artificial Life, 4,* 237–257. doi:10.1162/106454698568576

Solé, R. V., Bonabeau, E., Delgado, J., Fernandez, P., & Marın, J. (2000). Pattern formation and optimization in army ant raids. *Artificial Life*, *6*(3), 219–226. doi:10.1162/106454600568843

Somayaji, A., Hofmeyr, S., & Forrest, S. (1997). Principles of a computer immune system. In *Proceedings of New Security Paradigm Workshop* (pp. 75-82), Langdale, Cumbria.

Soro, S., & Heinzelman, W. B. (2009). Cluster head election techniques for coverage preservation in wireless sensor networks. *Ad Hoc Networks*, *7*, 955–972. doi:10.1016/j.adhoc.2008.08.006

Soro, S., & Heinzelman., W. (2009). A survey of visual sensor networks. *Advances in Multimedia*.

Sözer, E. M., Stojanovic, M., & Proakis, J. G. (2000). *Initialization and routing optimization for ad-hoc underwater acoustic networks*. Paper presented at OPNETWORK 2000, August 2000, Washington, US.

Space Solar Power Workshop, M. I. T. (2007, May). *Terrestrial energy generation based on space solar power: A feasible concept or fantasy?* Cambridge, MA. Retrieved March 8, 2010, from http://web.mit.edu/space_solar_power/

Spector, L., & Robinson, A. (2002). Genetic programming and autoconstructive evolution with the push programming language. *Genetic Programming and Evolvable Machines*, *3*(1), 7–40. doi:10.1023/A:1014538503543

Sporea, I., & Grüning, A. (2010a). Modelling the McGurk effect. In M. Verleysen (Ed.), *Proceedings of the 18th European Symposium on Artificial Neural Networks* (pp. 363-369). Bruges, Belgium: Dside pub.

Sporea, I., & Grüning, A. (2010b). A distributed model of memory for the McGurk effect. *Proceedings of IEEE International Joint Conference on Neural Networks*, (pp. 120-123). Barcelona, Spain.

Stadler, P. F., Fontana, W., & Miller, J. H. (1993). Random catalytic reaction networks. *Physica D. Nonlinear Phenomena*, *63*, 378–392. doi:10.1016/0167-2789(93)90118-K

Starner, T. (1996). Human-powered wearable computing. *IBM Systems Journal*, *35*(3-4), 618–629. doi:10.1147/sj.353.0618

Steel, J. M. (1988). Growth rates of Euclidean minimal spanning trees with power weighted edges. *Annals of Probability*, *16*(4), 1767–1787. doi:10.1214/aop/1176991596

Stevens, W. R. (1994). TCP/IP Illustrated: *Vol. 1. The protocols*. Reading, MA: Addison-Wesley.

Stibor, T., Timmis, J., & Eckert, C. (2005). A comparative study of real-valued negative selection to statistical anomaly detection techniques. In *Proceedings of 4th International Conference on Artificial Immune Systems (ICARIS2005). LNCS 3627*, (pp. 262-275). Springer.

Strogatz, S. H. (1994). *Nonlinear dynamics and chaos. Studies in nonlinearity*. Westview Press.

Stroop, J. R. (1935). Studies of interference in serial verbal reactions. *Journal of Experimental Psychology*, *18*, 643–662. doi:10.1037/h0054651

Sudame, P., & Badrinath, B. R. (2001). On providing support for protocol adaptation in mobile wireless networks. [Hingham, MA: Kluwer Academic Publishers.]. *Mobile Networks and Applications*, *6*(1), 43–55. doi:10.1023/A:1009861720398

Sudhaakar, R. S., Yoon, S., Zhao, J., & Qiao, C. (2009). A novel Qos-aware MAC scheme using optimal retransmission for wireless networks. *IEEE Transactions on Wireless Communications*, *8*(5), 2230–2235. doi:10.1109/TWC.2009.080294

Sutton, R. S., & Barto, A. G. (2002). *Reinforcement learning: An introduction*. Cambridge, MA: Bradford Books, MIT Press.

Szathmáry, E. (1991). Simple growth laws and selection consequences. *Trends in Ecology & Evolution*, *6*, 366–370. doi:10.1016/0169-5347(91)90228-P

Takeuchi, Y., & Adachi, N. (1980). The existence of globally stable equilibria of ecosystems of the generalized Volterra type. [Springer-Verlag.]. *Journal of Mathematical Biology*, *10*, 401–415. doi:10.1007/BF00276098

Tamaoka, K., & Makioka, S. (2004). Frequency of occurrence for units of phonemes, morae, and syllables appearing in a lexical corpus of a Japanese newspaper. *Behavior Research Methods*, *36*(3), 531–547.

Tamayo, P., Berger, C., Campos, M., Yarmus, J., Milenova, B., & Mozes, A. ... Myczkowski, J. (2006). Oracle data mining. In O. Maimon & L. Rokach (Eds.), *Data mining and knowledge discovery handbook* (pp 1315-1329). United States: Springer.

Tempesti, G., Mange, D., & Stauffer, A. (1998). Self-replicating and self-repairing multicellular automata. *Artificial Life, 4*, 259–282. doi:10.1162/106454698568585

Teuscher, C. (2007). From membranes to systems: Self-configuration and self-replication in membrane systems. *Bio Systems, 87*, 101–110. doi:10.1016/j.biosystems.2006.09.002

Texas Instrument. (2009). *CC1100 data sheet.* Retrieved March 8, 2010, from http://focus.ti.com/lit/ds/symlink/cc1100.pdf

The VINT Project. (n.d.). *UCB/LBNL/VINT network simulator - ns* (version 2). Retrieved from http://www.isi.edu/nsnam/ns/

Thomé, G. (1972). Le nid et le comportement de construction de la fourmi *Messor Ebeninus*, Forel (Hymenoptera, Formicoidea). *Insectes Sociaux, 19*, 95–103. doi:10.1007/BF02224727

Thompson, D. W. (1992). *On growth and form: The complete revised edition.* Dover.

Thompson, G. P. (2010). *The Quine page.* Retrieved June 22, 2010, from http://www.nyx.net/~gthompso/quine.htm

Tomforde, S., Cakar, E., & Hähner, J. (2009b). Dynamic control of network protocols - A new vision for future self-organised networks. In J. Filipe, J. A. Cetto, & J. J. Ferrier (Eds.), *Proceedings of the 6th International Conference on Informatics in Control, Automation, and Robotics* (pp. 285-290). INSTICC.

Tomforde, S., Hoffmann, M., Bernard, Y., Klejnowski, L., & Hähner, J. (2009c). POWEA: A system for automated network protocol parameter optimisation using evolutionary algorithms. In S. Fischer, E. Maehle, & R. Reischuk (Eds.), *Beiträge der 39. Jahrestagung der Gesellschaft für Informatik e. V.* (GI) (pp. 3177-3192). Gesellschaft für Informatik e.V. (GI).

Tomforde, S., Hurling, B., & Hähner, J. (2010). *Dynamic control of mobile ad-hoc networks - Network protocol parameter adaptation using Organic Network Control.* Paper presented at the 7th International Conference on Informatics in Control, Automation, and Robotics, June 2010, Madeira, PT.

Tomforde, S., Steffen, M., Hähner, J., & Müller-Schloer, C. (2009a). Towards an organic network control system. In J. G. Nieto, W. Reif, G. Wang, & J. Indulska (Eds.), *Proceedings of the 6th International Conference on Autonomic and Trusted Computing (ATC09)* (pp. 2-16). Berlin/ Heidelberg, Germany: Springer Verlag.

Tomforde, S., Zgeras, I., Hähner, J., & Müller-Schloer, C. (2010b). Adaptive Control of Sensor Networks. In: Proceedings of the 7th International Conference in Autonomic and Trusted Computing (pp. 77 - 91). Berlin / Heidelberg, Germany: Springer Verlag.

Trinh, T. A., & Molnar, S. (2004). A game-theoretic analysis of TCP Vegas. In *Proceedings of QofIS 2004,* Oct. 2004.

Tschudin, C. (2003). Fraglets – A metabolistic execution model for communication protocols. In *Proc. 2nd Annual Symposium on Autonomous Intelligent Networks and Systems (AINS)*, Menlo Park, USA.

Tschudin, C. (2007). *Fraglets home page.* Retrieved June 22, 2010, from http: // www. fraglets. net

Turgut, D., Daz, S., Elmasri, R., & Turgut, B. (2002). Optimizing clustering algorithm in mobile ad hoc networks using genetic algorithmic approach. In C.-K. Mao, L.-S. Lee, & K. C. Chen (Eds.): *Global Telecommunications Conference* (GLOBECOM '02), (pp. 62–66). IEEE, Los Alamitos, US.

Turing, A. M. (1952). The chemical basis of morphogenesis. *Philosophical Transactions of the Royal Society of London. Series B, Biological Sciences, 327*, 37–72. doi:10.1098/rstb.1952.0012

Turner, J. S. (2000). *The extended organism: The physiology of animal-built structures.* Cambridge, MA: Harvard University Press.

Twycross, J., & Aickelin, U. (2006). Libtissue - Implementing innate immunity. In *Proceedings of the IEEE Congress on Evolutionary Computation* (CEC2006) (pp. 499-506). Vancouver, Canada.

Valverde, S., Corominas-Murtra, B., Perna, A., Kuntz, P., Theraulaz, G., & Sole, R. V. (2009). Percolation in insect nest networks: Evidence for optimal wiring. *Physical Review E (Statistical. Nonlinear, and Soft Matter Physics, 79*(6), 066106. doi:10.1103/PhysRevE.79.066106

van Dam, T., & Langendoen, K. (2003). An adaptive energy-efficient MAC protocol for wireless sensor networks. In I. Akyildiz, D. Estrin, D. Culler, & M. Srivastava (Eds.), *SenSys '03: Proceedings of the 1st International Conference on Embedded Networked Sensor Systems,* (pp. 171–180). New York, NY: ACM.

van Renesse, R., Birman, K. P., Hayden, M., Vaysburd, A., & Karr, D. (1998). Building adaptive systems using ensemble. [New York, NY: John Wiley & Sons, Inc.]. *Software, Practice & Experience, 28*(9), 963–979. doi:10.1002/(SICI)1097-024X(19980725)28:9<963::AID-SPE179>3.0.CO;2-9

van Renesse, R., Birman, K. P., & Maffeis, S. (1996). Horus: A flexible group communication system. [New York, NY: ACM.]. *Communications of the ACM, 39*(4), 76–83. doi:10.1145/227210.227229

Varga, A. (2001). *The OMNeT++ discrete event simulation system.* Paper presented at the European Simulation Multiconference (ESM'2001), June 2001, Prague, CZ.

Varga, A. (2001). The OMNET++ discrete event simulation system. In *Proceedings of the European Simulation Multiconference* (ESM 2001).

Varga, A., & Hornig, R. (2008). An overview of the OMNET++ simulation environment. In *Proceedings of the 1st International Conference on Simulation Tools and Techniques for Communications (SIMUTOOLS '08),* (pp. 1–10).

Volterra, V. (1931). *Variations and fluctuations of the numbers of individuals in animal species living together, translation by Chapman, R. Animal Ecology* (pp. 409–448). McGraw Hill.

von Neumann, J. (1966). *Theory of self-reproducing automata.* Champaign, IL: University of Illinois Press.

Vuran, M. C., Gungor, V. C., & Akan, O. B. (2005). On the interdependence of congestion and contention in WSNs. *Proceedings of ICST SenMetrics.*

Waage, P., & Guldberg, C. M. (1864). Studies concerning affinity. *Forhandlinger: Videnskabs – Selskabet i Christiania, 35.*

Wagner, K. (2000). Cooperative strategies and the evolution of communication. *Artificial Life, 6,* 149–179. doi:10.1162/106454600568384

Wan, C.-Y., Eisenman, S. B., & Campbell, A. T. (2003). CODA: Congestion Detection and avoidance in sensor networks. *Proceedings of the 1st Int. Conf. on Embedded Net. Sensor Systems,* (pp. 266-279).

Wan, C.-Y., Eisenman, S. B., Campbell, A. T., & Crowcroft, J. (2005). Siphon: Overload traffic management using multi-radio virtual sinks in sensor networks. *Proceedings of ACM SenSys.*

Wang, Y., & Wu, H. (2007). Delay/fault-tolerant mobile sensor network (DFT-MSN): A new paradigm for pervasive information gathering. *IEEE Transactions on Mobile Computing, 6*(9), 1021–1034. doi:10.1109/TMC.2007.1006

Waxman, B. M. (1988). Routing of multipoint connection. *IEEE Journal on Selected Areas in Communications, 6*(9), 1617–1622. doi:10.1109/49.12889

Weimer, M., Paing, T., & Zane, R. (2006, January). *Remote area wind energy harvesting for low-power autonomous sensor.* Paper presented at the IEEE Electronics Specialists Conference, Jeju, South Korea.

Weingärtner, E., vom Lehn, H., & Wehrle, K. (2009). *A performance comparison of recent network simulators.* Paper presented at ICC 2009: IEEE International Conference on Communications, June 2009, Dresden, DE.

Whiteson, S., & Stone, P. (2004). *Towards autonomic computing: Adaptive network routing and scheduling.* Paper presented at the International Conference on Autonomic Computing (ICAC'04), May 2004, New York, US.

WildCharge Technology. (2010). *Website.* Retrieved March 28, 2010, from http://www.wildcharge.com/

Wilfredo, T.-P. (2000). *Software fault tolerance: A tutorial. Technical report.* NASA.

Williams, R. J., & Peng, J. (1990). An efficient gradient-based algorithm for on-line training of recurrent network trajectories. *Neural Computation, 2*, 490–501. doi:10.1162/neco.1990.2.4.490

Williams, B., & Camp, T. (2002). Comparison of broadcasting techniques for mobile ad hoc networks. In *Proc. of the 3rd ACM International Symposium on Mobile Ad Hoc Networking & Computing, MOBIHOC '02*, Lausanne, Switzerland.

Wilson, S. W. (1995). Classifier fitness based on accuracy. *Evolutionary Computation, 3*, 149–175. doi:10.1162/evco.1995.3.2.149

Wong, A. C. W., Kathiresan, V., Chan, C. K. T., Eljamaly, O., Omeni, O., & McDonagh, D. (2008). A 1 V wireless transceiver for an ultra-low-powerSoC for biotelemetry applications. *IEEE Journal of Solid-state Circuits, 43*(7), 1511–1521. doi:10.1109/JSSC.2008.923717

Woo, A., & Culler, D. E. (2001). *A transmission control scheme for media access in sensor networks* (pp. 221–235). ACM MobiCom.

Wu, J., & Li, H. (1999). On calculating connected dominating set for efficient routing in ad hoc wireless networks. In *Proceedings of the Third International Workshop on Discrete Algorithms and Methods for Mobile Computing and Communications (DiaLM)*, Seattle, Washington, United States.

Yamamoto, L., Schreckling, D., & Meyer, T. (2007). Self-replicating and self-modifying programs in fraglets. In *Proceedings of the 2nd International Conference on Bio-inspired Models of Network, Information, and Computing Systems (BIONETICS '07)*.

Ye, T., & Kalyanaraman, S. (2001). *An adaptive random search algorithm for optimizing network protocol parameters* (Tech. Rep. No. 1). Rensselaer Polytechnic Institute, US.

Ye, T., Harrison, D., Mo, B., Sikdar, B., Kaur, H. T., & Kalyanaraman, S. … Vastola, K. (2001). *Network management and control using collaborative on-line simulation*. Paper presented at IEEE International Conference on Communications (ICC'01), May 2001, Helsinki, FI.

Yoshida, A., Aoki, K., & Araki, S. (2005). Cooperative control based on reaction-diffusion equation for surveillance system. *Proceedings of KES International Conferences in Knowledge-Based and Intelligent Engineering & Information Systems, 3*, 533–539. doi:10.1007/11553939_76

Yu, J. Y., & Chong, P. H. J. (2005). A survey of clustering schemes for mobile ad hoc networks. *IEEE Communications Surveys and Tutorials, 7*, 32–48. doi:10.1109/COMST.2005.1423333

Yusoff, N., & Grüning, A. (2010). Supervised associative learning in spiking neural network. In K. Diamantaras, W. Duch, & L. Iliadis (Eds.), *ICANN2010*, Springer.

Yusoff, N., Grüning, A., & Browne, A. (2009a). Modelling the Stroop effect: Dynamics in inhibition of automatic stimuli processing. *Proceedings of the 2nd International Conference in Cognitive Neurodynamics (ICCN)*, LNCS, Springer.

Yusoff, N., Grüning, A., & Browne, A. (2009b). *Competition and cooperation in colour-word Stroop effect: An association approach*. Frontiers in Behavioral Neuroscience. Conference Abstract: 41st European Brain and Behaviour Society Meeting. doi: 10.3389/conf.neuro.08.2009.09.353

Zhang, Z. (2006). Routing in intermittently connected mobile ad hoc networks and delay tolerant networks: Overview and challenges. *IEEE Communications Surveys & Tutorials, 8*(1), 24–37. doi:10.1109/COMST.2006.323440

Zhao, W., Ammar, M., & Zegura, E. (2005). Multicast routing in delay tolerant networks: Semantic models and routing algorithms. *Proceedings of the ACM SIGCOMM Workshop on Delay-Tolerant Networking*, (pp. 268-275).

About the Contributors

Pietro Lio a Senior Lecturer in the Computer Laboratory which is the department of Computer Science of the University of Cambridge and a member of the Artificial Intelligence group of the Computer Laboratory. He has an interdisciplinary approach to research and teaching and holds a PhD in Complex Systems and Non Linear Dynamics (School of Informatics, dept of Engineering of the University of Firenze, Italy) and a PhD in (Theoretical) Genetics (University of Pavia, Italy). His current research interest is the investigation of biomedical processes employing a combination of techniques, ranging from machine learning to deterministic and stochastic models.

Dinesh Verma is a researcher and department group manager in the IT & Wireless Convergence area at IBM T J Watson Research Center, Hawthorne, New York. He received his doctorate in Computer Networking from University of California Berkeley in 1992, the Bachelor's in Computer Science from Indian Institute of Technology, Kanpur, India in 1987, and a Master's in Management of Technology from Polytechnic University, Brooklyn, NY in 1998. He holds over thirty US patents related to computer networks, and has authored over sixty papers and eight books in the area. He is the program manager for the US/UK International Technology Alliance in Network Sciences. He is a fellow of the IEEE, and has served in various program committees and technical committees. His research interests include topics in wireless networks, network management, distributed computing, and autonomic systems.

* * *

Andre Gruning is currently a Lecturer in the Computing Department at University of Surrey and has been working as a researcher at SISSA, Trieste, Italy, and University of Warwick, UK. He obtained his PhD in Computer Science from the University of Leipzig, Germany and his first degree in Theoretical Physics from the University of Goettingen, Germany. His research interests are in the field of learning algorithms for neural networks, cognitive modeling, and evolutionary systems.

Andrea Perna is a Biologist interested in the common properties observed at different levels of biological organization. He graduated in molecular biology at the University of Pisa and at the Scuola Normale Superiore of Pisa, Italy, and received a PhD in neurosciences again from Scuola Normale Superiore with Concetta Morrone, working on the mechanisms of visual perception in human brain. He has been a post doctoral researcher at the Research Centre on Animal Cognition in Toulouse, France, and in the Laboratory of Informatics of Nantes, France. He currently holds a research position at ISC-PIF. His current research mainly focuses on the formation of spatio-temporal patterns as a result of collective behavior of animals.

Andreas Pitsillides is a Professor at the Department of Computer Science, University of Cyprus, and heads the Networks Research Laboratory (NetRL). He is also a Founding member and Chairman of the Cyprus Academic and Research Network (CYNET) since its establishment in 2000. He has published over 200 research papers and book chapters, and he is the co-editor of the book on modeling and control of complex systems. His research interests include fixed and wireless networks (ad-hoc and sensor networks, TCP/IP, WLANs, UMTS Third Generation mobile networks and beyond), flow and congestion control, resource allocation and radio resource management, and Internet technologies and their application in mobile e-services, e.g. in tele-healthcare, and security issues. He has a particular interest in adapting tools from various fields of applied mathematics such as non-linear control theory, computational intelligence, complex systems, and nature inspired techniques, to solve problems in computer networks. He received the B.Sc. (Hns) degree from University of Manchester Institute of Science and Technology (UMIST) and PhD from Swinburne University of Technology, Melbourne, Australia, in 1980 and 1993, respectively.

Bernát Wiandt received his BSc degree from Budapest University of Technology and Economics (BUTE) in 2010. He is currently an MSc student at BUTE, conducting research in the field of self-organizing and adaptive networks, and evolution of communication protocols for his MSc thesis. His primary interests include programming languages and protocol evolution.

Borbála Katalin Benkő is a research fellow at the Dept. of Telecommunications at BUTE. She received her MSc degree in Technical Informatics in 2003 from BUTE and finished the Doctoral School there in 2006. Recently, she participated in two European Union integrated projects (CASCADAS FP6 IST-FET, Ambient Networks FP6 IST), in numerous national research projects, and as member of a data mining team she won 6th place award at the ACM KDDCup challenge in 2008. She published 20+ papers in journals and conferences, and regularly contributes to events as TPC member or organizer. Her research interests include autonomous systems, knowledge modelling, and data mining.

Christian Jost obtained his Doctoral degree from Institut National Agronomique Paris-Grignon in 1998 in the area of temporal dynamics of predator-prey systems. He has since then been working at CNRS; Centre de Recherches sur la Cognition Animale in Toulouse, France, and researching the phenomenon of social behavior in insets. He is currently working in the area of mathematical modeling of social insect behaviors.

Christian Tschudin is a Full Professor for computer networks at the University of Basel. Before joining Basel, he was at Uppsala University as well as ICSI in Berkeley. He received his PhD from the University of Geneva and holds a Master's degree in Mathematics. Christian Tschudin is interested in network architectures and mobile code, bio-inspired and wireless networks, as well as security.

Daniele Miorandi is the head of the iNSPIRE Area at CREATE-NET, Italy. He received a PhD in Communications Engineering from Univ. of Padova, Italy, in 2005, and a Laurea degree (summa cum lauda) in Communications Engineering from Univ. of Padova, Italy, in 2001. He joined CREATE-NET in Jan. 2005, where he is leading the iNSPIRE (Networking and Security Solutions for Pervasive Computing Systems: Research & Experimentation). Since Mar. 2007 he is the coordinator of the European project BIONETS (www.bionets.eu). Dr. Miorandi has co-authored more than 90 papers in internationally refereed journals and conferences. He serves on the Steering Committee of various international events (WiOpt, Autonomics, ValueTools), for some of which he was a co-founder (Autonomics and ValueTools). He also serves on the TPC of leading conferences in the networking field, including, e.g., IEEE INFOCOM, IEEE ICC, and IEEE Globecom. He is a member of IEEE, ACM, and ICST. His research interests include: bio-inspired approaches to networking and service provisioning in large-scale computing systems, modeling and performance evaluation of wireless networks, and prototyping of wireless mesh solutions.

David Lowe is the Director of the Centre for Real-Time Information Networks in the Faculty of Engineering and IT at the University of Technology, Sydney. From 2002 to 2008 he was the Associate Dean, Teaching and Learning for the Faculty of Engineering at UTS, and prior to that he was the Director of Undergraduate Programs and the Head of Computer Systems Engineering. He has active research interests in the areas of Web development and technologies, and software engineering. In particular, he focuses on real-time control in a networked environment, as well as the development and use of remote laboratories. He has published widely in these areas, including three books (most recently Web Engineering: A Practitioner's Approach, McGraw-Hill, co-authored with Roger Pressman). He is also on numerous Web conference committees and journal editorial boards.

Ederson Rosa da Silva is currently working toward the PhD degree in Electrical Engineering from Universidade Federal de Uberlândia (UFU). He received his BE degree in Electrical Engineering from Universidade Federal de Uberlândia (UFU) in 2007. He is a research scientist in the Computer Networks Laboratory of UFU. His research interests include performance analyses of communication networks, delay and disruption tolerant networks, and genetic algorithms.

Endre Sándor Varga received his MSc degree in Technical Informatics in 2007 at the Department of Telecommunications at BUTE and finished Doctoral School in 2010. He participated in the EU ICST-FET FP6 BIONETS research project. He was recently involved in a simulation based evaluation and validation of the P802.1Q revised IEEE standard at Ericsson. His primary interests are discrete-event simulations, programming languages, internet technologies, and biology inspired computing.

Feng Gu is PhD student in the Intelligent Modelling & Analysis (IMA) group, School of Computer Science at the University of Nottingham, UK. He received his Bachelor degree in Computer Science at Harbin Engineering University, China, and his Master degree in Engineering at the University of Warwick, UK. His research interests include: artificial immune systems, bio-inspired computing, intrusion detection systems, and machine learning.

Go Hasegawa received ME and DE degrees in Information and Computer Sciences from Osaka University, Osaka, Japan, in 1997 and 2000, respectively. From July 1997 to June 2000, he was a Research Assistant of Graduate School of Economics, Osaka University. He is now an Associate Professor of Cybermedia Center, Osaka University. His research is in the area of transport architecture for future high-speed networks. He is a member of the IEEE and IEICE.

Guy Theraulaz is research director and head of team working on Complex Dynamics and Interaction Networks in Animal Societies at Centre de Recherches sur la Cognition Animale in Toulouse, France. He obtained his PhD in neurosciences and animal behavior from University of Provence, Marseille in 1991. He has been subsequently working at CNRS. His research interests include swarm intelligence in natural and artificial systems, self-organization in biological systems, collective behaviors and collective intelligence in animal and human societies, and systems biology.

Ioana Sporea graduated from Politehnica University of Bucharest, Romania, with a degree in Computer Science. She is currently working towards her PhD in the Computing Department at University of Surrey, UK, where she is studying the modelling of multisensory processes using neural networks and learning algorithms in spiking neural networks. She is part of the Nature Inspired Computing and Engineering research group and her main areas of research interests include neural networks and artificial intelligence, psychology, and cognitive science. She is also an IEEE, IET, and SSAISB member.

Jason H. Li received his PhD degree in Electrical and Computer Engineering from the University of Maryland at College Park. He currently leads the Network & Security Group at Intelligent Automation Inc. Dr. Li's research interests include: computer networks, networks and systems security, network management and control, multi-agent systems, artificial intelligence, distributed systems, and intelligent software agents. Dr. Li has worked on various R&D projects including analysis of QoS routing under heavy-tailed traffic, seamless soft handoff for ad hoc networks, integrated graphical models for intelligent security management, cyber attack assessment, reliable networking over airborne networks, network services for airborne networks, secure routing in airborne networks, key management, et cetera. Dr. Li authored more than 40 publications in the area of communication networks, network protocols, network security, and multi-agent systems. He is a member of the IEEE, ACM, AFCEA, and USENIX.

Julie Greensmith is a Lecturer in School of Computer Science at the University of Nottingham. She is a member of both the Intelligent Modelling & Analysis (IMA) group and the Mixed Reality Lab (MRL). She gained a BSc in Pharmacology from the University of Leeds, UK in 2002 and a MSc in Multidisciplinary Informatics in 2003, also from the University of Leeds and completed a PhD in Computer Science at the University of Nottingham in 2007. Her research focuses on the development of novel AIS algorithms applied to computer security and bio-sensing for the entertainment industry.

Jörg Hähner received his Diploma in Computer Science from the Darmstadt University of Technology, Germany in 2001 and the 'Dr. rer. nat.' degree in Computer Science from the University of Stuttgart, Germany in 2006. He worked in the area of data management in mobile ad-hoc networks and was appointed as an Assistant Professor in the System and Computer Architecture Group at Leibniz Universität Hannover, Germany in 2006. His research focuses on architectures and algorithms in the field of Organic Computing (e.g. distributed smart camera systems, mobile ad-hoc and sensor networks, and global scale Peer-to-Peer systems).

Karina Mabell Gomez Chavez was born in Chillanes, Ecuador. She received the engineering degree (cum laude) in Electronic and Telecommunication Engineering from the National Polytechnic School in Ecuador, in 2006. She received her Master's degree in Wireless Systems and Related Technologies from the Turin Polytechnic, Italy, during 2007. In year 2007, she joined FIAT Research Center, becoming part of the Infomobility-Communication and location Technologies. Since July 2008, she is part of the iNSPIRE Area at Create-Net, working on the WING project. She is a PhD candidate at University of Trento. Her current research activity is mainly focusing on Green Networking. Her research interests include: WSNs, wireless mesh networks and ad hoc networks, green networking and Simulation (Omnet++, Matlab)

Masayuki Murata received the ME and DE degrees in Information and Computer Science from Osaka University, Japan, in 1984 and 1988, respectively. In April 1984, he joined Tokyo Research Laboratory, IBM Japan, as a Researcher. From September 1987 to January 1989, he was an Assistant Professor with Computation Center, Osaka University. In February 1989, he moved to the Department of Information and Computer Sciences, Faculty of Engineering Science, Osaka University. In April 1999, he became a Professor of Cybermedia Center, Osaka University, and is now with Graduate School of Information Science and Technology, Osaka University since April 2004. He has more than five hundred papers of international and domestic journals and conferences. His research interests include computer communication network architecture, performance modeling and evaluation. He is a member of IEEE, ACM, and IEICE. He is a chair of IEEE COMSOC Japan Chapter since 2009. Also, he is now partly working at NICT (National Institute of Information and Communications Technology) as Deputy of New-Generation Network R&D Strategic Headquarters.

Nooraini Yusoff is currently a PhD student in the Computing Department at University of Surrey (UK). She is a lecturer in Computer Science at Universiti Utara Malaysia, UUM (Malaysia). She obtained her MSc in Intelligent Systems from UUM. The topic of her PhD is focused around learning aspects in complex networks. Her research interests include spiking neural networks, intelligent systems, and cognitive modelling.

Pascale Kuntz received the MS degree in Applied Mathemaics from Paris-Dauphine University and the PhD degree in Applied Mathematics from the Ecole des Hautes Etudes en Sciences Sociales, Paris in 1992. From 1992 to 1998, she was Assistant Professor in the Artificial Intelligence and Cognitive Science department at the Ecole Nationale Superierue University (France) where she is currently Professor of Computer Science in the LINA Laboratory. She is head of the team "KOD - KnOwledge and Decision". She is member of the board of the French Speaking Classification Society. Her research interests include classification, graph mining, graph visualization, and post-mining.

Paulo Roberto Guardieiro is a Full Professor at Universidade Federal de Uberlândia, Brazil, where he has worked since 1978. He received his B.E. degree in Electrical Engineering from Universidade Federal de Uberlândia (UFU) in 1978, the degree of M.E.E. from the Instituto Tecnológico de Aeronáutica (ITA), in 1984 and the Ph.D. degree in Electrical Engineering from UNICAMP in 1991. He is the coordinator of the Computer Networks Laboratory of UFU and a member of the Brazilian Society of Telecommunications (SBrT). His research interests include mobile communications, multicast, QoS guarantees, and DTN's.

Pavlos Antoniou is currently a PhD student at the Department of Computer Science of the University of Cyprus under the guidance of Prof. Andreas Pitsillides. He received the Diploma Degree (M.Sc. equivalent) from the School of Electrical and Computer Engineering of the National Technical University of Athens, Greece, in 2005. He serves as a Research Associate at the University of Cyprus and he was working for the EU-funded GINSENG project and the locally funded MiND2C project dealing with Performance Control in WSNs. His current research interests include overload control based on nature-inspired techniques such as swarm intelligence and population biology for providing adaptation, robustness, and self-organization in autonomous decentralized environments.

Shouri Chatterjee received his BTech degree in Electrical Engineering from the Indian Institute of Technology (IIT), Madras, in 2000, and his MS and PhD degrees in Electrical Engineering from Columbia University, New York, NY, USA, in 2002 and 2005 respectively. He has been an Assistant Professor in the Department of Electrical Engineering, IIT Delhi since 2006. Dr. Chatterjee has previously worked at Silicon Laboratories Inc., NJ, USA (2005-2006) as a design engineer. His research interests are in the areas of active and passive filter design, ultra low power and ultra low voltage analog circuit design, energy scavenging, and high speed oscillators and frequency synthesis. Chatterjee is the author of the book, "0.5-V Analog Circuit Design Techniques", (Springer publications, 2007.) He was the recipient of the Edwin Howard Armstrong memorial prize for the best graduating Master's student from Columbia University in the year 2002. He was the recipient of the Analog Devices' 2004 Outstanding Student Award. His paper titled,"0.5-V analog circuit techniques and their application in OTA and filter design," was cited among the top 10 most read articles in the IEEE Journal of Solid State Circuits, 2005. His paper titled, "A 0.5-V 1-Msps Track-and-Hold Circuit With 60-dB SNDR", in the IEEE Journal of Solid State Circuits, was ranked as 31, in the list of top 100 most accessed papers in the entire IEEE site, in 2006.

Song Luo received his BS in Electrical Engineering from North China Institute of Electric Power in 1995, and received his Master and PhD in Computer Science from the University of Central Florida in 2002 and 2005. Dr. Luo is currently a senior research scientist at Intelligent Automation, Inc. His research interests include wireless ad hoc networking, design of high-performance routing protocols, network management, network traffic engineering, and network security. Dr. Luo has been a PI or key personnel in various research projects on computer networking: "Bio-inspired Robust and Secure Routing Protocol for MANET," "Adaptive Network Service Discovery," "An Integrated Architecture for Seamless Soft Handoff in Mobile Ad Hoc Networks," "Predictable, Scalable QoS Routing for Ad Hoc Wireless Networks Based on Heavy-Tailed Statistics," "A Cross-layer Approach for Reliable Communication in Airborne Networks," "A Distributed Cluster-based Emulation Test Bed for Large Wireless Communication Networks," and "An Intelligent Approach to Enable Space Networking."

Swades De received his BTech in Radiophysics and Electronics from the University of Calcutta, India, in 1993, MTech in Optoelectronics and Optical Communication from the Indian Institute of Technology (IIT) Delhi, in 1998, and PhD in Electrical Engineering from the State University of New York at Buffalo, NY, USA, in 2004. Before moving to IIT Delhi in 2007, he was an Assistant Professor of Electrical and Computer Engineering at New Jersey Institute of Technology, NJ, USA (2004—2007). He also worked as a post-doctoral researcher at ISTI-CNR, Pisa, Italy (2004), and has five years industry experience in India in telecommunication hardware and software development (1993—1997, 1999). His research interests include performance study, resource efficiency in multihop wireless and high-speed networks, broadband wireless access, and communication and systems issues in optical networks.

Sven Tomforde is a PhD candidate at the System and Computer Architecture Group of Leibniz Universität Hannover, Germany, where he also received his MSc in Computer Science in 2007. His current work focuses on distributed, self-organized, and collaborative control mechanisms (e.g. applied to data communication networks or urban traffic control systems).

Tadashi Nakano received the BE, ME, and PhD degrees in Information Systems Engineering from Osaka University in 1999, 2000, and 2002, respectively. He was with Department of Computer Science, Donald Bren School of Information and Computer Sciences, University of California, Irvine, where he was a Postdoctoral Research Scholar from 2002 to 2007 and an Assistant Adjunct Professor from 2007 to 2009. Since 2009, he has been with Frontier Research Base for Global Young Researchers, Graduate School of Engineering, Osaka University, where he is currently an Associate Professor. His research interests are in the areas of network applications and distributed computing systems with strong emphasis on interdisciplinary approaches. His current research is focused on the Biological-ICT (Information and Communications Technology) including design, implementation and evaluation of biologically inspired systems, and synthetic biological systems. Dr. Nakano is an editorial board member of ICST Transactions on Bio-Engineering and Bio-inspired Systems, and Elsevier Journal on Nano Communication Networks. Dr. Nakano is an MSR (Microsoft Research) IJARC fellow and a member of IEEE.

Thomas Meyer is a PhD student at the University of Basel, Switzerland. He received his MSc degree in electrical engineering from ETH Zurich in 2000. After that, we worked as software architect with Patton-Inalp Networks, where he contributed to the development of protocols and embedded software for Voice-over-IP devices. In 2007 he joined the Computer Networks Group headed by Prof. Dr. Christian Tschudin where he is exploring chemical and self-healing networking protocols.

Uwe Aicklein received a Management Science degree from the University of Mannheim, Germany, in 1996 and a European Master and PhD in Management Science from the University of Wales, Swansea, UK, in 1996 and 1999, respectively. He worked in the Mathematics Department as a lecturer in Operational Research at the University of the West of England in Bristol. In 2002, he accepted a lectureship in Computer Science at the University of Bradford. Since 2003 he works for the University of Nottingham in the School of Computer Science where he is now a Professor of Computer Science and leader of the Intelligent Modeling & Analysis (IMA) group. Prof. Aickelin currently holds an EPSRC Advanced Fellowship focusing on AIS, anomaly detection, and mathematical modeling.

Vilmos Simon received his PhD from Budapest University of Technology and Economics (BUTE) in 2009 and is currently a senior lecturer at the Department of Telecommunications. His research interests include self-organizing and adaptive networks, evolution of communication protocols, opportunistic and delay-tolerant networks, mobility management, and energy efficiency in 3G and 4G mobile systems. He participated in several research projects including the EU ICST-FET FP6 BIONETS where he also acted as a WP leader. He published 20+ papers in international journals and conferences, and acts as a reviewer or organizer for numerous scientific conferences.

Yalin Evren Sagduyu received his MS and PhD degrees in Electrical and Computer Engineering at the University of Maryland, College Park, and his BS degree in Electrical and Electronics Engineering at Bogazici University, Turkey. He worked as a postdoctoral fellow at Northwestern University for the DARPA project on IT-MANET (Information Theory for Mobile Ad Hoc Networks). He is currently a Research Scientist with Intelligent Automation Inc, where he has been the principal investigator of several STTR/SBIR projects on cyber superiority, heterogeneous network management, and network monitoring. His research interests are in the areas of design, optimization, and analysis of wireless networks, network coding, information theory, network security, optimization, game theory, and biologically inspired networking. He authored more than 40 papers on network architecture, design, optimization, and analysis of wireless networks, and he has been on technical program committee of major IEEE conferences.

Index